Patience and Power:
Grace for the First World

Jean-Marc Laporte, S.J.

PAULIST PRESS
New York • Mahwah

Imprimi Potest: William M. Addley, S.J.
January 22, 1987

Chart design: Ellen Whitney

Library of Congress Cataloging-in-Publication Data

Laporte, Jean-Marc, 1937–
    Patience and power : grace for the first world / Jean-Marc
    Laporte.
      p.   cm. —
    Bibliography: p.
    Includes index.
    ISBN 0-8091-2966-3 (pbk.)
    1. Grace (Theology)   2. Civilization, Modern—1950–   I. Title.
II. Series.
BT761.2.L277   1988
234—dc19
                                                   88-2478
                                                     CIP

Published by Paulist Press
997 Macarthur Boulevard
Mahwah, NJ 07430

Printed and bound in the
United States of America

CONTENTS

Chapter One

THE FIRST WORLD:
PLIGHT AND OPPORTUNITIES

How does God's grace pertain to the pressing dilemmas of our divided planet? Juan Luis Segundo and Leonardo Boff have spoken about grace from their standpoint within the third world. Segundo's *Grace and the Human Condition*[1] begins the move from a more general analysis based on Vatican II, especially *Gaudium et Spes*, towards a theology out of the Latin American context. Boff's *Liberating Grace*[2] is more pointed and specific in its references to that context, in which the dynamic of sin and grace is recast in terms of oppression and liberation.

By contrast the concerns of this book emerge out of the first world. To be sure, the insights of Segundo and Boff shed light on our first world: oppression is a part of our world just as technology is of theirs. Nevertheless we need to develop our own language in order to express in a distinctive way the cutting edge of God's action, anticipated or experienced, in our own world. We must address the plight of that world and its particular need of salvation. At the same time we must not set aside the theme of liberation: we are all travellers on the same earthship and theologies out of first and third worlds, while keeping their own colour and texture, must reach out to each other and mesh. As we attempt to portray the visage of grace in the first world a broad theme will emerge. At this point I will simply offer a preliminary description of it in terms of a spontaneity which holds patience and power together in inescapable oneness. The meaning of this theme will emerge in more precise and systematic terms as the chapters of this work unfold. Just as essential to my purpose, the relationship of first world empowerment to third world liberation will also be clarified.

In the process of this exploration we intend to keep in mind the full sweep of the traditional doctrine of grace. Liberation and empowerment are distinctive visages of a grace that meets the human situation in its diversities and *heals* it. At the same time grace also *elevates* us to intimacy with God. These themes of healing and elevating grace, as well as those of justification, sanctification,

1

salvation, actual and habitual grace, sufficient and efficacious grace, nature and the supernatural, will also find their due place as this essay unfolds.

We will begin to deal more technically with grace and the language of grace in Chapter Two. In this one we will focus on the first world and its particular experience of the dynamic of sin and grace. First we will set the first world in its global context, distinguishing it from second and third worlds, and relating Walbert Bühlmann's typology of first, second, and third church to these worlds. Then, beginning from the standpoint of an immediate although limited experience, we will turn to the first world's need of grace. Finally, moving towards a broader and more systematic perspective, we will survey recent literature on the plight of our first world and the avenues of radical transformation now before it, avenues which are genuine pathways of grace.

THE CONTEXT: OUR DIVIDED PLANET

Breathtakingly beautiful photos of our earth taken by astronauts have had a more powerful impact on us than all the eloquent and learned words about human solidarity spoken in our day. We can now easily pass from the notional assent that comes from passing Astronomy 101 to a real assent that we are one planet. This assent however is based not just on the triumph of space travel but also on the sobering realization that the science which makes possible such triumphs also has put into our hands the power of ultimate destruction. The life and death issue for humankind is not just whether this or that civilization will flourish or perish, but whether we will be able to maintain the precarious equilibrium that makes life possible in any form on this earth. Pollution steadily corrodes and clogs our biosphere, and nuclear technology constantly threatens us with the final cataclysm that could wipe all life from this earth. Like it or not, we are caught up for weal or woe in a single web, and more and more the actions of each have repercussions that touch us all. Will this cause us to huddle in terror or draw us into effective solidarity? That is the agonizing question. No theology of grace can circumvent or ignore it.

According to a classification which has gained wide acceptance, the human race that faces this question does so from the standpoint of three "worlds", the first (West), second (East), and third (South). Though this classification may be open to some question, it is in common use, and will help us to begin our reflection.[3] Aware of it or not, theologians begin their theological enterprise from the standpoint of their own world. We will begin ours from a first world stance. But we will do so deliberately and critically, reaching out to all three "worlds" as our reflections progress. This outreach is especially fitting in a theology of grace, for is not reconciliation one of the prime dynamics of grace, and is not humankind's need for reconciliation in our day massively evidenced by the difficult relationships of the three worlds with each other?

The *first world*, that of the West, is professedly free and democratic in its institutions. It arose out of the Middle Ages of Western Christendom. Since the sixteenth century, it has been at the forefront of technological change on our planet and has embarked upon a career of unbridled technological expansion which is just now beginning to come up against very serious limits. In its medieval stage the contacts of this world with what was outside itself were still fleeting and infrequent, and lacked the systematic pattern which could promote that "outside" to the status of a distinct "world". You simply had a familiar Christendom and, on the periphery, Muslims and other pagans who, it was expected, would soon give up their benighted state. But little by little the newly explored and discovered "outside" (new not from its own viewpoint but from that of Western Christendom) came to present itself as a vast human reality to be defined in distinctive terms. Unfortunately it was above all seen as endowed with highly desirable physical resources. The discovery of these resources coincided with the nascent capitalist phase of the first world; and this world outside became for the first world an object rather than a subject, an object, first of commercial relationships, and then of an outright colonization, which a concurrent missionary outreach failed to counter, and even at times abetted. Thus arose the *third world*, now predominantly situated in the Southern hemisphere, comprising nations and peoples who in the centuries following their "discovery" by the first world were outright dependencies. In spite of a recently won nominal independence they continue to be underdeveloped and exploited, fueling the ceaseless expansion to which the first world is still addicted.[4]

Just as the first world over the last few centuries has consciously proclaimed itself the main vehicle of progress and dynamism on our planet, so too the third world in the last century has become aware of itself as subject rather than object, a subject long treated as a mere object but now called to become itself in freedom and equality. The movement which flowed from this painful raising of consciousness has had an occasional flawed success (e.g. the American Revolution and the gradual accession of other former British colonies to independence);[5] but by and large colonization continues, albeit in more subtle forms which respect the illusion of political sovereignty and self-government. Indeed, if we accept the analysis offered by the *Center of Concern*, in its current stage first world industrial capitalism requires secure access to the valuable resources and cheap labour of the third world; and it is marked by a repressive and defensive preoccupation with national security. This repression, beginning to affect the first world itself, has become even more virulent in satellites of the third world.[6]

Like the third world, the *second world* has also emerged out of the first world. In the first phase of industrial capitalism (19th century), characterized by cut-throat competition and thorough exploitation of factory workers, a bone-crushing consciousness of oppression within the first world came to expression in Karl Marx' analysis of class struggle and his proposal for a communist system of economic organization. This has had its effect in the Western world, contributing to the greater share in economic goods achieved by its working class, but its main impact was elsewhere. As it turned out, Marx occasioned the development of a significantly different economic and political system in a part of the world which had up till then been on the margin of the Western world, namely Tsarist Russia. That system took root in Eastern Europe and later spread into China, thus forming an alternative to the Western capitalist world, a second world.

There are many nuances and variations in communism as practiced in the second world, and one can seriously question the extent to which Marx's insights have been truly implemented. The original Russian Marxist system has continued the conservative, cautious, authoritarian state apparatus of Tsarist Russia. In general the second world holds up a mirror so the first world can look at itself and see written in bold letters what it has not yet dared to be but could become if no force effectively counterbalances the momentum of its technology, which seeks to rationalize and control all resources, physical and human. Indeed, the latest phase of first world capitalism, that of the national security state, bears an increasing resemblance to what communist regimes have been for years.[7]

The current consciousness of oppression in the third world has often found expression in terms borrowed from Karl Marx, even if many Christian proponents of liberation within the third world claim that distinctions can be made between valid generative insights found in Marx and the atheism which has vitiated the embodiments of his system in the second world. In this way the struggle between the first and second worlds has in good part become a struggle for the third world.

Let us now pass from the three worlds to the three Churches. Walbert Bühlmann, in *The Coming of the Third Church*,[8] makes a helpful distinction between the first (East), second (West), and third (South) Churches. A synoptic view of how these three Churches and the three worlds intersect will show both convergences and divergences:

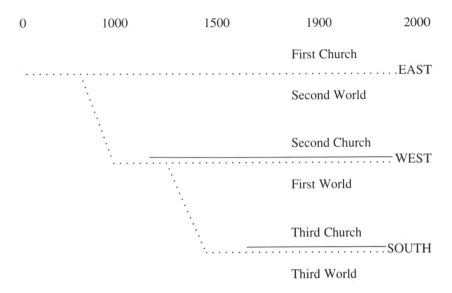

This diagram warrants careful scrutiny. The line representing the three Churches is a dotted one: (. . . . . . .) and that representing the three worlds is a solid one: (————). As can be seen, first, second, and third Churches are in a clear chronological sequence, the second Church emerging from the first, and the third Church from the second. The relation of the three worlds to the three churches is somewhat more complex. What is now known as the first world emerged out of the Western (second) Church. The second world which emerges as a reaction to the first world turns out to be located mostly in the East, where the first Church had already existed for centuries. In contrast, the emergence of the third world and the third Church out of the West takes place along clearly parallel lines.

The first Church received its impetus in the very first centuries after Christ, and attempted to live out the Gospel message primarily within the complex environment of the *eastern* half of the Roman Empire, in Hellenistic cultural terms. Partially submerged by the invasion of Islam in the second half of the first millennium, it has been, as we move towards the end of the second millennium, in greatest part reduced to a Church of silence within the communist world. The second Church, originating in the *western* half of the Roman Empire, and Latin in culture, began its period of creative expansion after the silence of the Dark Ages, and its dynamics have been uneasily intertwined with those of the Western capitalist world. It has not been silenced, but has in large part become marginal and ineffective. The third Church, that of the third world, emerges from the second Church as the first world reached out in its desire to expand, principally but not exclusively in the *southern* hemisphere. That Church was just as much colonized as the world to which it belonged. It is only now coming into its own, through the pastoral creativity, moral witness, and theological reflection it offers to the universal Church, and through its increasing numerical preponderance. Not surprisingly, the second Church takes the third Church and its characteristic theological trends, above all liberation theology, very seriously; at times it looks to that Church for leadership, and at other times views it with apprehension.

Much needs to be said about the perspectives on grace which unfold within each of these three Churches. That is a task for the next chapter. Having set a broad context for the first world, we will in this chapter explore the first world's characteristic need for grace, first in a more experiential and second in a more systematic vein.

A PERSONAL EXPERIENCE:
DISARRAY AND GLIMMERS OF HOPE

Many wise words have been spoken and written about the plight of the first world, but my theological reflection and yours must begin with our own experience of that plight. To stimulate your theological reflection on the reality of that world, and to be honest about the genesis of my own theology, I offer a brief account of my own experience. It is a limited experience, and yours is no doubt equally valid. It is as foundational for my own theology, however, as your experience is for yours. This experience will be given a broader sociocultural context later in this chapter, and in Chapter Two will be set in a yet broader theological context.

The first world and its plight emerged in full vividness for me when I was invited to move beyond teaching into administration, by serving as president of a theological college and accreditor of many others. Since then I have been exposed in an unexpected and relentless way to a wide range of experiences involving both personal and institutional dynamics. At first these experiences seemed to have little to do with grace. Rather they were leading me to explore the secular texture of the well-established first world within which North American theological institutions must survive and flourish. Soon, however, they opened me to a whole new realm of responsibility, of self-transcendence and failure. I began to discern in them the familiar patterns of grace, but these patterns emerged in a different guise, illuminating not my struggles within myself and with other persons but the efforts of institutions to survive and to serve.

What is significant in these experiences is its institutional focus. At this point a quantum-leap takes place. Institutions do far more than add up the resources and energies of each individual: they multiply them and thus create a reality of a higher order. I had to come to theological terms with this new reality. In the process I was led to a conviction that sanctification is not just an addendum to one's personal justification but its indispensable complement, as social as it is personal. The heady wine of personal spiritual experience, the exhilaration of letting go and trusting one's spontaneities, so much to the fore in the sixties and the early seventies, had to come to terms with our collaboration, warts and all, in building up and tending a little corner of God's Kingdom in this world. Thus the forms of discipleship proper to an ambiguous world began to loom large in my theology of grace, as did the dynamics of incarnation and kenosis. The liberation theology of the third world Church deals with the social dynamics of the third world. What kind of theology will address those of the first world?

In addition to being endowed with a rich and perplexing inner dynamic of their own, the theological schools I became acquainted with interface with many similar and complementary institutions within society. Their complex functioning involves financial, legal, academic, and political dimensions; and each of these institutions is drawn outwards to other corporate bodies, each of which has its own purposes and problems. I became alert to this dimension by a gradual learning process. As I continued in my administrative position, I found that this outward dimension absorbed more and more of my time and energy.[9]

I soon began to find the institutions within my purview deeply marked—precisely as institutions—by the struggle of sin and grace. Ultimately they mirror the sin and the grace which already permeate our hearts and minds.[10] However, in this matter one cannot count on a one-on-one correspondence between the persons who make up the institution and the institution itself. Individuals within the institutions I am familiar with are persons of integrity, good will, and undoubted competence. Yet their coming together for a praiseworthy purpose unfortunately does not guarantee the results they pursue so intently. Inertia, failure to communicate, deficient social skills, the setting up of "we" and "they" categories, the overlapping of energies, and fatigue often frustrate their efforts. The positive results they often achieve seem paltry in comparison with the immense amount of time and energy that goes into them. As a general rule, the more significant and necessary the cooperation of persons within institutions, the more difficult it is to bring that cooperation about.

Those chosen to be leaders are especially vulnerable to the struggle of sin and grace within institutions. In the large number of theological colleges I visited, I would find a special place where the portraits of former presidents were displayed. In an earlier era these persons often stayed in office for twenty or thirty years. But beyond the middle of our own century, the life span of an administrator becomes much shorter. Recent data suggests 6 or 7 years is the average tenure of the theology school president today. The same pattern of rapid change obtains in other walks of life.

No doubt, institutions were touched by the dynamic of sin and grace in earlier years, but now the struggle appears to exact a greater human cost. Stability and regularity once were the order of the day: over the years of a lengthy tenure, the same leaders would face a limited number of new or pressing issues and could repeat much the same routines year by year. The wisdom they acquired would serve them well during their entire term of office. Burnout would be much less likely.

Faculty members are also caught up in this institutional travail, and all the more so when their school belongs to an ecumenical cluster of collaborating theological schools. The calls upon their energy are numerous and diverse. Time for the essential duties of teaching, research, and publication is eroded by faculty meetings, departmental meetings, meetings of professional associations, committee meetings of every size and description. Creativity suffers. Faculty members chafe, and rightly so, at having to deal with the same issues at different points in the complex governing structure. Poorly prepared meetings lead to resentment, and resentment means that participants are even less likely to prepare themselves for further meetings. But then resentment and suspicion would only come to an unprecedented peak should someone seriously suggest non-participatory modes of governance.

Why have these struggles become more intense? The *accelerating tempo* of change in our society has had a drastic impact on theological institutions. They feel they have to keep up to remain viable and pertinent. Given the ever more intricate network of relationships that weaves us together, and an exponential increase in the means of communications, change anywhere in the system brings about change everywhere. The repercussions are dizzying. Humanly speaking, no individual with institutional responsibilities can develop the flexibility needed to keep adjusting over many years to the new situations and challenges relentlessly facing him or her each day, to adopt new technologies and procedures, to reassess, redefine, and re-implement in a ceaseless cycle. Infusions of new blood are needed more frequently. The old guard ages more rapidly; the new guard must often step in before it has learned the ropes—but then in a period of rapid change how worthwhile is any prior learning?

A neuralgic point that aptly reflects this accelerating tempo is long-range institutional planning. Since in our unstable world to drift is to decline, such planning becomes essential and is required by the bodies that accredit educational institutions. But how does one go about this kind of planning in our day? Who can identify, let alone master, the total range of factors that impinge upon the setting and achieving of goals for an institution? Given the swift transformations of the last ten or twenty years, the only safe assumption is that there are no safe assumptions. The long range planning we consider more and more crucial has become more and more unreliable.

The accelerating tempo of change has made *expansion* the law of survival for theological institutions. Like many other institutions, if they are satisfied with their particular "share of the market", our technological world condemns them to obsolescence. Thus they seek out new areas in which they can contribute, new categories of students, more abundant resources to cope with change. While at one time expansion or development emerged as an occasional issue on the institutional agenda, now it appears to be a constant undertow, if not a recurring priority item, and more and more it has led to the creation of development offices, calling upon a whole new brand of specialized institutional expertise. This means that chief executive officers usually find themselves at greater remove from the central commitment of the institution and more explicitly involved in the service functions of development and promotion.

The *complexification* which accompanies this change warrants consideration in its own right. I soon became painfully aware of it during my term as an administrator. Any institution seeking insertion into the modern world must foster a vast number of relationships and become accountable to a large number of constituencies. This creates overload. How much material passes across the desk of a chief executive from various governmental agencies, from professional associations, from other schools and clusters, from groups seeking support for various worthy social causes, from the sponsoring church body at different levels of its governance, from other church bodies, from associations representing various specialized functions within theology schools, each one wishing to bring its own interests and concerns to the fore? In many cases their material receives a cursory scan and ends up in the wastepaper basket, but in other cases a recurring pattern develops, which involves the receiving and assessing of data from other parties, the generating of data for those other parties, correspondence, meetings, and often travel. The creation of specialized departments within the school to handle these new relationships serves to generate more data which ends up on the chief executive officer's desk, and so on and so on far into the night (sometimes literally so).

This complexity affects all sectors of the school. The disciplines move apart from each other, speak diverging languages, and become mutually suspicious. Considerable energy goes into facilitating communication between functions and departments of the school. In the process communication becomes a discipline with its own lingo and adds yet another story to the tower of Babel.

To sum up thus far: institutions today are pulled into different directions, are distracted, frazzled, and scarcely have the time to foster what unifies them from within and gives them life. Often they go through motions, satisfy themselves with shallow compromises; because the pain of facing complex issues is unbearable they end up in a rut, time and time again facing the *déjà vu*. The person in charge struggles to be recollected, to nurture the vision which animates the institution, but the task is monumental. This heretofore unimagined complexity makes unification more essential than ever before but at the same time hampers its achievement.

Does not modern expertise offer us ever more effective means to break out of these vicious circles? Do we not have easy access to means of instantaneous communication, convenient airline connections, word-processors and computers that will spin out a statistical web in no time (and get countless people entangled in it), management techniques and facilitators a mere phone call away? These means are not without effectiveness. However, those who are recognized for their skills in helping institutions are the first to admit that they cannot solve problems for the institution but can only create the context for persons within the institution themselves to work at the required solutions. Even at their best, modern institutional devices do not achieve their purposes with automatic ease. The superficial alleviation they bring heightens the real problems underneath.[11] The possibility of an increased tempo of communications soon becomes a necessity, and the intended targets of the incredible array of messages thus generated are frazzled and bewildered. More and more is being communicated about less and less.

It is time to pause and take stock. Has this simply been the jeremiad of an ex-administrator licking his wounds after his stint in the corporate jungle? Where does grace fit into all this? To this question I now turn.

1. The realities I have described could be seen as purely secular ones: mission statements, development goals, statistical compilations, meetings, computers, all far removed from the proper arena of God's grace. But is there such a thing as a purely secular activity, an activity marked by neither the acceptance nor the refusal of grace?[12] No matter how deftly wrapped up in the glitter of up-to-date technology, everything that human beings do and fail to do is contextualized, whether they acknowledge it or not, by God's enduring

offer of himself to us. The task at hand is to discover the concrete visage of God offering himself in our experience of institutions within the first world.

2. The above account stressed the quandaries which I experienced within and around me. This is only natural: the asperities, the incongruities of life grasp our attention, whereas what functions smoothly and regularly is more often than not taken for granted. Still on balance my experience was positive. I was privileged to meet individuals who were competent, balanced, concerned, genuinely seeking the best way for themselves and the institutions to which they were committed. They evoked my admiration as they struggled in difficult situations, and I often looked to them for inspiration and example. Moreover I found that in spite of considerable difficulties, almost all the institutions I knew managed to survive and in many cases to flourish. Often they were able, in the pattern of the Paschal Mystery, to face up to painful situations and make the creative adjustments which led to new life. Moreover the Spirit was not limited in her action to processes of deliberation and implementation within the institution: often the synchronicity of outer events conspired to help along a worthy purpose in unforeseen and amazing ways. The scriptural text which best says it for me is one in which Paul reflects on his own apostolic labours, recognizes the difficulties which dogged his every step, but nonetheless exclaims:

> But we have this treasure in earthen vessels, to show that the transcendent power belongs to God and not to us. We are afflicted in every way, driven to despair; persecuted, but not forsaken; struck down, but not destroyed; always carrying in the body the death of Jesus, so that the life of Jesus may also be manifested in our bodies. For while we live we are always being given up to death for Jesus' sake, so that the life of Jesus may be manifested in our mortal flesh. So death is at work in us, but life in you. (2 Cor 4:7–12)

I am convinced that the institutions I have come to know are earthen vessels in the Pauline sense. Threats to the integrity of their endeavours differ from those that afflicted Paul two thousand years ago, but the unbreakable thread by which they securely hang over the abyss is the same. Faith, love, and hope in the midst of tribulation are just as much at home in our computerized offices as they were in the gathering places of Paul's rebellious flock.

3. In our description of the negative dynamics at work in theological institutions today, we are not pointing a finger at individuals whom we hold personally responsible for causing them. Persons can connive with or contribute

to these dynamics, but basically the sinfulness of institutions is structural rather than personal. This explains the marked contrast between the sincerity of individuals who seek the Lord's will and the effectiveness with which they achieve it. Try as we may, the work of transforming the structures of human collaboration is at best slow and painful. The mystery of iniquity still at work in our world until the final triumph of grace is just as much a thorn in our flesh as it was in Paul's. In our inmost hearts and even our personal lives we have begun to be transformed, but our institutions experience to the full the groanings of a great act of giving birth to transformed social structures (Romans 8). The birth-pangs are acute, but they produce endurance, "and endurance produces character, and character produces hope, and hope does not disappoint us, because God's love has been poured into our hearts by the Holy Spirit which has been given to us." (Romans 5:4–5)

4. These were preliminary points. The central question is how should we characterize the dynamic of grace and sin in the experience I have related? From this point on the theme of empowerment announced at the beginning of the chapter will begin to emerge.

Let us begin with grace-fulness, a quality which the very word "grace" suggests to us. Gracefulness is based on spontaneity and is at the root of any authentic power. Let us evoke the familiar image of the ballerina. Poured into her dance as a total action, not anxiously focusing on any of the countless small acts which make it up, whether they be relaxing and tensing her muscles, calculating distances, directions, and speeds, maintaining her equilibrium, intricately coordinating her steps with those of an ensemble of dancers, she appears to be exerting no effort. The myriad components into which her performance can be broken up have become second nature to her, thus she can concentrate on the meaning and shape of her dance as a whole. A contrasting image might emerge from our own past, that of the awkward adolescent whose limbs keep on sprouting. Tripping over himself, ungainly, flustered by a bodily puzzle he can't quite put together, he is plagued with the obsessive consciousness that everyone in the room is watching him.[13] The ballet dancer concentrates on *what* she is doing. The awkward adolescent is hung up on the *how*, appears to concentrate on but more precisely is dis-centrated by individual bits of coordination which do not feel right and by the faulty image he self-consciously projects to others.

These contrasting images lead us into one of the recurring themes of the theology of grace. Power is the term which usually capsulizes it; but the reality is at root one of spontaneity, a reality expressed in Paul as the fruits of the spirit and the cheerfulness of the loving giver, in Augustine as the injunction to love and do what you will, and in Aquinas as habit or second nature. This spontaneity gives the power to do graceful acts. The accomplished ballet dancer is at the height of both power and spontaneity; whereas at the most we would acknowledge that the powers of the adolescent are as yet undeveloped and hope that awkward and laborious repetition will generate genuine ease and skill.

A third image will help us clarify the relationship of spontaneity and power, that of the worker who uses a tool (for instance a typewriter, a hammer, a musical instrument, or his own hand) to achieve his purpose. To the extent that the tool obtrudes on his consciousness, and he has to pause on this or that particular sub-gesture contained within his total action, he will be hampered, in extreme cases even paralyzed. Try to be very attentive to the movement of each of your fingers as you type, and you will start to make mistakes much more frequently; you should be focusing on the words you wish to transfer from one sheet of paper to another, and not on the tiny sub-gestures which, if you are a typist, have passed into the realm of the sub-conscious. If you securely possess your own action, you can focus on its intentionality and creatively rise to various challenges. Spontaneity empowers; compulsive attention to each step of an action paralyzes.

There are many definitions of power, sociological and psychological, and we do not intend to go into them here. Suffice it to say that one gifted with genuine power can achieve the goal he or she intends, and thereby foster self-fulfillment or the fulfillment of some other person(s), thing(s), or situation(s). It is when we lack that gift that we fall back on coercion and manipulation to achieve what ends up being the empty shell of that goal. We violate our own spontaneity as well as that of the other.[14]

5. Let us return to the experience of institutional dynamics we have described. Sin and grace, under the form of spontaneity/power and their opposites, are at the heart of what goes on within them.

In the first place, like persons, institutions act towards substantive and constructive purposes. In the case of the theological institutions we used as examples, purpose has to do with teaching students, creatively doing theology, advancing the tradition. Schools are able to acknowledge this purpose in general terms but usually find it difficult to formulate it with sufficient clarity and precision to guide programmes of action. This is the point at which process becomes a painful and obtrusive reality and the limpid beauty of a unifying goal becomes muddied.

In the second place, much of what we described under the heading of institutional pluralism or dis-integration corresponds to the partial focusings which keep us from attention to the whole and from the smooth achievement of objectives. Partially in response to internal pluralism and to communication breakdown, partially in response to the expectations of external agencies, we continually get tangled in this or that aspect of our organization, caught in a repetitive reassessment of particular procedures, techniques, or objectives. We are unsure of our purpose and continually need to reformulate it, like the person who compulsively keeps checking his back pocket to see if his wallet is still there. At this point institutional spontaneity breaks down, and lassitude takes over.

In the third place, battered by rapid and relentless change, having to react and make adjustments each day, institutions are like the adolescent who is awkward and lacks balance. Unlike the adolescent, however, they can't be sure that their pains are growing pains, to be followed some day by ease and maturity. We are only too aware of the ambiguities of progress. We have seen institutions die as well as flourish.

In the fourth place, the attention which institutions continually have to give to development and public relations often parallels the unhappy consciousness of the worker whose attention is diverted to the purely instrumental. Tools and techniques get in the way of substantive goals. Similarly, rather than point beyond themselves, development and public relations end up unpleasantly obtruding within institutional consciousness.

In the fifth place, far from solving problems for us, the incredible array of management techniques, labour-saving devices, computers, sophisticated media campaigns simply make the nature and extent of our powerlessness more painfully obvious to us. Yet that fuller realization of powerlessness is a crucial first step towards the power of grace.

In the sixth place, in spite of all these negative factors, we still manage to survive and to move a good way towards the achievement of our institutional goals. To return to the instance with which I have some familiarity, while administrators and faculty groan under the burden of it all, good articles and books get written; and students receive a formation which enables them to do effective work in the ministry. This is evidence of grace at work in the face of all the negative dynamics I have mentioned, empowering institutions to do what is beyond their human capacities.

Narrow as it may be, this experiential perspective has led us to suggest that empowerment is the cutting edge of grace in the first world. The sin of our world is bound up with its illusion of power. As it painfully realizes its powerlessness it moves towards grace. The grace it receives is that of a power and a spontaneity that enable it to resolutely function in the face of the forces of disintegration at work within it, a power, we shall see, permeated with patience and respect.

Is this impression verified as we look at the first world as a whole? My experience and yours does not limit itself to what is going on within one institution or category of institutions. The many institutional relationships we carefully nurture lead us to people in many walks of life who share a common concern about what is happening in our world; and we begin to discern more and more clearly the pertinence of our individual experience to a much wider set of phenomena. At this point, however, that experience begins to be situated in a perspective at once broader and more reflective. What validity does it retain within that perspective? That is the question we are about to address.

THE BROADER PATTERN:
THE OLD AND THE NEW ORDER

Though the institutional standpoint which each one of us has on the vast and complex reality of the first world is particular and limited, it cannot but lead beyond itself. The many components that make up the life of any institution are intrinsically relational. They function in and are shaped by a broader political, social, cultural, and economic context. In this way the institutions familiar to each one of us mirror the first world as a whole, and, like segments of a holograph, enable us to reconstruct it. Writ large, the assets and liabilities of these institutions are the assets and liabilities of the first world.

In the last twenty years or so numerous authors have offered us strikingly convergent insights on what is really happening in our world. Reflection on their work will be uppermost in this last section. We will begin in a somewhat less technical vein, articulating apprehensions shared by many within the first world and reflected in the work of these authors. We will then move to a broader survey of these works, and in the process bring out more clearly the positive aspects of our present situation.

1. Linear progress is perhaps the most striking feature of our Western society. Bigger, better and faster is the ever recurring refrain. Should we ever begin to entertain doubts when we stand before the altar of technology, well-orchestrated advertising campaigns will soon bring us back into line. Every product is touted as new, improved, a giant step towards the utopia which is dangled before us like the proverbial carrot. There are no problems, only glitches that a competent technician can deftly handle in a moment with the appropriate service manual and a "One moment please" spoken in a tone of quiet authority. But deep down we are beginning to discern illusion from reality. We know the frightening ambiguity of technology, which can devastate as well as build up. Its rapid proliferation brings greater efficiency, but it also mercilessly lays bare the confusion of our own hearts and minds. It helps us to achieve many goals, but does it bring us any closer to the values that really

fulfill us? This ambiguity comes home to us as we watch television. More and more there opens before us a chasm between the illusions of our age of technology as they emerge in advertising and in many serial programmes, and the jarring reality brought home to us by the newscasts.[15]

2. We have looked at pressures on the leadership function within theological institutions. But these institutions are symptomatic of society as a whole. Board-room struggles in periods of retrenchment and financial loss lead to rapid turnovers in business leadership. Still more distressing is the quality of leadership available to society as a whole. This distress is especially acute when we cast ballots for elected officials. Too often we have a choice between lack-luster candidates, cosmetically warmed over, chosen for their ability to win elections rather than for their integrity or wisdom in government, and reluctantly we select the least of the evils before us. These candidates often claim that their policies are the sure-fire solution to our difficulties, that they will even usher in a bright new world; but we are left jaded and cold. We know that once elected, they will forget their brave promises and follow the path of least resistance. Even with many bureaucrats and computer printouts to offer them guidance, they appear to be powerless to head off the drift into chaos. We oscillate between periods of left-wing centralization and right-wing laissez-faire, but both policies prove to be simplistic, vague, ineffectual.[16]

3. The imbalance between the quantity and quality of products available for our use/consumption continues to grow. These products, whether material (in the form of machinery, equipment, food, clothing, housing, etc.) or personal (in the form of services, professional or technical) are becoming more numerous and diverse. But this quantitative increase is not matched by a qualitative one. To the contrary: our present economic system is condemned to feed on its own expansion, to produce more and more goods, whether useful, elegant, durable or not.[17] Professional and service relationships, which used to enjoy an unhurried, leisurely, human quality, are now often harried, perfunctory, carried out under the threat of expensive legal suits. Highly touted improvements to products are often utterly insignificant. Indeed advertising, which locks up considerable human and financial resources, tries to cover up the shoddy quality, unreliable service, planned obsolescence needed to feed our economy, and to shore up at any cost a fragile profit margin which becomes less and less meaningful as the economy continues to deteriorate. The less satisfactory the substance, the more ingenuity and resources must be applied to the wrapping, and the fewer resources are available for quality control and genuine improvements.

4. The same people who consume the goods of the economy also produce

them, thus we need to look at the other side of the coin. Our dissatisfaction as consumers is only compounded by our dissatisfaction as producers.[18] The stress on efficiency at all costs, the fragmentation and specialization of the work process which condemns workers to repeat over and over the same mindless gesture to fulfill the technocratic hope of maximizing the efficiency of the enterprise (quantitatively rather than qualitatively, as we have seen), the adoption of capital intensive means of production, have embedded severe unemployment into the very structures of our society. In spite of all the rhetoric, in spite of what at times are well-meaning intentions, our governments fail to rise above their narrow vision: too often they adopt priorities far removed from the compassionate but resolute reshaping of structures needed to give meaningful work to the millions now condemned to eke out a bleak existence on a dole which will soon prove too expensive for the economy to provide. What counts is the survival of traditional business enterprises and the security of their profits. The dream is that high technology will provide the quick fix, but thus far it has not: many of our young adults find no work, lead lives of futility and escape, and become part of our disintegrating social fabric. Youth used to be generally associated with hope. If we ask the young themselves, too many of them will associate youth with numbness and despair.

"Hidden unemployment" today usually refers to the persons who have given up hope of finding work, and who are not counted among the unemployed in economic statistics. Another form of hidden unemployment is ultimately even more devastating. So many people today work simply to survive economically. They are not committed as persons to the work they are doing. At best they tolerate what they do, at worst they find it degrading, even destructive.[19] This ties in with the quality factor mentioned above. Whoever is not convinced that his or her work is socially valuable or does not find in it pride and self-satisfaction, is ultimately alienated from it. By and large we have moved beyond the crass exploitation prevalent in nineteenth century industries, but what has replaced it may prove to be even more insidious and destructive of human values.[20]

5. The fifth factor is the immense pluralism of our society; the pluralism within theological institutions which we mentioned is but a small hint of it. The specializations, academic and administrative, which make it very difficult for persons within institutions supposedly as unified as theological schools to understand each other's language and perspective on things that really matter already evidence some dis-integration. On the scale of society as a whole, a pervasive fragmentation has accentuated the tendency to put forward one's own interests, whether they be those of an individual or of a class. Increasingly legislative assemblies are surrounded by lobbyists seeking to maintain or in-

crease the status, the slice of the economic pie, the exemptions from taxes and regulations of the special interest groups they represent. It becomes more and more difficult for legislators to actually concentrate on the common good they have been elected to promote. Engaged in a constant battle of conflicting interests, they bend this way or that depending on who shoves hardest and last.[21]

6. Just as fragmentation encourages the pursuit of selfish interests, so the dizzying pace of change encourages the adoption of short-term solutions. More and more we are willing to buy time for a few years by means of patchwork and piecemeal programs. The bottom line is not the welfare of society for future generations but the next meeting of stockholders or the next election. Indeed if the times are out of joint, it is in large part because of a succession of short-term solutions often disguised as long-term solutions by persons dressed in lab coats and speaking a reassuring scientific jargon. This awful truth is beginning to dawn on many people. Bernard Lonergan speaks of it in *Insight* when he describes the social surd:

> For just as progress consists in a realization of some ideas that leads to the realization of others until a whole coherent set is concretely operative, so the repeated exclusion of timely and fruitful ideas involves a cumulative departure from coherence. The objective social situation possesses the intelligibility put into it by those that brought it about. But what is put in, less and less is some part of a coherent whole that will ask for its completion, and more and more it is some arbitrary fragment that can be rounded off only by giving up the attempt to complete the other arbitrary fragments that have preceded or will follow it. In this fashion social functions and enterprises begin to conflict; some atrophy and others grow like tumours; the objective situation becomes penetrated with anomalies; it loses its power to suggest new ideas and, once they are implemented, to respond with still further and better suggestions. The dynamic of progress is replaced by sluggishness and then by stagnation. In the limit, the only discernible intelligibility in the objective facts is an equilibrium of economic pressures and a balance of national powers.[22]

7. The above points touch close to home. If, as suggested by Lonergan, one is willing to look at the broader world picture, the situation appears even more ominous. Nuclear posturing by East and West threatens to engulf us all, finishing off in one blast what unrestrained pollution has not in the meanwhile succeeded in destroying. Between North and South there is an economic

chasm. The first world acknowledges it, but addresses it not with effective measures but with a rhetoric at times sincere if ineffectual, at other times serving to conceal blatant intervention and subjugation. The ensuing international financial arrangements are like a castle of cards upon a flimsy table: everyone tiptoes around to avert catastrophe.

8. The ultimate result of this is a global sense of powerlessness, especially acute in the first world because the illusion of power is precisely what it clings to.[23] Achievements incredible twenty years ago are within our grasp, but are these achievements really worthwhile? In what really counts, our power is negative rather than positive, it is the power to manipulate, kill, instill terror, a power brought to a stalemate because of the equal and opposite power it has generated. What we lack is the power to influence minds and hearts, break down barriers, and achieve effective collaboration, for instance, between labour and business, East and West, North and South.[24] Technology takes away with one hand what it gives with the other. Its by-product is complexity; this means more and more of our resources have to be allocated to promoting communication between and unity of fragmented parts. Its by-product is also rapid obsolescence, which means that we have to expend much time and energy on the constant task of re-assessing, re-defining directions for a tomorrow that will be as unstable as is today. Bureaucracy swells. Paralysis sets in. We are ready to face anything except the real issues. We are cast adrift. Some through drug addiction try to deaden the pain of this headlong rush towards destruction but only succeed in destroying themselves. In moments of despair others, like moths near a light, experience a fascination for the final nuclear catastrophe that will deliver us from this social body doomed to death.

As we move into this broader picture, the dynamic of sin becomes terrifying. Nonetheless grace abounds; a resilient hope enables most human beings to survive and keep up the struggle. Plight recognized as plight is opportunity. Powerlessness acknowledged becomes the locus of a new power, that of grace. Can we discern the features of that grace more clearly?

This leads us to survey and consolidate the analyses of recent critics of the current first world scene, among them Theodore Roszak, Philip Slater, Fritjof Capra, James Ogilvy, Charles Hampden-Turner, E.F. Schumacher, Marilyn Ferguson, Jeremy Rifkin, Daniel Yankelovitch, and Morris Berman. They function within the parameters of their own secular disciplines, but we will be on the lookout for convergences between themes which emerge in their work and the themes of an explicit theology of grace.

The theme of the vicious circle has occasionally come to the surface in our descriptive survey. The author who expresses it most clearly is Philip Slater, in *The Pursuit of Loneliness*:

Technological change, mobility, and individualistic ways of thinking all rupture the bonds that tie a man to a family, a community, a
kinship network, a geographic location—bonds that give him a comfortable sense of himself. Yet his efforts accelerate the very erosion
he seeks to halt.[25]

Americans love bigness, mostly because they feel so small.
They feel small because they're unconnected, without a place.
They try to overcome that smallness by associating themselves
with bigness—big projects, big organizations, big government,
mass markets, mass media, "nationwide", "worldwide". But it's
that very same bigness that rips away their sense of connectedness
and place and makes them feel small. A vicious circle.[26]

Americans thus find themselves in a vicious circle in which
their community relationships are increasingly competitive, trivial,
and irksome, in part as a result of their efforts to avoid or minimize
potentially irksome relationships.[27]

Every possession we acquire loads us with more responsibilities
and cares, to which we respond by retreating into infant orality and
"consuming", thereby acquiring still more possessions. This vicious circle has inspired our economy for thirty years now, so that
we've come to view an "expanding" economy as an inevitability,
like the expanding waistline of middle age.[28]

We turn continually to technology to save us from having to
cooperate with one another. Technology, meanwhile, helps preserve
the competitiveness and render it even more frantic, thus making cooperation at once more urgent and more difficult.[29]

It's true that if I manufacture shoddy goods, create artificial
needs, and sell food that looks good but is tasteless or contaminated, I'll make money. But what can I do with this money? I can
buy shoddy goods and poisoned food, and satisfy ersatz needs.
Our refusal to recognize our common economic destiny leads to
the myth that if we all overcharge each other, we'll be better
off.[30]

Economists assume that jobs must be created even for things
that don't need to be done so people can have money to spend on
things they don't need. And to get people to buy things they don't
need, we create a huge industry to get them to want them. Meanwhile the things people really need—food, shelter, safety, health, a
pleasant environment—they can't afford.[31]

Slater's "catch 22's" powerfully evoke the classical theological doctrine of moral impotence, which involves a vicious circle of its own. According to Augustine and Aquinas, the sinful will can of itself generate only sinful actions and thus will never, without the gift of the grace that justifies, turn to God in conversion and allow God to break the stranglehold of evil. Its efforts originate within the confines of the ego and are doomed to failure. Thus like these two classical authors, Slater in effect is describing for us the moral powerlessness so vividly dramatized by Paul in Romans 7, doing so not in personal terms but in broader structural terms that speak to our first world as a whole.

Paul trusts in a God who has promised intervention on behalf of those who are bound and oppressed by their own sin and, more subtly, by their self-induced illusions of being powerful and blameless. But Paul's God waits for the opportune moment: evil carries with it the seeds of its own self-destruction and, in the analysis of Romans 7, the coming to term and the naming of its dynamic is part of God's saving action. Again Slater:

> Technological advance has its own self-destruct mechanism built into it. For as change becomes more rapid, reaching to the point of almost instant obsolescence, it becomes more and more impossible to plan for the future. But the whole structure of technological society is built on planning, looking ahead, living in the future, postponing gratification in favour of attending to tasks, and so on. So as technology pushes into the future, it also undermines the future, forcing people to turn to the present for security and gratification.[32]

In *Earthwalk* Slater further develops this theme under the heading of social eversion, the process "whereby the intensification of some social form leads directly to its opposite."[33] Theodore Roszak in his *People/Planet* puts the same point in terms of a feedback loop:

> As the scale of the industrial system mounts, so also—at least along one important line of contemporary dissent in Western society—do our expectations for freedom and fulfillment, together with our intolerance for whatever denies us the right to achieve our unique being in the world. This, in turn, becomes an obstacle to the further growth and integration of that system; and accordingly, it begins to dis-integrate, but for reasons that are essentially creative. Might we not say that the yearning of people to realize their full personal potentiality is in the nature of a feed-back loop that works to restore the

human scale of things? In seeking to save our personhood, we assert the human scale. In asserting the human scale, we subvert the regime of bigness. In subverting bigness, we save the planet.[34]

As Marilyn Ferguson says in *The Aquarian Conspiracy*: "Our pathology is our opportunity."[35] The seeds of hope are deeply planted within the detritus of our society. Earlier I discerned the presence, in a more direct and religious mode, of such seeds in first world institutions of my own experience. The authors we have been surveying manifest the secular mode of that hope. A few of them, for instance Alvin Toffler in *Future Shock* and *The Third Wave*, and Charles Reich in *The Greening of America*, fascinated by explosive but superficial signs of progress in our own world, fail to discern the depth of transformation that will be required for that hope to come to fulfillment. Others face the negative elements squarely. Whether they denounce the present or proclaim the future, they discern in our current bewilderment the building blocks of a new order, but stress that this new order will not emerge of itself: to use a biblical image, they invite us to resolutely set our faces towards Jerusalem and make the hard and painful choices which alone will instill a genuine forward movement to our journey.

Are these recent perceptions of what is germinating within our world unprecedented? If there is anything novel in them, it resides in the specific application to the dilemmas of the first world of a lofty intuitive grasp already available to thinkers of a more philosophical cast of mind. For instance Teilhard de Chardin, who had a wide experience of the struggles of humankind in the twentieth century, saw in its agony the birth of a new order of reality, a higher integration he calls the noosphere. Bernard Lonergan concludes that our age is characterized by the move from a classical mind-set in which everything is basically fixed according to an abstract and invariant pattern and any change of this pattern is a deviation from perfection, to a historical mind-set in which evolution is not downgraded as a temporary aberration but appropriated and fostered as the expression of a human transcendence which has no limits because only God can fulfill it. The personalist John Macmurray formulates a similar shift in terms of a movement from a mechanistic through an organic to a personal order of being and action.[36]

How do the more recent authors we have been surveying flesh out this lofty intuitive grasp? We shall survey their convergences and divergences on a) how to formulate the differences between the old and the new order, b) where to situate the beginnings of the old order, and c) how to envisage the movement towards the new order.

a) These authors show a striking convergence in how they see the new order differing from the old. Fritjof Capra can serve as a spokesperson here. In *The Turning Point*[37] he bases the shift from old to new world orders on a fundamental paradigm transformation which touches every domain of human life, including the ways in which physicists model the universe which they study.[38] To briefly evoke this transformation, I will use two images, one relating to Isaac Newton's classical physics, and the other to modern medicine's attempt to grasp what is going on in victims of cancer, in the hope that these images will lead to the basic insight shared by Capra and many others.

Newton's universe is composed of physical masses situated in space and time. They come together and separate according to various laws of causal attraction, repulsion, and impulsion, as, for instance, the solar system whose orderly movement is regulated by the laws of gravity. Once a body has received an impulse to move in a certain direction, it will continue to move in that direction unless stopped or diverted by some force outside itself. These physical entities, whether astronomical or microscopic, are essentially atoms, inert building blocks not only distinct but also separate from each other.[39] Their interaction is mechanical, extrinsically devised, expressed in mathematical terms which alone are considered to be objective and impartial.

The underlying assumption of this form of thought was already operative in Descartes' fateful methodological injunction to divide large problems into smaller sub-problems which are to be tackled one by one, as if each situation can be dealt with independently of all others; it was furthered by Locke and Hume in the social sphere, where individuals are seen as essentially self-sufficient, coming together only by social contract; it was further transposed in the epistemology of Immanuel Kant who, in more general terms still, expressed the Newtonian world-view in his *Critique of Pure Reason*. Operative here is a model in which reality appears not as an interrelated whole but as a juxtaposition of discrete elements going their separate ways unless they happen to be yoked together by some extraneous intervention. Movement is primarily linear. Whatever is moving in any given direction will continue to move in that direction unless stopped. Space and time are boundless, and, of themselves, any change, growth, or expansion will continue indefinitely. This leads to the assumption that more along the same line is always better.

But then contemporary post-Einsteinian physics has moved beyond this model. No longer is reality ultimately described in terms of matter and motion; no longer are the phenomena of the world the same whether we are there to observe them or not. In modern physics, the universe, in the words of Capra, is experienced "as a dynamic, inseparable whole which always includes the observer in an essential way".[40] We know the physical universe by being participants within that universe. The experiments we set up to know events within it are themselves events with inevitable repercussions on the events we wish to know. It is not "a collection of physical objects" but "a complicated web of relations between the parts of a unified whole."[41]

Our second image, that of cancer, offers us a vivid grasp of what is at stake in the newer physics. Realization in the twentieth century that cancer is essentially a form of linear growth run amok within the body is a salutary shock, as is the extension of this image to other areas of "cancer" within our society and our polluted environment. This image helps us to realize that the body is not a machine but an organic whole to be dealt with as a whole, a whole whose every part is in solidarity with every other part, a whole regulated by inner laws which set the limits of its healthy growth. This view helps us understand how more cell proliferation is not necessarily better. In the earlier stages of organic development some proliferation is good, but in maturity the normal rate of growth and change decelerates. Disease comes from linear expansion; good health from proper attention to the inner rhythms and fluctuations of growth and decline.[42] This applies not just to the physical body but to the intricately woven whole of our society in all its aspects. Repairing the body politic is like healing the human body rather than like fixing a bicycle. Zeroing in on the defective part and putting in a new one will not work in the long run: the essential interconnection of all parts of the body must be heeded at all times.

A diagrammatic comparison of the two orders, based on the authors we have studied, might be helpful. (See p. 25).

This diagram does no more than evoke the many ramifications of this shift from old to new orders. The economic implications are especially significant. Both capitalism and communism are to be subsumed under the old order, since in both expansionary industrialism reigns, with its vision of centralized control of every factor of consumption and production, with its Cartesian fragmentation of human activity into repetitive gestures which make possible efficiency and control.[43] In contrast the vision emerging in these recent authors leads to a new socio-economic order, one which the third world is beginning to lay before us and religious leaders to formulate, as Pope John Paul II does in his encyclical *Laborem Exercens*. Similar shifts can be charted for the political, educational, medical, psychological worlds. The prophets of the new order see all these different sectors as profoundly interrelated and expressing, each in its own way, the same profound world-view. Proponents of the older view—and this is an essential point of difference[44]—do not treasure nor do they even grasp that interconnectedness.

A final word of caveat. This contrast between old and new does not intend to re-enact in secular terms the biblical separation of the sheep from the goats

The Old Order	The New Order
MECHANISTIC world-view	ORGANISMIC world-view
The *parts* are prior to the whole	The *whole* is prior to the parts
linear growth: more and more of same: acceleration	*rhythmic growth,* according to inner law of development: deceleration
problems are solved by *isolating* individual components, treating them as separate from all others: the short-term fix and *profit motive*	*interrelating* all components within the whole is crucial, as are the long-range implications of any change: *ecological awareness*
expansion mentality gives rise to a *cult of bigness* for bigness' sake: the multinationals	*small is beautiful:* the human scale community & local enterprise
relationship is an extrinsic *self-sufficiency* to be cultivated above all else; self-enclosed systems	things defined by their interrelatedness; *openness* to the other in his otherness; the unexpected is welcomed
competition is the essential mode in which these unrelated beings end up relating	the essential mode is that of *cooperation*
stress on *quantity*	stress on *quality*

on the last day. For instance Capra in his book[45] offers a bi-polar approach based upon the Chinese yin/yang rhythm, an approach in remarkable continuity, we shall see, with some key themes of the theology of grace. The transition he advocates is not so much from old to new as it is from a situation where the values characteristic of the new order are subsumed under those characteristic of the old, to a situation where the exact reverse takes place. Technology, rationalization, proper distinctions between domains of human activity are not to be eliminated but relativized. Far from a return to a still older pattern which was undifferentiated, even animistic, he and many others envisage a movement forward from a competitive individualism to an ecologically sensitive and interdependent personalism.

b) The authors we have been studying retrace the steps by which our world has moved into its present sorry state. Though different, their viewpoints complement one another.

The authors we have studied, Capra more explicitly than others, attach great importance to the Cartesian-Newtonian revolution in the physical sciences. Newton's physics offered a simple and clear model of the universe, and from it much scientific and technological progress ensued. Not surprisingly, many transposed its basic mechanistic principles to their own forms of human pursuit, including medicine, economics, politics, and psychology. What essentially was a partial increment of knowledge to be relativized and set within a broader context became the sum and substance of our world. Thence our dilemma.

A number of these authors point out the key role played in this epochal shift by the Protestant reformers, especially John Calvin. According to Max Weber's classical study *The Protestant Ethic and the Spirit of Capitalism*, Calvin was the primary source of the work-ethic which underlies the emergence of mercantile capitalism in the seventeenth and eighteenth century, and the industrial revolution in the nineteenth. The author who espouses this position most clearly is Jeremy Rifkin in *The Emerging Order*.[46] He develops it in some detail but also refers to the scientific developments we referred to above.

Theodore Roszak attaches more importance to the contribution of Bacon and Descartes, because it is their framework which enabled Newton to come up with his successful model of the universe. Roszak sees this framework as an instance of a narrow "single vision". This vision counters the Old Gnosis, for which all reality is transparent, pointing beyond itself to numinous forces within the universe.[47] For him the Protestant Reformation gave considerable impetus to this denial of the sacramentality of being, though the Catholicism in which he was raised fares no better at his hands. All of these movements conspired to make normative a view in which things are only themselves, to be approached, analyzed, dealt with as inertly objective, self-enclosed realities over which we are entitled to exercise complete mastery.

In many ways Morris Berman's *The Reenchantment of the World* offers an account which strikingly resembles that of Roszak. He finds in alchemy a powerful instance of the earlier participatory, enchanted consciousness against which the scientific revolution took place in the sixteenth and seventeenth centuries. He puts that revolution in a broader context which includes the late medieval and Renaissance revolution in commerce and the break-down of the feudal system. Along with Barfield and Capra he would see the roots of this revolution going back to the Greeks. Already in Plato the shift from an earlier participating consciousness to an objectifying one begins. While elements of this earlier consciousness remain down through the Christian Middle Ages, from the sixteenth century the newer consciousness is given free rein.

These interpretations need not be seen as ultimately contradicting each other. I would only add for consideration another key transition which none of these authors refers to, that between the *via antiqua* of earlier and the *via moderna* of later medieval scholasticism. The *via moderna* offered a new universe, or rather a pluriverse, of isolated individual entities related extrinsically by divine decree; it contrasted with the universe of the *via antiqua*, relational through and through, suffused with the type of participation sought by Roszak in an earlier pre-Christian gnosticism, yet open to critical rational inquiry. This *via moderna* of Ockham aptly crystallized a newer set of basic assumptions beginning to emerge within the mercantile classes, as well as the sense of dislocation which permeated that period. The pioneers of modern science at work in the late Middle Ages would feel quite at home in the *via moderna*, and Descartes would find precedents in their work for his philosophical and methodological tasks.[48] The complexities of this key transition will be dealt with in Chapter Two.

c) When these authors delineate the new order to which they aspire significant differences begin to emerge, some of them already latent in how they view the origins of the old order. These differences are formulated by Berman. For him Western consciousness stands at a crossroads. One fork, corresponding to the old order, is quite clearly defined, while the other fork, corresponding to the new, remains somewhat vague:

> One fork retains all the assumptions of the Industrial Revolution and would lead us to salvation through science and technology; in short, it holds that the very paradigm that got us into trouble can somehow get us out. Its proponents (and they generally include the modern socialist states) view an expanding economy, increased urbanization, and cultural homogeneity on a Western model as both good and inevitable. The other fork leads to a future that is as yet somewhat obscure. Its advocates are an amorphous mass of Luddites, ecologists, regional separatists, steady-state economists, mystics, occultists, and pastoral romantics. Their goal is the preservation (or resuscitation) of such things as the natural environment, regional culture, archaic modes of thought, organic community structures, and highly decentralized political autonomy. The first form clearly leads to a blind alley or Brave New World. The second, on the other hand, often appears to be a naive attempt to turn around and return whence we came; to return to the safety of a feudal age now gone by. But a crucial distinction must be introduced here: recapturing a reality is not the same thing as returning to it.[49]

Among the authors we have surveyed, only Alvin Toffler and Charles Reich describe the new order in a way that resembles Berman's first fork. In *The Third Wave* Toffler stresses that the emerging new order will be found not by going backwards but by going forward. The first wave, that of the agricultural age, is completely spent, and the second, that of the industrial age, is definitely on the wane. We must pin our hopes on the third, technological wave about to wash over us, rejoicing in the unprecedented virtualities it makes available. Toffler's sense of the spiritual conflicts which underlie the epochal shift implied by the emergence of the new order is underdeveloped. His technological optimism clearly leaves him within the mindset of the second wave, which he claims is already spent. His injunction that we not look backward as we search out patterns for the new age is not taken seriously by analysts who are in touch with the profound spiritual crisis implied in our present peril. Though they are not interested in bringing back the dirt and squalor of an earlier form of economic organization, they do want to get in touch with the authentic values of our world which we have loved and lost, because without them we will flounder.

All the authors who seek this synthesis of originating and newer values agree in rejecting root and branch the approach to change which, centralized, bureaucratic, lavish in scale, prevails within the old order. For them renewal will come from the grass-roots, through small communities of persons whose consciousness has been raised and who share a concern that touches all walks of human life. Marilyn Ferguson in the very title of her book *The Aquarian Conspiracy* offers a telling image. She wishes not to conjure up cloaks and daggers but to remind us of the etymological roots of ''con-spiracy'': a breathing together, which calls to mind the synchronous, community-building role traditionally ascribed to the Holy Spirit who, in the words of Hopkins, ''broods over the world with warm breast, and with, ah, bright wings.'' Networks of persons who support one another in a common vision are beginning to emerge on a world-wide scale; and according to Ferguson, the impetus of these groups will little by little bring about transformation in all areas of human endeavour. In Roszak we find a longing for contemporary monastic communities which would function much as the Benedictines did in nurturing the gradual movement from the Dark Ages to the Middle Ages.[50]

Nonetheless significant differences do remain. Roszak deliberately seeks a form of religious commitment which leaves behind the traditional Christianity he himself has jettisoned because of the preoccupation with guilt which he found in his own Catholic upbringing and the connivance of Protestantism with the single vision which poisons our world.[51] He seeks this commitment in the confluence of a number of non-Christian, especially Eastern traditions[52] and appears willing to accept a Christianity diluted by occultism.[53] In a similar vein Capra in *The Tao of Physics* is taken up with the correspondences between contemporary physics and eastern mysticism, whether Hindu or Buddhist or Taoist. Berman uses Bateson to define a new order beyond the archaic and religious form of participation: ''What would be worshipped, if anything, is ourselves, each other, and *this earth—our home*, the body of us all that makes our lives possible.''[54] In the end, however, he offers us more questions than answers.

Some evoke the possibility that an emerging new order, thoroughly grounded in an organicist or holistic world-view, might degenerate into a fascism whose abuses would be even more frightening than those we have depicted. If we seek to replace the pernicious individualism of the old order with pseudo-mystical impersonalism, we will provide little bulwark against totalitarianism of any kind. In contrast, if we are rooted in and further develop the central position of the Judeo-Christian tradition that at heart God is personal, we find a basis for vindicating our own personhood as inalienable. In this vein Jeremy Rifkin in *The Emerging Order* looks for a revival of the old-time religion to move us towards constructive social change. We can say yes to revival, however, only if it gets in touch with what is most authentic in the Western tradition. Otherwise it will be short-lived.

This quest for authenticity is central to the remaining chapters of this book. We will seek to speak of God's gracious working for us and with us in terms which are faithful to the Christian tradition of the West, yet open to the authentic values of other religious traditions, Christian and non-Christian. As we uncover that tradition and transpose it into contemporary categories, we hope to speak insightfully to the plight of a first world caught up in the illusion of a technological power based upon a single-minded and partial vision, closed to the gift of a power to achieve what is authentic and worthwhile and fulfilling; and we intend to offer a fuller religious and Christian context for the opportunities which are beginning to emerge out of our disarray.[55]

Faithfulness to the Christian tradition is no easy thing. We will try to delicately ferret out the well-meaning but insidious aberrations of the later Middle Ages. They greatly contributed to the assumptions that distorted both Reformation and Counter-Reformation movements within the Church, keeping them from dialogue with each other until our century. They set the stage for the technological and scientific vision which has mortally flawed the old order still prevailing in our world. At the same time we will try to re-articulate the Western theological tradition in terms that are comprehensive, constructive, attentive to the relational dimension of reality, that can provide the space needed both to recover what is genuine and worthwhile in the ebbing industrial age and to welcome the contribution of East and South. That tradition gives life and meaning to the Western Church and to the first world of which the Western Church is the matrix. It enables that Church to enter more fruitfully into relation with the ancient Church of the East and the newer Church of the third world. Divorced from that tradition, the new order will be built on sand, like the house in the parable of Jesus.

NOTES

1. Juan Luis Segundo, *Grace and the Human Condition* (Maryknoll: Orbis, 1973), Spanish original published in 1968.

2. Leonardo Boff, *Liberating Grace* (Maryknoll: Orbis, 1979), Brazilian original published in 1976.

3. It appears that the first, second, and third world nomenclature finds its origins in the 1950's when, under the leadership of statesmen such as Nehru and Sukarno, the newly independent Afro-Asian countries of the world sought to forge and name a new solidarity between themselves. This theme is developed by Paul Johnson, *Modern Times: The World from the Twenties to the Eighties* (New York: Harper and Row, 1983). For instance he says of the newly emerging *tiers monde* terminology: "The concept was based upon verbal prestidigitation, the supposition that by inventing new worlds and phrases one could change (and improve) unwelcome and intractable facts. There was the first world of the West, with its rapacious capitalism; the second world of totalitarian socialism, with its slave-camps; both with their hideous arsenals of mass-destruction. Why should there not come into existence a third world, arising like a phoenix from the ashes of empire, free, pacific, non-aligned, industrious, purged of capitalist and Stalinist vice, radiant with public virtue, today saving itself by its exertions, tomorrow the world by its example . . . An ex-colonial state was righteous by definition. A gathering of such states would be a senate of wisdom" (p. 477). Even should the above quotation contain elements of truth, and even if in recent years in their wish to expand the three world typology some have pointed out sharply differing levels of economic development within the third world· as well as the presence within the first world of third world enclaves of oppression, such as the blacks, the natives, the unemployed, women, etc., still in recent theological conversation surrounding theology of liberation the typology maintains its usefulness and corresponds with what we will discover later to be a helpful typology of the Churches.

4. Certain areas of the world, such as North America, were originally included within the colonial empire of Western Europe but became part of the first world rather than of the third. In many cases however the original population of those areas continues to exist in enclaves, reminding us of a third world dynamic of oppression still very much

at work within the first world. The Indians of North America stand out as an example of this.

5. The independence gained by the descendants of European settlers in North America did not break but rather consolidated the oppressive structure implied in their earlier relationship to the mother country. They simply became members of the first world club. From oppressed colonials they became oppressors of the native populations, carrying forth a programme of relentless expansion.

6. Joe Holland and Peter Henriot, S.J., *Social Analysis: Linking Faith and Justice* (Washington: Center of Concern, 1980), Chapter 4.

7. Ibid., pp. 34–38.

8. Walbert Bühlmann, *The Coming of the Third Church: An Analysis of the Present and Future of the Church* (Maryknoll: Orbis, 1977).

9. This was just as true of the institution over which I presided as it was of myself. This perception was no doubt enlivened by one of my first major tasks: to implement a decision to move our school to a location contiguous with one of the major university centers of Canada. What for years had been a sheltered seminary-type institution, on the margin, entered into a bracing atmosphere and had to learn to breathe much more vigorously.

10. This relates to the constitutive function of meaning described by Bernard Lonergan, *Method in Theology* (London: Darton, Longman, & Todd, 1972), p. 78.

11. In this vein Theodore Roszak in *The Cult of Information: The Folklore of Computers and the True Art of Thinking* (New York: Random House, 1986), especially on pp. 105–107, 129–134, reflects on the role of computerized information in our society. Raw data is as useful as the ideas which preside over its gathering and organization are valid. That computers will give us instant access to the information we need to improve our society is a myth. They are machines that operate only according to how they are programmed; programmes, and the questions they are designed to answer, embody the ideas and assumptions of those who frame them. In no way do computers allow us to bypass our responsibility as human beings to sift out, in a delicate and open-ended process, right ideas from wrong ones. Apart from this process, computers will magnify our predicament rather than contribute to its solution. In other words dialectic, a functional specialty which emerges in Lonergan's *Method in Theology*, is an inescapable part of any human endeavour.

12. That there is no human activity which is salvifically neutral is a traditional position espoused by Aquinas. One is either *conversus ad Deum* or *aversus a Deo*. In the first case human acts can lead us to God, in the second case they are powerless unless the yearning enfleshed within them, the natural desire they embody, is fulfilled by God's grace.

13. For this analysis, see Chapter Four of Michael Polanyi's *Personal Knowledge* (Chicago: University of Chicago Press, 1958).

14. A contemporary psychologist, Rollo May, and a contemporary sociologist, Philip Slater, converge in their analysis of power. It will be worthwhile to summarize their thought. In his *Power and Innocence* (New York: Norton, 1972), May lists five

forms of power in the order of their increasing authenticity (pp. 105–112): *exploitative* (power = force), *manipulative* (power over), *competitive* (power against), *nutrient* (power for), and *integrative* (power with). There are situations where force is called for, but in the long run "power ought to move with the affirmation of the spontaneity of the person it encounters" (p. 102). In his *Earthwalk* (New York: Bantam, 1975), Slater distinguishes between negative power, "the ability to control, force, imprison, invade, terrify, and kill others", and positive power, "the ability to influence others, to arouse love and respect, and to get one's needs met—without pressure and in a socially naked and unadorned state, devoid of status, position, or other weaponry" (p. 137). Negative power in balance leads to a terrifying stalemate (e.g. the phrase "balance of terror"); positive power in balance leads to fruitful interaction and mutual development. Also cf. Morris Berman, *The Reenchantment of the World* (New York: Bantam, 1984), pp. 277–278.

15. In recent years there has been a more thoroughly orchestrated effort at managing the news, at softening hard edges and muting hard questions. Law suits and attempts at taking over networks that present or appear to present a picture unfavourable to this or that interest within society evince a tendency which, unchecked, would subsume genuine reporting under advertising and public relations.

16. James Ogilvy in *Multi-dimensional Man* (New York: Oxford University Press, 1977) offers an analysis of the powerlessness at the very nerve center of our society. He claims that a profound shift is taking place in which the traditional loci of power are becoming obsolete. The presidency is dead, Ogilvy tells us. Bureaucrats have power to limit, to constrain, to reduce all to the lowest common denominator, but not to lead and direct. For him, "The attempt to locate a single source of power in contemporary society is as *pointless* as a corresponding attempt in nature: the project is reminiscent of the earliest religious impulse to account for thunder as the wrath of God." (p. 31)

17. Berman in *Reenchantment* . . . offers a striking insight based on Gregory Bateson into the nature of this expansionary process. A healthy system is marked by self-correction: " . . . the results of past actions are fed back into the system, and this new bit of information then travels around the circuit, enabling the system to maintain something near to its ideal, or optimal state" (242). The perfect example of the contrasting runaway system is addiction: "The heroin addict needs an increasingly larger fix; the sugar addict finds that the more pastry he eats, the more pastry he wants; the imperialist power starts out seeking particular foreign markets, and eventually winds up trying to police the globe" (242). In Berman's terms, the obsession of our system with bigger, better, faster, defined in quantitative terms is an addiction and not a normal healthy activity: "Unlimited expansion, ideologically ratified by the French Enlightenment and the economic theory of laissez-faire, began to make sense, and the need for an increasingly larger 'fix' was regarded as part of the natural order of things rather than as aberrant. We are by now completely addicted to maximizing variables that are wrecking our own natural system. The emergence of holistic thought in our own time might itself be part of the general process of self-corrective feedback" (263).

18. Cf. Jeremy Rifkin, *The Emerging Order* (New York: Random House, 1983), pp. 175–180.

19. Cf. Theodore Roszak, *Person/Planet* (New York: Anchor Press, 1979), ch. 8.

20. This is not to deny that a good number in our world find their work significant. We all know many such people. Because they have caught sight of a redeeming purpose they can gracefully put up with annoyances which characterize the work-place: this is the dynamic of grace which is at work within and against the dynamic of sin.

21. In the second world system, where such factors do not overtly come into play, pluralism seems to occur at a lower level: condemned to spend most of their lives drably fulfilling the plans established from the isolation of some central office, citizens find ways of investing large amounts of time in their own pursuits, diverting public resources and personal creative energies towards them. Thus, if anything, the phenomenon of inertia is even more noticeable.

22. Bernard Lonergan, *Insight* (New York: Philosophical Library, 1956), p. 229. Cf. pp. 228-232.

23. The language here deliberately alludes to Phil 2:6–11. What the West clings to is a genuine gift, but the sin is in the clinging, and the clinging stifles the gift and renders it unavailable. The illusion is that of power; the reality is that of powerlessness. The kenotic paradigm for Paul applies not only to Jesus Christ but to all of human reality. This point will be developed further in Chapter 2. This point is further developed in my article, "Kenosis Old and New", in *The Ecumenist*, 1974, pp. 17–21.

24. Slater, *Earthwalk*, pp. 137–8, also pp. 171–176.

25. Philip Slater, *The Pursuit of Loneliness: American Culture at the Breaking Point*, revised edition (Boston: Beacon Press, 1976), p. 11.

26. Ibid., p. 11.

27. Ibid., p. 17.

28. Ibid., p. 28.

29. Ibid., p. 147.

30. Ibid., p. 148.

31. Ibid., p. 172.

32. Ibid., p. 181.

33. Slater, *Earthwalk*, p. 145, also pp. 185 ff.

34. Roszak, *Person/Planet*, pp. 37-38. Berman in *Reenchantment* . . . develops this point more theoretically, in terms of homeostasis and self-corrective feedback, along the lines of Gregory Bateson's cybernetic approach. Cf. pp. 256 ff.

35. Marilyn Ferguson, *The Aquarian Conspiracy* (Los Angeles: Tarcher, 1980), p. 25. Also cf. pp. 39 and 42.

36. His contribution, above all found in his 1953-54 Gifford Lectures published as *The Self as Agent* and *Persons in Relation* (London: Faber, 1957 and 1961), consists above all in the clarification that in moving away from the mechanistic it is not sufficient to get to the organic. We must go beyond the organic to the domain of persons-in-

relation. This provides a corrective to a vision which, emerging from a perhaps hasty assimilation of the subtleties of Eastern religious experience, prizes impersonality and fails to do justice to the authentic values which the first world must recapture to be itself once again. More on this later.

37. Fritjof Capra, *The Turning Point: Science, Society, and the Rising Culture* (New York: Simon and Schuster, 1982).

38. This latter point Capra develops at greater length in *The Tao of Physics* (London: Fontana, 1983), showing the affinities of modern physics with Eastern mystical traditions. It will be our contention that, valuable as these traditions may be to us in our search for new forms of life, there are considerable resources to be exploited in the authentic traditions of the West, and that these resources bear within them an inalienable affirmation of the human person as free, essentially related to other persons, and endowed with intrinsic worth.

39. In *Tao* . . . Capra shows how the Newtonian universe in effect goes back to the Greek atomists Leucippus and Democritus (26).

40. Ibid., p. 93.

41. Ibid., p. 150. Cf. Berman, *Reenchantment* . . . , pp. 135–140, 237. Capra does not eliminate the classical model of physics but integrates it within the organic (336–337). His account ought to be contrasted with that of Bernard Lonergan in *Insight* on the complementarity of what he calls the classical (Galileo & Newton would be examples) and the statistical modes of scientific investigation, leading to a world-view based on emergent probability. These insights are helpful in supporting the point we make later that the emerging new order should not without further ado turn its back on the old, but incorporate within the newer perspective what is of lasting value in the older.

42. Yet another instance of the principle of homeostasis, of self-corrective feedback emerges here.

43. Again Berman offers us keen and pertinent insights. For him classical science and modern capitalism form a gestalt (*Reenchantment* . . . , p. 38). In both of them exact mathematical calculation is the key to success, and in both of them there is a linear infinity, whether found in the vast emptiness of space or in money, which in the capitalist system can indefinitely reproduce itself (44). Moreover a view of nature as essentially mechanical offers less resistance to those who wish to exploit it for profit (117). This latter point offers a perceptive approach to current debates on the environment, marked by the contrast between long-range respect for ecological balance and short-term profitability.

44. Cf. Ferguson, *Aquarian* . . . She does this type of analysis throughout her book.

45. Cf. *Tao* . . . , chapter 1. Also cf. Slater, *Earthwalk*, who puts the polarity in terms of masculine/feminine or agency(tendency of an organism to maintain its separate existence)/communion (tendency of it to participate in a larger organism). We have already alluded to the complementarity of the older classical and the newer statistical models which Lonergan develops at length in *Insight*.

46. Rifkin, *Emerging Order*, pp. 18–27.

47. Cf. especially Roszak, *Where the Wasteland Ends* (New York: Doubleday, 1974).

48. This is a point to which Capra could have paid more attention, as for instance on pp. 53–54 of his *Turning Point*.

49. Berman, *Reenchantment* . . . , p. 189.

50. Cf. Roszak, *Person/Planet*, chapter 10. One can surmise that he would approve the emergence of basic communities, so crucial to the third world Church, within the Church of the first world as well. Our sophisticated analysts from within the first world might well find some of the values they are seeking to realize already at hand in the third world. The ethical philosopher Alistair MacIntyre finishes his recent work *After Virtue* (Notre Dame, University of Notre Dame Press, 1981) on the same note, seeking a Benedict of Nursia for our own age.

51. *Person/Planet*, p. 95; *Where the Wasteland Ends*, ch. 4.

52. Cf. Roszak, *Unfinished Animal* (New York: Harper Colophon, 1977).

53. Cf. the note on p. 106 of *Where the Wasteland Ends*.

54. Berman, *Reenchantment* . . . , p. 283.

55. For a parallel assessment of this literature on the new age, cf. J.L. Schlegel, "La gnose ou le réenchantement du monde", *Etudes* 1987, 389–404.

Chapter Two

THE FIRST WORLD:
LIGHTS AND SHADOWS FROM THE PAST

Our first world is in dire need of a theology of grace which is both new and old, old in its faithful return to authentic traditions, new in its willingness to face up to today's unprecedented crisis. This is easier to talk about, however, than to achieve. The reality we must face is complex, and the thought-processes we must enter into are subtle and intricate. I invite you to patience as we enter into technical matters and historical developments which seem far removed from our urgent needs, but will prove to be of considerable importance.

The main focus of this chapter will be a sketch of the growth, decline, and future possibilities of the theology of grace which has emerged in the Church of the first world. But we will set the stage for this sketch by giving a brief account of our methodology and by contrasting first, second, and third world theologies of grace. Finally we will in the broad terms of a horizon analysis recapitulate the themes of this chapter. Having done all of this, we will be ready in subsequent chapters on Paul, Augustine, and Aquinas to recover elements of the authentic Western tradition on grace in order to move that tradition forward in response to today's urgent needs.

GENETIC AND STRUCTURAL PRESUPPOSITIONS

The two terms "genetic" and "structural" evoke the main approaches used today in attempting to enter into any author's thought. For instance in scriptural exegesis we now find earlier critical methods which patiently piece together the elements which enter into the genesis of the author's thought alongside more recent methods which study the texts themselves rigorously and structurally. While I do not claim to have knit the two together to my own or anyone's satisfaction, they have been for me essential tools in interpreting the thought of others and in elaborating my own.

These two methodological approaches can be expressed diagramatically as follows:

The *genetic* or *diachronic* approach	tradition experience challenge	→	author's thought
The *structural* or *synchronic* approach	author's thought	←	the text available here and now

In the *genetic* approach one attempts to understand someone's contribution to theology by recreating its genesis, attending to the three components it must include if it is to be authentic, which we will term tradition, experience, and apostolic challenge. How did the author over a period of time (*diachrony*), in struggle with these components, come to shape his or her thought? In the *structural* approach, one approaches the author's thought from the text in which it is embodied, one tries to be as sensitive to the relational elements implicit and explicit in the text as they come to light here and now (*syn-chrony*) in the act of interpreting them.

Genetic: The academic tradition in which theology is done can easily lead to an overemphasis on tradition at the expense of experience and apostolic challenge. During my seven years of administration I often heard the refrain, ''What a shame that you had to withdraw from theology and drastically curtail your research just when you were beginning to hit your stride!'' This understandable reaction is short-sighted. Balanced theology requires attention to experience and apostolic challenge just as much as research into the received tradition. Thus, far from being a diversion or set-back, this unexpected and relentless exposure to a wide range of experiences involving both personal and institutional dynamics in the long run facilitated my theological development and sharpened my perception of the challenge presented by our world. These three components, *tradition*, *experience*, and *apostolic'challenge*, are present in the genesis of any constructive contribution to the ongoing theological tradition.

To draw your attention to these three components is not a superfluous methodological nicety. It will help you, the reader, to understand and assess my work and that of others, but more important, it will invite you to identify the corresponding components in your own life context and to engage in a theological reflection of your own, which will criticize, complement, and carry forward the work of others. This latter point is crucial: more than ever before without collaboration no theological achievement is possible.

My enumeration of these components is not atypical within the Roman Catholic theological community. More specifically it re-expresses in a simpler way the gist of the functional specialties found in Bernard Lonergan's *Method in Theology.*[1]

Lonergan's scheme of eight functional specialties is well known. The first set—research, interpretation, history, and dialectic—lead the theologian from an examination of the documents of the *past* to the point where he or she is invited to a personal event in the *present*, a conversion, which, among other things, implies a commitment to God as a member of the community whose tradition he or she has examined, interpreted, judged, and evaluated. If this pivotal event takes place, then the theologian enters into the second set of functional specialties—foundations, doctrines, systematics, and communications—in which he or she collaborates in the ongoing development of that tradition. Turned towards its *future* the theologian strives to understand an ambient culture and be understood by it.

Tradition, experience, and apostolic challenge stand outside the eightfold functional pattern but they are integral to it. *Tradition* is the documented past which the first four functional specialties deal with in indirect discourse (X or Y says that . . .); *experience* corresponds to the personal conversion which is the pivot between the two sets of functional specialties, seen not so much as an event narrowed in space and time but as an ongoing dimension of the theologian's life; *apostolic challenge* is the situation of the world in urgent response to which he or she carries forward the tradition by a creative contribution in direct discourse (I say that . . .), which to a later generation will be a tradition with which to begin the cycle once again.

Each of the three components deserves fuller elucidation:

Tradition is input from the past, whether remote or recent, to which I open myself in order to understand and to assess it. It usually consists in documents, but not to the exclusion of the wider set of embodiments in which Christian meaning and commitment are expressed, ranging from the witness of individual lives to vast historical movements. The tradition upon which I will focus above all in this book is that of the classical authors of the theology of grace in the Western Church, a tradition which lives on, theoretically and practically, in authentic and inauthentic forms, in the Church of the first world today. This tradition speaks with many voices and accents, and at times they appear to contradict one another. To test them accurately involves a personal struggle. Where do I myself stand? Though this question may have a technical and theoretical side, it is at root experiential, existential.

The *experience* which has by now entered into the picture is unique, complex, shaped by my own stance towards the living God but reaching out into all the facets of my life. It centers around my conversion or lack of it, but conversion is not just a moment's event that I recall from my past or anticipate in my future, a turning point, a breakthrough in my journey to my God, but also an ongoing reality which follows me every step of the way and adopts different nuances and forms as it takes flesh in the events of my life. Key elements of that experience have already emerged in the first chapter, especially as I related my shift from a personal to an institutional focus when I took on administrative duties, and began to experience in a new way the dynamic of grace and sin within and around me.

My wrestling with the texts of tradition in the context of my own experience has led me to a renewed desire to do theology as someone fully inserted within the first world. What is the texture of that world, and what contribution can I make to its enlightenment and healing? Who are my allies in this task? Together with them we reach out to the future, and face the *apostolic challenge* of our times. I offer them what I hope is an authentic and life-giving theological tradition, and I receive valuable insights and telling words from their body of perceptive comment on what in final analysis is our world's desperate need for grace. I respect them as bearers of a genuine non-theological tradition and allow that tradition to enter into my personal struggle for conversion, but at the same time they help me understand the texture of our world and find the way to communicate to it effectively.

The riches of a tradition, the authenticity of an experience, and the urgency of an apostolic challenge: these three in a mysterious con-spiration lead to a theology which does not hide behind the repetition of old formulas but steps out in faithfulness and creativity, enriching the tradition, and bringing it to bear on the future. The classical authors who have made an indelible mark on the theology of grace have done so because these three components felicitously came together in their work. They must come together in our own.

Structural: The structural side of our theological methodology has a link to contemporary structural linguistics, of which Ferdinand de Saussure is a founder. It invites me also to consider the text in front of me simply as it is in itself. In what elements, what movements of thought and structures, is its meaning to be articulated? How are these elements linked to each other, and how does this text relate to wider unities beyond itself? These are questions of structure, language, grammar.

Grammar is preferable to language as a term to use in this setting: for de Saussure it is a more precise and specific term than language. Language is a broad reality at once individual and social. It straddles the realms of the physical, physiological, and psychic.[2] Grammar focuses more narrowly on the system of relationships which, by their consistency and reliability, ground the inner coherence of a language and its use as a vehicle of communication across space and time. In a sense grammar limits and confines, but it is only by respecting it that we can successfully explore the limitless virtualities of nuanced expression available within any language.[3]

Grammar emphasizes the stable relational structure which underlies a variable content. In analyzing classical texts on grace, I have been very attentive to their structures, whether stated clearly or deeply embedded, and to the transpositions by which the same structures over the centuries have served to express in varied forms the same basic insights. This structural approach will help us trace the profound continuities of the theology of grace as it develops in history and seeks different modes of theological expression adapted to the different worlds of our complex planet. It will also help us discern the hidden affinities of contemporary non-theological thought with the authentic tradition we seek to defend and illustrate.[4]

It should be clear by now that we are not seeking to find a definition of grace that will finally capture its elusive substance to the satisfaction of all, but rather to unearth the significant structures and dynamics of God's action in, for, and with the human world God has created. These structures and dynamics can be expressed in terms, theological and non-theological, far removed from the term ''grace'', and one's effort to trace them must be as subtle as they are wide-ranging. Our quest is for a language, or even better a grammar of grace.

This structural dimension can be further fleshed out in terms of the genesis of this work. In earlier work on healing and elevating grace in Aquinas,[5] I found that an exegesis in terms of relations and proportionalities[6] opened up the architectonics of Thomas' thought on grace, and allowed broad shifts within his thought to stand out. What struck me above all in my study of Thomas' texts, and confirmed the key role that he has always played in my own theology, was their effective emphasis on the *dynamic* element of grace. The older standard presentations on grace, even those purporting to be *ad mentem divi Thomae*, had left me dissatisfied. I saw them as some kind of reified algebra of God's workings in human persons. A return to Thomas himself, a close structural reading of his texts, led me to see the preponderance in his thought of verbs and participles over nouns and adjectives. Healing and elevating are not adjectives adding to the sum of intricate distinctions evolved over the centuries by theologians of grace. They are participles, verbal forms connoting various active relationships. This healing and elevating—Thomas develops the point more explicitly in relation to healing—unfolds over the life of a person, from the initial inward healing of the person's relation to God in justification, through the gradual healing of psyche and body in the sanctification achieved by the repetition of meritorious acts,[7] and culminating in the fulfillment of glory to which grace and the activity it empowers are ordered.

Teaching a survey course on grace led me to begin exploring with a similar approach other classical authors on grace. This opened up for me a new perspective on the deep continuity among Aquinas, Augustine, and Paul. The conclusion of recent research[8] that finally the roots of Aquinas' theology in Paul and Augustine counted more than the terminology and philosophical principles he borrowed mainly from Aristotle was vindicated when I discovered an underlying structural pattern in Aquinas' theology of grace which is also found in Augustine and in Paul. In Aquinas the pattern is aimed at discovering the sapiential order of the universe, in Augustine at grasping his own personal experience, in Paul at calling forth and channelling the apocalyptic energy of his communities.

My struggle with the texts of the tradition was bound up from the very beginning with a search for ways to communicate effectively with my students. The terminology and concerns of classical authors often left them anxious and bewildered, since the earlier philosophical formation which ought to have made them more at home within the world of these authors was deficient. This prompted me to seek other modes of expression in my teaching, something I would have done anyway in order to do justice to the current insight into the universality of grace, which ranges beyond the ecclesial and the sacramental and enters into the secular and the day by day realities of life, even when they lack explicit Christian or religious motivation. Thus I began to consider the dynamics of healing and self-transcendence at work in persons and society, as described from the viewpoint of various secular disciplines, hoping that the structures and dynamics they delineate would be helpful in re-expressing those found in the classical theologies. I started exploring a contemporary approach to grace. Some students were excited by the discovery of links between the theology they were learning and the world to which they were being missioned, but others were just as unfamiliar with the world of the present as they were with that of the past.[9]

The structural approach, which seeks the similar structures which underlie and unify different contents applies not only to the comparison of classical theologies of grace with each other but also to efforts to relate these theologies to contemporary authors and concerns. Together with the genetic approach, it can be of invaluable assistance in making sense of the past and exploring pathways for the future.

THE CONTEXT: THE CHURCHES OF THE
FIRST, SECOND, AND THIRD WORLDS

To grasp the history of the theology of grace within the first world, its growth, decline, and future possibilities, we must attend to historical context as well as to method. In this section we will compare and contrast the first world theology of grace with those which emerge within the Churches of the other two worlds. If the context set by these other two theologies is neglected, the recovery of the authentic Western tradition will be imperilled, and the empowerment to which a renewed Western theology seeks to contribute will be an illusion.

None of the three traditions on grace has a corner on the truth. Indeed it is only to the extent that each allows itself to be enriched by the other two that it can develop a balanced theology of grace. The more one reaches out in and is shaped by relationship with others the more one grows in one's own genuine reality. Indeed one can rightly interpret the first world's plight as the enfleshment in secular terms of the structures and dynamics of a Western theology of grace gone amok, bereft of the balance which comes from the give and take of interaction with the other two traditions.[10]

The contrast between the three theologies of grace is best seen if we consider grace concretely in the person of Jesus Christ and his redemptive work. In their attempt to understand how Jesus Christ redeems us by his grace, each Church has tended to pinpoint a particular moment of his life. In summary, the two traditional approaches, those of the East (first Church) and West (second church), seek in the mysterious beginning of that life (*incarnation*) and in its mysterious ending (*death*) the principal moment of redemption. The more recent approach of the South (third Church) seeks in the *earthly life* of Jesus its key to understanding the mystery of redemption.

For the Church of the East, Christ is above all the *priest*, and the preferred focus is the liturgy which celebrates the action of God on our behalf and draws us into the sacred space in which we are already saved. For the Church of the West, Christ is above all the *king* who has gained a kingdom by obeying the Father at terrible price to himself, and the focus is the canonical structures by which proper patterns of subordination and obedience are maintained. For the Church of the South, Christ is above all the *prophet* who denounces injustice and gives a powerful witness which leads him to his death, and the keynote is the praxis by which the people of God in response to the promptings of the Spirit takes risks in its own efforts to free itself.[11]

Eastern Church: The God of Hellenistic thought is absolutely other, comes from the realm of immutability, immortality, and incorruption in order to deliver us from transience, mortality, corruption; in other words, in order to divinize us. Redemption is primarily *ontological*. God and humanity are reconciled in Christ Jesus who is both divine and human. God shares our human nature that we might share his divine nature. The key to redemption is the Incarnation itself, for precisely in that event does the union of God and humanity take place.[12] Grace is primarily elevating, divinizing: it raises us up into the realm of incorruptibility and stability which we long for in this uncertain world.[13]

The danger of the Eastern approach in isolation is that redemption could be seen as something which God does, leaving humanity without the need to painfully take up the cross of its own liberation from sin. We are not just redeemed out of the limitation of finitude which prevents access to intimacy with the infinite God, we are also redeemed out of the self-inflicted limitations of sin. Redemption is not an effortless growing up to the stature of God: it involves pain, struggle, rupture, and ultimately death, to be followed by resurrection. We don't live in a pollyanna universe. The mystical/liturgical space to which even now we have access must not be allowed to blot out the not yet reality which permeates our world, the agony of a childbirth that still continues. Putting this point in terms of the theology of grace, one must, not clinging to the new life imparted in justification, get in touch with the other side of the bi-polarity, which is the labour of sanctification, stressed in both Western and third world approaches.[14]

The beauty of this Eastern approach is its contemplative stress on the already now presence of God within our world: it has enabled Christians of this Church to sustain persecution for centuries and maintain their dignity in situations where the power of Christianity to shape society was and is hampered.

Western Church: The emphasis of this Church is more *juridical*, as befits its roots in the Roman mentality, a mentality later re-echoed in the feudal categories of the Middle Ages and paradoxically re-expressed by the Reformers. The classical expression of this emphasis is found in the theology of redemption of Anselm of Canterbury. God is the law-giver and we humans are the obedient ones. By our sin, we have opened a chasm between ourselves and God. We need a healing and a forgiveness which we cannot give ourselves. A sacrifice of infinite worth is needed to bridge an infinite distance. Only a human being who is also God can perform this sacrificial deed. This Jesus does by dying on the cross for us.

In this account stress is laid on human response. Though the initiative is ultimately God's, God empowers our freedom, and takes with utmost seriousness what that freedom chooses. Adam's disobedience radically changes the relationship between God and each human being. The effects of an act of human disobedience has to be undone by an act of human obedience.[15] Implied here is a covenantal relationship to be maintained or restored, through a divine initiative of love that empowers our own human response of love. But if that relationship is seen apart from its origins in an act of divine love, it becomes a narrow juridical reality. God becomes distant and exacting, even angry and vindictive. Our efforts are fraught with anxiety and insecurity. Apart from the corrective offered by the Eastern approach, the Western approach falls into inauthenticity. The covenant becomes juridical rather than dialogical. Redemption becomes individualistic and is fraught with a false sense of isolation and competition.[16] On this view God is angry and we change his anger to grace by our efforts. In terms of the bi-polarity of grace, what is needed as a corrective is attention to the transforming event of justification which underpins all else in the life of grace. God loved us while we were still sinners and already the inner reality of the deed of salvation has taken place within our hearts.

These deviations, actual and possible, do not detract from the inherent value and beauty of the first world view of redeeming grace, a value which emerges in all its attractiveness when it allows itself to be shaped in interaction with other values. Authentic personalism is the genuine value of which individualism is the excess. That personalism is expressed in respect for the freedom of persons to be themselves, to make choices, to do work which is both disciplined and worthwhile. Pauline justification takes away the fear, anger, and insecurity which plague the first world, and enables persons within it to lead lives of selfless service in which others are valued for themselves. Luther makes this point very tellingly in *Christian Liberty*,[17] and countless Christians have based their lives on this truth.

Third World Church: A profound continuity between Western and third world Churches arises from their common stress not so much on the divine initiative in grace and redemption as on the onerous human response which follows from it, that of Jesus and ours. However they view that response differently. The classical Western tradition stresses the individual human being, whether the Jesus who dies on the cross or each one of us saved through his death. The contemporary approach of the third world Church stresses the *historical* and *social* dimension. Jesus did not just act to help individuals in distress but bore witness to the fact that the significant social structures of his day were in need of profound transformation by making himself totally vulnerable to those who presided over those structures. Our response to him is to initiate and sustain concerted action within human history, in willingness to face suffering and even death.

This recent approach is buttressed by the results of the new quest of the historical Jesus and is expressed in liberation theology. For the third Church of the South Jesus is above all the liberator. What counts is his kenosis-in-action, as evidenced by his handling of the temptations in the desert, his pro-existence (i.e., being person-for-others), his solidarity with the oppressed, his call to a selfless love of others and an abandonment to the Father which he lived out to the full. If Jesus did not show himself to be a liberator in his life, then his death would have had no salvific meaning. If in our own lives and in our involvement within history we fail to mirror forth the pattern of Christ's activity of liberation, then we do not appropriate the salvation he brings us. Rather than an ontological or a juridical scheme, this approach offers us a historical one, history being seen as the arena of human praxis.

The third world approach also has its dangers. Both traditional approaches by their focus on the mysterious beginning or ending of Jesus' life clearly see that life as constitutively open to the Transcendent. This contemporary approach, focusing upon the life of Jesus, which parallels our lives because of similar social and political concerns, can lose sight of that mystery and fall into a shallow secularism. A new form of Pelagianism becomes possible, that of social action. Salvation takes place within history, yes, but—this is the corrective which must be kept in mind—history is the vehicle, the embodiment of a transcendence which leads us to the very mystery of God, and only in the power of that mystery can our human action contribute to salvation. Otherwise our action is shallow, ineffective, and truncated. This newer approach is largely untested. There are potential dangers—the Roman magisterium keeps pointing them out—but also a tremendous power for renewal in the light of the Gospel.

The above can be summed up in the form of a diagram. (See p. 46.)

Each tradition achieves balance in conjunction with the other two, each has its own unique standpoint which is enhanced rather than diminished in the resulting tension. In this tension grace appears not as escape, not as juridical status, not as good example, but as the mysterious power of love calling forth love, of labour calling forth our labour. If grace is power, it is also patience. The death of Jesus is not a substitution or mere good example. Ratified by the resurrection, it offers us the only pattern for our authentic human response, and empowers us to embrace that pattern.

In this book we are concerned with the approach to grace of the Western Church. The East reminds the West that God is the initiating mystery and our response, no matter how noble or disciplined or technologically proficient, is derivative. The contemporary third world Church reminds it that salvation is not just individual but also social and historical, that the individual becomes a person only in relationship to other persons within a community of endeavour and suffering, of action and passion. In these reminders, the Churches of the

Eastern Church	Western Church	Third World Church
key moment is incarnation	key moment is death	key moment is public life
Christ as Priest	Christ as King	Christ as Prophet
ontological pattern	juridical pattern	historical pattern
Church focus on liturgy, mysticism	Church focus on authority, obedience	Church focus on praxis, witness
divine initiative	human response	
	individual	collective
justification	sanctification by individual good works	sanctification by collective action
danger is withdrawal into an already now ghetto, pollyanna	danger is individualism, lack of relationship, manipulation, raw power	danger is historical immanence, horizontalism, Pelagianism
redemption by escape	redemption by juridical status	redemption by good example

THE THREE IN BALANCE: LOVE CALLING FORTH LOVE

East and of the third world call the Western Church not away from but into its deepest and most authentic self. A recovery of the authentic tradition of the West on redemption and grace cannot bypass the values of the ancient East and the contemporary third world.

The time has come for our sketch of the history of the theology of grace in the Church of the first world, which will be carried out under three headings: growth, decline, and future possibilities.

THE WESTERN TRADITION ON GRACE: GROWTH

''Il faut reculer pour mieux sauter''. This French adage is most pertinent to the task we are about to undertake. To move ahead more securely, we must begin by retracing our steps, especially because the single vision[18] which presided over the emergence of the old order in the 15–16–17th centuries has also, in its theological form, led to a minor and a major breakdown in the Western tradition on grace. We need to get in touch with the earlier and more authentic Western tradition on grace before we leap forward to our own era and its daunting challenges.

Unity in the faith does not require uniformity of theological expression. It requires that theologies in their pluriformity be open to and find their equilibrium in each other,[19] because in their original impetus they are one. They not only can but also must develop in different directions because they find in the New Testament a common point of origin and a model for a pluralism of standpoints which not only coexist but interact and enrich each other. Because Jesus is one person with many facets, the various theologies that deal with his person and his work are complementary rather than disparate. Paradoxically the unity of Christian truth is not diminished but enhanced by such diversity.

This paradox applies to the richly diverse theologies of grace. Their unity is rooted in the simple fact that in dealing with us God's initiative is entirely God's own, unmerited by our efforts or our status: a fact which the term grace clearly bespeaks. But the agreement of Paul and John, the main theologians of grace in the New Testament,[20] is based on more than this. The dynamic structures they develop to account for how God deals with us in his grace parallel each other. Both begin with an action by which God enters into our lives and transforms us, an action which John develops in the Book of Signs under the headings of regeneration (Chapter 3) and faith (passim), and which Paul develops under the heading of justification. This divine initiative is continued and fostered in us as we, under God's grace, live out our response to it, a response which Paul develops under the heading of sanctification and John, mainly in the Book of Glory, under that of indwelling and bearing fruit. The fulfillment of that initiative/response is eternal life in John, an eternal life we already share but whose fulness we will receive only on the last day. In contrast Paul speaks about the salvation of which we receive the first fruits now and the fulness later. This dynamic structure is present in distinctive forms within the thought of Augustine and Aquinas, the classical authors on grace that we deal with in this book. Indeed a case might be made for using its presence as a criterion of a balanced theology of grace. The convergence of these authors will emerge in greater detail later, but it is worth offering its main headings. (See p. 48.)

The diversity which coheres with this unity is remarkable. While John and Paul[21] agree on the central affirmations of the theology of grace, they stand in sharp complementarity to each other. In this they serve as the theological models which preside over the evolution of the Eastern and Western Church theologies of grace respectively. John is much more attuned to the already-

	Beginning	*Continuation*	*Fulfillment*
Paul	justification	sanctification	salvation
John	rebirth, faith	bearing fruit, indwelling	resurrection on the last day, eternal life
Augustine	gift of *posse*	*agere*	*beatitudo*
Aquinas	justification of the ungodly	meritorious deeds	vision of God

now reality of God present in our midst, to the intimacy with God already given to those who believe in Jesus Christ. The elevating function of grace is uppermost: grace introduces us into an unprecedented communion with God utterly beyond the resources of our nature. For Paul the not yet of a world still to be healed is more urgent. The dynamic of sin is still very much at work in ourselves and in our world, and grace is needed to forgive sins, to make each person upright in the sight of God, to empower us in the struggle to bring to birth the new creation. Yet in spite of sharply differing accents, these two perspectives do not exclude each other. Intimacy with God and the already now are part of the Pauline picture[22] as forgiveness of sins and the not yet are part of the Johannine picture.[23]

The contrasting emphases of the theologies of grace that emerge in the Eastern and the Western Churches find their origins in the contrasting emphases of John and Paul. The already now intimacy with God valued within the Johannine Gospel surfaces in the theology of the Eastern Fathers under the heading of divinization.[24] With our cooperation, God gradually brings his creation to its intended fulfillment, which is participation in the very nature of God and escape from the transitoriness and corruption inherent in created nature. While not denying the need to have sins forgiven, the Eastern tradition lays stress on our transcending, already now in contemplation and later in the fulness of vision, the limitations of our creaturehood. Western theology of grace shifts that emphasis. Deriving from Paul,[25] who was very sensitive to the not yet dimension of our graced reality, to the onerous aspect of the human struggle before grace and under grace, it attaches much more importance to our waywardness, rebellion, blindness, impotence, even depravity, as, for instance, in the work of Augustine, who more than anyone else shaped the doctrine of grace in the Western Church. Without grace, Augustine maintains, we cannot be our true human selves. We must be converted from the illusory quest of God on our own terms and with our own resources.

While Aquinas is firmly situated within the Western Church, his quest, rooted in the creative openness of the earlier Middle Ages and the emergence of a concern for theory within theology, is to integrate into one view the many sources, both Eastern and Western, which were available to him. As a result his theology of grace, seeking balance above all, interrelates nature and grace, the healing and elevating functions of grace, the various modalities of grace, in terms which remain with us today in spite of the limitations which we may find in them.

This growth of the Western tradition can be put into diagrammatic form:

PAUL
affirms
the not-yet dimension
forgiveness of sins
healing function of grace

JOHN
affirms
the already-now dimension
intimacy with God
elevating function of grace

AUGUSTINE
in his struggle with Pelagius
he affirms human depravity
and grace as
prevenient
internal

EASTERN FATHERS
they affirm human deprivation
and grace as
divinizing
synergizing

AQUINAS
in his systematic bent
he seeks to integrate
East and West
nature and grace
healing and elevating

A few additional points:

1. Without the sense of equilibrium which characterizes Paul, Augustine, and Aquinas, their conscientious attention to how other strands of thought or tradition complement their own, their work would not be recognized as classical, as essential to the development of a tradition. While Aquinas remains within the Western tradition, his systematizing bent leads him to incorporate

the Eastern strand more thoroughly than other authors within his tradition. But the other classical authors, Paul and Augustine, are also quite open to complementary dimensions of grace affirmed by the East. Paul does not contradict John but complements him. While the Western characteristics of Augustine are more prominent, the latter is quite familiar with the main outlines of the Eastern thought on divinization and incorporates it into his theology, especially when he is not engaged in polemics.[26] Disregard for the contribution of the Eastern tradition characterizes not the authentic but the inauthentic Western tradition.[27]

2. It will be quite instructive for us to contrast Paul, Augustine, and Aquinas in terms of the periods in which they lived. Paul lived at the time of the secular *Pax Romana*, but as a religious Jew he saw the world as highly volatile and charged with apocalyptic energy. Augustine lived when the Roman Empire was in turmoil and breakdown, but also when the Christian Church for the first time was beginning to experience peace and cope with unaccustomed mass conversions, was mounting administrative structures parallel to those of the Empire and settling in for the long haul rather than proclaiming the imminent end.[28] When Aquinas came on the scene, the Dark Ages had passed. A new civilization was in the making, with the attendant tensions between the older hieratic structure of a Church which had served as a beacon of sanity and continuity through an incredibly difficult period and the emerging dynamics of a secular society which was just beginning to flex its muscles.

This varied life experience helps to shape our three authors' theologies of grace. Paul envisages grace predominantly as an external sphere which affects him and within which he dwells. The forces of sin, grace, the law, death, life, the flesh, the spirit are like so many magnetic fields whose pull on his human consciousness is unmistakable. Caught in the present in-between state, he experiences and expresses the scission between sin and grace as external to himself: "Now if I do what I do not want, it is no longer I that do it, but sin which dwells within me" (Rom 7:20).

By contrast, Augustine, faced by dissolution and breakdown in society around him, found solace in the movements of grace which he felt within himself. He developed unparalleled skills in accounting for his own interiority. His preoccupation, pastoral and personal, to effectively counteract the position of Pelagius led him to lay even more stress on his inward self and its mysterious transformation by grace. He pulled together elements of interiority present in Paul's theology of grace and gave them a powerful and elegant articulation. Clearly the titanic struggle described by Paul is operative not just between my will and what is outside it; it most properly rests within my will, a house divided within itself.[29] The moral struggle intimate to each person replaces salvation history as the urgent focus of theology of grace. Indeed recent interpreters of Paul have set us straight on our tendency to read him as if he were an earlier Augustine journeying from painful impotence when faced with the allurements of sin to the joy and spontaneity that comes when he can once again do the good.[30]

By contrast Aquinas lived in a much more objective universe. His own person and the movements which stirred within his heart remained in the background as he opened his eyes upon the world as its potential unfolded before him. His simple acceptance of the rich and varied tradition of East and West in the forms available to him invites him to make room for the more cosmic and objective side of grace treasured by the East. Augustine remains the doctor of grace *par excellence* for Aquinas, but Aquinas transposes to an objective and ontological register the experiential categories which Augustine devises to express the inward transformation wrought by grace. Augustine dwells on delight, on love as a force of attraction akin to that of gravity, on spontaneity healed from within by grace. Aquinas would have denied nothing of this but preferred the language of potency, habit, and act, cast in the systematic perspective which his new-found acquaintance with Aristotle made possible. Yet while Aquinas writes with an objective un-self-consciousness, when the need arises he does succeed in marshalling apt examples from his own experience.

3. A final point of contrast between our three authors emerges when we situate them in terms of Lonergan's differentiation between the world of common sense, of theory, and of interiority.[31] Paul and Augustine belong to the world of common sense. At heart pastors, they are trying to achieve not so much a broad theoretical perspective on grace-in-itself as the resolution of pressing problems affecting their flock: grace-for-us, as it were, is their bailiwick. Yet neither of them is a total stranger to interiority and theory. This is especially true of Augustine: he makes ample use of the philosophical categories available to him, and his attention to interiority is unparalleled until our own twentieth century. By contrast, Aquinas decidedly moves into the world of theory. His overriding concern is to achieve an ordered knowledge of grace consistent with what the authors available to him had to say—and here the root meaning of author as authoritative source is of vital importance. These authorities at first glance appear to be in considerable conflict. What they have to say, however, he must treat with respect. Nothing of the truth which they vehicle can fail to be incorporated in the whole. In consequence, what Aquinas leaves to us is not so much a new theology of grace as a new way of systematizing the theology of grace. He diligently seeks and to an unprecedented degree achieves a higher systematic viewpoint which enables theological conflict to be overcome, to be exposed as apparent rather than real.[32]

To sum up: there is profound continuity between Paul, Augustine, and Aquinas. The deep structures and underlying themes of their theologies are remarkably alike, but express different mind-sets and have different aims: in Aquinas to discover the sapiential order of the universe, in Augustine to grasp his own personal experience, in Paul to bring about a state of tolerant yet expectant equilibrium within communities of Christians living in apocalyptic times.

THE WESTERN TRADITION ON GRACE: DECLINE

While Paul, Augustine, and Aquinas were agents of authentic growth within the tradition, that growth was not without its limits and shadows. Only in the later Middle Ages, however, did significant decline set in. We will analyze the emergence of this decline and relate it to the plight of our own age. As we shall see, the upheaval of this period was multifarious, comprising the bubonic plague, the papal schism, and the emergence of nation states. The sharply different vision of reality it stimulated was expressed in a new theology, a *via moderna* corresponding to the distemper of the times, and it presided over the emergence of Western science, technology, and capitalist expansion, achievements whose ambiguity has become so clear to us today. Here begins the "single vision" which Roszak sees as central to the present quandaries of the first world.[33]

So let us go back to Aquinas and continue our journey from his day to ours. In retrospect what is especially impressive about his theology of grace is its synthetic sweep. Out of the Eastern approach to grace, rooted in John, stressing our participation in the divine nature, and the Western approach, rooted in Paul, stressing forgiveness and the healing of a wounded and powerless nature, he created an inextricably organic whole, bringing to their fruition many creative suggestions emanating from the lively theological world of the twelfth century. His synthesis was open rather than rigid in its conceptual expression; it easily embraced shifting nuances and echoed in their diversity the disparate voices of the past whose truth he was retelling.[34] Aquinas' system was a system-on-the-move. What stands out above all is his faithfulness to the revealed paradox of a God who is totally free yet utterly reliable, infinitely loving and infinitely wise.

The achievement of Aquinas was not recognized in his own day as it is in ours. Three years after his death the Latin Averroists, members of the Paris faculty of philosophy for whom Averroes was *the* commentator of Aristotle, were condemned. More traditional theologians—Pope John XXI, the Bishop of Paris, and the Archbishop of Canterbury—were fearful of the inroads made by the necessitarianism implied by Aristotle's view of scientific/philosophical knowledge. They felt that this pagan trend of thought, unmitigated in its Averroist version, jeopardized the faith, failed to safeguard the transcendence and freedom of God, over-emphasized the powers of nature apart from grace, of reason apart from faith. They did not explicitly condemn Aquinas but in effect made his theology suspect. How could someone be so open to these newer elements and incorporate them so organically in an account of revealed faith? In retrospect this reaction is understandable. Historical assessment requires the lapse of centuries. It was too soon to discern the profound transformation of Aristotelian insights brought about by Thomas, a transformation possibly paralleled only by the shaping of Hebraic and Hellenic categories by the authors of the New Testament to express the Christ event.

Formed by Divine Wisdom, the universe of Aquinas was harmonious and coherent, ultimately grounded in the consistency of the Divine Intellect to itself. Its many components were permeated through and through by an intricate order. Relation as a reality is at the very heart of Aquinas' universe, so much so that it remained in the background as something taken for granted. He gives the tag of *ens debilissimum* to relation as an Aristotelian category, but in its wider reality relation is an *ens potentissimum* which keeps his whole system together.[35] This universal coherence has epistemic ramifications as well. The Wisdom that permeates the universe means that even if our reason is not able to penetrate the mysteries of revelation and deduce their truth from necessary reasons, as the strict Aristotelian ideal would demand, it can and does come up with arguments which show their fittingness, on the basis of our fruitful grasp of their relation to truths of reason and to one another.[36] In this kind of *argumentum convenientiae* Aquinas excelled.

Necessitarianism was the danger which the more conservative church establishment saw lurking in this attractive and wide-ranging presentation of an ordered universe which, based on a Wisdom invariably faithful to itself, was totally reliable. They did not grasp the crucial difference between the *argumentum convenientiae* and the proof that demonstrates without the shadow of a doubt. They feared that such a reliance on Wisdom was an attack on divine freedom, that the next step would be to establish with our reason the necessary truth of what is known through revelation. Thus theology would slip into a denial of the utter freedom and transcendence of God so consistently affirmed by Holy Writ and by so many Church Fathers, above all Augustine.

As a result, what for Thomas and the earlier scholastic tradition was intricately and thoroughly relational was splintered into fragments. God would be more clearly in command of a universe made up of disparate elements which he could yoke and unyoke at will. Moreover forces were at work within that period of time to move beyond Aristotelian science, bound up in logical categories, to a more empirical and actively questioning approach to physical nature akin to that which pertains to our own age.

The Averroist condemnation did not stick to Aquinas, but in the atmosphere it engendered the breadth and inspiration of the Thomist synthesis was belittled and eventually eclipsed. Even those who continued to valiantly protect the positions of their master little by little allowed themselves to be penetrated by the very positions they were trying to overturn.[37] Many followers of Thomas, impressed by his achievement but insufficiently aware of the difference between the context in which it was formulated and the context for which they ought to have translated it, have been content to repeat its formulas to themselves and prescribe them to others, not disdaining external appeals to authority in the process.[38] Not acknowledging that Thomas' synthesis was fragile,[39] even premature given the historical circumstances in which it came about, they missed an opportunity to do what their master did in the thirteenth century, which was to transpose the richness of the tradition he had received into a new key. Free regarding its re-expression in Aristotelian terms, he was faithful in maintaining its substance. Their literal fidelity to the tradition as they received it from him was in effect a betrayal.

The movement away from the sapiential perspective of Aquinas, which reconciled freedom and reliability, was a gradual one. A first step is the genuine achievement of Duns Scotus, synthetic, balanced, yet leaning towards divine voluntarism. The pendulum did not, however, stop there. The ensuing nominalism of William of Ockham was spontaneously recognized by the theologians of subsequent centuries not as a further conservative reaction but as the breaking of new ground, a *via moderna* contrasted to the *via antiqua* of Thomas and Scotus.

In the theology of Scotus, characterized by the development and use of the notion of the *formalitas*, God created a universe which maintained a measure of intrinsic order and of necessity.[40] However in the nominalist position human reason reaches out to an arbitrary God who in his absolute power (*potentia Dei absoluta*) can put together and take apart the isolated elements of the universe in any way he wishes, because they are nothing but in-dividual entities (a-toms), constitutively separated from rather than related to each other. Revelation gives access to the *potentia Dei ordinata* (power of God as he freely chooses to use it in ordering the elements and activities of the universe), but behind this revealed truth there is the inscrutable and terrifying mystery of a God who might have determined a completely different set of game rules and who could still change them, leaving the players in utter confusion and bewilderment.

Little by little the theological exploration which paved the way for the giants of the thirteenth century was replaced by the rigidity of scholastic sects. Positions were attacked and defended with the arsenal of a subtle and complex logic; slowly and insidiously, in spite of their lively disagreements, the schools became more narrow-minded, reflecting the insecurities and deficiencies of their age. Even those who combatted nominalism as a position could not entirely ward it off as an ethos.

This relatively minor breakdown culminated in a major breakdown in the unity of Christendom, the Protestant Reformation of the sixteenth century. By then many experienced the God of nominalism not just as arbitrary and elusive but as angry and inaccessible. As we saw, they took God's grace to be a scarce commodity, gingerly measured out, obtained through religious observances with a quantified value. Luther's indignation at this galvanized many Christians. Together with him, they sought out the gracious God promised in the Gospels, condemning the system of observances which, stemming from and leading to religious anxiety, helped to finance the Renaissance Church. He invited them to flee from the turmoil within themselves to the security of the Word which beckons them from outside themselves. This was a step in the right direction, but the underlying malaise was more covered up than overcome.[41] The focus was on the egoic "I", threatened from within and without, seeking a gracious God. The community dimension so integral to the earlier organic view remained in the background. The Catholic Church reacted against the lacunae of his position, but failed to recognize and incorporate what was positive in it.

The divisions brought about by this reform have lasted to this day. Anathemas were hurled back and forth, doctrinal battle lines were drawn. At a deeper and scarcely conscious level, however, the Church was being rent by the birth-pangs of a new way of doing theology. Luther sensed this new way when he defined the path of the theologian as living, indeed dying and being damned rather than understanding, reading, or speculating.[42] Unfortunately no one on either side was able to recognize the radical newness of which Luther was the vehicle, and lift it out of a context which did not work in its favour. This failure hampered efforts to open and sustain a fruitful dialogue between the old in desperate need of reform and the new which had so much to contribute. Each side according to its own mindset read the positions of the other side, magnified their lacunae, and impugned their orthodoxy. *Odium theologicum* was given free rein.

With the distance of four centuries, scholars are beginning to put their finger on what was going on at the time. For instance Otto Pesch[43] offers us a very helpful distinction between the sapiential mode of doing theology favoured by Aquinas and the existential mode favoured by Luther. Aquinas dwelt in peaceful and insightful contemplation of the reality ordained by a good and wise God. Luther urgently sought the answer to a personal quest: how could he find a gracious God in the midst of the anguish that he suffered, placate a God who seemed angrier the more he tried to please him? As we have seen, the focus of Luther's theology was the individual's *relation*, problematic and anxious, between himself and God, whereas Aquinas put grace into the Aristotelian category of *quality*, taking for granted the massive and secure reality of God's relation to humankind.

We have drawn a contrast between Aquinas and Luther, but the struggle of the Reformation was between Catholic theologians of many different schools and the theologians of the Reformation. Thus Pesch's simple contrast must be amplified. Most Catholic theologians and bishops at Trent still followed as best they could the *via antiqua*: they shared, with limitations, the objective/sapiential approach to theology traditional in the Church up till that time. Differences between schools of theology at Trent, however, tended to cancel each other out. Providentially, that council had to rely on an earlier, less theologically sophisticated and more biblically based tradition. Those influenced by the *via moderna* of nominalism were critical of the traditional mode of doing theology, of its efforts without much prior fuss and bother to formulate the intelligible pattern of God's activity, and they attached much more importance to the positive sources of theology. Luther shared this critical bent of the *via moderna*, extolling a naked faith in the word of God over the idolatrous pretensions of human reason to achieve wisdom. Others, such as Calvin, developed similar positions, with less existential impact but with more systematic scope.

How did Roman Catholic theology pursue its development in the aftermath of this major breakdown? Centrifugal pressures generated from the fourteenth century onward were heightened by the Protestant Reformation. The Council of Trent established parameters for the theology of grace, but did nothing to lessen the intensity of theological debate among Roman Catholics. If anything, it raised the stakes for the adversaries: more often than before theologians were not satisfied to vindicate their own positions; they tried to tar their adversaries with the brush of heresy. Incredible amounts of energy were locked into the ultimately sterile quarrels of the sixteenth and seventeenth centuries. Highly complex, these quarrels are not worth retelling here. However let us briefly describe the three schools involved in them.

a) There was an Augustinian school based upon a rigid and juridical interpretation of Augustine, above all his later writings. Its main proponents, Baius and Jansenius, held positions which were akin to those condemned by the

Council of Trent. They sought theological truth in the positive study of the authoritative writings of Augustine. In this they were influenced by nominalism, with its tendency to seek theological truth exclusively in positive revealed data and to adopt an extrinsic and juridical cast of mind.

b) There was a Dominican school, based on an interpretation of Aquinas hardened by years of scholastic debate. The main proponent of this school, Dominic Bañez, is famous for his advocacy of *praemotio physica*, which to his adversaries was the death knell of any real freedom under grace. Lonergan shows how this position fails to take seriously the primacy Aquinas gives to the universal and the all-encompassing dimension of providence. When all is said and done, on Lonergan's interpretation, God controls each action because he controls all of them.[44] This Bañez fails to acknowledge. The ethos of nominalism, with its stress on *individual* action, was too strong.

c) There was a Jesuit school of thought which was more free- wheeling in its speculative attempts to resolve the thorny issues of divine dominion and human freedom. It set out from the emphasis on freedom which characterizes Ignatius Loyola. The most famous proponent of this school is Luis de Molina. His overly subtle theory of *scientia media* tried to reconcile God's dominion with human free activity, and for many it watered down the divine transcendence. The Jesuit school misinterpreted Thomas in the same way the Dominican school did, failing to recognize the primacy Aquinas gave to the whole over the part.[45]

The rigid Augustinians of the first school were condemned by the Church.[46] The other two schools were forbidden by Pope Clement VIII to call each other heretics, and they continued their debate for centuries afterwards.

The presupposition that quietly but effectively shaped theological positions across most of the spectrum of that period was the basic nominalist option for expressing the dialogue of God and humankind as a set of extrinsic and quasi-juridical relations added on to the self-enclosed human reality. The Protestant Reformers saw grace and nature as realities alien from one another. Should these two components enter into relation, it would only be by some kind of divine intervention from without. By itself nature is powerless, depraved, and alienated from God's grace. The Augustinian school went along with this negative assessment of nature, though it made a distinction between the two historical states of human nature: after the fall, the Protestant positions were basically true, but before the fall, in the state of pure nature, nature was rightfully entitled to grace. For theologians within the Roman Catholic mainstream, though nature after the fall was not depraved but kept its essential goodness, it remained a self-enclosed reality, with its own finality and aspirations, and grace was something added on extrinsically, by divine decree.

Grace was seen as a second story added on afterwards to the edifice of nature. Beyond the reach of human experience, it was the object of dogmatic faith. Aquinas' doctrine of the natural desire to see God was in eclipse, even among those who claimed to be his disciples. A distortion with immense consequences was inserted into the life of the Church.[47] In sum Catholics and Protestants of the era shared the presupposition that grace and nature are elements extrinsic to one another, but differed about the nature to which grace is added. It was depraved in the eyes of the Protestants, enjoyed a certain autonomy and goodness of its own in the eyes of the Catholics. That presupposition remained unmasked for centuries.

After this account of the decline which took place within the Western tradition on grace, we need to pause and take our bearings. The emergence of the *via moderna* and its aftermath are not isolated phenomena. They are in effect part of a profound mutation which affected all aspects of human life, encompassing the fragmentation of the political order in the late Middle Ages, the emergence of modern science and technology, the rise of capitalism, a different experience of God and conceptualization of grace. As we saw in Chapter One, this mutation in effect sowed the seeds of the flawed old order we are now trying to uproot. A better understanding of this mutation will help us to shape a theology of grace which will bring to light the true motivation and rationale for the struggles of our day towards a new order.

a) *The Wider Scene*: From the fourteenth century on the organic texture of medieval society was being relentlessly unravelled. The ideal of unity which permeated the earlier Middle Ages was shattered against a persistent papal schism and eroded by the emergent nation states setting off on their long career of bellicose expansion. The terrible plagues which traversed Europe left people in a state of bewilderment, anguish, insecurity. The universe in which each individual eked out survival and the God to whom he or she related were arbitrary, frightening. The support one used to find in a divine fidelity which expressed itself in a consistent, organically interrelated universe was no longer there. Individuals were more preoccupied with their own survival, their relationship with God having become fragile and fraught with anxiety. The parts had to fend for themselves because the whole was no longer seen as benevolent.

b) *The Epistemic Shift: Divide et Impera*: This pervasive sense of fragmentation is accompanied by a far-reaching shift in the ways of human knowing. As we saw, the intellectualism of Thomas is open: the intellect's act of understanding is conscious, and consciously expresses itself in structured concepts whose elements are intrinsically related to each other and to the whole. In the final analysis the Thomist intellect is ecologically sound: it gives primacy to the whole over the part. By contrast, for the conceptualist position of Scotus, which paves the way for the more radical nominalism of William of Ockham, each concept, generated within the mind prior to the conscious act of understanding, is atomistic, given in its own absolute (as opposed to relative) and isolated reality, and the further act by which concepts are related to one another is derivative.[48] This approach invites us to see the universe not as an organic whole but as a mechanistic assembly of parts, and opens the way for an attitude of scepticism and suspicion.[49]

Many late medieval thinkers entered upon the Ockhamist path. The *via moderna* they espoused goes hand in glove with a fragmented universe over which presides a God of absolute power who at will yokes and unyokes its basic building blocks. This epistemic shift goes beyond the realm of theology to include the newly emerging physical sciences of that time. It underpins the *divide et impera* methodology that has served the modern sciences so long and so well. This methodology was enshrined in Descartes' *Regulae ad directionem ingenii* and *Discours de la méthode*: in order to understand, break the larger problem into its constituent simple problems. Priority is given to the parts and not to the whole.[50]

Some of the key insights of the Protestant Reformation gave further impetus to this method. Nature was in and of itself lifeless and inorganic, fragmented, because the God who created it and acted upon it had to remain sovereign over it. The view that it was under the control not of a humanly devised *a priori* system but of divine sovereignty only strengthened the tendency to attend to the here-and-now *de facto* empirical data which Aristotelian science belittled.[51] This method yielded amazing results, above all our mastery, scientific and technological, over the universe,[52] but we now are faced with its limitations. Disregard of the whole, exclusive concentration on the parts which can be measured, isolated, controlled, manipulated has become a hindrance to the development of science in our day; in addition the untrammelled application of this method carries with it the seeds of self-destruction, as we saw in Chapter One.

c) *The New Capitalism: Quantity Reigns Supreme*: Berman insightfully links the emergence of the new mechanistic vision of the universe and the rise of capitalism.[53] Money is no longer seen as a purely instrumental medium of exchange to facilitate the consistent and ordered intermeshing of complementary human activities and values. It begins to be prized for its own sake: the more plentiful one's store of it, the greater human worth and dignity one enjoys in one's own eyes and in those of others, the more one is able to fend off the sense of fragility and isolation gnawing within. It is absolutely essential that it be subject to exact numerical calculation, defined in terms of a precise quantitative more or less which can fuel comparison and competition. It is not so much the intrinsic value and enjoyment of the goods produced and enjoyed as the state of the bank account that defines the value of the person.

Quantity was a part of Aquinas' organically interrelated universe, belonging to the predicamental categories he derived from Aristotle. Aquinas never highlighted quantity, but it becomes the linchpin of the emergent single vision: the really real consists in quantified and measurable particles moving in space and time. As is true in the economic order, the fragmented parts are related to one another in quantitative terms, the precise measurement of which becomes the means of major scientific advance. (This quantification becomes valid in the religious realm as well, affecting above all God's grace, but more on that later.)

d) *Achievement and Anxiety*: At the root of this drive to measure and to increase quantities we find scarcity, real or imagined, and anxiety. If I am secure in the plentiful possession of something, I generally do not bother to count it. If I am insecure about how much I have now or am likely to have in the future, I begin counting and accumulating: the quantitative element obtrudes.

This leads us to the consideration of the economic scarcity, mentioned by Berman, which prevailed in the fourteenth century. A vicious circle was at work here. Scarcity spawned anxiety. Anxiety fueled the drive to achieve in monetary terms, and contributed to a world in which isolation and competition reigned supreme. This in turn intensified the culture's awareness of scarcity:[54] a vicious circle which could be added to the ones so tellingly developed by Slater, quoted in Chapter One.

What is anxiety all about? What leads one as an individual to seek a totally unassailable position apart from genuine relations, in this case through monetary self-sufficiency, is the basic insecurity which R.D. Laing expresses very well.[55] This basic insecurity is very much present in the late Middle Ages and in the Renaissance, and presides over the emergence of capitalism and of the "single vision" of the universe as made up of essentially inert entities subject to precise physical measurement and manipulation.

Rollo May offers us a helpful amplification of this point. The Renaissance above all valued the *uomo universale*, the powerful individual[56] able to compete and come out on top. The point May makes is that the *uomo universale*'s drive towards and achievement of success was accompanied by an undercurrent of insecurity, anxiety, even despair, due to "the state of psychological isolation and the lack of the positive value of community, both results of excessive individualism".[57] To mask this undercurrent success and wealth in the eyes of others were needed. Work lost its intrinsic value as providing something worthwhile for self and others, and became above all the means to shore up one's fragile self-esteem.[58]

The anxiety which presided over the emergence of expansionary capitalism and of the technological/scientific vision continues unabated today, and is at the very core of the old order. Its consequences are now much more to the fore. The anxiety of the Renaissance man was latent, but now anxiety is a recognized and pervasive phenomenon.[59] The signs of mental breakdown surround us. In his *Pursuit of Loneliness* Slater in effect holds that the anxious and insatiable pursuit of artificial goals is essential for the old order to maintain itself.[60] In his *Earthwalk* he discloses the link between the need to be a high achiever, a wielder of power in our world, and basic personal insecurities linked in great part with the patterns of upbringing which obtain in our world.[61]

e) *Anxiety and the Angry God*: The anxiety we have spoken about touches the deepest nerve of the human psyche and distorts our relationship to God. That distortion we have already touched on: it is what happens to the Western tradition on grace when it falls out of touch with its roots and refuses to be complemented with the emphases of other traditions.

This anxiety prompts us to set up barriers between ourselves and God, to consider God as our oppressor, the angry and arbitrary judge whom we must at all costs placate. Our confusion and resentment is projected upon a God who is falsely seen as angry and resentful. Instead of being recognized as the one who is com-passionately present to his Son dying on the cross for us, the Father is seen as the one who wreaks vengeance on a Jesus who stands in our place, alienated, in a state of enmity, and who releases Jesus to his death once Jesus has fulfilled his required quota of suffering. In subtle secular guise this false relationship with God permeates and poisons the achievements of the old order. The vaunted technological power of that world is at the service of a need to control, to expand, to snuff out life and spontaneity.[62] If I can't be sure of my status before the angry God, at least I can be resourceful in assuring my status here below. If my salvation consists in imitating God, and if I perceive God's perfection as consisting in the cold juridical purity which leads him to make such demands of his Son, I will enflesh this false image in my relations to others and thereby diminish their lives. My striving, my achievement, my good works are poisoned and counter-productive. The dynamic of oppression is unleashed within my psyche, my very self.

f) *Grace Measured out*: In accord with the prevailing *Zeitgeist*, grace begins to be conceptualized in quantitative terms. It had been subsumed by Aquinas under the descriptive category of quality, a quality linked to the transforming relationship with God which I can count on in a totally secure and abiding way.

But now it is quantified and given a price tag. As the power and freedom of God begin to seem arbitrary and frightening in the human experience of that period, the relationship with God becomes problematic, and the quality of life which grace bestows becomes hardened into a quantity which I measure in order to possess more securely. In this realm as in that of human secular activity, anxiety leads to quantification. Grace becomes a scarce possession for which I have to compete.[63] I go through complex quasi-mechanical procedures in order to make sure that in the end my account will be on the credit rather than on the debit side. The preaching of indulgences, against whose excesses Luther reacted so strongly,[64] graphically puts before our eyes the climactic conjunction of grace and money. The scarce resource of money made its way from the anguished faithful to the administrative center of the Church, and from its spiritual treasure the Church allowed the scarce commodity of grace to flow in careful measure to the faithful.

This reification of grace is not part of the authentic tradition of the Western Church but a theological sclerosis which parallels the emergence of the single vision and the old order. As in the twentieth century we move away from the single vision to a more organic and relational view of the universe, so too we are seeking to renew the authentic Western tradition on grace.

This renewal has already begun. By the mid-twentieth century theologians began to question this presupposition and to seek recovery of the authentic tradition. The history of the breakthrough they achieved is beyond our scope, but we will at least evoke Maurice Blondel, philosopher of human action, Henri de Lubac, whose historical studies on the supernatural, problematic as they were thought to be by the magisterium in the '50's, were crucial in bringing back the forgotten tradition of the centuries to which Aquinas was faithful, and Karl Rahner, who systematized these new insights and brought them into the mainstream of Catholic theology.

THE WESTERN TRADITION ON GRACE:
NEW POSSIBILITIES:

The age of all-embracing *Summae* may be over, but this ought not deter us from trying to explore the paths of integration now beginning to open up. The trailblazing work of Blondel, de Lubac, and Rahner, a hermeneutically and historically sounder understanding of what was happening in the confrontation of Reformers and Council Fathers in the sixteenth century, emerging models for a new theology of grace in continuity with the old, and a more collaborative approach to theology: together these factors encourage us to resume in the twentieth century the constructive task of the thirteenth.

We have briefly presented the historical context for the shift that has taken place between Aquinas' day and ours. Let us now reflect on the deeper implications of that shift, and sketch out the possibilities now open to us.

For all its attractiveness and architectonic sweep, Aquinas' synthesis proved ephemeral. In the wake of the 1277 condemnations, many rejected it in favour of a safer, more conservative approach. More important, those who professed their fidelity to Thomas often misunderstood him in subtle but far-reaching ways.

Why is this so? Reasons external to Aquinas' thought entered in, as we have seen, but we must not forget the inescapable discrepancy between the Aristotelian model of reality which Aquinas employed and the revealed mysteries of which he was attempting to render a faithful account. Grace is as mysterious as God is. No humanly derived philosophical categories will do justice to it, because the experiential, concrete grounding for such categories is found in created reality and not in the reality of God.

The language of Aristotle is meta-*physical* (beyond physics). Though Aristotle is interested in developing concepts that touch being as such and thus go beyond the realm of the physical, his springboard is physical reality, a reality organic, alive, subject to growth and decay. His basic categories of potency and act are taken from his experience of living things that fulfill their potential for development, his four causes are based upon interactions he observed with his senses, and his categories most aptly apply to the descriptive classification of physical phenomena.[65]

Thomas uses the conceptual armature of Aristotle's metaphysics, but with the intent of leaping much deeper and further from the springboard than Aristotle himself. He wishes to leap into a world which is suffused with the mystery of a personal God. Openly at times, at other times very subtly, he uses that armature as a tool, he refines it, makes it less inadequate, at times transforms it.[66]

Aquinas was walking a tightrope. At every step of the way he deeply communed with the eminently personal nature of the mysteries of which he sought an imperfect understanding, but the very language he used, though purified and adjusted to communicate revealed mystery less inadequately, still smacked of the impersonal and necessitarian universe of Aristotle.

Like Aquinas we are not exempt from the inherent limitations of philosophical language. Unlike him we are in a position to explore the use of new languages, in continuity with the old, possibly less inadequate than his as a vehicle for mystery. Would the meta-*psychological* or meta-*sociological* languages unavailable to Thomas but available to us[67] not give us a better springboard for leaping into divine mystery? Because the realities which serve as the base for these languages are properly human, less distant from the mystery of God than the infra-human and im-personal reality of the physical universe, would they not be less removed from the reality of God and his actions towards us, less inapt to express them? And are not such languages better attuned to the dimension of interiority which has begun to pervade theology?

Luther was the first theologian to urgently seek out such a new personal language for theology. As we saw, without realizing it he initiated a move from theory to interiority, opted for relation rather than quality as a category for his definition of grace, and made his personal relationship with God the central burning question of his theology. In this, however, he played the essential but disturbing role of the precursor. A well-rounded synthesis could not but elude his grasp. In spite of the reliance on the Word of God which he advocated, the relationship with God which was so central to his thought continued to be fraught with anxiety, and the resulting theology failed to do full justice to the diverse ways in which God may touch each and every human being.

Recent ecumenical efforts—we have mentioned Pesch's work—have enabled us to see that the struggle between Martin Luther and the Fathers of the Council of Trent was not a clear-cut confrontation of heresy and orthodoxy. Rather it was the non-encounter of ships passing in the night, of persons who used the words of their shared vocabulary in different ways because their contexts had drifted far apart. A basis for recovering Luther's precious contribution and incorporating it into the authentic Western tradition on grace is now emerging in the human sciences of the twentieth century. Their grasp of the dynamics of how human beings interact with each other in freedom and in community is a less inadequate springboard from which to leap into the mystery of how God deals with us than the analyses of Aristotle. The personalist mode in which the theology of grace has been done in the last thirty years or so has prepared us to enter upon this path with resolution and dispatch.

Yet a firm caution must be expressed at this point. We must not rest with the achievement of an exclusively personal/interpersonal model for grace. The drawback of such a model would be that it sets aside the social, cultural, political, economic, even planetary realms in which we so keenly experience the absence of grace. The relational virtualities of contemporary psychology need to be exploited to the full. Indeed that discipline reminds us that without exception persons are not only persons-in-relation but also persons-in-community.[68] Psychology cannot but call for the complementary investigations of sociology, economics, politics, ecology. More recent developments in the Roman Catholic theology of grace, in sympathy with theology of liberation, take this social dimension of sin and grace with the utmost seriousness. We stress the meta-sociological implications of the meta-psychological more than will the meta-sociological on its own terms—with the exception perhaps of our analysis of Paulo Freire's work in the next chapter.

THE WESTERN TRADITION ON GRACE:
HORIZON-ANALYSIS

We wish to end this complex chapter by depicting in even broader terms the context of our efforts to recover and advance the Western tradition on grace. We will do this by expanding the elements of horizon-analysis which emerged in the last section.

We will center our reflections on the epochal shift brought about by Christian revelation, a shift which has irrevocably changed the horizon of human thought. (The late medieval mutation we have just described is but a phase of this shift.) These reflections relate to the topics which this chapter has thus far touched upon:

a) The recovery and advance of the tradition on grace has *methodological* implications, of which we have given an account in the first section of this chapter. Bernard Lonergan, as we have seen, develops these implications in greater detail in *Method in Theology*, where he carefully situates his method within an emerging new phase of human thought which gives pride of place to history and interiority. It is our contention that this new phase derives its power and impetus from the epochal shift brought about by Christian revelation.

b) That recovery also has *ecclesial* implications, which we have dealt with in the second section. The Western Church will not recover its authentic tradition without *ipso facto* re-engaging in symbiotic interchange with the Eastern and third world Churches. This interchange is needed to foster and develop the new horizon brought about by that epochal shift.

c) That recovery also needs to be situated in its *historical* context. The growth, decline, and possibilities of the authentic tradition of the Western Church which we have just finished sketching, are an essential part of the growth, decline, and possibilities for further unfolding of that new horizon.

Many have tried their hand at horizon analysis in this century, hoping to make some sense out of the accelerating tempo of change which engulfs us. Thomas S. Kuhn describes paradigm shifts within the field of science.[69] At a certain point new discoveries can no longer be added to other discoveries and integrated within an older and familiar context of thought. They destroy the parameters of that earlier context, call for a new, broader context which can integrate the new with the old and open up the possibility for sustained advances on a higher level.

Others have paid attention to the horizon within which philosophy and theology advance and have sought to describe the phenomenon that corresponds to paradigm shifts in the physical sciences. For instance in his Gifford Lectures the English personalist philosopher John Macmurray has described the journey of Western thought in recent centuries as a movement from the form of the material through that of the organic to that of the personal.[70] The German theologian Johann Baptist Metz has written on the properly Christian anthropocentric *Denkform* (thought-form). Grounded in the Gospel, that thought-form, quite distinct from the cosmocentric thought-form of the Greeks, systematically affects Christian thought from the time of Thomas Aquinas on, and becomes an explicit theme in our own age.[71] Macmurray offers us three thought-form categories: the personal, the material (or mathematical), and the organic; and Metz two: the cosmocentric and the anthropocentric (which in part dovetails with Macmurray's personal). We will take these categories as a source of inspiration for our own reflections rather than as models to be followed rigidly.[72] In broad terms, Metz' categories will help us account for earlier developments, Macmurray's for later.

What do these authors mean by thought-form? Macmurray distinguishes between the content of a philosophy and the form which enables that content to be rationally determined, understood in a unified and systematically interrelated way.[73] Metz develops his distinction between thought-form and thought-content more thoroughly. The thought-content has to do with the *explicit* themes and concerns which emerge as important within a given view of the world. The thought-form is the world-view itself as a stance, perspective, angle of vision which powerfully acts on and sets the parameters of a thought-content, but itself remains *implicit* and hidden. If you will, thought-content has to do with what one knows, thought-form with how one knows it. In scholastic terms, thought-form is the formal object, thought-content the material object.

It is above all the introduction and unfolding of the personal[74] and the anthropocentric as thought-forms which relate to our efforts at unifying and contextualizing this chapter. To recover the authentic tradition on grace one has to be able to do theology in the light of a personal, anthropocentric horizon.

Let us begin our analysis with the broader categories of Metz. The contrast he depicts can be diagrammed as follows:

	Hellenistic world-view	**Judeo-Christian world-view**
thought-form:	cosmocentric	anthropocentric
thought-content:	anthropocentric	theocentric

The Hellenistic world-view provided both a counterfoil and a treasure-trove for early Christian theology. Spanning many centuries, the contact of Hellenistic and Judeo-Christian world-views began with the later strata of the Old Testament, fruit of the contact of diaspora Judaism with its ambient culture; it constituted a major theme of New Testament times, and it culminated in the struggles of the Fathers of the Church to re-express the deposit of faith in terms both faithful and recognizable to a person of Hellenistic culture. Christians in good part derived the conceptual armature of their thought from Hellenistic thought; they also kept a distance from it within their own minds and at the appropriate moments transformed it.

How does the Hellenistic world-view differ from the Judeo-Christian? The diagram expresses the difference quite succinctly: Metz contrasts the Hellenistic cosmocentric thought-form which permeates an anthropological thought-content, with the Judeo-Christian anthropocentric thought-form which permeates a theocentric thought-content.[75] In other words—and here we go beyond the terms used by Metz—the major focus and concern of Greek thinkers was the human reality, but they set that reality within the horizon of the cosmos,[76] whereas the major focus and concern of Judeo-Christian thinkers was the divine reality which freely discloses itself, but they set that reality within the context of the subjective/personal relation which is operative in that disclosure and which, permeating the human reality, places it on a level utterly beyond that of the physical cosmos.[77]

In Metz's perspective the stages of the Judeo-Christian world-view's advance are as follows:

a) Christian revelation has contributed not just a new thought-content but has also invited humankind to respond to reality in a different way, the way of the anthropocentric thought-form. At first the power of that thought-form remained tacit, but—this is a point that Metz does not develop—it achieved effective results in a few strategic instances, as in some of the early Councils of the Church.

b) It is only in the Christian Middle Ages that this Christian thought-form, while still remaining implicit, began to shape theological thought in a systematic and thoroughgoing fashion. This occurred especially in the work of Thomas Aquinas.

c) Between the thirteenth and twentieth centuries this thought-form has become more clearly recognized and has had a greater impact.

This brief account needs to be fleshed out in more detail:

Since Christian doctrine is taken up with the mystery of God's self-disclosure in the person of Jesus Christ, it approaches that mystery in a mode which is at root personal and calls for a personal response. That mode becomes thematic in the notion of person-in-relation, applied to the doctrine of Jesus Christ and of the Trinity from the very beginning, and subsequently to Christian anthropology.

The God of both Testaments[78] reveals himself freely as a subject, with all the mysterious interiority that implies. In his passionate caring for human beings God invests them with unparalleled value, invites them to see themselves and their companions on the human journey as subjects and to be as caring as he is. In contrast, Greek thinkers, though more and more aware of the properly human,[79] viewed divinity as impersonal, tragically unconcerned with the unique destiny of each human person, and they dealt with natures and essences as situated within the cosmos. Personal uniqueness, freedom, and relationships were largely beyond their ken. While the Christian Church used Hellenistic terminology to vindicate and illustrate its own doctrines, it began, in the struggle to maintain their distinctiveness, to forge a new terminology, one able to differentiate between person and nature, in order to speak about the unprecedented subject-related dimension of Christian faith.[80] For many centuries the Christian churches have been working out the implications of this breakthrough for the dignity and status of each human person. This process is far from complete.

While remaining in the background, this thought-form of the personal began to consolidate its sway over Christian theology as it developed beyond the first contact of the Fathers and Councils with the world of Greek thought. It comes to sharper expression in Augustine, who was aware of himself as a person with an acuity far beyond his time, and shaped his theology of grace in the light of that awareness. It comes to further expression in the early Middle Ages, which were disarmingly naïve, spontaneous, creative, and in some ways very much under the aegis of the personal. We find these attractive characteristics in the Trinitarian theology of Richard of Saint Victor and in the spiritual writings of monks such as Aelred of Rielvaux. These persons enjoyed a genuine experience of interpersonal and communitarian dynamics and were able to use it in their spiritual and theological writings to bring to the fore in a new and creative way the relational dimension entailed by the personal thought-form.

The first medieval author in which the personal or anthropocentric thought-form can be grasped in its systematic ramifications over a whole body of knowledge is Thomas Aquinas.[81] This fact leads Metz to acclaim Thomas as the agent of the epochal breakthrough of the anthropocentric thought-form.

In explaining the unique contribution of Aquinas Metz covers some of the same terrain as Lonergan does. The latter reflects on the shift from the world of common sense in which the Fathers lived to the world of theory which emerges in the Middle Ages. The Fathers were concerned above all with pastoral and practical issues. If from time to time they allowed a properly theoretical concern to come to the surface, it was with some reluctance, as when they were forced to explicitate in quasi-philosophical terms the exigencies of the Christian thought-form against a Hellenized and overly simplified version of the Christian faith. But it is only in the Middle Ages that the theoretical concern became uppermost, as the first *Summae* made their appearance.

For all the significance of the breakthrough achieved by Thomas the Christian thought-form remains implicit in his thought. At first blush what strikes us is the organized body of knowledge concerning the universe of nature and grace which he devised on the basis of the principles of Aristotelian philosophy. The subtle but far-reaching transformation of those principles in the light of the Christian thought-form lies beneath the surface and went largely unacknowledged in the years that followed his death.[82]

It is only after Thomas that the exigencies of the anthropocentric thought-form become urgent, that the world of the subject becomes the object of concern and conceptualization. This emergence of the subject is central to the emancipation which leads to modernity. Typically that emancipation is thought to begin only with the Renaissance and Reformation, but Metz shows how it is firmly rooted in the work of Thomas Aquinas, the one who mediates the personal thought-form to our modern age. The continuity between his world and ours is far deeper than their discontinuity.[83] Yet modernity's promotion of the anthropocentric thought-form to the point that it has become an explicit theme, a value espoused for its own sake, entails serious limitations. Modernity has failed—understandably so—to acknowledge its Judeo-Christian roots, and as a result the subjectivity it so prizes has lost its moorings.[84] However we should not call our era back to an orthodoxy based on the thought-content of Aquinas but invite it to acknowledge the personal thought-form in which alone modernity will recover its authenticity and overcome the impasse of our age.

Metz offers no detailed account of how the anthropocentric thought-form has since Thomas Aquinas gradually lost touch with its roots. Finding inspiration in Macmurray's categories, we will trace this development under the headings of the organic, the mechanical, and the personal.

Let us begin with the *organic*. As we saw in Chapter One, the organic, interrelated nature of medieval life and thought has attracted a number of contemporary authors. They have been taken up with science's rediscovery, in a similar vein, of interrelations at the very heart of the material world, ranging all the way from the intricate micro-dance of space/time and mass/energy to the macro-concerns of ecology. In some instances, these authors suggest the kinship of this organic view with the religions of the East,[85] and offer an approach in which the ultimate, irreducible, and ultimately perduring value of each human person appears to be downplayed in favour of some impersonal, all-encompassing reality into which persons are absorbed. That they should think this way is understandable: our world, we hope, is on a path of convergence, and Eastern traditions have much to offer our Western world. These authors sense how important it is to counteract a tight-fisted emphasis on person as self-sufficient, competitive, needing to make it on its own, and insights and disciplines from the East can be of immeasurable help to us.

At the same time these authors fail to realize that the value and attractiveness they perceive in the Middle Ages ultimately stems from the Christian anthropocentric thought-form, for which each individual human subject has an irreducible value grounded in his or her relation to the divine Subjects. They perceive an attractive organic dimension in medieval thought and life, but fail to penetrate to the form which animates it. The modern West needs to recover what is authentic in its originating Christian tradition. In this process we will be led to the mystery of each person, which has its organic and relational dimension, yes, but also carries with it a unique value. We should not belittle that uniqueness, even if it has been caricatured for the last four hundred years of competitive self-assertion. Persons are fulfilled not by being dissolved into the All, thus losing their selfhood, but by the self-forgetfulness which alone makes genuine relationships possible. The Christian, like the grain of wheat, falls into the ground and dies not to be absorbed but in order to produce a distinctive new life.

The organic and the personal are profoundly linked: one of the paradoxes of being a person, which has come to expression in recent theology of the Trinity, is the mutual enrichment which unrestricted relationality and unique subsistence bring to each other. The relational element is central to the form of the organic. The form of the personal does not deny that element but brings it to a higher level of realization by setting it in symbiosis with another element, the inalienable uniqueness of the person. It is precisely by reaching out in risk, establishing genuine relationships, that persons find their fulfillment. At the same time it is precisely out of the ontological strength of a personhood that is fully acknowledged and accepted that genuine emptying out towards others can take place. These two elements do not compete with one another but enhance one another. This paradox is integral to the form of the personal. For the Christian it is rooted in a divine personhood in which the absolute and the relative, the self-sufficient and the relational, the utterly secure and the totally vulnerable clasp hands in a marvellous *coincidentia oppositorum*.

Unfortunately, in the Middle Ages this paradox central to Christian revelation had not yet come to the light of day. Thus it could not counteract a predisposition to see relation and self-sufficiency as competing rather than as mutually enriching. The Aristotelian dimension of Aquinas' thought stood out in the minds of his interpreters both friendly and hostile. They detected the surface structures of that thought, saw it as affirming the reliable, the organic, and the relational, but failed to discern its deeper structures, deriving from the revealed mystery of God, structures which have to do with self-identity, self-assertion, self-originating freedom. They took Aquinas' thought to be less personal than it really is, stressed its links with the cosmocentric universe of the Greeks, criticized it or tried to correct it in misguided ways.[86]

This reaction to Thomas was motivated by a unspoken need to safeguard certain aspects of the personal thought-form, but it ended up occasioning the rise of another thought-form, that of the *mechanical*. Critics of Thomas attempted to give greater prominence to what they perceived to be lacking in his thought: the freedom, the transcendence, the self-sufficiency of the person, above all of God. They ended up in the other extreme, however, with a person so self-sufficient that it becomes monadic, and with a universe which is no longer organic and relational but disjointed and atomistic, essentially open to mechanistic description and manipulation. As we have seen, this paves the way for the "old order" which prizes self-aggrandizement at the expense of relations.[87] This order many are seeking to overthrow in our day by returning to something which is older and more authentic, but that something is also radically new because it is part of the new creation in Christ Jesus.[88]

A struggle to get out of the strait-jacket of the mechanical has been going on for well over a century. It began with the Romantic movement[89] and includes Hegelianism, Darwinism and other allied forms of thought. Not having recovered the personal thought-form in its fullness as rooted in the Judeo-Christian dispensation that particular struggle has been in vain. For Macmurray the movements which it comprises are united under the form of the organic, which is a half-way house between the form of the material (mechanical) and of the personal. His insight is most helpful: the pervasive sense of the organismic, of the holistic, of the dialectical which characterizes these movements brings us out of the mechanical but by itself fails to lead us to the personal.

Macmurray includes Marxism under his heading of the organic. In a very true sense Marxism arises out of a powerful reaction to a merely mechanical vision of the human world, and its dialectical structures do have Gospel roots.[90] But its failure to acknowledge the Judeo-Christian source of its own vitality means that its protest against the mechanistically structured world of industrial capitalism has led to an even more thorough and terrifying apotheosis of the mechanistic model.

The form of the *personal* as envisaged by Macmurray has religious underpinnings which we hope to clarify in this book. At heart it is the Christian anthropocentric form which Metz points to, seen with a focused clarity which will enable it to be effective in today's world. It helps us discern the hidden heart of the new order which is arising out of the gray ashes of the old. It does justice to the paradox of the person which subsists as relation. It offers us a synthesis of the earlier organic form, which celebrates the relational and reliable character of God's universe while leaving the paradox which animates it in the penumbra, and the later mechanical form, which in reaction is at pains to stress the autonomy of each self within the universe, and ends up unleashing a tremendous power over everything except that which counts, namely the achievement of genuine personal fulfillment.

The odyssey of the form of the personal can be summarized in the following way:

a) Adumbrated in the Old Testament and in Greek thought, which raise key aspects of the essential human question, and is more fully revealed in Jesus Christ, the form of the personal becomes an implicit vector shaping Christian and human thought.

b) At critical moments during the first centuries of the Church it leads to the explicitation of certain personal values in the struggle to protect the genuineness of the Christian dispensation from Hellenistic impersonalism.

c) In the Middle Ages, especially in Thomas Aquinas, it systematically influences Christian thought not just in this or that critical area but in a thoroughgoing and systematic way. For the first time it fully acts as a thought-form, though it still remains implicit.

d) The process of becoming explicit is a dialectical one:

i) The organic texture of Aquinas' thought aptly expresses the relational side of the form of the personal. The person is *emergent*.

ii) In reaction the form of the mechanical emphasizes the self-sufficiency and autonomy of the person, adopts a relation-free mechanistic approach to reality rather than an holistic one. The person is *self-assertive*, but this self-assertion is clouded in an atmosphere of anxiety and isolation.

iii) In reaction to the mechanical some returned to organic elements, but to the extent that they overlooked Judeo-Christian roots of the personal, they allowed the sway of the mechanical to continue unabated, even exacerbated it. The person is *crushed*. This is the case with Marxism.

iv) Others are now seeking a fuller and more explicit reinstatement of the form of the personal, one faithful to its roots in Judeo-Christian revelation. What is sought is the *integrated* person, one in which autonomy and relation are both fully realized.

As we can see from this chapter, the struggle to overcome the powerlessness at the heart of a first world enamored of the trappings of technological might engages us in issues of absolute moment. We are not dealing with mere technological adjustments to the system but with a dynamic which is truly apocalyptic in scope. Paul of Tarsus, and in his wake Augustine and Thomas, will be guides to us as we resolutely enter into the struggle of our age. The full reinstatement of the form of the personal is integral to that struggle.

NOTES

1. Cf. Chapter 5 of that work.
2. Ferdinand de Saussure, *Cours de linguistique générale* (Paris: Payot, 1971), p. 25.
3. Cf. ibid., pp. 185 ff. for a discussion of this point.
4. This attention to relations and affinities blends in with the convergence we have seen emerging in our own day: social critics within the first world applaud the new order's emphasis on ecology and relationship and decry the old order's refusal to take interdependence seriously as constitutive of human being and doing, its constant exaltation of the rugged individual, isolated except for those relations which he or she chooses to cultivate, and self-reliant to the extreme in the competitive struggle for success.
5. This work, done for my doctoral degree at the Université de Strasbourg, was published in modified form under the title *Les structures dynamiques de la grâce: grâce médicinale et grâce élevante d'après Thomas d'Aquin* (Montréal: Editions Bellarmin, 1974).
6. My article "The Dynamics of Grace in Aquinas: A Structural Approach", in *Theological Studies*, 1973, pp. 203–226 offers a more detailed presentation of these matters.

7. The distinction between *justificatio impii* and merit, which corresponds to Paul's distinction between justification and sanctification, is of key structural importance in Aquinas' treatise on grace. Cf. *Ia–IIae*, 113, intro.

8. I am thinking above all of Henri Bouillard's *Conversion et grâce chez S. Thomas d'Aquin* (Paris: Aubier, 1944).

9. Initially this effort at structural transposition centered around the work of Paulo Freire. His *Pedagogy of the Oppressed* (New York: Herder and Herder, 1971) set the direction for much of my quest of a new language for grace. His analysis of oppressor and oppressed, of the process of liberation which overcomes their opposition, and of the typical distortions of this process, dovetailed with the dialectic process involving Jew and Gentile, strong and weak, which Paul formulated to promote an understanding of the process which leads to true community in the body of Christ. This opened for me a more dialectical and liberationist approach to grace than that of Aquinas. The oppressor/oppressed model, seen not so much in its later Marxist utilization as in its original Pauline roots, could help to describe the dynamics of God's relation with each human person, of the relation of persons among themselves in community, of the relations within each person between soul and body, and between what we would look upon today as different parts of the psyche; it could help us to better grasp what Paul meant by the reconciliation which he sees as central to the grace event. More on this in Chapter Three.

10. We are concerned with the first world tradition. Someone else could do the same for the other two traditions. To the extent, for example, that the tradition of the East is balanced by proper attention to aspects stressed in the Western and third world traditions, it also has a signal contribution to make to our world. That I do not take on this task does not imply that I do not consider it equally worthwhile.

11. This use of the priest/prophet/king typology is suggested by the way in which Karl Barth in the fourth part of his *Church Dogmatics* relates salvation to the ascending and descending modes in Christology. The Eastern model in this understanding is above all descending (God takes an initiative, comes down to earth), the Western is above all ascending (the man Jesus Christ does what needs to be done to win our salvation), the third world model is one in which the two converge in the earthly life of Jesus. In summary, Barth's architectonics would be as follows:

Descent: Incarnation → Death		Justification		Christ as Priest
Ascent: Death → Resurrection	=	Sanctification	=	Christ as King
Convergence: Earthly Life		Call to Glory		Christ as Prophet

12. This is not to deny that this descending movement of God towards humanity stops with the incarnation. The kenosis of God, as the Letter to the Philippians points out and as the Christian tradition affirms, continues unto death, for in the end God does not spare his only Son. However in this perspective, the death and resurrection are seen as the act of God not sparing his Son rather than the act of the human Jesus commending himself in total obedience to God, and therefore they are considered as the continuation

of an act of God which is already in principle complete when the Word becomes flesh. Cf. B. Sesboüé, "Esquisse critique d'une théologie de la rédemption'', *NRT*, 1984, pp. 801–816, and 1985, pp. 68–86.

13. A striking expression of this Eastern Church understanding is found in 2 Peter 1:4. A fuller account of Eastern theology would show great complexity, because the Church of the East, like that of the West, encompasses great cultural and ritual variety within itself.

14. The inconsistency between this description and the traditional contrast between East and West expressed in terms of the West's preoccupation with prevenient grace and the East's with the synergy of God and humankind in the redemptive process is more apparent than real. The reason for the West's preoccupation with our powerlessness, which comes to its sharpest expression in Augustine, is precisely the onerous nature of the redemptive process which is initiated and sustained by grace. Conversely the synergistic approach of the East supports a position in which a specific divine initiative need not be stressed, because God's action smoothly blends within the overall fabric of the redemptive process.

15. At this point the roots of this Western approach to redemption in Paul are quite evident. Cf. Romans 5:12–21.

16. As we saw in Chapter One, this sense of isolation and competition, this denial of intrinsic relations, is central to the old order. While at their best Western Church structures are attuned to personal and organic values, at times that Church succumbs to a tendency parallel to the ones which have distorted the reality of our world. Persons and groups are seen as intrinsically untrustworthy, to be controlled, hemmed in by a central authority which knows best. Claims to authority and obedience become a preoccupation. To the extent that this takes place within the Western Church, that Church is out of touch with its roots, and reflects the ambiguous reality of the world to which it is precisely called to be a counter-witness.

17. Martin Luther, *Christian Liberty*, edited by H.J. Grimm (Philadelphia: Fortress, 1970).

18. This apt expression is used by Roszak in *Where the Wasteland Ends*, ch. 3. Single vision is mechanistic rather than organic or personal. It singles out isolated parts which it can control rather than be attentive to the interrelations which make up the whole.

19. Paul uses the kenotic principle exposed in Phil 2:6–11 precisely to encourage the toleration and interaction by which a greater truth emerges out of different personal and theological standpoints within the community at Philippi. It is in going out to others that each one finds his or her own authenticity in the truth. What applies within the Pauline communities also applies in the interaction of the different communities which make up the apostolic Church. R. Brown's *The Community of the Beloved Disciple* (New York: Paulist, 1979) offers us a plausible account of one such interaction.

20. We are not denying that there are other theologies of grace in the New Testament, above all in the synoptic gospels, much more theologically sophisticated than might appear at first glance. However Paul and John develop their theologies of grace

more fully, and the contrasts between them are reflected in the distinction between the first and second churches.

21. We are referring here to the Paul of what the Germans call the *Hauptbriefe*. Colossians, Ephesians, and the Pastoral Epistles belong to a later stratum, and their relation to the Apostle Paul is understood in different ways by different authors. Likewise we are stressing the John of the Fourth Gospel, which, in contrast to the First Epistle, stresses the already now and the individual rather than the not yet and the communitarian dimensions.

22. The already now dimension above all comes to the fore in Paul's struggle against the Judaizers. He calls their attention to the here and now breaking in of the Kingdom into our hearts, the most intimate and personal aspect of ourselves.

23. The not yet dimension comes to the fore in the fact that when the chips are down John's Gospel does refer to the resurrection on the last day, as for instance in Chapter 5. It is wrong to read John's Gospel entirely in terms of realized eschatology.

24. Already the language of divinization emerges in the New Testament. Cf. 2 Peter 1:4.

25. Paul of Tarsus is the litmus paper of Western theology of grace. Much of that theology arises out of repeated attempts to come to terms with his thought. Augustine's reading of Paul (tradition) was just as strategic in his evolution as was his need to account for his own conversion (experience) and to craft a response to Pelagius (apostolic challenge). The Aquinas whose indebtedness to Aristotle is so often stressed was more deeply still a student of scripture. For all its Aristotelian armature, his theology of grace is in its deepest reality Pauline and Augustinian. This is especially true when we study the evolution of Aquinas' thought from his earlier and more enthusiastic use of Aristotelian categories to his unequivocal reaffirmation in later works of basic scriptural and Augustinian insights. Cf. H. Bouillard, *Conversion et grâce chez S. Thomas d'Aquin*. His conclusions are corroborated in my own *Les structures dynamiques de la grâce*.

Paul's thought and images have had a powerful impact not just in Western theology, but, transposed into secular terms, on the structures and dynamics of the first world. They instill a recurring apocalyptic sense in our culture of struggle for something new to be born. As we see illustrated in the work of the Canadian political philosopher Abraham Rotstein, they ground the categories with which Marx critiqued the first world structures of the nineteenth century and which have given the impetus for a second world more harshly technological than the first. The programmatic text of Gal 3:28 urges an ideal of equality between human persons at times fulfilled more thoroughly in the world than in the Church. A late medieval interpretation of his thought, K. Stendahl tells us in his "The Apostle Paul and the Introspective Consciousness of the West", in *Harvard Theological Review*, 1963, pp. 199–215, gave rise in the West to an introspective, guilt-laden consciousness which scholars such as Max Weber relate to the systematic development of disciplined capitalist structures of production and distribution. As a result our chapter on Paul will be of pivotal importance to our quest for a renewed grammar of grace for the first world.

26. Cf., for instance, his *Enarr. Ps* XLIX, 2, and his *Letter 140*, 4, 10.

27. An outstanding contemporary instance of an open-minded Western thinker is Teilhard de Chardin, who incorporates many Eastern elements in his thought while at the same time being powerfully rooted in Paul's cosmic vision.

28. Did Augustine obscurely sense that the patient and hidden labour of the Church on behalf of and with the invading tribes, beginning in his day, would set the stage for the renaissance of human values which took place in the early Middle Ages?

29. *Confessions* 8:8–9.

30. Cf. Stendahl, "The Apostle Paul and the Introspective Consciousness of the West" in *Harvard Theological Review*, 1963, pp. 199–215, together with J.C. Beker, *Paul the Apostle* (Philadelphia: Fortress, 1980) and J. Munck, *Paul and the Salvation of Mankind* (London: SCM Press, 1959). For many centuries the tendency within the Western Church has been to continually return to Romans 1 to 8 as the core of that Epistle, the one which offers Paul's mature theology of grace. While the point about mature theology of grace may be correct, it is clear that Paul was interested in developing that theology so as to be able to deal in Chapters 9 to 11 with the agonizing issue of the rejection of Jesus by the chosen people.

31. Lonergan, *Method in Theology*, pp. 91-96.

32. Later on in the writings of Luther and his Catholic adversaries we find documented the re-emergence of the world of interiority, this time the limited interiority of one individual, and the struggle between this newer theology and a theoretical approach to grace which had lost touch with its roots and become desiccated. In a sense, we are passing from grace-in-itself to grace-for-me, without paying sufficient attention to the fact that grace-in-itself emerged out of an earlier grace-for-us. Cf. Paul Hacker, "Martin Luther's Notion of Faith", *Catholic Scholars Dialogue with Luther*, edited by J. Wicks (Chicago: Loyola University Press, 1970), pp. 85–105.

33. Roszak, *Where the Wasteland Ends*, ch. 3.

34. What distinguishes a classical text from a scholastic one is that the latter succumbs to the illusion that an absolutely clean and consistent conceptual system enables one to possess the truth. The classical text shows evidence of an intellect that is alive and on the move. Terms shift according to contexts, and bear a wealth of hidden connotations and connections. Upon each reading something new is gleaned.

35. The technical term for relation in its narrow sense is predicamental relation and in its broader, all-encompassing sense, is transcendental relation. Some twentieth century students of Aquinas have rightly concentrated on the theme of relation in his thought. A. Krempel, *La doctrine de la relation chez S. Thomas: exposé historique et systématique* (Paris: Vrin, 1952) is helpful but does not succeed in breaking through to the immense significance of relations in the thought of Thomas. C.G. Kossel, *Relation in the Philosophy of Saint Thomas Aquinas*, doctoral manuscript (Toronto: University of Toronto, 1952) is of greater value in this respect. B. Lonergan offers a succinct but very perceptive summary of the Thomist doctrine on relations in his *De Deo Trino, Pars Synthetica* (Rome: Pont. Univ. Greg., 1964), pp. 291–315.

36. An earlier and highly enthusiastic exponent of the use of reason in matters of

faith is Richard of Saint Victor, especially in his treatise on the Trinity. By contrast, Aquinas is quite sober and realistic in his approach.

37. This is especially true of the fifteenth and sixteenth century Thomist commentators, who in many ways are very much under the influence of their age. This applies to the foundational area of epistemology. Cf. *Insight*, p. 413. As concerns our topic of grace, we can allude to Henri de Lubac's *Le mystère du surnaturel* (Paris: Aubier, 1965) on the gradual loss among scholars even of high calibre of the authentic Thomistic position on the intrinsic relation of a nature to supernatural fulfillment in the vision of God, in favour of a position in which nature is a building block which may or may not by divine fiat be brought into significant interface with God. Lonergan documents a similar process in the matter of the relationship between grace and freedom. Cf. *Grace and Freedom* (New York: Herder and Herder, 1971), pp. 139–145.

38. For example, the twenty-four Thomist theses of the early 1900's, which certain Church authorities hoped would be a touchstone of ecclesiastical orthodoxy at a time when they felt especially threatened by the modernist movement.

39. Cf. Copleston's *History of Philosophy*, Vol. III, revised edition (London: Burns, Oates, & Washbourne, 1953), pp. 3 ff.

40. This does not preclude the presence in Scotus' position of a measure of the contingent and arbitrary, dependent upon the fiat of the divine will. Indeed his universe is made up of what is necessary and what is contingent. Aquinas would not deny this distinction. However Aquinas conceives the necessary less rigorously (compare his proofs for the existence of God with that of Scotus), and for him the contingent, especially as it emanates from the Divine Freedom, is reasonable, appropriate, encompassed within the Divine Wisdom and accessible in part to human wisdom.

41. As Luther puts it graphically: "Fides facit ut stercus non foeteat." To be fair, there is a similar Catholic position according to which the guilt (*culpa*) of sin is removed, but the penalty (*poena*) remains to be undergone by the penitent. The approach is different however. Luther is quite loath to admit that there is a gradual process of transformation and healing in this life, for fear that this very achievement will become yet another bulwark against the angry God. This was understandable in terms of his own personal experience and his perception of the religious sensibility of his flock. The tone which he introduced can be further gathered by contrasting his slogan, "*Pecca fortiter et fide fortius*", with Augustine's, "*Ama et fac quod vis.*"

42. Luther's phrase is "*vivendo, immo vero moriendo et damnando fit theologus, non intelligendo, legendo, aut speculando*". (*Operationes in Ps. 5:12*)

43. Otto Pesch, *Theologie der Rechtfertigung bei Martin Luther und Thomas von Aquin* (Mainz: Grünewald, 1967).

44. Cf. *Insight*, p. 664. This position of Aquinas, highlighted by Lonergan, shows a remarkable correlation with the holistic insights of current physics, for which any one event in the physical universe is influenced by every other event, so much so that the very act of observing the event impinges upon the event one wishes to observe. Cf. Capra, *The Turning Point*, Chapter 3, and J. Campbell, *Grammatical Man: Entropy, Language, and Life* (New York: Simon & Schuster, 1982).

45. Cf. *Insight*, p. 664.

46. A broader and more traditional Augustinian tendency remained. It continued to play a moderating role in theological discussions. Cf. Henri de Lubac's *Augustinisme et théologie moderne* (Paris: Aubier, 1965).

47. Rahner develops this point in an article which evidences his typical combination of pastoral acuteness and historical erudition. Cf. "Nature and Grace", in *Theological Investigations*, Vol IV, esp. pp. 166–187.

48. Lonergan develops this point in *Insight* but above all in *Verbum—Word and Idea in Aquinas* (London: Darton, Longman, & Todd, 1968), esp. pp. 141–191. On the intellectualist view, insight is the conscious intellectual act which takes place before and generates the concept, and concepts are expressed in terms and relations which mutually define one another (*Insight*, p. 493). On the conceptualist view, concepts are fixed formal realities given before the act of knowledge, and they are joined together or divided by the intellect. Relations are extrinsic rather than intrinsic. Indeed conceptualism introduces a confusion "which places conception before understanding and things before their orders" (*Insight* p. 695, also cf. p. 664). The article "The Natural Desire to See God" utilizes these points very clearly in a significant grace-related issue. Cf. *Collection* (London: Darton, Longman, & Todd, 1967), pp. 84–95.

49. A scepticism against which Descartes struggled. The *Deus verax* on which he was able to rely did not stem the tide in later centuries.

50. Cf. Berman, *The Reenchantment* . . . , pp. 20–22.

51. The article of G.B. Deason, "The Protestant Reformation and the Rise of Modern Science", in *Scot. Journ. of Theol.*, Vol 38 (1985), pp. 221–240 is especially instructive on this matter. Two quotes: "Protestant criticism of Aristotelian rationalism and insistence that theology must begin with the direct study of scripture proved a useful precedent for seventeenth century scientists arguing against Aristotle's deductive methods and in favor of the empirical study of nature" (p. 231). "The mechanical philosophers turned to the Protestant doctrine of the radical sovereignty of God in arguing for their belief in the passivity of matter. The conviction that matter could not possess active powers if God were sovereign (in the Reformation sense of sovereignty) helped the mechanical philosophers in constructing arguments for mechanism and against Aristotelianism" (p. 237).

52. At first glance one might think that late medieval philosophy, with its recondite speculations and logical hair-splitting; has little or nothing to do with the developments which we associate with Galileo, Bacon, Descartes, and Newton. But this is not the case. Already John Buridan (ca. 1300–1358), a key philosopher/scientist of that period, ventured into areas later explored with great insight by Isaac Newton: matter, motion, and gravity. Speaking of Buridan and others of his time, E.A. Moody says "the background of ideas within which the seventeenth century physicists worked stemmed in large measure from the later Middle Ages and undoubtedly influenced the direction in which modern physics developed." *Studies in Medieval Philosophy, Science, and Logic* (Berkeley: U. of Cal. Press, 1975), pp. 200–201.

53. Berman does this especially in Chapter 2 of *The Reenchantment* . . .

54. Sources and further amplifications of this are found in Berman, *The Reen-chantment* . . . , pp. 40–45 and Rollo May, *The Meaning of Anxiety*, revised edition (New York: Norton, 1977), p. 164.

55. R.D. Laing, *The Divided Self* (Harmondsworth: Penguin, 1965), esp. pp. 94–95.

56. *The Meaning of Anxiety*, p. 155.

57. Ibid., p. 159. R. Bellah et al. in *Habits of the Heart* (New York: Harper and Row, 1985) present the shapes and subtleties of this individualism as it emerges in American life. Cf. esp. pp. 142–163.

58. *The Meaning of Anxiety*, p. 164. This point is developed very tellingly by Morris Berman with respect to the inner evolution of Isaac Newton. The emptiness of his inner psychic space is a counterpart to that of the absolute space depicted in his physics: cf. *The Reenchantment* . . . , ch. 4.

59. Cf. *The Meaning of Anxiety*, p. 162.

60. Cf. *Pursuit of Loneliness*, Chapter 4.

61. Cf. *Earth-walk*, p. 117-150.

62. Cf. Slater, *Pursuit of Loneliness*, Chapter Two, entitled "Kill anything that moves". Later in the book he makes this point in a striking sentence that many would judge excessive: "Most scarcity in our own society exists for the purpose of maintaining the system that depends upon it. Americans are often in the position of having killed someone to avoid sharing a meal which turns out to be too large to eat alone." (p. 114)

63. This topic of grace as abundant and grace as scarce is further developed in my article "Grace: The Mystery of God's Abundance" in *Word and Spirit* (Toronto: Regis College Press), pp. 371–409.

64. Luther sought to overcome the basic anxiety which led to the frantic quest for reassurance exploited in the preaching of indulgences. He preferred to consider grace as a relation rather than as a quality, but what he inveighed against was grace as a thing one possesses and clings to, as that which is included in the heart "like a jewel" (LW 12 377–8: Commentary on Ps. 51:10). While Luther was on the right track in advocating a view of grace as relation, relation for him is in effect problematic relation, the relation which obtrudes on his consciousness because he can never in his heart of hearts be sure about it, in this case the relation to a God in whom he believes against the evidence of his own perduring anxiety and inner struggle. Luther signally contributes to the emergence of the world of interiority, but his contribution is that of a pioneer.

65. This point is made by Lonergan in *Insight*, p. 395.

66. Perhaps the most familiar instance of this transformation is the distinction between essence and existence, which touches on a dimension of reality quite beyond Aristotle's ken. This is the instance typically adduced by 20th century Thomists such as Gilson and Maritain.

67. The secular scholars who will help us in our quest are not those who are still under the spell of the mechanistic approach now subject to profound re-evaluation but those who are willing to treat the human reality, psychological and sociological, on its own terms. For instance, behaviourist psychology is of precious

little use to us, whereas humanistic psychology is. Herbert Fingarette in *The Self in Transformation* (New York: Harper Torchbooks, 1965), esp. ch. 1, offers a fascinating discussion of the struggle between some of the seminal insights Freud was achieving into human behaviour and the infra-human scientific world-view within which he felt constrained to express them.

68. This point the doctrine of the Trinity, especially in its Western form, has already made with great forcefulness, above all by Richard of St. Victor as he argues for the appropriateness of more than two persons in the Trinity, and it also has been developed, perceptively and at great length, by the contemporary personalist John Macmurray. It has been corroborated by recent research into developmental psychology, as for instance that of R. Kegan, *The Evolving Self* (Cambridge: Harvard University Press, 1982), esp. pp. 113–116, 256–257.

69. Kuhn's classic work is *The Structure of Scientific Revolutions* (Chicago: University of Chicago Press, 1962).

70. These lectures, given in 1953–1954, were published in the volumes we have already alluded to, *The Self as Agent* and *Persons in Relation*.

71. *Christliche Anthropozentrik* (München: Kösel Verlag, 1962). In his article "Freedom as a Threshold Problem between Philosophy and Theology" (Eng. trans.), *Philosophy Today*, 1966, p. 267, Metz shows his affinity with the person-language of Macmurray. The anthropocentric thought-form is that in which the human reality is seen precisely as personal and free, rather than subsumed under nature and its categories.

72. This is especially true of Macmurray's categories. My analysis and his, though not incompatible, show some differences. His sequence is from the form of the material (the "single" mechanistic vision decried by Roszak) through that of the organic (the dialectical, romantic, evolutionary vision) to that of the personal (the new order). Cf. *The Self as Agent*, pp. 17–38. While this is a very helpful way of surveying a complex development, I would also use the category of the organic to account for the earlier medieval matrix out of which the mechanical emerges.

73. This is gleaned from pp. 28 and 33 of *Self as Agent*.

74. "Personal" is not to be taken in a narrow atomistic sense. To do so would be to ignore the distinction Metz recalls between person and nature (cf. note 71 above) and to revert to the mechanistic thought-form against which we have mightily struggled thus far. The doctrine of the Trinity, especially in the Western Church, makes a great point of referring to persons as subsistent relations, a tradition which Macmurray at least implicitly respects by choosing *Persons in Relation* as the theme and title of the second volume of his Gifford Lectures. Thus the personal includes the interpersonal. But this point needs to be pushed even further. Indeed I have already done so when in a different context I suggested that we must move beyond a purely meta-*psychological* to include a meta-*sociological* language for grace. Put in trinitarian terms, the fact that there are three persons rather than two shows that the form of the personal implies not just the interpersonal but also the communitarian. This latter point was most effectively made by Richard of St. Victor in the twelfth century. Kegan in *The Evolving Self* dis-

tinguishes between an earlier stage of personal development characterized by mutuality closed upon itself and a later characterized by open reciprocity.

75. Metz, *Christliche Anthropozentrik*, p. 47.

76. At this point the analysis made by Eric Voegelin in *The New Science of Politics* (Chicago: University of Chicago Press, 1952), will offer an indispensable complement to Metz. For Voegelin the breakthrough of Greek thought lies in the emergence of a concern for the human reality as it emerges out of a broader cosmic context. The psyche is discovered as the instrument by which human beings discover and relate to transcendence, and thus themselves become transcendent. The concern is anthropological, but the context continues to be cosmological. The new reality is in part expressed in cosmological terms: man is the being that is open to the transcendent, that is drawn to it as to a prime mover which is also a final cause. Judeo-Christian revelation brings an answer to the question posed by human openness. There is established between human and divine reality a personal dialogue which enables the human reality to focus on and affirm its own subjective, personal dimension (cf. pp. 67 and 78).

77. Metz has other ways of expressing his crucial cosmocentric/anthropocentric distinction. In proportional equation form, they are as follows (cf. *Christliche Anthropozentrik*, p. 111):

$$\frac{\text{``things and their objective structures}}{\text{the irrepressible originating self}} = \frac{\text{objectivity}}{\text{subjectivity}} = \frac{\text{substance}}{\text{subject}} =$$

$$\frac{\text{objective/ontic understanding of the subject}}{\text{transcendental/ontological understanding}} = \frac{\text{world}}{\text{humankind}} = \frac{\text{nature}}{\text{history}} =$$

$$\frac{\text{abstract universality}}{\text{concrete universality}} = \frac{\text{things in space}}{\text{persons in time.}}$$

One can readily see from this enumeration a relation with the Lonerganian shift from classical to historical consciousness which implies a whole new way of doing theology.

78. On this point Metz' analysis might be amplified. Did the event of Jesus Christ introduce a thought-form that was radically and utterly new, or did it unlock and unleash a force already latent in the relations which Yahweh had with the chosen people of the Old Testament?

79. Voegelin's appreciation of the contribution of the Greeks to the unfolding pattern of revelational thought is very clear. Metz's approach seems to belittle that contribution, but Metz is at pains to dispel that perception. Cf. *Christliche Anthropozentrik*, p. 114 note 28.

80. We are referring to the lengthy struggle which led to the *physis/ousia / / prosopon/hupostasis* distinction formulated at Chalcedon. Cf. J. Ratzinger, "Zum Personenverständnis in der Theologie" in *Dogma und Verkündigung* (München: Wewel, 1977).

81. Metz, *Christliche Anthropozentrik*, pp. 110–113.

82. This is an appropriate context in which to situate recent attempts to show how

Thomas' epistemology is rooted in the experience of the subject. This is the project of transcendental Thomists such as Rahner, in his *Geist in Welt* (München: Kösel, 1964), and Lonergan in his *Verbum*. It is precisely this patient work of detecting the impact of the Christian thought-form in Aquinas' theory of knowledge that enables Lonergan to develop a contemporary method for theology in continuity with the thought of Aquinas. Some secular authors we took up in Chapter One seek in the Middle Ages a treasure which to them is lost. It is my contention that the work of theologians such as Rahner, Metz, and Lonergan is most germane to their quest.

83. Metz, *Christliche Anthropozentrik*, pp. 120–128.

84. Metz, *Christliche Anthropozentrik*, p. 128. He makes a similar point in his article "Future of Faith in a Hominized World", *Philosophy Today*, 1966, p. 297. The anthropocentric thought-form has liberated forces by which humans have begun to take charge of the world, to *hominize* it. But more and more we are realizing the ambiguities of this. Technology is more exacting than nature. The hominized world is also *dehumanized*. With technology there is given, however, the potential for greater humanization.

85. An outstanding instance of this is Fritjof Capra's *The Tao of Physics*.

86. A striking instance of this arises out of the lengthy debate on Thomas' doctrine of the natural desire to see God, to receive a fulfillment which is utterly beyond nature. In the absence of clarity regarding the personal form that animates his thought, interpreters have gone through many contortions to safeguard the gratuity of the supernatural order, as documented by de Lubac in *Le mystère du surnaturel*. Can there be such a thing as a genuine natural desire for a supernatural fulfillment? For how could God refuse the fulfillment of a such a desire? And if we can count on this fulfillment with such assurance, how can we truly assert it is a supernatural fulfillment to which we have no claim? If our model is infra-personal, we are at an impasse here. If our model is personal, then we are open to the paradox of personal relationships which are utterly gratuitous and utterly reliable, of fulfillments which are utterly essential to the person yet unfulfilling unless they come to the person out of the free disposition of another person. Thomas did not at this point express the form of the personal which was animating his thought, so the cogency of his thought was missed for centuries.

87. Again from his own perspective Voegelin offers us some keen insights. The current breakdown, which he sees not as a pagan re-divinization of the cosmos but as a gnostic deviation of Christianity, results from a flight from the mystery of the personal, from the relation with God. Within both of these faith, fragile yet unmanipulable, is central. Cf. *The New Science . . .* , pp. 120–130, 164–167.

88. Interestingly enough, some of the recent literature on what persons are all about in effect amplifies what the Gospel said so strikingly: unless the grain of wheat fall into the ground and die, it remains alone; but if it dies, it bears much fruit (Jn 12:24). Cf. my article "Kenosis Old and New", in *The Ecumenist*, 1974, pp. 17–21.

89. It is not surprising that Theodore Roszak, an outstanding prophet of the new order, finds in William Blake such a powerful source of inspiration for his protest against the old order. Cf. *Where the Wasteland Ends*.

90. Paulo Freire offers an alternative dialectical vision in his *Pedagogy of the Oppressed*, one which is in touch with the Christian roots of Marxist categories. These roots are examined in A. Rotstein, "The Apocalyptic Tradition: Luther and Marx" in *Political Theology in the Canadian Context*, ed. B. Smillie (Waterloo: Wilfrid Laurier University Press, 1982), pp. 142–208. In his own way—this we shall see in the next chapter—Paulo Freire in his *Pedagogy of the Oppressed* liberates Marxist categories from their atheistic context.

Chapter Three

PAUL: GRACE FOR
THE BETWEEN-TIME

Many of the non-theological works we examined in Chapter One reveal a definite end-time perspective. The human race, they tell us, is at a crucial cross-roads, it faces an unprecedented moment of truth. Expressed in the apocalyptic terms of his own religious culture, a similar perspective permeates Paul's theology of grace. Given its rightful prominence in recent Pauline studies, for instance J.C. Beker's *Paul the Apostle*,[1] such a perspective will prove most illuminating for a theology of grace that speaks to the situation of our world. As Paul of Tarsus faced the conflicts which emerged within his communities caught in the ambiguities of the time between the resurrection and the parousia, his apocalyptic vision of final reconciliation in Christ led him to preach a loving dialectic in which unity is based on the recognition of diversity. In this he provides the original pattern for a twentieth century namesake, Paulo Freire. As a philosopher and adult educator, Freire reflects on the implications of educating illiterate adults within the oppressed situation of Latin America in his *Pedagogy of the Oppressed*, and opens the way for a renewed yet profoundly Pauline theological/pastoral understanding of how grace is at work in our world.

In this chapter we will first delineate the basic apocalyptic perception common to our age and that of Paul, then present the dynamic structures of grace which Paul develops out of this perception, and finally attempt to re-express these structures in contemporary terms, using Freire as a starting point.

APOCALYPTIC UNDERPINNINGS

As we have seen in Chapter One, technological progress within the first world, until recently so highly touted, has begun to show its frightening ambivalence. It was supposed to transform, enrich, facilitate, fulfill us in so many ways, but in effect it has been little by little strangling our environment and has put in our hands the means for ultimate catastrophe. Far from ensuring a steady course upwards and onwards to the illusory prizes held out to us by advertising, it is bringing to an ugly climax the dynamic of sin and grace latent in every age of humankind.

Behind the wonderful facades created by modern technology, the forces of disintegration and chaos in our world have reached unparalleled fierceness. The vicious circle is becoming a vertigo and we are collapsing into it. Countering these forces, however, there is also at work in our world a quiet and persistent drift towards transformation and integration. Many have become aware of this movement and in their own way are contributing to it. Their convergence has, to use Marilyn Ferguson's terms, become a conspiracy. Yet humanly speaking the odds against its success are overwhelming. The agony of our world appears to be not so much that of new life coming to birth as that of a spent life struggling against its inevitable fall into emptiness.

So many people are willing to bear this agony. What resource within them makes this possible? The Christian answer is faith, hope, and love. Springing from the unobtrusive Mystery within each of us, they lead, in ways which escape our fathoming, to the fullness of that Mystery, the Pleroma. In the context they provide, the throes we are in are part of the *thlipsis* which announces that this Pleroma is at hand.

Down through the ages various Christian sects, at times obsessively, have centered their hope on an early return of the Lord and inauguration of his Kingdom. Their desire to spell out the time-table known only to the Father of Jesus and to proclaim it with unbending certitude made them suspect to the majority of Christians, and they were relegated to the fringes. But in the process something crucial has been lost. The urgent New Testament proclamation of the end has been attenuated within most Christian denominations and in some cases narrowed into a personal/existential transformation with scarce relevance to the world and its history.

Nonetheless a mood of fragility, disjointedness, and apocalyptic expectation has at certain moments come to the fore within Western Christendom. This was the case as the Western Church approached the beginning of the second millennium after Christ. The Dark Ages were at their darkest. The Papacy was in dire straits. The time was ripe: millenarist expectations and end-time scenarios abounded. More intensely and on a planetary scale, the same phenomenon is recurring in our own day. Not only are the times out of joint, but time itself is threatened with dissolution. The end of the world has become a widely acceptable topic among Christians today. The apocalyptic theme has once again found a fertile spawning ground, and was, to mention one significant example, evoked in the inaugural address of Pope John Paul II in 1978.[2]

By alluding to the end of the second millennium which could well come within his reign, he implicitly reminded his listeners of the heightened expectancy that emerged as the Dark Ages were moving towards the year 1000, and is shaping our consciousness as we move towards the year 2000, whether that expectancy is expressed in religious/apocalyptic or in secular/catastrophic terms.

For many authors today, including Beker, apocalyptic constitutes the basic framework of Paul's thought. Beker is not a pioneer in this view but builds upon an emerging scholarly consensus. It is perhaps difficult to single out a key breakthrough in that emergence, but one might allude to the programmatic articles of Ernst Käsemann, "The Beginnings of Christian Theology", and "On the Subject of Primitive Christian Apocalyptic",[3] which have had considerable influence in exegetical circles.

To help us focus on Paul's particular views, we will first hazard a broad sketch of apocalyptic, adverting to the differences between Paul's context for apocalyptic, a Jewish one, and ours, a secular one. We will then consider how he modifies the Jewish apocalyptic in the light of his momentous encounter with Christ.

Apocalyptic Then and Now: The apocalyptic perspective emerges within societies whose aspirations are in sharp dissonance with a bleak and hopeless reality. It is intended to foster perseverance in those who are called to endure in a humanly untenable situation. Beker lists four major characteristics of this genre: vindication, universalism, dualism, and imminence.[4] The original instances of this genre are found in the two hundred years which precede the coming of Christ. Apocalyptic is represented in the canonical literature by the Book of Daniel, and further develops the proclamation by earlier Old Testament prophets of the coming day of the Lord. What specifies apocalyptic within the more general eschatological/prophetic genre is its sense that an imminent divine intervention will not so much fulfill history as abolish it, ushering in a new world in discontinuity with the old. It enables eschatological imagery to live a life of its own, not bound by the concrete events of history, since history has gone completely sour.[5]

Let us flesh out this description. Though the Jews still gloried in the promises God made to their ancestors and called to their attention through the prophets, during the two hundred years immediately before Christ they laboured under successive forms of political oppression which invaded their lives in various ways, but above all made it impossible for them to worship their God with pure and unsullied observance. In 167 B.C. Antiochus Epiphanes withdrew his tolerance of Jewish religious practices and rededicated the temple in Jerusalem to Zeus. This abomination of abominations occasioned the Maccabean revolt. But as the situation gradually deteriorated in the years subsequent to this successful movement of liberation, a more subtle form of oppression came into being. The priestly class gained a certain amount of space for the external observances of Jewish religion, but the hypocrisy and compromises with oppressive powers through which they gained it were too much for many faithful Jews to stomach. At best such arrangements were precarious; they ebbed and flowed according to the vagaries of local politics. From about 65 B.C. onwards, direct Roman overlordship over Judea ensured a greater stability, but the price was too high.

How humanly and spiritually could faithful Jews cope with this utterly gloomy situation? Apocalyptic literature through its detailed and confident descriptions of how God very soon would act to fulfill his promises and vindicate his chosen people kept their hope alive. This action of God was foreordained from all eternity[6] and till this moment of revelation (*apocalypsis*) had remained a secret. The climax of this action was proclaimed to be imminent. It would entail a struggle of stark opposites: good and evil, the forces of light and the forces of darkness, life and death. The cataclysmic events surrounding it would profoundly mark all peoples, who would be destroyed or subsumed under the anticipated *dénouement* in which the people of the promise were to hold a place of honour. The present age of turmoil and suffering would give way to the coming age of the Messiah's triumphant lordship. His triumph was proclaimed to be imminent.

In our period a secular version of apocalyptic is gradually beginning to emerge. The end of the world is no longer the possibility of astronomical catastrophe, so remote it remains out of mind, but the terrifying possibility of a holocaust triggered by human error or insanity. Yet at the same time a completely different path is open before us, a heightening of human consciousness and the building of a new order of human integration, on a scale which respects the rhythms of human development and the resources of our planet. Many people, stopping their ears against the blandishments of technology, have resolutely set out on this path. They lead their daily lives, establish personal contacts, explore new patterns of global interaction, all in the hope of a radically different kind of future. In this secular apocalyptic we find realized three characteristics of classical apocalyptic, imminence, dualism, and universalism. The theme of vindication is not developed—except among those who believe that there is a God on the side of humankind who in any event will save us and vindicate himself—nor does the notion of a revelatory vision of the mystery of God play a part in this secular apocalyptic.

The Structures of Paul's Apocalyptic: During Paul's life the *Pax Augustana* still held sway. This period was not generally marked by bleak despair or nameless hope, except perhaps in persons of extraordinary sensitivity such as

Virgil who in his Fourth Eclogue sings of the transition from the iron to the golden age and of the child who will bring peace to the world. The Jewish people to whom Paul belonged constituted an apocalyptic enclave. If anything, the different religious movements within Judaism at the time—pharisaic, es-senian, and zealot—only served to heighten within the people a sense of being violated, and raised vivid hopes that very soon the Messiah would appear, to vindicate them and overthrow their oppressors.[7] Jesus of Nazareth carried out his ministry in this inflamed atmosphere, and struggled to draw the people away from their naïve and materialistic pictures of how God's Messiah, deliv-ering them out of political oppression, would introduce them to the land of plenty. Following in the footsteps of the canonical prophets of Judaism, he tried to direct them towards the transcendent perspectives of his Father's king-dom.

Scholars might disagree on the relative weight of Palestinian Jewish over against Hellenistic Jewish traditions in Paul's upbringing, but none deny that the apocalyptic perspective is deeply engraved in his mind and heart. His apoc-alyptic fervour appears to have been channeled by his Pharisaic upbringing, which brought with it the conviction that rigorous observance of the law in the teeth of Roman oppression and priestly connivance with Rome would only has-ten deliverance by God. But he met Jesus on the road to Damascus and his fervour was radically redirected. From a persecutor of the Christian commu-nity he became a builder of that community within the Greco-Roman world. In the process he (1) radically reworked the structures of his apocalyptic, and (2) developed a more nuanced understanding of how God is present to the new age.

(1) The structural shift in Paul can be presented in diagrammatic form:[8] The diagram on page 90 brings out both a striking similarity and a sharp con-trast between Paul's teaching (bottom half) and that of the milieu out of which he sprung (top half). Note the dualism of the two ages (the present evil age and the age to come) common to both, yet the difference in where they situate the NOW of the present moment.

Oppressed Jews lived in the hope that God's promise would be fulfilled. The more painful the evidence that this promise remained unfulfilled, the more intense their hope and the more vivid their anticipation of what God would do in the end. Situated within this present evil age, their experience of ''now'' was extremely distressing. The transition between this present evil age (broken lines) and the age to come (continuous line) still lay ahead: it would take place on the Day of the Lord. Yahweh would not let his chosen people languish. He would decisively intervene and vindicate himself before humankind.

For Paul apocalyptic fulfillment has been ushered in through the death and

OLD TESTAMENT, APOCALYPTIC, RABBIS:

Creation	Promise	Law		Day
and	and	and	NOW	of the
Adam	Abraham	Moses		Lord

. . . . This present evil age . . . . . .) (the coming age

PAUL:

			Dying		
Creation	Promise	Law	and		Day
and	and	and	Rising	NOW	of the
Adam	Abraham	Moses	of		Lord
			Christ		

. . . . This present evil age . . . . | . . . .)
(The age now coming . . . . . .

THE BETWEEN TIME:
Already now
and not yet

resurrection of Jesus Christ. Having experienced the Risen Jesus on the road to Damascus and within the nascent Christian community, Paul knew that the Father had vindicated Jesus as his Son, and that the new age had already broken in. The NOW he once situated in the future becomes a present reality. Like the apostles and evangelists he proclaimed the good news that the promises of God had been fulfilled in Jesus. Indeed the adverb "now" takes on a special meaning in his writings, as for instance in the key text of Romans 3:21–23 which offers us his formulation of the very core of the good news: "But *now* the righteousness of God has been manifested apart from law, although the law and the prophets bear witness to it, the righteousness of God through faith in Jesus Christ for all who believe.'' ''Now'' denotes a moment of great significance, a *kairos*. It is eschatological rather than chronological.[9]

However elements of future expectation still remain. Hence the difference in structure between the diagrams depicting Jewish and Pauline apocalyptic thought. The beginning of the new age does not mean that the old age with its hope for a better future has vanished. The old and the new overlap, and the ''now'' of the Christian is situated within the zone commonly referred to as the between-time.[10] However the new and the old are not present in the same way. The old age is in the process of passing away, and as a result we are to live our lives in this world as if we were radically detached from it (1 Cor 7:29–31). The new age is at hand (Rom 13:12). It has broken in but its coming is still in process.

Christians simultaneously experience the drawing power of both ages: of the old towards a past to be firmly repudiated for its idolatry and slavery, of the new towards a future which gives them hope in the midst of their tribulation. This leaves them in a state of inner division often depicted by Paul, notably in Romans 7 (the division within the not yet redeemed, in which the old age dominates) and Romans 8 (the division within the redeemed, in which the new age dominates). When will this division cease? At root the redemption wrought by Christ Jesus has already overcome it, but the full manifestation and the secure grasp of this victory will come about at the *parousia*. Like his Jewish coreligionists, Paul still looked forward to a final act in which God would judge humankind and vindicate himself. Unlike them he saw that the essential reality of that act had already taken place and its power was already unleashed within the world.[11]

(2) What are the modalities of the divine presence to the new age? As intimated in the Old Testament, two shadowy and mysterious agents are also at work on the side of Yahweh in the dawning of this new age. The figure of a *Messiah* anointed to be the instrument of the Lord in bringing about his reign became clearer over the centuries, but by the time of Jesus its focus had become unduly narrowed, its mystery hardened by precise political expectations. Apocalyptic fervour was vulnerable to a tendency to mistake for the divine plan its own vivid, at times materialistic imaginings. One figure of messianic proportions whose mystery had remained intact was that of the Son of Man who comes on the clouds of heaven and is exalted by the Ancient of Days (Dan 7:13). In his preaching about the imminent end, Jesus preferred the term ''Son of Man'' to ''Messiah''.

The Old Testament also evidences the expectation of an extraordinary end-time outpouring of the *Spirit*. Indeed the Messiah himself is to be anointed with the Spirit (Is 11). During the old age the Spirit was given in a transitory way to certain individuals for a function such as prophecy. But at the end all would receive a new heart and a new spirit (Ex 36:22–32). The Lord would pour out his spirit upon all flesh, and make prophecy, dreams, visions a common and permanent phenomenon rather than a rare and transitory privilege (Joel 2:28–29).

The inauguration of the new age brings greater clarity to these two shadowy end-time figures, as we see in New Testament writings.[12] The Christian community proclaims that the promise of the Messiah/Son of Man has been fulfilled in Christ Jesus risen from the dead, and that he has poured out the end-time Spirit in full abundance. A significant text in which Paul expresses the parallelism between Son and Spirit is found in Galatians:

> But when the time had fully come, God sent forth his Son, born of woman, born under the law, to redeem those who were under the law, so that we might receive adoption as sons. And because you are sons, God has sent the Spirit of his Son into our hearts, crying, "Abba! Father!" (Gal 4:4–6)

The phrase "when the time had fully come" sets the context. This sending of Son and Spirit, which in turns reveals God as Father, is an essential feature of the unveiling of the new age. The sending of the Spirit adds a personal appropriation to what might otherwise be an objective transformation without any conscious repercussion. The Son makes us sons and daughters; but the Spirit empowers us to claim that filial relation, to cry out "Abba" to the one who henceforth is our Father.

The theology of grace more directly reflects on the Spirit poured into our hearts than on the Son sent into the world. Indeed much of Paul's struggle centers around distorted views concerning the Spirit's presence/absence within Christian communities and Christian hearts. As we have said, that presence is no longer a transitory gift imparted upon chosen individuals for specific purposes, e.g. prophetic utterance, but the permanent outpouring upon all humankind promised by the prophet Joel (Joel 3:1–2). This prophecy, evoked by Acts in its narration of the Pentecost experience, has, for Paul, been fulfilled by the Spirit already poured into our hearts (Rom 5:5) and destined to permeate our corporeal existence (Rom 8 and 1 Cor 15). However the essential link of this gift of the Spirit with the sending of the Son is often reiterated in Paul's thought, as we shall see.

Let us recast the diagram which expressed Paul's apocalyptic thought by inserting the following into it:

a) The Father who stands as both the origin and the goal of the process. He sends Jesus to usher in the new age and gives the Spirit.
b) Jesus who inaugurates the end time through His death and resurrection, and fulfills it at the moment of his *parousia*, when he submits all things to the Father, having recapitulated and redeemed them in himself (1 Cor 15:20–28).
c) The Spirit, sent into our hearts that we might with Jesus cry out "Abba, Father!"

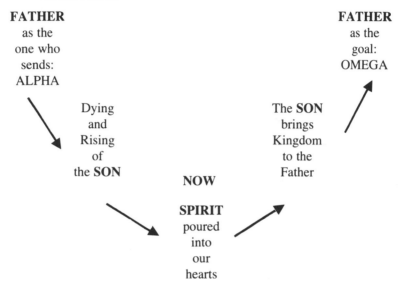

FATHER
as the
one who
sends:
ALPHA

Dying
and
Rising
of
the **SON**

NOW

The **SON**
brings
Kingdom
to the
Father

FATHER
as the
goal:
OMEGA

SPIRIT
poured
into
our
hearts

Within this new structure of understanding Paul's major pastoral concern was with the "now": with the behaviour and attitudes of his communities of Christians, caught as they were in the crucifying tensions of the between-time. They found it easier and more comfortable to adopt one-sided approaches to their new life, in continuity with what their earlier religious tradition taught or their social situation suggested. This led to rifts within the community, against which Paul struggled with might and main.

This prompted Paul to reformulate the apocalyptic scheme in bi-polar terms. He speaks of the *already now* of the new age that has already broken in, the now of a righteousness that has appeared in the event of Jesus Christ, and of the *not yet* of a fulfillment which still awaits the final demise of the old age.

Already now and not yet entail for Paul a genuine temporal dualism. There is a before, an after, and a between-time situation in which the Christian is subject to the simultaneous tug of both ages.[13] How does he or she react to this bi-polar tension? There is room for different styles of response, some of them allowable within the parameters of human temperament, but others clearly excessive, and, what is important for Paul, destructive of genuine community. Thus to those Christians who are so enamored of their experience of the already now in the Spirit that in immature enthusiasm they simply gloss over the not yet, Paul has to emphasize that the sufferings of our present condition are to be fully and redemptively lived out in imitation of the cross of Jesus. To those Christians who are not convinced that the already now is for real, remaining as they do under the sway of religious attitudes characteristic of the old age, he stresses the full reality of the victory of Christ manifested in the resurrection. To simplify somewhat, he develops the not yet dimension in his letter to the Corinthians and the already now dimension in his letter to the Galatians, whereas in his letter to the Romans he formulates a calm and mature synthesis of his thought. We shall develop this in the next section.

This simultaneous tug of old and new, before and after, entails for Paul a type of anthropological dualism. Paul distinguishes between two aspects of the unitary human self, one of which situates him or her in the new age, the other in the old. For him the inbreaking of the new age has already taken place in the most inward dimension of the person, which he refers to as the *heart*: "The love of God has been poured into our hearts by the Holy Spirit which is given to us." (Rom 5:5) But the *body*, which bespeaks the outer dimension of the person, relating it to the world, still awaits its liberation and permeation by the Spirit, as does the world as a whole (Rom 8:20–23), still under the sway of the old age. In this way the temporal dualism of already now/not yet yields an anthropological dualism of heart/body.

The interplay of the new and the old is a matter of some subtlety. For Paul the dying/rising of Christ is not just another sign that God is going to be faithful to his as yet unfulfilled covenant promises, nor is it, at the other extreme, the total realization of those promises. To put across his middle position Paul calls upon two images, that of the first-fruits, and that of the down-payment. The promises have already been fulfilled in Jesus Christ risen from the dead, who thus becomes the "yes" to God's promises (2 Cor 1:20), and they have begun to be fulfilled in us. We have received the first-fruits of the eschatological harvest, a down-payment which not only guarantees more to come but in a mysterious hidden way already bestows upon us part of that "more". The delicate line Paul draws between the absence and the presence of the end-time fulfillment is in effect an osmotic membrane. He is dealing with a spiritual reality, a mystery in which possession and non- possession, desire and fulfillment coexist and mutually reinforce one another.[14] Paul develops his thought on this paradox as he struggles to correct the distorted expectations generated within some of his communities. His thought is dialectical, dedicated to a reconciliation which does not destroy but affirms the differing aspects of the apocalyptic experience. This leads us into the second section of our chapter.

THE DYNAMICS OF GRACE ACCORDING TO PAUL

As we explored the apocalyptic underpinnings of Paul's theology of grace we began to notice the dynamic movement of grace in his theology. In this section we will analyze that movement, which envelops both individual and community.

Initial Overview—Justitification/Sanctification/Salvation: A diagram which follows the pattern of the previous two will help us grasp how Paul inserts the individual human being into his view of emerging apocalyptic reconciliation. The terms of his contrast between old and new age are noteworthy. The triad of justification, sanctification, and salvation, however, is of crucial importance in defining the dynamic of grace for the individual:

OLD AGE   **NEW AGE**

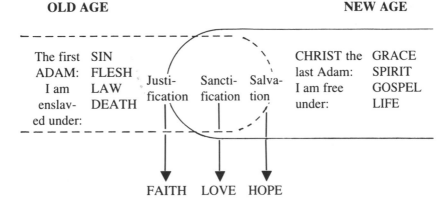

According to Paul, each human being in the unredeemed, "*old-age*" state is under the headship of *Adam*, who by his disobedience brought sin and death into the world (Rom 5:12–21). Each one of us experiences the reality of *sin* in his life, and because of the congenital opacity towards God of our being, signified by the word "*flesh*", we cannot but make sin our own and therefore are doomed to be engulfed by *death* (Rom 6:21; 7:13–23). The *law* which God reveals is good, but by itself it only points out the path to salvation, leaving us powerless to achieve it. It makes us aware of our utter helplessness, thus raising our sense of sinfulness to the point that each one of us cries out in despair: "Wretched man that I am! Who will deliver me from this body of death''? (Rom 7:25) Thus Paul treats sin, flesh, law, and death as forces which hold us in thrall until we are freed through justification.[15]

As the transition to Romans 8 brings out, deliverance comes thanks to Jesus Christ. For those who are under the headship of *Christ* (''in Christ Jesus'' is the phrase Rom 8:1 uses) the *new age* has already begun. His single act of obedience has canceled out the disobedience of Adam, won for the world a *grace* which is more abundant than sin (Rom 5:12–21), made possible the transformation of our hearts by the *Spirit* pouring love into them (Rom 5:5), and opened the path to *eternal life* (Rom 6:21–22). The law of the Old Covenant heightened the sense of sin; now the *Gospel* announces that God in Jesus Christ has fulfilled his promises to save us from our sin. However the old age is still with us. Thus we are saved in hope. The great act of giving birth to the new age is still going on, with its mixture of anticipation and agony (Rom 8:18–25).

The above comparison of old and new ages offers a helpful context in which to understand the three steps Paul discerns in the journey of the Christian from the old to the new age:

a) from the old age to the between-time: JUSTIFICATION (faith)
b) within the between-time period: SANCTIFICATION (love)
c) from the between-time to the new age: SALVATION (hope)

The first and third of these ''phases'' take place at a given moment, the second is a process which takes place over a period of time. Paul generally associates justification and faith, sanctification and love, salvation and hope. Faith, love, and hope are three basic attitudes which coexist within Christians, relating them to God as he has acted in the past, is acting now, and will act in the future.

Justification is the term Paul uses to point to the event by which I personally enter, or rather am drawn into, the death and resurrection of Jesus Christ, and thus appropriate the redemptive power present in that event. Just as the death and resurrection which has ushered in the new age has an apocalyptic connotation, so too does justification. It is the new age which takes over my life, the overcoming in principle of the power which the forces of sin, death, and the law exert over me.

The term ''justification'' connotes the final act by which God, in fulfillment of his promises, comes as judge to vindicate himself and his chosen ones. He not only vindicates those whose righteousness the world fails to recognize and respect, but makes just those who are really sinners.[16] Thus God's judgement is at the same time forensic, eschatological, and creative.[17] It does not simply bring to light an already existing situation between myself and God but creates a new situation, one of total reconciliation. In the deepest part of myself I have become a new creation in Christ (2 Cor 5:17–19), and strive to become more and more in my total self what I already am.

The basic attitude which Paul normally associates with justification is faith. God takes an initiative to which I respond in faith, trusting no longer in my own illusory resources or vain efforts to achieve status before him, but in what he has done in Jesus Christ to fulfill his promises, and in that alone. Faith and hope are very closely linked in this initial step, but the difference is that faith is essentially rooted in the past, in what God has done to ground my security in his presence; whereas hope is essentially turned to what God will accomplish in the future.

The fruit of my justification is *sanctification*, and its end is eternal life (Romans 6:22). Having been set free and radically empowered, I am called to walk in the Spirit, to live a fruitful life of good deeds, growing towards and waiting for the "prize of the upward call in Christ Jesus" (Phil 3:14,20; 1 Cor 1:7), dealing lovingly, patiently and constructively with what remains of the old age within myself and my world (1 Cor 13), enduring through the end-time tribulations (Rom 5:3), working out my salvation in fear and trembling (Phil 2:12). In a word, according to Gal 5:6, my faith (justification) operates through love (sanctification). Though love as a basic attitude of the Christian is given in the initial event of justification (Rom 5:5), it receives special emphasis within the process of sanctification. Paul constantly invites his between-time communities to a life of love, not any love but one which is patterned after Jesus' own kenotic love. Justification has freed them, given them the rights and prerogatives of the new age, but sanctifying love for Paul does not stand on these rights but rather empties itself out. The reward is salvation, patterned after the exaltation which Jesus receives from his Father.

While in the main epistles of Paul justification is a past event, *salvation* is a future one:

> Since, therefore, *we have now been justified* by his blood, much more *shall we be saved* by him from the wrath of God. For if while we were enemies we were reconciled to God by the death of his Son, much more, now that we are reconciled, shall we be saved by his life. (Rom 5:9–10)

Corresponding to the past/future distinction found in this text is the fact that though I have already participated in the mystery of the Lord's *death*,[18] I still await the day of Christ, on which I hope to be united to him in a *resurrection* like his (Rom 6:5), to be established pure and blameless in his sight (Phil 1:10;

1 Thess 3:13), as well as to experience the total transformation of my body and of the world which will remove all precariousness in my relationship to God. Until my body and my world share what my heart has already received, I only have the down-payment and not the total reality promised by God. I am saved, but only in hope (Rom 8:24). That hope is the third of the basic attitudes of the Christian, turned to the future, and, with faith, a powerful stimulus to live out my present life in loving alertness (Rom 13:11–14).

Justification, sanctification, and salvation, like faith, love, and hope, are interior to one another. They are not to be conceived as successive and separate elements of a temporal process, one taking over where the other leaves off. This is immediately clear as regards faith hope and love, which are solidary and simultaneous with each other, since there is no genuine human here and now without the there and then of past and future being at least tacitly present. I do not receive faith initially, then love, and finally hope. Though faith comes to the fore in justification, I also receive the gift of love in that initial experience (Rom 5:5) as well as that of hope (Rom 4:16 ff). All three are given together, grow together, and together find fulfillment.

The same is true of justification, sanctification, and salvation. Justification is salvation begun; salvation is justification in its fullness; sanctification is the dynamic power of justification and salvation in the "now" of the Christian. All three are permeated by the double reality of Jesus Christ and the Spirit. I am justified by faith in Jesus Christ and his saving deed. My sanctification consists in living my life in imitation of the kenotic pattern of Jesus' life. My salvation consists in fully sharing in the glory of Christ's resurrection. My justification consists in receiving the outpouring of the Spirit. My sanctification consists in doing the deeds inspired by the Spirit rather than those of the flesh (Rom 8:1–17; 1 Cor 3:16, 6:19). The glory I hope to receive from the Lord when he comes again is a permeation by the Spirit (Rom 8:11; 1 Cor 15:44–46). In this way justification, sanctification, and salvation dwell in a circumincession whose mystery points to that of God, their origin and object.

In justification we receive the gift of the Holy Spirit poured into our *hearts* (Rom 5:5). In the deepest part of ourselves we are re-oriented (cf. Phil 3:4–11). Our relationship to God is transformed. Instead of coming before him with our accomplishments we approach him with humble, contrite, and trusting hearts. In salvation that gift finally penetrates our *bodies*: we become totally transformed, permeated by the reconciliation that has already begun to possess us (Phil 3:20–21; Rom 8:22–23). The intervening period, that of the between-time, is one of tribulation,[19] of the agony of giving birth to something radically new. The process by which the deepest and most interior part of the self transformed by grace gradually pushes out to and encompasses the entire human person and the world in which that person lives is slow and painful, threatened by the ever present possibility of falling away from what he or she has received. When Paul speaks about justification, he uses the indicative mood: we are saints, we have been justified, sanctified, put on the way to glorification. But when he speaks about sanctification he usually shifts to the imperative: become what you already are, live out day by day the identity you have received. Though the dynamism of faith operating through love (Gal 5:6), the power of God at work within us, makes us triumphantly hopeful (Rom 8:28–39), we still must work out our salvation in fear and trembling (Phil 2:12–13). Our freedom to say yes does not remove our freedom to say no. The indicative grounds the imperative, but does not denature or abolish it.

The justification/sanctification/salvation triptych describes the individual's life of grace. Paul, however, elaborates his doctrine of grace in response to conflicts within the communities which he founded. If one wishes to grasp the dynamics of grace in his thought, one must attend to the community context which emerges in his letters. Put in basic terms, he fleshes out his doctrine of justification in pastoral response to a group of Christians at work in Galatia who in effect fail to recognize that anything is essentially changed: as Paul sees it, they remain under the bondage of the law, they ignore the already now ushered in by Christ. He fleshes out his doctrine of sanctification in response to a group of Christians at work in Corinth for whom apocalyptic fulfillment is already a total reality, and the not yet does not count. In his letter to the Romans, he presents a less polemical and more systematic view of his position. In his letter to the Philippians, he lays bare the key Christological dynamic of his theology of grace.

Galatians: The polemical thrust of Paul's letter to the Galatians is indubitable, but the identity of Paul's opponents is not. For Beker[20] these opponents were itinerant Jewish Christian missionaries who impugned Paul's apostolic status as well as his doctrine. They insisted that in order to inherit the promise through Christ the Gentile Christians of Galatia first had to become members of the Jewish people through circumcision, and had to observe the times and seasons of the Jewish religion (Gal 4:10).[21] For Schillebeeckx, the opponents of Paul were propagating a syncretistic doctrine and practice, but in addressing the situation Paul chose to treat them as if they were straight Judaizers.[22]

Paul's argumentation is quite complex, and we will only present those elements that are essential to our purpose. Its main thrust is that with Jesus Christ and the Spirit the fullness of time has come (Gal 4:4–6). Jesus gave himself for our sins to deliver us from the present evil age (Gal 1:4) and the weak and beggarly spirits that control it (Gal 4:9), and to impart upon us the promised Spirit (Gal 3:2,14). His opponents in Galatia wished to shift the focus from Christ and the Spirit back to the Law and its demands. But the Law has fulfilled its role; it is now a curse (Gal 3:13),[23] a step backwards to the slavery of the old age from the freedom of the new age, from the new creation which is essentially constituted by faith operating through love (Gal 5:1,6; 6:15). Paul's opponents attempt to persuade these Gentile Christians that they should incorporate the best of Judaism,[24] observing not the whole law but only major features such as circumcision and various feasts. Paul unmasks their subtle ploy by reminding them that to reintroduce any part of the law is to introduce it entire.

The letter to the Galatians stresses what God has already done for humankind. By his own *death* on the cross under the law, Jesus has annulled the curse of the law. The apocalyptic fulfillment yet to come, which finally conforms us to the mystery of the *resurrection*, is scarcely mentioned. Yet there are a few hints in this letter of the "not yet", of that mysterious fulfillment (Gal 5:5,21; 6:7–8). Faith operates through love (Gal 5:6), and that love invites the Galatians to be servants to one another (Gal 5:13). The fruits of the Spirit include patience, gentleness, self-control, which remind us of salient features of love described in the quite different First Letter of Paul to the Corinthians, which we will examine as the counterpart to Galatians. If it were not for these hints, Beker opines that Galatians could easily be taken as a document of realized eschatology and Paul as the greatest of all the Gnostics.[25]

Corinthians: In Galatians the issue is fairly straightforward. A particular group has with some success urged the Galatians to depart from the Gospel Paul had preached, and Paul fights it tooth and nail. In his letters to the Corinthians, especially the first one, he deals with a more complex situation. Different parties, mentioned in 1 Cor 1:12, are at work in the Corinthian congregation.[26] Above all there are the strong and the weak, characterized mainly by their attitudes towards consuming meat sacrificed to idols (1 Cor 8). Though no total consensus on the precise nature and interrelation of these groups is available, current scholarship is moving towards some convergence. The work of Gerd Theissen[27] and Wayne Meeks[28] offers us a helpful approach to relating these groups with the social classes to be found in the urban setting of Corinth.

The community at Corinth, as well as other Pauline congregations, reflected a wide range of social status.[29] Most of its members were likely to be slaves, artisans, small traders, but those whom Paul usually mentions in his letters are persons who, without belonging to the Roman establishment, have achieved a certain wealth and position, upwardly mobile persons of high status inconsistency open to radical change within themselves and their society.[30]

Let us begin with the "*strong*", those of a higher level of education, more in touch with the ambient religious culture and its incipient Gnostic tendencies. Many of them may have been "God-fearers", persons who accepted the monotheism of the Jewish religion without becoming proselytes, since this would jeopardize the social relationships so crucial to their status. Given the heavy hopelessness beginning to pervade the Empire, these more cultured people would be sympathetic to a gnostic, knowledge-oriented approach to salvation, and would naturally translate the temporal categories of Jewish apocalyptic (already now/not yet) into spatial categories (above/below, inner/outer) befitting the Gnostic view. They would consider salvation to be purely spiritual, they would seek to achieve it in the here and now by withdrawal to inner space out of the confusion and bustle of the market place, by the cultivation of various ecstatic phenomena occurring in their prayer. They would also resonate to visiting missionaries who proclaimed the Gospel with greater rhetorical effectiveness and show of wisdom than Paul. From their position in society, they would already be accustomed to social intercourse with pagans in meals which featured meat sacrificed to idols and feel they could continue to do this with a free conscience, since now they knew the idols did not really exist. They buttressed their position with arguments which Paul reflects in his letter and to some extent accepts (1 Cor 8).

The *weak*, if we accept Theissen's interpretation, were Jews and Gentiles of lower social standing and education who would not take well to the free and easy social intercourse of the strong with pagans. A rare occurrence for them, eating meat bore a numinous quality. Thus when they saw the strong partake of meat sacrificed to idols, their consciences were bothered.

How did Paul grasp this complex nettle? He perceived that the problem here was quite opposite to that in Galatia, and developed a different set of emphases in his teaching. His approach was more subtle and open to practical compromise. However a basic principle remained intact: even if the observances of the Law were abrogated, as he stated in Galatians, the temporal structure of Jewish apocalyptic thought with its "not yet" dimension was a nonnegotiable. In writing to the Galatians he could take this structure for granted, but in Corinth he had to spell it out. Yes, the new age has broken in. But its full emergence was to be accomplished by means of a gradual process. The Corinthians thought they were experiencing eschatological fulfillment, but that was an illusion: they were still living in the ambiguities of the between-time. Apocalyptic tension was still the order of the day.

To those who gloried in their gnostic-like wisdom and their social standing, he opposed the folly of the cross, the choice which God made of those who are weak and negligible to confound those who are high and mighty (1 Cor 1:26–28). They felt they had achieved the fullness of the resurrection in their own individual and communitarian spiritual experiences, but, he emphasized, the fullness of that resurrection lay ahead of them, when their mortal bodies would be glorified with a new life and the whole universe under Christ delivered to the Father (1 Cor 15). In theory they may have been right in their judgement that idols did not exist and in their decision to eat meat sacrificed to idols. In practice they still had to deal with the tender consciences of their weaker brethren, and what might have been lawful was not to be done (1 Cor 8; 10:23–33). They gloried in their various ecstatic gifts, but Paul expressed some very clear criteria to distinguish genuine from illusory gifts, taught that charismata were given for the good of the community, and pointed out to them the way superior to all other ways, that of the self-sacrificing love without which the community founders (1 Cor 12–13).

Galatians and Corinthians Compared: In 1 Corinthians as in Galatians, the cross of Jesus is at the center. In the letter to the Galatians, the cross neutralized a boast in the works of the Mosaic law. In the first letter to the Corinthians the cross neutralized a boast in wisdom and pneumatic experience. In the first case the cross is the means by which Jesus has already submitted to the depths of human bondage, overcome it, and radically disabled the old age. In the second, it is something which we ourselves also have to experience before we share the Lord's triumph on the day of his *parousia*.

In Galatians Paul dealt with opponents who had apocalyptic expectations like his own. Thus he took for granted rather than highlighted the expected return of Christ, and brought to the fore the unprecedented *already now* of Jesus Christ. In Corinthians Paul dealt with a group of people more at home in the spatial categories of Hellenistic religion than in the temporal ones of Jewish apocalyptic, so to them he stressed the temporal, *not yet* dimension which they overlooked.

Galatians underlines the inward transformation effected by justification by faith. The Spirit has been sent into our *hearts* (Gal 4:6), and we now stand in freedom (Gal 5:1). Corinthians stresses the *body* in all its complexity: the body of the individual Christian sown corruptible and raised incorruptible, the body of the Church with its messy plurality, its strong and weak members, and the need for the strong to forego their privileges in the interests of the weak.

Galatians invites to a celebration of *unity*: In Christ Jesus we are all one; in him there is neither Jew nor Greek, slave nor free, male nor female (Gal 3:27–8). Corinthians celebrates the indispensable *plurality* of Christ's body (1 Cor 12), composed of many diverse members, all of them knit together by a love which bears all, hopes all, endures all (1 Cor 13:7).

Each letter has its characteristic emphasis, but what is dominant in the one is recessive in the other. As we saw above Paul in Galatians does not deny the end-time in the sight of which we remain unfulfilled, and includes self-sacrificing love as a fruit of the Spirit. Likewise in 1 Corinthians the doctrine of justification by faith is marginally present. Christ is said to be our justification in 1 Cor 1:30, and 7:19 reflects the polemic against circumcision which is central to Galatians.

Not many years after Paul wrote these two letters he had the opportunity of recasting somewhat more eirenically his doctrine of grace. He does this especially in Chapters 1 to 8 of his letter to the Romans. Moreover in his letter to the Philippians he clearly articulates a pervasive kenotic thought pattern which emerges especially in 1 Corinthians. The perspectives opened by Romans and Philippians will enhance our perception of the systematic nature and dynamic sweep of Paul's theology of grace.

Romans: It appears that Paul's letter to the Romans was not based on intimate acquaintanceship with the problems current in that community. It was more of a way for Paul to introduce himself to that milieu in view of future apostolic action, and, according to some, may have served as a sort of encyclical letter. In it he carries on a more dispassionate theological reflection, pulling together the strands found in Galatians and 1 Corinthians, and adding to them.

Rom 1:6–7 expresses the thesis of the letter in typical ABCBA structure:

A) The Gospel is the power of God unto salvation
B) to everyone who has faith
C) to the Jew first and also to the Greek.
B) For in it the justice of God is revealed through faith for faith
A) as it is written, He who through faith is righteous shall live.

A) represents the not yet perspective in which Paul refers to the salvation and life to come, B) the already now perspective of justification by faith, and C) the theme of Jews and Gentiles, unique as well as central to Romans, developed especially in ch. 9–11.

In Chapters 1 to 4 Paul speaks about justification by faith, first setting forth the universal bondage to sin which prevails apart from Christ among both Jew and Greek, and then in 3:21 proclaiming the eschatological ''now'' inaugurated by Jesus Christ and accessible to us through justifying faith. In Chapter 5 he develops the theme of salvation which we have not yet attained, but which in the midst of end-time tribulations (*thlipseis*) we hope to attain because of the love of God poured into our hearts. In this chapter justification is something we have already received, and salvation from the wrath of God and our reign in life something we expect in the future (Rom 5:9–11,17).

In Chapter 6 Paul, replying to objections raised in 3:1–8 (esp. 3:8) and brought to the fore in 5:20, shifts from a broader salvation history perspective to that of individual Christians in the period between justification and salvation, characterized by sanctification through the deeds in which their members yield themselves to righteousness (Rom 6:13,19,22–23). In Chapters 7 and 8 he draws a contrast between the experience of human beings under the bondage of sin and the law and their experience now that they are freed in the Spirit. Chapter 8, a high point in Pauline literature, describes the dynamics of grace within the Christian. "If the Spirit of him who raised Jesus from the dead dwells in you (your *heart*), he . . . will give life to your mortal *bodies* also through his Spirit which dwells in you." (Rom 8:11) The between-time is not one of passive waiting for God to do something but an entry into the sufferings of Christ (Rom 8:17), a "groaning in travail together" (Rom 8:22) to bring forth the fullness of the new creation. Given what God has already done for us in Christ, there is nothing that can separate us from the love of God in Christ Jesus (Rom 8:31–39): the assurance of future salvation is based upon the truth and firmness of what God has already done for us.

Philippians: Whether written before or after Romans, the value of Philippians is in the light it sheds upon the dynamic which underpins justification/sanctification/salvation.[31] The pattern of this dynamic is as follows: though Christians, strong in being who they are, enjoy certain rights and privileges, they should not cling to them and stand upon them, but identify themselves with the weak who are bereft of them. Paul urges the strong to give up the privilege which comes from their knowledge and guiltless conscience lest they become a stumbling block to the weak (1 Cor 8). He offers himself as an example of this pattern. Though his apostolic mission gives him certain rights, he foregoes them in the interest of a universal outreach:

> For though I am free from all men, I have made myself a slave to all, that I might win the more. To the Jews I became as a Jew, in order to win Jews; to those under the law I became as one under the law—though not being myself under the law—that I might win those under the law. To those outside the law I became as one outside the law—not being without law towards God but under the law of Christ—that I might win those outside the law. To the weak I became weak that I might win the weak. I have become all things to all men that I might by all means save some. I do it all for the sake of the Gospel, that I might share in its blessings. (1 Cor 9:19–23)

Paul concludes his section in 1 Corinthians on this topic with the words "Be imitators of me as I am of Christ" (1 Cor 11:1). This phrase leads us into the letter to the Philippians, because it is there that the Christological basis of the kenotic pattern is more fully developed. In an exhortation to community in Christ, which implies putting others first and looking to their interests, he points to the example of Christ by quoting a hymn familiar to the Philippians, known as the kenotic hymn (Phil 2:6–11) after the words, "he emptied himself, taking the form of a servant".[32]

This hymn poetically depicts the kenosis of Jesus Christ. Though Christ Jesus was in the form of God, he did not cling to his equality with God, i.e. avail himself of the right of recognition which flowed from his being God's equal, but emptied himself of that right, becoming human in weakness and vulnerability, even taking the ultimate step of being obedient unto death on the cross for us. He does not exchange his strength for weakness, but precisely out of his strength which abides, he chooses to be weak.[33] His *kenosis* was rewarded by the Father's gracious act of exalting him, in that way bringing that state of equality and those rights to full recognition.[34]

According to a common explanation, the hymn refers to three stages: in the first stage intimated by the hymn,[35] Christ exists in his state of primordial equality with God; in the second, that of the earthly life, he exists in a state in which that equality is hidden in weakness; in the third stage, that of the risen life, the strength becomes transparent within his total human self, and he is recognized for who he is. There are two movements, one of abasement, the other of exaltation. The beginning and the end of the process are not the same. In the final exaltation, the originating divine glory incorporates a human life to itself and makes that human life transparent. Divine glory becomes divine/human glory.[36]

For Paul this pattern is at the heart of our imitation of Christ. The call to imitate the movement from the first to the second stage is clear in the way he uses the kenotic hymn itself in Philippians and its underlying pattern in 1 Corinthians, exhorting the Christian to genuine vulnerability out of inner strength instead of illusory boasting out of an unacknowledged state of inner weakness.[37] The same call to imitate the crucified form of the Lord's life is expressed in terms of the movement from the second to the third stage: "For if we have been united with him in a death like his, we shall certainly be united with him in a resurrection like his" (Rom 6:5).[38] The first movement is downwards: from a state of original strength and glory to a radical self-divestment. The second movement is upwards: from that state of radical self-divestment to the reward in glory with Christ.

The downward movement corresponds to the passage from justification to sanctification which is central to 1 Corinthians. We are not originally in the form of God, but the gift of God which in justification has been poured into our hearts has inaugurated for us a new form of existence, and henceforth we can let go out of strength and enter into the limitations and ambiguities of the human situation.[39] The Corinthians, in the enthusiasm of their first taste of the new life, possibly involving pneumatic phenomena, wished to stay on Mount Thabor in the illusion that all had been consummated. Paul was urging them to come down from the mountain, and divest themselves in favour of the weaker members of their community.

Likewise the upwards movement corresponds to the passage from sanctification to salvation: in our struggle we taste the weakness and precariousness of human life to the full, but in and through it we strive for the prize of the upward call in Christ Jesus, and firmly expect to receive a share in his glorification.[40]

We can summarize this movement in the form of a diagram:[41]

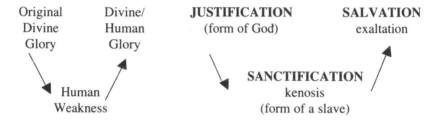

Original   Divine/   **JUSTIFICATION**   **SALVATION**
Divine   Human   (form of God)   exaltation
Glory   Glory

        Human   **SANCTIFICATION**
        Weakness   kenosis
                              (form of a slave)

The difference between the beginning and the end of this process corresponds to the difference between the life which Christ had from the beginning and that same life having triumphed over death by allowing death to exert its full power over it. In other terms, the gift of love which from the very beginning is given to us passes from attractive innocence through conflict, self-scrutiny, anguish, infidelity, forgiveness, and thus reaches its full maturity and security. As we are told in Romans 5:1–5, tribulation produces endurance; endurance character; and character a hope that does not disappoint us.

THE DYNAMICS OF GRACE FOR TODAY:
A THIRD WORLD INSIGHT

The starting point of our exploration of a contemporary language of grace based on Paul's theology will be a twentieth century namesake from the third world, Paulo Freire, who in his *Pedagogy of the Oppressed*[42] outlines the various components of a process of reconciliation between oppressors and oppressed. His thought, at once dialectic, dynamic, and structural, strikingly transposes that of his forebear. We will then return to Paul of Tarsus, in order to open up a different dimension of his approach to the graced relationship of God and humankind. In subsequent sections we will apply our new understanding to the world in which we live.

For Freire, teaching illiterate men and women in South America the basic skills of written communication provides them with far more than familiarity with the alphabet. Alphabetization implies humanization. In other words it fosters in them the ability to reflect upon and analyze their situation and to devise steps by which they can improve it.

But what does such humanization have to do with grace? In classical theology humanization and divinization are the two essential functions of grace.[43] These two functions are distinct but not separate, like the two natures, human and divine, of Jesus Christ the prime exemplar of grace. In him the human enfleshes the divine, and the divine is the mystery at the core of the human. It is our contention that the process of humanization Freire describes has an implicit reference to God and is quite open to divinization. Indeed without divinization there is no humanization. The thought of these two namesakes can be brought to a most useful convergence.

Paulo Freire's Model: Having and being are two central categories in Freire's thought. The new humanity comes about when human beings are no longer separated from each other in terms of those who have and those who have not but are seen in their radical unity as persons and brought to reconciliation. The essential category is that of simply being. Oppressors define themselves in terms of having rather than being:

> Analysis of existential situations of oppression reveals that their inception lay in an act of violence—initiated by those with power. This violence, as a process, is perpetuated from generation to generation of oppressors, who become its heirs and are shaped in its climate. This climate creates in the oppressor a strongly possessive consciousness—possessive of the world and of men. Apart from direct, concrete, material possession of the world and of men, the oppressor consciousness could not understand itself—could not even exist . . . For them *to be is to have* and to be the class of the "haves". The oppressors do not perceive their monopoly on *having more* as a privilege which dehumanizes others and themselves. They cannot see . . . that they suffocate in their own possessions and no longer *are*; they merely *have*.[44]

In turn the oppressed are the ones who have not. In their own eyes and in those of the oppressors they are less than fully human, a reality owned by the oppressor, whose survival is tolerated in the interests of the oppressors' accustomed standard of living. To the extent that they are under the spell of oppression, to be for them is not so much simply to be, but to be like the oppressor[45] or to be under the oppressor.[46]

The final state for Freire is one in which the opposition of oppressor and oppressed has been overcome, in which all human beings enter into a dialogical process of ever more fully becoming who they are, as they engage in the historical task of transforming reality. This is filled out in the diagram on p. 109 (references are to *Pedagogy of the Oppressed*).

The resemblance of the above with our comparison in Chapter One[47] of the old and the new order as it emerges in the work of contemporary first world analysts of the human scene is striking. From his third world perspective Freire spells out in urgent terms the implications of the first world's espousal of and persistence in the mechanistic "*divide et impera*" approach to reality. He uses Marxist categories to do this but sets them in a humanistic context which leads to their transformation. The convergence of the first world analysts we alluded to and Freire corroborates an emerging perception that communism and capitalism are two sides of the same denatured coin, and that the alternative to them is radically different from either of them.[48]

How does one in Freire's thought get from the situation in which the rift between oppressor and oppressed is paramount to that of the new humanity in a free and open process of becoming? Again let us begin with a diagram:

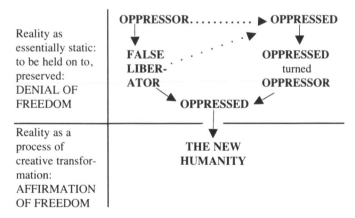

The top of the diagram depicts for us the basic division between oppressor and oppressed. The arrows with broken lines indicate the direction in which the oppression takes place. Those with solid lines indicate the direction in which the oppressive structure is overcome.

OPPRESSOR-OPPRESSED	NEW HUMANITY
anti-dialogic, oppressive relations	dialogical relations, cooperation
cultural invasion: artificial uniformity imposed (PO 150 ff.)	cultural synthesis: unity in plurality (PO 180)

How human beings are viewed:

as passive receptacles	as active/passive knowers/doers (PO 61 ff.)
as a-historical	as historical (PO 71)
as cut off from self-reflection	as present to themselves in their active presence to the world (PO 87)
as to have (PO 44) or to be like (PO 33)	as to be
as in the world, but isolated from the world	as with the world: mutual interaction (PO 62)

How reality is viewed:

as static, unchangeable	as dynamic, in a process of constant change (PO 61)
as fragmented, known in a constricted, shackling way	as a totality known as such (PO 60, 94, 99, 110, 137 ff.)
as a hard impenetrable block	as a problem to be tackled together by human beings
limit situations as the boundary between being and non-being: untested feasibility of new possibilities is a threat	limit situations as the boundary between being and being more human: untested feasibility of new possibilities welcomed as a task, a risk worth taking (PO 93)

Both oppressor and oppressed are dehumanized:

a) the *oppressor* by his attitude towards the oppressed, whom he treats as things not persons (I-it rather than I-thou relationship). He defines himself as the one who has possessions, thus ignores what is primordial to his own essence.
b) the *oppressed* by not being able to possess the means of human fulfillment except to the extent of being allowed to subsist in order to make possible the maintenance by the oppressor of his own domination. He is further dehumanized by being manipulated: not only is he unfree but he fails to perceive his own unfreedom.

The process of liberation itself carries with it the danger of subtle forms of oppression under the guise of liberation, akin to the evil which masquerades under the guise of good which Ignatius Loyola draws to our attention in the Second Week Rules for Discernment found in his *Spiritual Exercises*. Persons of the oppressor class can become *false liberators*. Having undergone a ''conversion'', false liberators attempt to play a role in the liberation of the oppressed. They reserve the role of actors to themselves, thus becoming oppressive, treating the oppressed as objects and not as co-subjects of their own liberation.[49] Likewise persons of the oppressed class can become ''*oppressed turned oppressors*''. Looking upon liberation as a simple turning of the tables, the oppressed turned oppressors seek to exchange roles with their former oppressors.[50] In both cases the basic oppressive structure remains intact.

At the bottom of the diagram one finds the elusive goal of this liberation, the *new humanity*, which is not a static reality but a process of continuing transformation of self and world through the praxis of recurring action and reflection.[51] As the arrows with the solid lines indicate, the central movement of liberation takes place from and through the oppressed. Only by a real identification with them can one take part in the genesis of the new humanity. They are as it were the eye of the needle through which the rich must pass.

What for Freire is involved in this process of liberation? Three aspects stand out: conscientization, dialogue, and action. For Freire they are indeed aspects of one process rather than distinct steps. They exist and function together or not at all.

In *conscientization*, the oppressed are helped to achieve a heightened awareness of their plight, of their painful relation to their oppressors. In this way their oppression becomes more oppressive still,[52] it is focused for them, it becomes a sharp pain that must be dealt with rather than a dull suffusive ache controlled through narcotization.[53] The oppressed are invited to enter into critical and liberating *dialogue*, so that they might reflectively participate in the act of their own liberation,[54] and share in the act of transforming the world and becoming fully human themselves.[55] *Action* is not a consequence but an integral part of this dialogue, since the word which is the instrument of dialogue is a "praxis" made up of both reflection and action.

Some two thousand years separate Paulo Freire and Paul of Tarsus. To trace the meanderings of history which account for the similar structures of thought found in the two of them is a formidable task which we will set aside.[56] At this point we will return to Paul, and seek out the similarities and contrasts between his thought and that of Paulo Freire.

Paul of Tarsus' Model Revisited: What distinguished the "haves" and the "have nots" of Paul's experience was not economic wealth or political power as such but "status" in the eyes of God, seen, in analogy to material goods, as a scarce commodity to which many are not entitled. Such status had many non-religious implications in Jewish society, which internally kept a strong theocratic bent as it tried to survive within the Roman imperial scheme. For Paul, who in his mission to the Gentiles had begun to adopt a more universal viewpoint, the primary instances of "haves" and "have nots" that needed reconciliation in the process that led to the new humanity were the Jews and the Gentiles. While he saw himself as the apostle to the Gentiles, he was also a Jew proud of his inheritance, longed for the day when both Jew and Gentile would be incorporated into God's kingdom on equal terms, and struggled with the mystery of Israel's apparent rejection of the message of Jesus Christ. Finally it would be through the "have not" Gentiles that salvation would come to the Jews. The distinctive mark of Paul's letter to the Romans is this struggle within his mind and heart. Where he deals with it in Chapters 9–11 he breaks new theological ground.[57]

Paul is very careful to recognize the priority God gives to Israel, the chosen people:

> They are Israelites, and to them belong the sonship, the glory, the covenants, the giving of the law, the worship, and the promises; to them belong the patriarchs, and of their race, according to the flesh, is the Christ.[58]

Paul's great sorrow and unceasing anguish (Rom 9:2) comes from Israel's option, as he saw it, to trust not in what it has received from God but in what it has achieved, not in the faithfulness of a God who freely chose it to be his people and who promised to be with it, but in its own efforts to achieve status in God's eyes (righteousness) by observing the law (Rom 9:30–33; 10:3). The Israelites clung to the law as a possession exclusively their own, boasted in their observance of it, and set themselves apart from the Gentile nations, who were excluded from this access to God. What was intended to be a privilege which they had received in order that salvation might come to all the nations, they turned into a means of domination. There is a subtle shift from playing a special role within the universal salvific plan of God to being an oppressor in the religious realm.[59] To shore up their own status, they pass judgement on their Gentile counterparts. Paul concurs with them in their view that the Gentiles fall short of the glory of God, as he makes abundantly clear in Rom 1:18–32. But in arrogating to themselves the right to judge the Gentiles and in setting themselves in a position of moral and religious superiority, blinding themselves to their own failures in observing the law, even more do the Jews fall short of the glory of God (Rom 2:2). Thus in this way all, Jew and Greek alike, are under the power of sin, and in the new creation which overcomes the power of sin, they exist equally and without distinction in Christ Jesus:

> For as many of you as were baptized into Christ have put on Christ.
> There is neither Jew nor Greek, there is neither slave nor free, there
> is neither male nor female; for you are all one in Christ Jesus.[60]

In this way Paul treads a very fine line between recognizing the privileges of the Jewish people, privileges which are never abrogated because God remains ever faithful to his promises, and affirming the radical equality of all human beings as sinners apart from Christ and as redeemed in Christ. He was most concerned with the radical equality before God of Jew and Greek, began to deal with the issue of the equality of slave and free, which was perhaps the outstanding secular division within his communities, as for instance in the letter to Philemon, and alluded to the equality of men and women, leaving our generation to deal with it.

This foundational issue of the relationship of Jew and Greek in the plan of salvation emerged as Paul dealt with the problems posed by the complex communities he nurtured in Christ. There the problem of Jew and Greek was a backdrop to more precise issues arising from the struggle of groups who, converted to Jesus Christ, had already left behind the basic dichotomy of Jew and Greek and were striving to unify their lives in Christ Jesus, but were still caught in the subtle tendency to erect barriers within the community, to oppress under the guise of liberation. The structure of oppression which they professed to have overcome they were reintroducing in new ways, and Paul was challenged to develop a theological and pastoral approach to this poisonous deviation. It would be a mistake to claim one on one correspondence between these groups and the avatars of liberation Freire describes in his book, but the resemblances are noteworthy.

The Judaizers, whether they were Gentile Christians who felt that Paul was cheating them of the total Judeo-Christian inheritance or Jewish Christians who happened to belong to what was a primarily Gentile community, were quite willing, so it seemed, to allow non-Jews to enter into the Christian community, but only if these accepted the basic Jewish observances, including circumcision. In this way the Judaizers falsified the liberation Jesus Christ had introduced: they replaced faith in Jesus Christ as the only source of salvation by confidence in the works of the Mosaic law. Against this, as we saw, Paul struggled with might and main.

His problem in Corinth was quite different. A good number of Corinthian Gentiles converted to Jesus Christ were of the conviction that there was no more need for any law or discipline. In their communal and personal experience they had found the fullness of the eschaton and now they could relish the ecstasy and freedom that fullness brought with it, much like the oppressed turned oppressors of Paulo Freire who for a time wallow in new found freedom and wealth. These Christians were styled the strong, but their strength was illusory, since they did not realize that the power of this present age was still influencing their lives, and that they would fall back into their previous existence unless they were willing to enter into the lengthy struggle leading to true liberation. In other words, they may have broken the fetters of justification by the works of the Mosaic law, but they had created for themselves those of justification by self-validating religious experience.

In these internecine struggles a good number of Christians, those Paul terms the weak (analogous to the little ones Jesus refers to in the Gospel) felt the brunt of these two forms of attack. Their conscience was scrupulous, they did not have the security—due perhaps to the psychic bent left in them by their earlier religious formation, to their sense of social inferiority, or to their own psychic disabilities—which would permit them to peacefully ignore the condemnations, spoken or tacit, of Judaizers and enthusiasts. They were manipulated, put upon, pulled in different directions. Paul is very sensitive to their plight. In Galatians he explodes with indignation that anyone would dare to impose upon them a whole series of unnecessary burdens pertaining more to the age that was passing than to the one in which they were called to henceforth live their lives.

Paul's purpose was not so much to create uniformity within his communities as to create a space where different people could collaborate in peace and mutual respect. The mystery of salvation is many-faceted, and the variety

of origins, talents, and perspectives found within the Christian community
opens the way for a rich synthesis. But without love there is no synthesis. All
of this can be summed up in a diagram parallel to the one we outlined above.
However a key difference deserves to be noted. Paul not only preaches the need
to enter into the lengthy process by which the new humanity is born, but also
proclaims the parousia that will bring this process to a successful conclusion.
Paulo Freire within his humanistic perspective does not go beyond a rebirth
corresponding to justification and a continual struggle corresponding to sanctification. Ultimate salvation does not enter within his explicit purview.

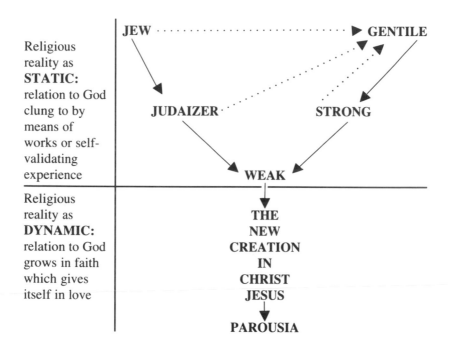

THE DYNAMICS OF GRACE FOR TODAY:
THE FULL RANGE

Paulo Freire and Paul of Tarsus both generate their insights within a
global perspective. Freire's oppressors and oppressed refer in first instance to
classes existing within Latin American society, but clearly point to the overall
situation in which the first world plays the role of oppressor vis-à-vis the third
world. Paul of Tarsus's broad categories of Jew and Gentile belong to the vast

sweep of apocalyptic fulfillment which touches all peoples. Both authors pay close attention to the subtle ways in which the process of liberation can break down, evil masquerading under the guise of good.

We now intend to apply their insights into oppression and liberation to other areas of human functioning. We will explore how the dynamic of oppression and liberation they have uncovered touches the most intimate zones of human reality as well as the broadest and most public. As it ranges over these zones, it keeps the same structure but takes on a different content. To anchor our discussion, we present these zones as a set of concentric circles:

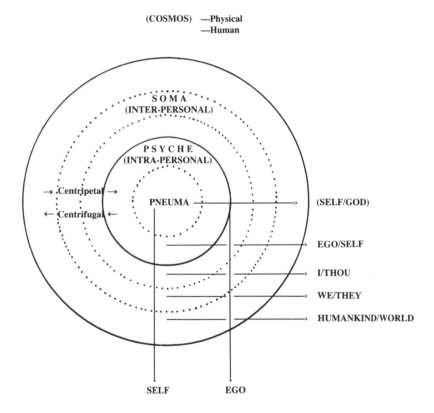

At the very centre of the series of concentric circles we find the *pneuma* or spirit. Strictly speaking it should be represented as a point which has a position but occupies no area. The inner circle represents the *psyche* or soul, the outer the *soma* or body, and the area beyond the circles the *cosmos* or world. These circles can be sub-divided. Within the inner circle is located the sub-conscious self, which is next to the supraconscious spirit at the centre, and the conscious ego which is closer to the body. Within the outer circle one finds three areas: the one which is closest to the soul has to do with inter-personal relations and primary groups (I-thou); the middle one has to do with the realm of the social and the political (we-they); and the one closest to the outer rim has to do with the ecological relationships of humankind to the physical world.

These components are listed in pairs to the right of the diagram. It is possible for the components within each pair to enter into an oppressor/oppressed relationship. The self/God pair is put in brackets because in this case one of the components, God, is the constitutive term of the relation which the self at root is, and to be represented would require adding another dimension to this two-dimensional diagram.

In the left half of the circle we find arrows both centripetal and centrifugal. These represent the mutual influence which oppression or liberation on any one level can have on the ones next to it. The influence can move from the centre to the periphery or vice-versa. To describe the modalities of this inter-influence at all levels would in effect be to transpose in contemporary terms the Pauline dynamic of grace and sin.

The diagram is based on the Pauline distinction of spirit, soul, and body (1 Thess 5:23). We need to look at each component separately:

a) The *spirit (pneuma)*, sometimes referred to as heart (e.g. Rom 5:5), is the deepest, most inward part of the person, the originating source of objective and explicit consciousness which itself is never grasped, controlled, objectified. It is there that the relation between the person and God comes to a point, it is there that the Spirit of God dwells. The medievals refer to it as the *apex animae*, some moderns as the self which is distinct from the ego.

b) The *soul (psyche)* is the feeling-laden intra-personal world which gravitates around this core. In medieval terms it would be composed of various faculties and appetites related to each other. In modern terms it would be diversely seen in terms of conscious and sub-conscious zones, ego, id, super-ego, anima, animus, shadow, etc.[61] For our purposes, the main distinction is between that part which is unconscious, close to the self, and that which is illumined by conscious objectification, which can be referred to as the ego.

c) The *body (soma)* is the conjoint instrument, the embodiment through which the person relates to other embodied persons and to the world. It makes possible a variety of relations which take the person outside himself or herself, ranging from the primary inter-personal relations which are so important in the development of the psyche, through the all-encompassing relationships of the three human worlds of our planet to each other, to the universe as an ecological whole.

d) Thus beyond the body there is the *world (cosmos)*. In modern usage the term bears many meanings. In order of increasing scope, it can mean networks of relationships and institutions constituted by human meaning and value; it can refer to the physical universe as an ecological unit which human value enhances and disvalue destroys; it can point to the physical universe in the widest sense, the object of theoretical research and exploration.[62] It can refer to the immediate habitat of the individual (I/thou relations); to the wider world in which he or she lives such as the first, second, or third worlds (we/they); to the planet earth as a whole or to the universe in all its aspects (humankind/world).

As we have seen, oppression and liberation occur on all these levels. As they occur on one level, they may exert a centrifugal and centripetal causal influx on other levels (left of the circle). The inner influences the outer, and the outer the inner.[63] For instance, *centrifugally*, some become oppressors of others on the social and political level because of an earlier experience of being oppressed or alienated, which leaves scars and insecurities within their psyches. To cope with that oppression they often cannot name, they project it outside themselves. The poor, the marginated, the idle, the good-for-nothing are a reflection of what is poor, marginated, idle, good-for-nothing within themselves. Others are no longer valued and recognized in their otherness but become a scapegoat. *Centripetally*, the effect of the oppressive stance is that these others will be diminished, alienated within themselves, oppressed in the more interior zones of their being. Structures of oppression without breed oppression within.

1) Within the outer circles of body and world, which, as we have seen, are in intimate correspondence, the dynamic of oppression is obvious in its various effects. We have explored some of them already:

a) In recent years ecological concerns have led us to focus on the widest rim of both circles. Disorder within the human heart is mirrored not only in the broken fabric of our political and economic relationships but also in a physical environment which is cluttered, ecologically unbalanced, threatened with nuclear catastrophe. In turn an unbalanced and threatened physical environment has already begun to deaden our psyches, robbing our human hearts of vitality.

This interaction of humankind and its environment has been brought more and more insistently to our attention in recent decades. We will not develop it further here.

b) Paul of Tarsus and Paulo Freire have been especially concerned with we/ they relations in the political/economic field (Freire) and in the religious field (Tarsus). As we saw, persons in their diversities can collaborate together as members of the one body, or else their differences can be rigidified and hierarchized in terms of us and them, haves and have nots. In this latter case, persons on both ends of the relationship are de-humanized, their inner reality belittled, obviously so in the case of the oppressed—Freire describes the state of apathy and human belittlement which they suffer—less obviously perhaps but just as profoundly in the case of oppressors, whose status as oppressors both conceals and confirms a more interior inadequacy. The dynamic of humanization, of reconciliation, described by Freire in secular terms and by Paul in religious terms, dismantles oppressive structures and brings about a state in which differences are celebrated in unity rather than hardened in division.

c) Closer to the psyche we find the realm of I/Thou relations. They are nurtured in the more primary groups of society, above all the family (*Gemeinschaft* as distinct from *Gesellschaft*). In the first formative years of human life (some would wish to include relations with the mother in intra-uterine existence), they are especially crucial for the organization of the psyche. It is at this point that the inter-personal and the intra-personal enter into symbiosis. Alienation and disjointedness within the psyche occurs because someone in the immediate environment is doing the alienating and the disjointing.[64] Integration and security within my psyche is the gift of the significant other who cherishes me and cares for me. Wholesome I-thou relations within the family in which one develops as a person are a *sine qua non* of psychic health.

2) We are ready to concentrate on the more interior reality of the psyche, the disruption of which is mirrored forth in conflicts between human beings, whether within the intimacy of the family or on a planetary scale. In intra-psychic conflicts I oppress myself, divide myself into that part of me that oppresses and that which is oppressed. An experience of such conflicts as they impinge on behaviour is expressed by Paul in Romans 7: "I do not do the good I want, but the evil I do not want is what I do" (Rom 7:19), and by Augustine as he reflects on the sickness of his will that both longs for and flees from conversion.[65]

Contemporary psychological literature enables us to discern the forms of oppression latent in such conflicts. A fruitful approach is suggested by Herbert Fingarette, in *Self in Transformation*.[66] His view can easily be transposed to the oppressor/oppressed mode of speech. Within the psyche there is a mental system often referred to as the ego, a high order set of perceiving, judging, synthesizing, and executing functions which mediate between inwardly generated drives and external reality in such a way as to maintain the reasonable long-term integrity of the person as autonomous agent.[67] But the other part of the psyche, closer, as depicted on the diagram, to the intimate mystery of the self, can in the process of ego-formation be relegated to the dark. The person refuses to advert to it, to receive new insights from it, to make it the material of responsible self-creation. From unconscious in the neutral sense of being potentially conscious it becomes unconscious in the negative sense of being repressed, buried, hidden.[68] There ought to be a free movement to and fro between ego and unconscious. To establish that kind of movement is central to the effort of the therapist: the unconscious and its contents are to be brought to consciousness within the self who is the subject of guilt, freedom, and responsibility, and dealt with in a process of mature self-transformation.

When we examine the state of inner alienation more closely we see the appositeness of the oppressor/oppressed model developed by Freire and adumbrated by Paul of Tarsus. The ego clings to center stage, it becomes estranged from what is unconscious, be it the elusive supra-conscious mystery of the pneuma or the sub-conscious remainder of the psyche. The ego wishes to protect itself against the vast inner mystery which underpins and permeates it. It fears other parts of the psyche, those it does not wish to acknowledge, look at, seek the meaning of, take responsibility for. It finds security in granting consciousness and attention only to certain contents and feelings, and in setting itself off against the rest of the psyche which becomes an oppressed or, in terms proper to psychology, a repressed zone. The osmotic membrane between the ego and the unconscious becomes an impermeable barrier. Communication has to pass through rigorous check-points. In the Freirian model both oppressors and oppressed are invited to enter into a process of gradual transformation by which, interacting with each other and with their common milieu, they together become the new humanity. In the transposition of this model, therapy works towards the reconciliation, integration and open communication between the ego and the unconscious which have been grown alienated from each other, and facilitates a crucial step towards the transformation of the self based upon the assumption of responsibility by the person for his or her reality as a whole, including what is not yet conscious.

Neurosis, the psychic disorder which in Fingarette's book serves as counterpart to integration, is a psychic state of frozenness, constriction, fragmentation. These are the very characteristics spawned by oppressive structures according to Freire. In both cases the victory of the oppressive element is pyrrhic. The political oppressor is dehumanized in a different way but just as profoundly as the oppressed. Likewise in putting down the unconscious the ego diminishes itself. The price it pays for air-tight control is rigidity and narrowness. Its adoption of an oppressive stance is an illusory attempt to heighten feelings of security, to ward off anxiety. It becomes characterized by a protruding, pathological self-consciousness. It is accompanied by ''repetitive fantasies''[69] and by:

> . . . the compulsive, obsessive, acutely self-conscious focusing of attention upon our feelings and our perceptions, our theoretical perceptions and logical proofs . . . the neurotic drive to achieve security by fitting all experience into a firm, clear, and neat logical system within which one can then manipulate the elements in an absolutely regularized way.[70]

The problem with this system is that it is arbitrary, partisan, fragmented, subjective.[71] It leads to stereotyped, repetitive attempts to avoid or seek certain types of situations.[72] Apparent control serves to mask deep fear and unfreedom. In therapy, according to the related approach of Eugene Gendlin[73] the experience of the client passes from that of a frozen whole, a rigid repetitive structure, to an ongoing process of interaction with the total environment.

R.D. Laing develops a theory along similar lines to deal with schizoid states in his *Divided Self.*[74] For him ontological insecurity and anxiety lead to the dissociation of the self from the body. The self needs to be in control, thus it steps back and disengages itself from the body, which is at the same time its only avenue of fulfillment in relationships and the greatest threat to its need for control and regularity. Thereby the self becomes an inner unembodied reality, untouched by and invulnerable to what is not itself; it spawns a false self system:

> If the individual delegates all transactions between himself and the other to a system within his being which is not 'him', then the world is experienced as unreal, and all that belongs to this system is felt to be false, futile, and meaningless.[75]

While it is not possible to work out a detailed correlation between Fingarette, Freire, and Laing, still it remains that in the schizoid person part of the psyche is oppressive: it pathologically sticks out in a heightened self-consciousness which is morbid, always concerned with how others perceive or fail to perceive the self;[76] and part of the psyche is oppressed, its perceptions unreal and its actions futile.[77]

3. We now pass from the soma and psyche to the pneuma, which is touched by oppression in ways that are as elusive as they are crucial. For this reason these observations about it are somewhat tentative. The pneuma, or spirit, or self,[78] is depicted in the diagram as the most interior of the concentric circles, but in reality it is the point at the centre rather than a smaller circle occupying an area within the larger circle. It is from perspective of the center point that the circle is circular, or to transpose, from the standpoint of the self that I am myself and relate to others and to the world. The self in this sense cannot be brought into explicit consciousness. It must remain as the mysterious lived presence 'behind' any effort to objectify anything, including itself. The relationship which most intimately constitutes the self is the relationship with God. In that sense the self is created spirit, a privileged receptacle which only God's own Spirit can fill.

The human pneuma is unitary, utterly indivisible, so we cannot speak about distinct oppressive or oppressed realities within it as we do in the case of the psyche. However just as the ego can oppress the unconscious zones of the psyche, so too it can oppress the pneuma, which is at the same time the highest, deepest, and most central ''part'' of the unconscious.[79] Here oppression consists not in preventing certain feelings, images, memories from coming into explicit focus so they can be dealt with in the ongoing task of living one's life but in refusing to accept as central to its own functioning a mystery that will ever remain elusive and out of its control.

Why would oppression occur at this deepest and most generative level of the person? At this point we touch the very roots of sin and oppression in our world. The pneuma is a mystery of emptiness totally related to the Mystery of fullness. God created our hearts restless until we rest in him. Fulfillment in God is beyond our control and our comprehension. We are attracted to it, but at the same time experience a powerful urge to ignore it, to set it aside as fraught with fear and mystery. Because the Holy is not only *fascinans* but also *tremendum*, we tend to replace the mystery of the living God who is totally and lovingly bent on our liberation, but in ways that we cannot fathom or control, by a God we construct out of the familiar categories of our own existence. We transmute the many-faceted mystery into a narrow, predictable, but oppressive reality. We work out the precise terms on which we can by-pass, neutralize, or change that oppression, and this lulls us into a false sense of security.[80]

It is easier to deal with God as an oppressor than as a lover. Part of me would rather deal with the illusion that I can grasp and control a hostile God than with the truth that I am defenseless before a God who is the very mystery of Love. Only too often my ego has the same bent in its dealings with God, who, in Augustine's terms, is more intimate to me than I am to myself, as it does in its dealings with the psychic unconscious: the ego is inclined to fear the unconscious, to ward itself against it and control it. Grace is that which breaks through this self-generated illusion. In the power of grace, I allow my attraction to mystery to overcome my fear of mystery. I destroy the God I have created in my own image and likeness and open myself to the real God who created me in his image and loves me into his likeness.

The right relation of the ego to God is the key issue in Paul's polemic against justification by works.[81] Justification by works implies a relationship with God in which I count on my own accomplishments, on what lies within my own power, as a way of gaining entry into and remaining within the grace of a God who otherwise is fickle, oppressive. Justification by faith is the opposite: humble and contrite in heart, letting go of the fear that makes me want to control, to define my relationship to God, I thrust myself in total confidence before him. My reconciliation with God is not the illusory one of pretending to change God's anger into acceptance, but the real one of accepting the mysterious acceptance which is there from the beginning. Beginning with the *pneuma*, this work of reconciliation expands into my psyche, and reaches out to the world as a whole: "In Christ God was reconciling the world to himself, not counting their trespasses against them, and entrusting to us the message of reconciliation" (2 Cor 5:19).

My stance towards God is central to justification. If God is at heart a liberator, then I need not rely on what is not God to assure my access to God. I will boast not in my own deeds but in the deed by which God has through Jesus Christ inaugurated his definitive presence in our world, and allow myself to be drawn into the mystery and the power of that deed. If God is at heart an oppressor, angry, unpredictable, then I need to assure my status in God's eyes by means of something which I possess and control independently of God. I will put my trust in something which is not God, not in the saving deed which God enacts through the cross of Jesus Christ. To use Pauline terminology, I will boast in my own observance of the law as that which will assure my entry into the realm of God and will distinguish me from so many others who are excluded from that realm. Do I fear the dawning of the new age in which God stands fully revealed or do I welcome it into my heart? This is the issue at stake between justification by works and justification by faith.

One could extend this pattern of analysis even more widely to other forms of religion, in some of whom the divinity is conceived as a numinous, ominous force that needs to be placated through sacrifices and other rituals. The structures that Paul was concerned with are widespread and basic. Generally stated, the issue might be seen as choosing between a personal God who calls for a personal relationship of trust and faith and an ultimately impersonal force which is tapped into, manipulated, controlled in one way or another.

The causal link between this most intimate form of oppression and the other two, intra- and inter-personal, is relatively unexplored. Martin Luther points to a centrifugal influx when he asserts that authentic faith gives us a basic security and freedom which enables us to live and act towards our neighbour in a gratuitous and anxiety-less way. Our good deeds and practices are no longer fraught with a burden too heavy for them, that of assuring our justification in the eyes of God. We are free to perform actions for their own sake, respecting their intrinsic meaning and value,[82] thus to act as liberators rather than as oppressors. Moving to the centripetal side, it is clear that the structures of oppression which exist inside and outside us strongly incite us to develop and act on a false image of God as oppressor. A simple and telling example. It is most difficult to bring a child who has been abused by his or her father to a real as opposed to a notional assent in God as Father. Often the pattern in which we conceive God and God's actions towards us is based on how other human beings have treated us when we were at our most vulnerable.

JUSTIFICATION/SANCTIFICATION/SALVATION: A TRANSPOSITION

We have considered obvious and familiar instances of oppression and liberation at work in our world. By steps we were led into the mysterious realm of the human heart. We have caught a glimpse of oppression and liberation at their most intimate, as they touch the relation to God that constitutes our deepest selves and determines the modalities of our own justification in the sight of God.

That oppression and liberation should pertain to justification should come as no surprise to one who is familiar with the broad context of Paul's doctrine of justification. Justification marks the personal entry of the Christian into the new eschatological age. It is clear from the tradition which shaped Paul that the transition from the old to the new age is one from oppression to liberation. Oppression reigns in the old age: this theme many prophets of the Old Testament developed with insistence and vigour. What God above all abominates is exploitation of the weak and the orphan; what he above all wishes to bring about for his people is deliverance from the powerful enemies who constantly surround them. Liberation is the hallmark of the new age. Initially the people longed for a political and economic liberation, but as time went on constant reverses led the prophets to proclaim that God had something more profound in store for them, a new heart and a new spirit leading to a new heaven and a new earth. At the deepest level liberation transforms the relationship of human beings to God: the secret attempt to control and manipulate God on human terms is extirpated and replaced by total trust and surrender in a God who fully reveals himself to be God, the Liberator and the Lord of history. Thus the new age inaugurates a new relationship to God. God does not become different: from all ages God is who he is. God's human creatures, however, would because of his decisive act of self-revelation finally be able to accept what has been true about him from the beginning. In this way liberation would be a passage from darkness into light, from illusion into truth.

The dynamics of oppression and liberation, ranging back and forth from a heart in need of conversion to a world in need of transformation, offers new possibilities for understanding and re-formulating Paul's doctrine of justification/sanctification/salvation. To substantiate this thesis, after briefly relating the sweep of justification/sanctification/salvation to *pneuma*, *psyche*, and *soma*, we will look more closely at distortions introduced by judaizers and enthusiasts, pointing to their convergences and divergences; finally in the main part of this section we will pull together some key bipolarities essential for grasping the contemporary ramifications of what Paul achieved two thousand years ago.

The relationship of the traditional trichotomy of *pneuma/psyche/soma* to Paul's doctrine of justification, sanctification, and salvation briefly came to the surface when we presented Paul's doctrine of grace. The Spirit, who is the already now of the new age, has been poured into our *hearts*, into the inmost part of ourselves where we surrender to the mystery of God in Christ. But we still await the permeation of our mortal *bodies* by the gift of the same Spirit, and the redemption of creation itself—in other words, we await our salvation. Sanctification is the lengthy and painful process which leads us from justification to salvation.

In sanctification the power of justification begins to permeate our psyches, to heal our tendency to cling to our ego-strengths, to what is familiar, easily controlled. Its freeing action then moves into the realm of the soma, makes possible authentic personal relations and respect of diversity within one's human world—a matter of real urgency in the Pauline communities—and effects not only the transformation of the *soma* into a copy of Christ's glorified body but also the renewal of creation itself. Sanctification is a cosmic struggle and, in Paul's unforgettable image, a great act of giving birth (Rom 8).

To return to our image of the concentric circles, justification is the Spirit's entry at the center point, sanctification is the painful and gradual stretching out of the area which the Spirit permeates and transforms, and salvation is the end of the process, the total and irrevocable permeation by the Spirit of the entirety of creation within and without ourselves: there is no more beachhead of unredeemed reality to threaten us.

Judaizers and Enthusiasts—Distorted Understandings: We have already touched on the judaizer and enthusiast distortions of the patterns of Christian life. These groups markedly differ in religious and cultural context, but both a) distort the reality of justification; b) refuse to enter into the redemptive pains of sanctification; c) in final analysis elude the mystery of the living God.

a) Both judaizers and enthusiasts distort the reality of justification by faith. In his polemic with the judaizers Paul spelled out the contrast between authentic justification by faith and inauthentic justification by works. We need not develop this point further. The theology Paul develops to counter the enthusiasts implies a parallel contrast of justification by faith and justification by self-validating religious experience. The illusory boasting of many Corinthian Christians is based upon their pretended possession of a superior gnostic wisdom, of an ecstatic religious experience which sets them apart from others. Basking in the warmth of justification and its attendant phenomena, unwilling to move beyond this warmth, their rebirth is defective. Yes, they have moved away from a stance of justification by works, but only to exchange it for another form of illusory justification, namely justification by gnosis (if one goes by the first chapters of 1 Cor) or justification by self-validating religious experience (the perspective which emerges later on in the letter when Paul deals with ecstatic religious experiences).[83]

In the final analysis both judaizer and enthusiast boast in what they think they possess or have achieved vis-à-vis God, works of the law or religious experience, rather than in the cross of Jesus Christ, which exhaustively manifests the love of God, inalterable and beyond our control, to which we have access only in the surrender of faith.

b) The refusal to accept justification by faith is also the refusal to enter upon the path of sanctification. This is very clear in the case of the enthusiasts. Sanctification is cruciform. They shrink from it. They huddle together in the illusory comfort of their ecstasies, refusing to deal with the divisions at work in the world and even in their own midst. Paul shows them what sanctification entails: letting go of what they have received in justification, putting themselves at the service of the community, struggling in an imperfect world with a love which bears all things, believes all things, hopes all things, endures all things (1 Cor 13:7).

The apparent zeal of the judaizers to perform the works of the law is in its own way just as firm a refusal to enter into the path of genuine sanctification. Rather than embrace the mystery of a life marked by suffering, ambiguity, uncertainty, lived in surrender to a God who is beyond their control, they narrow their focus to those illusory works which they think guarantee their acceptance by God. These works distinguish them in their own eyes from their fellow humans, who are deprived of this privileged access. That the mystery of life and the mystery of God are coterminous is beyond their ken.

c) What underlies their shared misconception of justification and sanctification is an unavowed effort to shield themselves from the mystery of the living God. To the liberating and loving God who entirely escapes their understanding and above all their control, the judaizers prefer an oppressive God whom they can harness and control to their own advantage, and the enthusiasts a pollyanna God who shelters them from their own inauthenticity and from the asperities of the world. Both close themselves off from the personal depths of a God whose self-communication, entry into the human situation, and respectful invitation to them are utterly beyond human measure. Both in effect envision God as infra-personal rather than a person who freely approaches them and invites their free response.[84] Refusing the mystery of their own personhood, they refuse that of God; refusing that of God, they refuse their own. Grace overcomes both refusals, both heals and elevates, humanizes and divinizes.

The underlying communalities of judaizer and enthusiast express themselves in strikingly diverse ways. The infra-personal God of the judaizer is a force to be controlled and manipulated; the infra-personal God of the enthusiast is a force to be tapped into. The judaizer fails by being stuck in the past, in obsolete patterns of legal observance which wear the musty smell of the old age. The "already now" is bypassed. The enthusiast fails by taking refuge in a future which does not yet exist, pretending that the beginning of liberation is already its end, the first fruits of the new age its pleroma.[85] The "not yet" is bypassed.

In sum the law of the cross would have us embrace the tension of the already now and the not yet. Both enthusiast and judaizer agree in refusing to accept that law, flee from the *thlipsis* which alone can bring the Christian and the world to their eschatological maturity.

The Bipolarity of Paul's Thought: In presenting a number of pertinent correlations between Paul's doctrine and contemporary concerns that emerged in Chapter One, we would note at the outset that the authors we cited in that chapter often share with Paul a predisposition to think in bi-polar terms. Like Paul, but less explicitly than he, they are faced with paradoxes generated when humans approach the mystery of the living God.

In the Pauline bi-polarities we have brought to light one of the poles is dominant, the other recessive.[86] This becomes most evident in Paul's controversy with the judaizers. For the judaizers, the works of the law are the be-all and end-all, the privileged and exclusive means of ensuring that God will be gracious to them. For Paul God's grace is radically abundant, as befits the age of eschatological fulfillment, and in principle it can be appropriated in faith by absolutely anyone apart from the works of the law. This faith, however, does not replace works; it relativizes them. In other words, rather than the role of bringing about a relationship with God that doesn't yet exist, works are given the role of enfleshing a relationship that already exists. Thus Paul reverses the order of priority: faith is to be dominant, works recessive.[87] The Corinthian enthusiasts go too far in the other direction: rather than relativize works within the Christian life, they consider themselves absolved from any striving to achieve the "not yet". Paul invites them to embrace the paradox, the struggle, the tension; to live not in the warmth of their own experience but in the arduous power of the cross.

With his bi-polar approach Paul wishes to do justice both to the fact that the new age has broken in and that the old age is still with us. If we go back to Chapter One[88] we shall see that in like manner the transition from the old age to the new age in secular terms does not entail the abolition of the values and the perspectives of the old age but rather their relativization. The cooperation, the radical abundance which characterizes the new age becomes the context in which elements of scarcity and competition maintain a rightful but secondary place.

We will now highlight three contemporary bi-polar themes, scarcity/abundance, adult/child, and militant/mystic, with the intention of further uncovering and clarifying the ramifications of Paul's doctrine of justification and sanctification for our day.

Scarcity/Abundance: This theme has come to the surface now and again, and deserves fuller development. As we have seen in Chapter Two, anxiety, scarcity, competitive isolation, and a distorted relation with God are features of the old age which came to the fore in the late Middle Ages. The transition we now hope for from this old age to the new age of cooperative relationship dovetails with the transition from oppression to liberation developed in this chapter. In both transitions the underlying assumption changes from one of scarcity to one of abundance. The need always to compete, to possess and to produce more is based on the fear that there will ultimately not be enough. My own share of this world's goods must be secured at all costs, and in this battle ultimately I depend on no one but myself, since all others are pursuing their own survival. At the most I can set up uneasy contractual relations to temper the savagery of this battle. In contrast the basic perspective of cooperation emerges out of a vision of abundance, one which gives primacy to the personal and whose values grow by being shared and distributed to others. The basic structures of the human world ought to be built on this abundance rather than upon scarcity—though, as we shall see, scarcity remains and needs to integrated within the prevailing abundance.

Philip Slater's *Pursuit of Loneliness* makes the point quite vividly: he analyses the emerging shift from "old" to "new" culture in terms of abundance and scarcity:

> The core of the old culture is scarcity. Everything in it rests upon the assumption that the world does not contain the wherewithal to satisfy the needs of its human inhabitants. From this it follows that people must compete with one another for these scarce resources—lie, swindle, steal, and kill, if necessary. These basic assumptions create the danger of a "war of all against all" and must be buttressed by a series of counternorms which attempt to qualify and restrain the intensity of the struggle. Those who can take the largest share of the scarce resources are said to be "successful", and if they can do it without violating the counternorms they are said to have character and moral fibre . . . [89]

> The new culture is based on the assumption that important human needs are easily satisfied and that the resources for doing so are plentiful. Competition is unnecessary and the only danger to humans is human aggression. There is no reason outside of human perversity for peace not to reign and for life not to be spent in the cultivation of joy and beauty . . . [90]

For the old culture, scarcity is the overall context in which abundance is pursued. If goods are not scarce in reality, advertising campaigns will create the illusion that they are scarce.[91] This results in an ever more anxious race to ensure one's own private abundance, which remains as the ever elusive carrot dangling at the end of the stick. The abundance generated within the context of scarcity is a material abundance, a pale and unsatisfying image of abundance on the interpersonal level which alone will satisfy the human hunger.

This does not mean that with entry into the new culture scarcity is abolished. Yes, abundance profoundly marks human living: basic personal values are abundant; as these values reach out to touch more and more people, they do not thin out but rather intensify. But scarcity we will always have with us: the material things which we need for our lives are not in endless supply; they must be used carefully, with attention to the needs of future generations, and they must be distributed equitably. Thus the spontaneity which enables us to give and to receive with no strings attached must share its place with the careful calculation of contractual exchange. To ignore the abundance is to condemn oneself to a life of anxious striving out of touch with a radical security available to everyone; to ignore the scarcity is to live in a world other than the real world. In sum, the passage from the old to the new age is the passage from a situation in which scarcity is dominant, abundance recessive, to one in which abundance is dominant, but scarcity indeed remains as a recessive factor.

One can look at Paul's analysis of old and new age in these terms. Scarcity prevails in the old age. The favour of God is bestowed within a narrow range and the means of drawing this favour to oneself are restricted to the privileged few who can accomplish the works of the law and gain what abundance there is. Justification reverses the roles of scarcity and abundance. The abundance of the new age becomes the central fact. Radically God's favour is open to all. Yet the old age still remains until the parousia, which means that within the between-time and its context of abundance, scarcity still has to be dealt with. Indeed the measure for the genuinity of abundance is the willingness of abundance to empty itself out in scarcity, trusting that it will never be exhausted. "Give, and it will be given to you, good measure, pressed down, shaken together, running over, will be put in your lap. For the measure you give will be the measure you get back." (Lk 6:37-38)

Let us from this perspective look more closely at what happens when justification takes place. The Pharisees' law is a scarce resource. To possess it securely one must be able to look down on others who do not possess it. This illusory scarcity is shattered in the justification experience: one enters into the realm of radical abundance, of salvation available to all, Jews as well as Gentiles, because of a saviour who died for all human beings while they were still sinners. One enters into and is transformed by the mystery of God giving himself unrestrictedly. One passes from radical insecurity to radical security because nothing on earth can separate us from the abundance which is in Christ Jesus. This insecurity can take many forms. It is repressed by the pharisaic conscience which has built air-tight defenses around its neat legal system; it painfully protrudes in the earlier Augustine, inhabited by anxious restlessness, and in the earlier Luther, driven by anxious striving. In the contemporary person it may emerge as the rigidity and narrowness of a neurotic work-ethic. Achievement in matters that ultimately are insignificant becomes an addiction.

The illusory abundance of the Corinthian enthusiasts is based upon the first fruits of salvation which they received, first fruits manifested in their own personal experiences of the Spirit and in the power and warmth which permeated their coterie. They focused upon this narrow circle and blocked out the wider circle in which the anguish and incompleteness of our world is so obvious: injustices, oppressions, people who lay burdens on themselves and on others. They refused to deal with their own continuing incompleteness. The modern counterpart to this would be found among those people who seek liberation and fulfillment through the techniques of psychic and interpersonal integration, who cultivate prayer experiences for their own sake, without being in solidarity with the wider world marked by injustice and suffering.

Adulthood/Childhood: This particular contrast is rooted in both contemporary and traditional themes. Let us start with the contemporary. The new culture, Slater tells us, is culturally neotenous, i.e. it tends to retain and foster earlier juvenile characteristics: "behaviour, values and life-styles formerly seen as appropriate only to childhood are being retained into adulthood as a counterforce to the old culture."[92] "Competition, invidiousness, status-seeking, authoritarianism" are replaced by "spontaneity, hedonism, candor, playfulness, use of the senses for pleasure rather than utility, and so on."[93] Thus the passage from the old to the new is a passage from adulthood to childhood, a going back, a rebirth, a recovery of spontaneity.

The image of justification is a legal, business-like, "adult" one, but many other New Testament images for the same process of entry into the Kingdom evoke a regression, a re-tracing of one's steps, a return to a more primitive state. Unless you are reborn, regenerated (Jn 3: the verb carries both meanings), unless you become like little children (Mt 18:3), you cannot enter into the Kingdom of God. In an attempt to ascertain the import of Paul's doctrine, (1) we shall in a first step turn to justification by faith and by contrasting it with justification by works show that it does indeed entail a re-gression, a return to the primitive side of man, as in other New Testament images, and (2) in a second step, by relating justification to sanctification, we shall show that this re-gression is not a return to the naïvetés and undifferentiation of childhood, to the ambiguities and dangers of primitivism, but it implies a new integration of childhood and adulthood.[94]

1. In a real sense justification by faith stands for the simple trusting attitude of the child, of the "primitive", and justification by works represents the veneer of adult sophistication covering over repressed anxiety about self and distrust of God. In his polemic against the judaizers Paul opposes a relationship with God which is like a good business transaction: "I have fulfilled my end of the bargain, now you come through with yours." Even more, in laying claims on God the judaizer is not just acting like a pursuant in a legal case, but he is also the judge, not immediately of God (though this is ultimately implied), but at least of others whom he supposes do not have the inheritance of the law which gives him security before God and enhances his status.[95]

What Paul calls for in justification by faith is the "impoverishment" of the child who totally forgets herself and her accomplishments and trusts her parent. The one justified has nothing by which she can lay claim to God's attitude towards her. Yet that God accept her, that God justify her once and for all is a matter of crucial importance to her. A person needs the fulfillment of human friendship in order to be herself, but precisely cannot lay claim to that which she so desperately needs, for to receive it other than as a totally free, unclaimed gift is not to receive it at all. Likewise the same person is totally dependent on God's radical acceptance of her if she is to be fulfilled, but to fulfill her this acceptance must be free on God's part, radically undeserved and unowed to her, unmotivated by any contractual or manipulative gesture on her part. In other words, we are not in the realm of the business relationship, with its juridical claims and counter-claims, but in a realm of personal exchange which is keynoted by spontaneity and abundance. By a deep paradox, I am openness to a gift which I can in no way claim for myself. I totally thrust myself upon, entrust myself to God and God's mercy. My gift to God is to become a child rather than cling to my adulthood, to let go of the illusion of contractual self-sufficiency; but that gift is already God's gift to me, God's free justifying grace embodied in my response.

2. Perhaps a sense of one-sidedness has gradually been growing in the reader. May the justified Christian use the abundance of his justification as a shield to protect himself against having to deal with the very real scarcities which remain within himself and the world? Is justification a return to primitivism with its ambiguous innocence? Is there no place within the Christian life for the serious, 'adult' side represented by faithful and disciplined commitment to a law? What about the 'not yet' side affirmed by those who at great cost strive for social justice in an unbalanced world? Is there no place for it in the theology of Paul? Though we must become as care-free as little children, are we not also enjoined, each one of us, to take up his own cross and follow Christ (Mt 10:38; 16:24–26)?[96]

No more than Slater does Paul advocate a simple regression to childhood. Rebirth, return to childhood is but the first step in a "way" which leads to the integration of childhood and adulthood. Grasped by the abundance of God, we are called to realistically deal with the remaining scarcities of our life as we reach out to grasp for the prize which is in Christ Jesus (cf. Phil 3:12–14).[97]

In brief, for Paul a justification which fails to open out to sanctification is inauthentic. In dealing with the judaizers he stressed the "already now" dimensions of the Christ-event: there is no need to strive actively and anxiously for a justice of our own making because God's justice has already appeared in Christ, and the *eschaton* is already upon us. But in dealing with the Corinthian community Paul stressed the corresponding "not yet" dimension. Drunk with the wine of their own justification experience, glorying in their new-found freedom, they failed to see the toilsome and painful path that lay ahead (1 Cor 9:24-27). For their benefit Paul had to spell out the better way, the way of the cross, the way of a love that finds its fullest expression in the midst of limitations, turmoil, ambiguity.

The radical abundance of justification brings total freedom, but out of that freedom Christians have to choose their particular self-commitment, and in a world marked by scarcity this will entail self-limitation (1 Cor 9:19–23).[98] Everything is lawful (justification perspective), but not everything builds up the kingdom (sanctification perspective) (1 Cor 10:21). The universal must embody itself in the particular.[99]

Once having passed through the "regression" of justification, the Christian has to take on a life of adult responsibility: "you should make every part of your body into a weapon fighting on the side of God; and then sin will no longer dominate your life, since you are living by grace and not by law" (Rom 6:13–14). "Now you must put your bodies at the service of righteousness for your sanctification" (Rom 6:19). The *eschaton* has already begun to exist in the heart of the Christian: this is her justification. But the old world of sin has not yet been done away with, and the Christian must take up a continual struggle with its power, she groans inwardly as she waits for her body, her world, to be set free (Rom 7:18–25). Thus the child of God must also be an adult; the newly born "primitive" who rejoices in the range of her new spontaneities must enter into a world of serious disciplined endeavour, working out her salvation in fear and trembling (Phil 2:12), having to render account for the talents that have been entrusted to her. In justification she is called upon not to *give up* her adulthood, the seriousness exemplified in the life of the zealous Pharisee, but to *let go* of it, to set it within the broader context to which it belongs, that of God's abundant grace, allowing it to bear real fruit, fruit unto salvation (Rom 6:20–23).

In sum we are called to let go of our adult state and become like little children in order to reappropriate that same adult state. To be a childish adult is a contradiction in terms; to be a childlike adult is to walk the path of genuine sanctification.

Militant/Mystic: This variant of the adult/child theme will help us to achieve a better perception of how the current transition from the old to the new age generates its own brand of judaizers and enthusiasts, of false liberators and oppressed become oppressors.

Like Reich in *The Greening of America*, Slater is keenly aware of the tensions which reside within the movement towards the new culture. Within it a split separates:

outward, political change from internal, psychological transformation. The first requires confrontation, revolutionary action, and radical commitment to changing the structure of modern industrial society. The second involves a renunciation of that society in favor of the cultivation of inner experience and pleasing internal feeling-states.[100]

The first strand is task-oriented, partakes of some old-culture traits such as postponement of gratification and preoccupation with power. It seems to be marked by future eschatology: the final state has not yet arrived, we must tighten our belts to make it come true. The second strand is a "salvation now" approach. It is less contaminated with old-culture values, but at the same time is far less realistic in dealing with a broken and suffering world, neotenous values having become an excuse for flight from adulthood. Both strands distort the relationship of abundance and scarcity.

The militant who is out of touch with the mystical side valiantly tries to overcome the injustices of the old culture, but in too narrow a way, because she fails to question at a sufficiently radical level the old-culture priority of scarcity over abundance. In her efforts to change the old culture she is caught up in characteristic old-culture distortions such as competition, violence, aggression. Her temptation is to disregard human values in the pursuit of human values. Thus her revolution is doomed before it starts:

> The dilemma of the radical, then, is that she is likely to be corrupted if she fights the *status quo* on its own terms, but is not permitted to fight it in any other way. And even if she succeeds in solving this dilemma, after a lifetime spent altering the power structure, won't she become old-culture—utilitarian, invidious, scarcity-oriented, future-centered, and so on? Having made the world safe for the enlightened, can she afford to relinquish it to them?[101]

The mystic who is out of touch with the militant side is "turned on" by features of abundance in the new culture and blocks evidences of scarcity out of his awareness. He seeks expanded consciousness, vivid experiences. He creates his cozy little island of comfort, not realizing that he is still in an antagonistic milieu in which he must survive in a state of highly vulnerable dependence.[102] Refusing to pro-gress into childlikeness, he re-gresses into childishness.

The mystic is right in stressing the primacy of abundance, but wrong if he denies the real scarcities of the world in which we live and the need to use effective power to overcome them. The militant is right in stressing the need for effective power, but is easily caught up in the assumption of scarcity which haunts the old culture she is trying to change. If they establish a relation of interdependence on each other, the mystic and the militant will find their own true nature and real effectiveness. It is in being integrated as parts of a whole that the parts are truly themselves as parts. It is in letting go of an illusory isolation that they find their unique value. Militancy must be grounded in mysticism. Mysticism must lead to militancy.

The above can be put into clear theological terms. The "mystical" state is that of the one who has been justified. Justification ushers one into the inner realm of pure receptivity, of primal simplicity, of unquestioning abundance. It enables one to be firmly anchored and deeply at peace because of what God has already done in Christ Jesus. Already now the justice of God, expected as the end-fulfillment, has been revealed, the justice of God which justifies us (Rom 3:21–26). Already now, even in the midst of tribulation, the love of God has been poured into our hearts (Rom 5:1–11). Through justification, one enters already now into the world to come. But if the justification is genuine, it calls to a life of toil and commitment within this present age. The "militant" state is that of the one who seeks the prize of the upward call in Christ Jesus, straining between the starting post of justification and the finishing line of salvation. If properly grounded in justification, its works are practical, earnest, yet not anxious, since the victory has already been won; it confronts injustice and oppression not with hatred and naked power but relies on the force of suffering and love. In this light the judaizer and the enthusiast, like the militant and the mystic, persist in refusing the complementarity of their indispensable partner, of the aspect of themselves which they relegate to the shadow-side of their psyche.

Recapitulation: We will now conclude our efforts to transpose Paul's theological discourse on justification and sanctification out of his era into our own, beginning with the diagram on p. 135.

In the first two columns we list the distortions combated by Paul and a number of contemporary authors, which consist in affirming one value to the detriment of its polar opposite. The third column depicts the synthesis of the two. The first mentioned member of each pair is the dominant, the second the recessive member.

The foundational categories of oppressor and oppressed remain in the background of this diagram. The first two columns refer to persons who have already begun the journey towards the new humanity, if only imperfectly. Thus this diagram, like our presentation thus far, is not so much about the oppressor in his primordial state as about the false liberator who still keeps his

ALREADY NOW	NOT YET	ALREADY NOW → NOT YET
Corinthians (enthusiasts)	Galatians (judaizers)	Justified → sanctified → saved (Paul's view)
Abundance without prior scarcity	Scarcity without prior abundance	Abundance → Scarcity → Abundance
Oppressed turned Oppressor	False Liberator	Genuine Liberator
inner (heart)	outer (body)	inner → outer
Mystic	Militant	Mystic → Militant
Child (childish)	Adult	Child → Adult (childlike)
spontaneity (permissiveness)	order (discipline)	spontaneity → order
false universality	undue limitation	universality → self-limitation
quietism	anxious striving	passivity → activity (operating → cooperating grace)

oppressive ways, not so much about the oppressed *tout court* as about the oppressed caught in the illusion of having made the grade because she enjoys the momentary triumph of being an oppressor. Only in the third column is oppression overcome by liberation. The false mystic of the first column finds herself oppressing not only the side of herself that needs the structures of responsible action, but also those who in their weakness still hang on to structures and laws for dear life. The militant is out of touch with the spontaneous, mystic, childlike side of himself, and oppresses others by laying unnecessary burdens upon them.

The diagram depicts where each group stands in terms of scarcity and abundance. The enthusiast mistakes the down payment for the final installment, the inbreaking of already now abundance for the pleroma. Thus there is no scarcity, only abundance. The judaizer lives in a context of scarcity within which he pursues a final abundance he will never attain. The integrated person receives the gift of an initial abundance, but lets go of it, fully entering into a world of scarcity, knowing that at the end of the struggle she will be given her full part in the pleroma which already dwells within her heart. Integration occurs in the kenotic pattern of abundance followed by scarcity followed by abundance.

The inner/outer duality corresponds to the Pauline heart/body, or to the transition from pneuma and psyche to soma and world. The false mystic is too concerned with his inner spiritual and psychic states, where he has already begun to feel the love of God poured into his heart, and achieves an integration which is turned in on itself and self-enclosed. The false militant is too concerned with the not yet, insufficiently attentive to the well-springs of her action within her own redeemed pneuma and psyche.

Central to both false mystic and false militant is a failure of incarnation, of an incarnation which in Pauline terms is a *kenosis*. The false mystic gets stuck in the universal transcendent perspective generated by the experience of initial rebirth. The whole world appears new, everything becomes possible. But actuality implies particularity, this rather than that, a very concrete destiny which eventually comes to a point of nothingness in death. The false mystic's celebration of life is ultimately a refusal to live because it is a refusal of the movement towards death which is a concomitant of life. It is a refusal to be embodied and become vulnerable. The failure of the false militant offers a striking contrast. In her case there is nothing to embody, nothing to be vulnerable about. She has not opened herself to the gift of the wider perspective within which kenosis becomes possible. She is wedded to the particular and the concrete: this law, this observance, this revolutionary cause; but the particular becomes an obsessive reality since it is not situated within a context of liberating transcendence. That reality embodies nothing, points to nothing beyond itself. It is inert and monadic rather than alive. Neurotic rigidity and *rigor mortis* are first cousins. This rigidity brings defenders of the first world's old mechanistic order and second world Marxian revolutionaries into a profound kinship.

CONCLUSION: PAUL'S LESSON FOR OUR DAY

Paul's role in the theology of grace as it has developed within the Church of the West is seminal, so much so that in principle our task has been achieved with this chapter. A thorough grasp of his theology and of its ramifications would suffice to offer a solid theological underpinning and justification for the wide-ranging Aquarian conspiracy of our day, in which many seek to go behind the impasses and inauthenticities which characterize our first world to find the seeds of a new order in the authentic values latent in the Western tradition. A thorough grasp of Paul's theological efforts to overcome the distortions which hampered his communities will give us a powerful tool with which to unmask and dismantle the distortions of our own world. However chapters on Augustine and Aquinas, and dialogue with other creative figures of the first world theology of grace—I am thinking above all of Luther—will help us immeasurably in this task.

In brief, what emerges from this study of Paul is that an incisive theology of grace for the first world will be apocalyptic, social, cruciform, and dialectical.

a) *Apocalyptic*: The broad context of Paul's thought was apocalyptic and the deep issue at stake within his communities was the proper understanding of God's *eschaton*. To what extent is the end already upon us, and to what extent does it still lie before us? The urgency of Paul's theology of grace was bound up with the imminence of a new age towards which the Christian was called to take a stance at the same time utterly passionate and utterly disciplined. This stance Paul tried to describe in all its paradoxical subtlety. He would not countenance a comfortable theology of grace, one that settles in, gets caught up in narrow concerns and closes itself to the wider vision, one that exclusively focuses on the private salvation of individuals. The gentle yet urgent demands of the living God encompass absolutely everything in the human world, everything in the cosmos. Fortunately the cries of our world, broken, on the brink of catastrophe, dimly aware of the apocalyptic nature of the struggle it is engaged in, are so loud that we cannot stop our ears. The cosmic vision of Paul will help us discern the voice of God in those cries, a God who in the earthly Jesus came to birth in our world and invited us to come to birth, a God who in the cosmic Christ is still engaged in the great act of giving birth to the new world. Thus the apocalyptic emphasis of Paul's thought on grace is not an exotic affectation we can afford to ignore: it is central to the issues of our world and ought to be at the heart of our theology.

b) *Social*: Paul's theology of grace above all flows from the down-to-earth pastoral concerns evoked by conflicts within his communities. Those of us who are accustomed to an approach to grace which is exclusively intimate and personal ought to learn from Paul that apart from interaction with the human world, with its ambiguities and failings, grace is not grace: it fails the test of cruciform love. Again we are called to the broader perspective. Grace is not just a matter of personal transformation but it encompasses and touches all the networks, social, political, economic, cultural, which define our interaction as human beings. It does this, however, not by offering a detailed blueprint and specific means for rapidly resolving conflict and ushering in a society without tension, but also without diversity. It offers the only available strategy for the transformation that would meet our deepest longings: a life lived out according to the pattern of Jesus' *kenosis*; the welcoming of diversity and plurality and tension as a source of enrichment on the way to a fulfillment which will always in the end elude merely human efforts.

c) *Cruciform*: Paul's recasting of apocalyptic, as we saw, led him to formulate the dynamic of grace by means of the triad of justification, sanctification, salvation. As we saw briefly in Chapter Two, and will see in more detail in subsequent chapters, this approach has proved foundational for later theologies of grace.

The apocalyptic context helps us define the tension within which Christians are to lead their lives as cruciform. We are able to see ourselves as caught between the vertical relation to a God who is *already now* present and the horizontal relation to a God we have *not yet* encountered, not having come to the end of our journey through the labyrinths of time.

d) *Dialectical*: In dealing with the unfolding of God's grace within our world, Paul uses a dialectical model which theologies of grace have only begun to exploit. This model, via Luther and Hegel, has led to the oppressor/oppressed dynamic central to Karl Marx's analysis and, derivatively, to Paulo Freire's pedagogy. The content and the context of this dynamic is quite different for Paul of Tarsus and Karl Marx, but there are significant affinities between Paulo Freire and Paul of Tarsus, and the resulting model for grace offers us a way of concretely describing the dynamic of healing and humanizing grace at work in the twentieth century. Grace heals by overcoming dichotomies and oppressive structures at all levels of our existence, ranging all the way from those embedded in our wayward hearts to those which poison our world. In this way it breaks the vicious circle of moral impotence and opens the path for genuine interchange and progress.

As we saw, the forms of oppression and of liberation that mark all aspects of the human reality are intimately linked. The dialectical approach of Marxism is not something simply to be cast aside as we struggle for an understanding of how grace is to act in the first world. Rather that approach must be purified by contact with its authentic and life-giving roots in the thought of Paul of Tarsus and broadened in its applications. This task has been begun by theologians of liberation out of the third world. It is to be continued by them as well as by theologians out of the first world. Fretful anxiety that theology will be infiltrated by Marxian categories if it enters into such a project must be replaced by a confidence that what is good in Marx comes out of the deepest and most authentic Christian tradition, and will find a powerful corrective in that tradition.

This implies that in final analysis we cannot independently of the liberation theme and the dialectical structures articulated by third world theologians come up with a description of the dynamic of grace needed to counteract the plight of the first world. To attempt this would be to fall into the typical first world trap of sterile self-sufficiency. If we truly believe that salvation and insight comes in a privileged way from the weak and oppressed, those who are nothing in the eyes of the powerful (1 Cor 1:26–31), we will heed what comes from the hearts and minds of theologians whose primary experience is that of an oppressed world. However we wish to name the dynamic of grace needed for our world, unless that name is spoken within the encompassing dialectical context the third world urges upon us, it will be fruitless.

Put more concretely—and this point will be developed at greater length later on in this book—Freire tells us that both the oppressor and the oppressed suffer in the oppressive structure. Both are dehumanized, but in different ways. The dehumanization of the first world, caught up in the illusion of power created by its technological and advertising expertise, calls for a dynamic of grace for which to liberate is most concretely and immediately to empower. That empowerment is to touch and transform a world which is oppressing rather than oppressed, taking away the rigid and obsessive self-consciousness which paralyses its best efforts to achieve human fulfillment, enabling it to appropriate its own authentic reality as it dialogues with the rest of humankind. At the same time, given the cruciform tension of the already now and the not yet, that empowerment calls forth as its indispensable complement the patience that enables us to sustain ambiguity and offers us the only access to the mystery of the living God.

NOTES

1. J.C. Beker, *Paul the Apostle. The Triumph of God in Life and Thought* (Philadelphia: Fortress, 1980).

2. Address of Oct. 18, 1978. Also cf. the dramatic ending of the homily John Paul II pronounced in Edmonton on Sept. 17, 1984, during his visit to Canada.

3. Both articles appear in translation in *New Testament Questions of Today* (Philadelphia: Fortress, 1969).

4. J.C. Beker, *Paul's Apocalyptic Gospel: The Coming Triumph of God* (Philadelphia: Fortress, 1982), p. 15.

5. Paul D. Hansen, *The Dawn of Apocalyptic* (Philadelphia: Fortress, 1975), pp. 11–12; Walter Schmithals, *Die Apokalyptik: Einführung und Deutung* (Göttingen: Vandenhoeck und Ruprecht, 1973), p. 60. C. Rowland in *The Open Heaven. A Study of Apocalyptic in Judaism and Early Christianity* (London: SPCK, 1982), tells us that there are other dimensions to apocalyptic than the ones Beker singles out in his enu-

meration. He stresses the revelational dimension, the access of the apocalyptic seer to the mysteries of God through visions.

6. Cf. Karl Kertelge, *Rechtfertigung bei Paulus* (Münster: Aschendorff, 1967).

7. Beker in *Paul the Apostle* discusses the relationship between Pharisaic and apocalyptic Judaism, and claims that in spite of their differences they are convergent rather than divergent. Sharp differences between them emerge only after the destruction of the temple. Cf. pp. 137 ff.

8. Our source here is Otto Kuss, in *Der Römerbrief* (Regensburg: Pustet, 1963), p. 290 (under Rom 5:21).

9. Cf. Kertelge, *Rechtfertigung* . . . , pp. 134–136.

10. For Schmithals this shift implies the reaffirmation of the view of the mainline canonical prophets, for which God does indeed act *within* this world and its history, rather than simply abolish it in favour of the new age. Cf. *Die Apokalyptik* . . . , pp. 60–61, 120–129. However the action of God within this world is already the new age coming into being. Christianity incorporates essential elements of apocalypticism within canonical eschatological thought.

11. Could we say that Paul's own stance towards this final act of God changed in the course of his apostolic career? For Beker Paul was consistently apocalyptic from the beginning to the end of his career. Others are more willing to postulate an evolution within Paul (*Paul the Apostle*, p. 142). For them the early Paul's sense of imminent *parousia* became less concrete and intense as his wait for God's final triumph become longer and as some members of his communities died without having participated in it. Thus Paul's theology of grace evolved as it began to address itself to the situation of a community settling in for the long haul. We will not attempt to resolve this matter here, but would offer two comments.

a) There is ample evidence in the Pauline corpus for differences of perspective between Paul and his communities. Could we have an instance of this here? Just as Jesus during his public ministry laboured mightily to correct wrong Messianic/apocalyptic notions, so too Paul might have been doing the same with his own communities, trying to counteract their preoccupation with the timetable of the Lord's final manifestation, transforming it into a more spiritual imminence. Thus if evolution there is, it may occur not so much within Paul as within his communities.

b) Could it be that since the passion and resurrection of Jesus Christ already essentially fulfilled the promise of God, the question of how long one had to wait for the *parousia* became less and less significant? In this perspective, the sense of imminence is derived from the massive impact of Jesus' resurrection from the dead rather than from artful calculations concerning the future (cf. Schmithals, *Die Apokalyptik*, p. 124).

12. The trajectory of this movement leads to the classical doctrine of the Trinity, but that is not our concern here.

13. This influence can be described meta-sociologically as that of two political spheres of power vying for dominance, or meta-physically as that of two magnetic fields which exercise their force of attraction upon the same object. Paul would be very much attuned to the first image, since the relation of different urban classes to Roman

authority was a significant part of his experience, and images from urban life readily flow from his pen. The second image is beyond his ken, but it is not unhelpful.

14. Schmithals, *Die Apokalyptik*, p. 170.

15. In the classic debate on whether Romans 7:7–25 refers to the conflict of good and evil within the unredeemed human being or within the Christian, basically I side with the first position, adopted, among others, by Beker (*Paul the Apostle*, p. 238). What convinces me of this, more than all else, is the transition from Chapter 7 to Chapter 8. However this does not imply the absence of conflict within redeemed Christians. Since the ultimate victory of Christ has already touched them, they experience the conflict as hope-filled tribulation, agony. In contrast, the conflict within the unredeemed is without hope because the power of sin prevails. Luther applied Romans 7 to the conflictual *simul justus et peccator* state of the Christian. His distinction of *peccatum regnans* (in the unredeemed) and *peccatum regnatum* (in the redeemed), however, can be taken to be quite compatible with the other position on Romans 7.

16. Cf. E. Schillebeeckx, *Christ, the Experience of Jesus as Lord* (Seabury: New York, 1980), p. 144, for a more ample treatment of this point.

17. For a fuller development of this theme cf. Kertelge, *Rechtfertigung* . . . , pp. 134, 160.

18. In the deutero-Pauline epistles the Christian initially participates in the death and resurrection as one event. Cf. Schillebeeckx, *Christ* . . . , p. 155.

19. The term Paul uses, *thlipsis*, refers precisely to the struggle of the end-time, e.g. in Rom 5:1–5.

20. Beker, *Paul the Apostle*, pp. 42–43.

21. Ibid., p. 44. A variant of this opinion is that the judaizing opponents of Paul seeking to undermine his work with the predominantly Gentile congregations in Galatia were themselves not Jewish Christians but Gentile Christians. Cf. Johannes Munck, *Paul and the Salvation of Mankind* (London: SCM, 1959), ch. 4.

22. Schillebeeckx, *Christ* . . . , p. 123. Cf. p. 166 as well, where a similar claim is made concerning Philippians 3.

23. According to Beker, *Paul the Apostle*, pp. 41–58, Paul takes a more polemical and negative view of the law in this letter than he does in Romans.

24. Ibid., p. 53.

25. Ibid., p. 58.

26. Munck rightly points out that these parties are not hard and fast theological factions but simply the outcome of bickering for non-theological reasons. Cf. *Paul* . . . , pp. 135–139.

27. G. Theissen, *The Social Setting of Pauline Christianity* (Philadelphia: Fortress, 1982).

28. W. Meeks, *The First Urban Christians: The Social World of the Apostle Paul* (New Haven: Yale University Press, 1983).

29. Meeks, *The First* . . . , ch. 2, esp. p. 73; Theissen, *The Social Setting* . . . , ch.2, esp. pp. 69, 106 ff.

30. Meeks, *The First* . . . .

31. The timing of the letter of the Philippians seems to be a matter of greater dispute than that of the other letters we have analyzed. If it was written in Rome during Paul's captivity there, it would come later. However there is a strong current of opinion that would put it fairly early, together with 1 Corinthians and Galatians, and before Romans. Our own analysis in effect argues for the rough contemporaneity of 1 Cor and Phil. These two letters concur in their kenotic emphasis, expressed more christologically in Philippians, more practically in Corinthians.

32. We make no attempt to determine at what points Paul may have modified or added to the original version of the hymn.

33. Paul is not talking about a process in which Christ exchanges the form of God for the form of man, but rather one in which being in the form of God he takes on the form of man.

34. For a fuller development of this topic, with reference to contemporary psychological literature, see my article "Kenosis Old and New" in *The Ecumenist*, 1974, pp. 17–21.

35. This first stage is affirmed by many exegetes, e.g. R.G. Fuller in *The Foundations of New Testament Christology* (London: Collins, 1965), p. 207. Others however dispute it. They see in the text a straight contrast between the earthly and the risen Christ. While the second position better fits the literary structure of the hymn, there is in the description of the earthly Jesus' kenotic life the intimation of a prior "stage" in which the original emptying out took place. While the text does not speak of pre-existence in clear words, its images begin to point in that direction.

36. For Karl Rahner the human nature of the risen Christ is not just an appendage without rhyme or reason, but essential in the continuing mediation of grace and vision. Cf. "Dogmatic Questions on Easter", *Theological Investigations*, Vol. 4 (London: Darton, Longman, & Todd, 1966), pp. 121–133.

37. This is also found in 2 Cor, but mainly in reference to the strength/weakness of his own apostolic career: 2 Cor 3:4; 6:10; and 8:9.

38. Also cf. Rom 8:17; Phil 3:11.

39. This theme is masterfully developed by Martin Luther:

> So a Christian, like Christ his head, is filled and made rich by faith and should be content with this form of God which he has obtained by faith; only, as I have said, he should increase this faith until it is made perfect . . . Although the Christian is thus free from all works, he ought in this liberty to empty himself, take upon himself the form of a servant, be made in the likeness of men, be found in human form, and to serve, help, and in every way deal with his neighbour as he sees that God through Christ has dealt and still deals with him (*Christian Liberty*, edited by H.J. Grimm [Philadelphia: Fortress, 1957], 29).

Luther does not give the same importance to the corresponding movement of exaltation, which culminates in a divine/human integration.

40. Another facet which could be developed is that of the upward movement as a reaching out for a goal, a striving upwards, a race. The image is found in both 1 Cor 9:24–27 and Phil 3:12–16. In it justification implies a receptivity to God's action, whereas sanctification implies our response to that action, a struggle, a co-operation. The initial moment of inward transformation is a passive one; the subsequent life, in which we make ourselves and the world in the image of Christ, is an eminently active one, grounded, however, in the prior action of God on our behalf.

41. This striking proportionality between justification/sanctification and form of God/form of a servant is found in the Luther text quoted above. The whole structure of Luther's treatise is kenotic, as we can see from its opening thesis. The Christian who is the perfectly free lord of all corresponds to Christ Jesus in his original lordship; the Christian who is the perfectly dutiful servant of all corresponds to the Christ Jesus who divests himself of that Lordship to take on the form of servanthood.

42. Paulo Freire, *Pedagogy of the Oppressed* (New York: Herder and Herder, 1971).

43. This basic distinction will be analyzed more thoroughly in Chapter 5 on Aquinas. He uses the terms a) healing and b) elevating, but the context clearly shows that what he means is grace enabling human beings to achieve a) what is proportionate to their own nature (thus humanizing them) and b) what totally exceeds their nature because it pertains to God alone (thus divinizing them).

44. Freire, *Pedagogy* . . . , pp. 44–45. Cf. also a telling quotation of Erich Fromm on p. 64. In his analysis of the contemporary American scene, Philip Slater says: "Old-culture Americans are peculiarly drawn to anything that seems to be the exclusive possession of some group or other, and they find it difficult to enjoy anything unless they can be sure that there are people to whom this pleasure is denied." (*Pursuit* . . . , p. 117)

45. Freire, *Pedagogy* . . . , p. 33.

46. Ibid., p. 51.

47. Chapter One, p. 25.

48. The fuller analysis of the sources and context of Freire's thought is beyond our scope. Such analysis would look into the affinities between his use of the having/being binomial and that of the French Christian existentialist Gabriel Marcel. It would likely deal with the striking convergences between the views which emerge in his book and those which emerge, for instance, in Charles Hampden-Turner's *Radical Man* (New York: Doubleday, 1971), in which normal psycho-social development (p. 37) and anomie (p. 79) are compared.

49. Freire, *Pedagogy* . . . , pp. 46–47, 53–54, 121.

50. Ibid., pp. 30, 43, 49, 121.

51. Ibid., pp. 71–74, 119–123.

52. Ibid., pp. 36–37.

53. One could draw an instructive parallel between this process and the description by Paul of the movement towards justification which involves, in Chapter 7 of

144 PATIENCE AND POWER

Romans, the paroxysmic heightening of the awareness of one's plight prior to being delivered from the body of sin and death through Jesus Christ.

54. Ibid., p. 52.

55. Ibid., p. 77.

56. The Canadian political philosopher and economist Abraham Rotstein has accounted for part of this genealogy in his studies of the roots of Marx in Luther, and, more fundamentally, in Paul. Cf. "The Apocalyptic Tradition: Luther and Marx", in *Political Theology in the Canadian Context*, edited by B. Smillie (Waterloo: WLU Press, 1982), pp. 146–208. The basic Marxian structures of Freire's thought are easy to pick out: the overriding goal of overcoming a situation in which many people are alienated, kept in subjection, exploited; the analysis of social and economic forces in terms of oppressors and oppressed, the heightening of oppression by the process of conscientization, are all rooted in Marx. Marx's debt to Hegel's doctrine of the master/slave dialectic, of alienation and sublation, of the resolution of thesis and antithesis by means of synthesis, is well known. What for Hegel is part and parcel of an idealist philosophy becomes for Marx something materialist, down-to-earth, with far-reaching consequences. The next step in this backward journey is Martin Luther, whose dialectical and paradoxical cast of thought very much influenced Hegel, especially in his younger years, when theological concerns were uppermost in his mind. Specifically the Hegelian master-slave dialectic which re-emerges in Marx and Freire in terms of oppressor/oppressed is central to Luther's programmatic *Christian Liberty* in which this dialectic is interiorized, adapted to the struggle of Christians to find a gracious God. They are at once masters of all because of their justification by faith and slaves to all because in sanctification they put themselves at the service of their neighbours, much after the pattern of Christ, as we saw in a text quoted earlier in this chapter. This brings us back to Paul of Tarsus, the first thinker in the Christian tradition to work out for us an approach to God and humankind which is at once dynamic and dialectical.

57. On this point, cf. Krister Stendahl, *Paul among Jews and Gentiles* (Philadelphia: Fortress, 1976), pp. 3–5.

58. Rom 9:4–5. Also cf. Rom 3:1–2.

59. These points are very aptly developed by Beker, *Paul the Apostle . . .* , Chapter 15, esp. pp. 335–337.

60. Gal 3:27-28. Cf. similar passages in Gal 5:6; 6:15; 2 Cor 5:17–21. The same theme emerges in the deutero-Pauline epistles: Col 3:10–11; Eph 2:11–16.

61. Robert Doran, in *Psychic Conversion and Theological Foundations: Towards a Reorientation of the Human Sciences* (Chico: Scholars Press, 1981) offers a clear delineation between psyche and pneuma. For him the psyche and the pneuma are distinct as are the realm of the sensitive consciousness (the Lonerganian term) or appetite (the traditional term) from the realm of the intellective (cf. pp. 29, 147). In my particular approach, the key distinction is between the implicit subject as subject (pneuma) and everything else, whether latent or explicit, whether intellective or sensitive. In practice these latter distinctions imply no separation. They occur within a field of consciousness of which the central focus is a spiritual self-presence. Only when the par-

ticularly human form of pneuma (*"infimus in genere intelligibilium"*, Aquinas would call it) relates to sensory input coming from its organismic environment can and does it function with an explicit focus.

62. The issue nowadays is not so simple. While the ideal of a certain type of physics may be to get as "objective" a grasp of the "universe in itself" as possible, now we know that there is no such a thing as an act of measuring which does not in some sense change the physical situation which it measures.

63. A more technical formulation of this influx/outflux can be found in Chapter 6 of Laporte, *Les structures dynamiques . . .* , pp. 179–189.

64. R.D. Laing and A. Esterson's *Sanity, Madness, and the Family* (Harmondsworth: Penguin Books, l970), among many books, analyses this kind of relationship. R.D. Laing's *Knots* (Harmondsworth: Penguin Books, 1970) presents a number of double bind situations in which adults alienate each other and destroy the possibility of any healthy and growthful interaction between themselves. In his *Politics of Experience* (Harmondsworth: Penguin, 1967), he states:

> In over 100 cases where we have studied the actual circumstances around the social event when one person comes to be regarded as schizophrenic, it seems to us that *without exception* the experience and behaviour that gets labelled schizophrenic is *a special strategy that a person invents in order to live in an unlivable situation.* In his life situation the person has come to feel he is in an untenable position. He cannot make a move, or make no move, without being beset by contradictory and paradoxical pressure and demands, pushes and pulls, both internally, from himself, and externally, from those around him. He is, as it were, in a position of checkmate (p. 95).

This emphasis on I/thou relations should not be construed as implying a denial of the role of patterns of we/they alienation within society upon the incidence of mental illness. Though more indirect, the effect of the latter is nonetheless broad and pervasive.

65. *Confessions*, 8,5 and 8,9.

66. H. Fingarette, *The Self in Transformation. Psychoanalysis, Philosophy, and the Life of the Spirit* (New York: Harper & Row, 1965), pp. 146–170, esp. pp. 162–170.

67. Ibid., p. 76.

68. Ibid., Chapter 1. Fingarette rejects the view that the unconscious is composed of fully-formed but hidden realities waiting to be teased out by the craft of the therapist (pp. 18 ff). At this point one of the inbuilt limitations of our spatial diagram emerges. It would be equally legitimate to put the ego at the center, the unconscious (including the supra-conscious self or pneuma) at the periphery, which is more exactly descriptive of what happens when their relationship is an oppressive one.

69. Ibid., p. 324.

70. Ibid., p. 319.

71. Ibid., p. 57.

72. Ibid., p. 43.
73. Cf. Eugene Gendlin, "A Theory of Personality Change", in *Personality Change*, edited by P. Worchel and D. Byrne (New York: John Wiley & Sons, 1964), pp. 100–148; and his more recent *Focusing* (New York: Bantam, 1981).
74. R.D. Laing, *The Divided Self. An Existential Study in Sanity and Madness* (Harmondsworth: Penguin, 1965).
75. Ibid., p. 80.
76. Ibid., pp. 106 ff.
77. Ibid., pp. 81–82.
78. In my article "Kenosis Old and New" in *The Ecumenist*, 1974, pp. 17–21, I develop an alternate language of subject as subject (self) and subject as object (ego).
79. The mysterious reality of the human pneuma is best approached by many images, even though mutually exclusive, than by one image alone. The un-conscious straddles between the mysterious self at the center and the unexplicitated areas of the psyche. In distinguishing this mysterious self from that part of the psyche which is made up of the unconscious residue of our relations with other persons and the world, we have adopted the convention of using "supra-conscious" to speak of the pneumatic self and "sub-conscious" to speak of the hidden areas of the psyche.
80. A later step in this process is that of denying existence to this false God, dismissing the urge to find what is beyond the emptiness of the human spirit as an illusion.
81. Cf. Käsemann's "Justification and Salvation History in the Epistle to the Romans", in *Perspectives on Paul*, pp. 72–73.
82. The outstanding development of this theme is found in his *Christian Liberty*. In Paul's view, however, central to our justification is the inhabitation of the human *pneuma* by the divine *pneuma*. At this deepest level God breaks down the oppressive barriers which we ourselves have put up. Luther's fear of appropriating the Spirit as a possession, quite understandable in the light of the excesses current in his day, may have led him to give undue stress, at the expense of the Spirit dwelling inwardly, to the Word breaking in from outside and calling us to dwell outside ourselves, *extra nos*.
83. Paul deals with many different problems in 1 Cor but this letter shows considerable unity. In the prevailing culture, gnostic wisdom was the boast of elite groups, privy to special religious experiences, and so enamored of their freedom, of their distinction from the *hoi polloi*, that they failed to see the very real needs of community members around them.
84. At stake here is the very dynamic of the Gospel which grounds what Macmurray terms the form of the personal and Metz the anthropocentric thought-form (cf. the last section of Chapter Two). In effect both judaizers and enthusiasts in their own way undermine the revelation of God as person.
85. The Freirian analogues are helpful at this point. The false liberator, like the judaizer, goes about the tasks of liberation from the obsolete mindset of the oppressor, wishing to control and to manipulate; the oppressed turned oppressor, like the enthusiast, wallows in what he thinks is triumph, but he has not yet begun the real struggle,

he has not yet embraced the toil and suffering which alone will break down the basic structure of oppression.

86. A similar approach to polarity runs through the work of Macmurray. What characterizes the form of the personal, which he distinguishes from the form of the mechanical and the form of the organic, is the polarity of positive and negative elements which coexist, both equally essential but the positive subordinating to itself and containing its own negative. (*The Self as Agent*, pp. 89, and esp. 98; *Persons in Relation*, pp. 62–63, 69–71).

87. G. Siegwalt's analysis in *La loi, chemin du Salut* (Neuchâtel: Delachaux et Niestlé, 1971), is very helpful in this respect.

88. Cf. pp. 24–25.

89. Slater, *Pursuit of Loneliness*, p. 113.

90. Ibid., p. 114.

91. Ibid., p. 117.

92. Ibid., p. 122.

93. Ibid., pp. 122–123.

94. Some of this material is developed in my article "Grace: The Mystery of God's Abundance", pp. 371–409.

95. Cf. Rom 2 where Paul berates the judaizer for passing judgement on the Gentiles, a prerogative which is God's only. Cf. quotation of Philip Slater in note 44.

96. Edward Edinger, in *Ego and Archetype* (Baltimore: Penguin, 1973), advocates the need for a similar balance in the context of child-rearing. He expresses it in Jungian terms. Permissiveness in his terms corresponds, it seems to me, to the "child" pole, and discipline to the "adult":

> permissiveness emphasizes acceptance and encouragement of the child's spontaneity and nourishes his contact with the source of life energy with which he is born. But it also maintains and encourages the inflation of the child, which is unrealistic to the demands of outer life. Discipline, on the other hand, emphasizes strict limits of behavior, encourages dissolution of the ego-Self identity and treats the inflation quite successfully; but at the same time it tends to damage the vital, necessary connection between the growing ego and its roots in the unconscious. There is no choice between these—they are a pair of opposites, and must operate together. (p. 12)

97. To be grasped corresponds to the passive, receptive attitude characteristic of the child; to grasp corresponds to the active, reaching out attitude characteristic of the adult. Classical theology of grace reflects this in its distinction between operating and cooperating grace: operating grace is God's work in us; cooperating grace is God's work, but also our own. (Cf. Aquinas, *Summa Theologiae*, Ia–IIae, 111, 2.)

98. Edinger describes this process in Jungian terms. One must cease being the *puer aeternus* and become a functional adult:

Such a person (e.g. identified with the *puer aeternus* image) considers himself as a most promising individual. He is full of talents and potentialities. One of his complaints is often that his capacities and interests are too wide-ranging. He is cursed with a plethora of riches . . . The problem is that he is all promises and no fulfillment. In order to make a real accomplishment he must sacrifice a number of other potentialities. He must give up his identification with original unconscious wholeness and voluntarily accept being a real fragment instead of an unreal whole. To be something in reality he must give up being everything *in potentia*. (*Ego and Archetype*, p. 14.)

99. The language of transcendence and limitation provides another way of making this point. (Cf. R. M. Doran, *Psychic Conversion and Theological Foundations*, pp. 139–141, as based on Lonergan, *Insight*, pp. 472 ff.) The only way of unfolding the patterns of one's personhood within the unbounded transcendent horizon which is disclosed in the original event of conversion is to be in touch every step of the way with one's own limitations and particularities. A transcendence which over-reaches itself collapses in on itself. But conversely one can remain stuck in limitation, refuse to budge, expand, unfold beyond the tried and tested routines of what appears to be adulthood but in effect is a compromise.

100. *Pursuit of Loneliness*, p. 124. The first edition of Slater's book used the more precise but dated terms of "militant activism" and "hippie movement". A similar distinction, that of the militant and the mystic, emerges in Harvey Cox's *The Feast of Fools* (Cambridge: Harvard University Press, 1969), ch. 7.

101. Slater, *Pursuit of Loneliness*, p. 126.

102. Ibid., p. 124.

Chapter Four

AUGUSTINE OF HIPPO: GRACE FOR A DYING AGE

Together with other New Testament writings, especially the Johannine corpus, Paul's epistles offer the normative basis for any theology of grace. No one can ignore the forgiveness and healing grace which are stressed by Paul but also found in John, or the divinization and elevating grace which are stressed by John but also found in Paul. While both adhering to this basis, the Eastern Churches have paid more attention to the Johannine patterns, the Western Churches to the Pauline.

The theologian who above all sets the *status quaestionis* of the Western theology of grace is Augustine of Hippo (354–430). His concerns recur in the constant discourse on grace which has marked the Western Church.[1] Paul's doctrine of grace responded to the situations and controversies surrounding the entry of Gentiles into the Church. The quest for personal moral conversion has a place in his theology, but the dominant notes are other: he agonized over the relation of Jew and Gentile, gave prime importance to the shift of allegiance from the law to Jesus Christ and the call to apostleship. Augustine personalizes and universalizes Paul: with a wealth of introspective detail Augustine describes his own conversion from a state of rebellion, of moral impotence, to one of delight in the law of God; and out of his experience he formulates dynamics of grace which apply to the journey towards fulfillment of every human being. At the same time he gives evidence of the balance one ought to expect from a *locus classicus*, in that he makes room in his theology for the Johannine themes of divinization and intimacy with God.[2]

The weighty impact of Augustine upon the Western Church is both positive and negative. He is the first to lay out, with unparalleled depth and loving care, the link between theology of grace and personal experience, especially in his *Confessions* (397–401). In subsequent writings he develops a balanced theology, which includes ringing affirmations of grace as internal, spontaneous, and prevenient, and which is subsequently received by all branches of

149

the Western Church. But the later Augustine hardens his theology of grace in polemical response to Pelagius and his followers. Mesmerized by the short-comings of Pelagius, he fails to incorporate the positive elements of Pelagius' vision. Thus Augustine's strong affirmation of the primordial passivity of humans under grace, also to be found in Paul, is not accompanied by an equal emphasis on the synergy of Christians with God in their life of grace. Augustine's vindication of God's absolute dominion in the life of grace leads him to a vision of a God who arbitrarily bestows his favours upon a chosen few in order to express his mercy, leaving the *massa damnata* to its fate in order to give rein to his just anger. Though there are indications in Augustine's thought that he recognizes that God only deserts those who have already deserted him,[3] the stronger impression which emerges from his work is that of a grace which has to be scarce rather than abundant.[4]

The backdrop of Paul's thought was Jewish apocalyptic, which he modified to fit the new situation created by Jesus Christ risen from the dead. Like Paul in the first century—and us in the twentieth, it goes without saying—Augustine lived at a time of profound and catastrophic mutations. An old order was passing away, and the new had yet to emerge.[5] However the experience of Paul and of Augustine were markedly different. The wider political and economic world in which Paul carried on his missionary activity was relatively stable. The benefits of the *Pax Romana* were considerable. By contrast the immediate worlds to which he belonged, that of Pharisaic Judaism and later that of the Christian mission to the Gentiles, experienced the wasting away of an old religious order, and, longing for the new to be born, was afire with apocalyptic fervour.

The reverse was true in the case of Augustine. In spite of controversies within the Christian Church, controversies in which Augustine was a willing protagonist, by and large the Church was settled in. Having gained recognition and protection at the highest levels, it was a haven for all peoples. Its orientation towards a heavenly, not an earthly fulfillment lacked the keenness and urgency of earlier centuries. The imminence of the *parousia* was the object of an assent more notional than real. By contrast the wider political and economic system of the fifth century suffered disarray. The fabric of the Roman Empire, so toughly woven at the time of Paul, was threatening to unravel. Breakdown and fragmentation were undermining the Empire from within, and the barbarians were smashing down the gates. The Goths sacked Rome in 410, and in the last years of his life Augustine saw the Vandals invade his own beloved Hippo. Augustine felt that he had to deal with the apocalyptic issues latent in these historic events, thus vindicating the ways of the Christian God against pagan philosophy. This he did in his monumental *City of God*.

Augustine's experience of apocalyptic disruption appears to be more like ours than like that of Paul. The breakdown of the old order and the emergence of the new of which we spoke in Chapter One is not an intramural Christian concern. Like the impending fall of the fifth century Roman Empire, it affects the fabric of human life as a whole, and keenly concerns men and women of many different religious stances. But there are vital differences. The apocalyptic stakes today are much higher. The impending breakdown is radical, universal. The barbarians at the gates were the end of an era, but not the end of the world: as we know, the eclipse of the Dark Ages was followed by unprecedented human development on all fronts. Moreover today there are no "outsiders" at the gates. As inhabitants of the one planet, we are all insiders. If we seek those responsible for the atmosphere of impending catastrophe in which we live, we have no choice but to point the finger at ourselves.

I will begin this chapter by trying to relate Augustine's theology of grace to his life experience, first centering around the *Confessions*, that unique biographical document which in effect grounds the balanced and psychologically realistic theology of grace developed by the middle Augustine, for instance in *Spirit and Letter*, then paying some attention to the *City of God* and its insights into the social dimensions of grace. Then I will focus on the positive contributions of Augustine's theology of grace and their contemporary ramifications, under the headings of grace as inner transformation, grace as total prevenience, grace as kenotic freedom.

CONFESSIONS/SPIRIT AND LETTER

The *Confessions* have immeasurably heightened the impact of Augustine upon the Western Church. His philosophic acumen, rhetorical skills, and pastoral concern suffice by themselves to give him a place in history: what makes of him a figure vividly present even to this day is his passionate quest for God. There is no reason for us go over the familiar biographical terrain of the *Confessions*. However to correlate in somewhat greater detail key events of his life and basic insights of his theology of grace found in both the *Confessions* (397–401) and the *Spirit and Letter* (412) is most germane to our purpose.

Augustine's conversion is not exclusively centered upon the *tolle lege* incident in the Milan garden, recounted in Book 8. To be sure, that incident is pivotal in both his life and in his *Confessions*. However that work makes a point of recounting the lengthy struggles leading up to it, as well as further struggles which followed from it. Indeed what Pelagius finds odious in the *Confessions* is not so much Book 8, which offers an exemplary model of initial conversion, as Book 10, in which Augustine lays bare the struggles and temptations he was experiencing as a believer who had become a bishop in the Catholic Church.[6]

"You have made us for yourself and our hearts are restless until they rest in you." These words in the opening paragraph of the *Confessions* set the stage for the entire work, and introduce the primordial element of grace. The first eight books relate Augustine's restless quest: time and time again he sought God where God was not to be found, and discovered the bitter taste of emptiness. His conversion did not remove that restlessness but altered it. It became, in his account, the restlessness of one who, though at heart peaceful, still has to live as a pilgrim in a precarious and threatening world, who longs for the full and definitive liberation of his total self. In Pauline terms, the "already now" does not in this life annul the "not yet".

In assessing the contribution of Augustine to the theology of grace one generally singles out his capable illustration and defense, against Pelagius, of the internal spontaneity of sanctifying grace which alone makes possible the observance of the law. We must remember however that the *Confessions*, especially the first eight books, also give massive witness to two other elements of grace which contrast with sanctifying grace, one external rather than internal, the other negative or primordial (an emptiness) rather than positive (a fullness).

Augustine includes the deep-rooted and innate desire for happiness among the plethora of natural gifts he has received[7]. It is the painful emptiness of which sanctifying grace is the fullness. From it stem dissatisfaction, bitterness, restlessness, which welled up within him whenever what he found proved to be less than the God who alone would fulfill his heart: "you were always present, angry and merciful at once, strewing the pangs of bitterness over all my lawless pleasures to lead me on to look for others unallied with pain".[8] In and of itself this emptiness is not an evil, a deprivation. It is rather a primordial absence at the heart of which there resides the unquenchable desire which urged Augustine to continue his painful struggle no matter what. Evil comes from attempts to fulfill this desire with what is not God.

Again in contrast to sanctifying grace, we find in the *Confessions* a manifold external grace, the marvellous pattern of a Providence orchestrating events both pleasant and painful, slowly but persistently paving the way for Augustine's surrender to God. Instances of this Providence are to be found in his early upbringing, which already instilled in him an inchoate faith in Jesus Christ;[9] the reading of Cicero as a law student, which altered his outlook on life: "All my empty dreams suddenly lost their charm and my heart began to throb with a bewildering passion for the wisdom of eternal truth";[10] the steps by which he was invited to move away from the Manichean to the neo-Platonist position and eventually back to the faith which he had originally received as a child. These events stirred up an awareness of the painful gap between what he sought and what he was finding. In retrospect he saw in them manifestations of God's love needed to steer him in the right direction.

Augustine's later polemical works against the Pelagian movement may give the impression that in his theology only internal or sanctifying grace counts, the "love of God poured into our hearts by the Holy Spirit who is given to us" (Rom 5:5). However, *Spirit and Letter*, an earlier, more irenic response to Pelagius, brings together with admirable clarity the three aspects of grace, internal, external, and primordial, in harmonious balance:

> Our own assertion, on the contrary, is this: that the human will is assisted to do the right in such manner that, besides man's creation with the endowment of freedom to choose, and besides the teaching by which he is instructed how he ought to live, he receives the Holy Spirit, whereby there arises in his soul the delight in and the love of God, the supreme and the changeless Good.[11]

The freedom to choose, *liberum arbitrium* in Augustine's text, is a *velle* (velleity) rather than a *posse* (power to make an effective choice), an inbuilt but ineffective orientation towards God, a restless and bittersweet quest for beatitude. Later on in *Spirit and Letter* Augustine distinguishes this *liberum arbitrium* from *libertas arbitrii*, the new spontaneity which results from the gift of the Spirit, the delight in and love of God which is needed to fulfill the law and achieve beatitude in God, in short sanctifying grace. This distinction dovetails with the contrast Augustine experienced between the ineffective love of God he had before his conversion in the garden, and the secure love he received from that moment onwards as God's gift. The first is the negative counterpart of the second.[12]

The external promptings of grace in *Spirit and Letter* center around the law, which, telling us how to live, but of itself leaving us powerless to live that way, only exacerbates our sense of bondage and futility. But later in that treatise Augustine gives a broader expression to this external element when he refers to events which prompt the will towards conversion, in some cases merely suasively and in other cases persuasively, for unfathomable reasons relating to the mystery of God's grace.[13]

Augustine and Pelagius agree on two elements of grace: the innate desire for fulfillment in God and, external to the will itself, the promptings of the law and of providential events. For Pelagius these two elements suffice.[14] Augustine insists on a third element, the love of God poured into our hearts, the inner delight which alone overcomes the countervailing attraction to the created values that ultimately leave us unfulfilled.

Is it a mere coincidence that Augustine ends up with three elements? Given his propensity to find various vestiges of the Trinity in creation, especially in spiritual creation, such a coincidence would be doubtful. Augustine's metaphysics of creation, as outlined by Eugene TeSelle,[15] offers us valuable clues on this point. The substrate of every created reality—and this applies to both material and spiritual creatures—is the formless void, the "tohu-we-bohu" of Genesis, of and by itself mutable, given over to the nothingness out of which it was created. In the case of the created spirit, this void is the innate desire for happiness. Attracting us to the Father and yet by itself never bringing us to the Father, it leads to restless and unstable activity.

For the created spirit to be complete as a creature, this substrate must be "formed", i.e. converted to the Word; and the formed substrate must be "stabilized", i.e. converted to the Spirit. The conversion to the Word is a form of illumination. The formless orientation of created spirit is given a name and a goal; that spirit in some sense knows that it will only find fulfillment in God. In experiential terms that orientation becomes a sharp pain rather than a dull ache. The conversion of the human spirit by the divine Spirit rescues the human spirit from its innate ineffectiveness and instability, from the fretful impotence of mere knowing, sets it in a secure, loving movement towards God. With this double conversion, the journey towards beatitude has effectively begun. Without difficulty one can discern in the above the three elements of Augustine's balanced doctrine of grace.

Linked with each other, these doctrines of creation and of grace are also linked to the mystery of the Trinity. The original gift of the desire which can only be fulfilled in God relates to the Father, the internal and external promptings which illuminate the path without of themselves giving the strength to follow it relate to the Word, and the gift of an effective and stable will orientation towards God above all else relates to the Spirit. In brief the Father creates us as receptive to the gift of intimacy with himself; the Son calls us repeatedly from without; and the Spirit transforms us from within.[16]

These are the broad strokes. Detailed and vivid traces of Augustine's trinitarian itinerary are to be found in the *Confessions*.

The truth that our spiritual nature is created by God and for God alone, in God alone finding its peace, is affirmed in the very first paragraph of the *Confessions*: "our hearts are created restless until they rest in you." This truth permeates the whole work, which is just as much prayer to the *FATHER* as it is autobiography. The evidence for it is seared into the psyche of Augustine as the restless, ever unsatisfied desire which relentlessly urged him forward on his pilgrimage.

Augustine's illumination by the *WORD* was gradual. His conversion from Manicheism to neo-Platonism was a turning point. It was soon after his reading of *Hortensius* that he became a Manichean "Hearer". But the more he probed, the less he found the Wisdom he was expecting, and the more flaws he discovered in the arguments of Faustus and other Manichees. Nevertheless Manicheism enabled him to postpone facing the bitter division within himself. One part of himself sought for happiness, wisdom, and spoke eloquently about them; another was enslaved by various sinful patterns and doomed to frustration. Augustine had chosen the tactic of repression, of pretending that the evil which he could not avoid facing *in* himself was not really *of* himself. His dark side was not so much something to be brought to the light and healed as something to be escaped from. However God in his Providence kept breaking through the illusions Augustine was fabricating in order to lessen the pain of the wound deep within him:

> I still thought that it is not we who sin but some other nature that sins within us. It flattered my pride to think that I incurred no guilt and, when I did wrong, not to confess it so that you might bring healing to a soul that had sinned against you. I preferred to excuse myself and blame this unknown thing which was in me but was not part of me. The truth, of course, was that it was all my own self, and my own impiety had divided me against myself. My sin was all the more incurable because I did not think myself a sinner.[17]

In 386 Augustine began avidly perusing works of the Platonists, especially Porphyry's *Return of the Soul* and Plotinus' *On Beauty*.[18] This conversion to philosophy, a dream of his since his much earlier reading of Cicero's *Hortensius*, was the first and most significant step in his conversion to the light. Pulled apart by pursuits which led him outside himself, having deserted both himself and God,[19] he now was led to return to his own self, and he found there a glimpse of the Light.[20] He began to see how spirit utterly transcends matter.[21] He even began to appreciate the Christian doctrine of the Word that was with God (but at this stage not of the Word made flesh). Indeed this illumination in great part consisted in a more and more explicit knowledge of the Christ whom he had always known since his earliest days as a catechumen. Knowledge of Christ and knowledge of self went hand in hand; appropriating his own self as spiritual, as present to its own knowing and willing, ineluctably led him to face the conflict within himself:

> One thing lifted me up into the light of your day. It was that I knew that I had a will, as surely as I knew that there was life in me. When I chose to do something or not to do it, I was quite certain that it was my own self, and not some other person, who made this act of will, so that I was on the point of understanding that herein lay the cause of my sin.[22]

No sooner was Augustine drawn to God's beauty than he was dragged away from God by his own weight and in dismay plunged again into the things of this world.[23] At once he wanted to follow the law of God and was utterly incapable of doing so. The light to which he was being converted acted like salt on the wound of his inner division. The pain reached a paroxysm in Book 8, where he describes his experience of his will's utter inability to give a command to itself, because it is divided, wrenched in two.[24] The light of philosophy had been a good pedagogue to him, like the Law was for the unredeemed "I" in Romans 7. He realized that, no matter how much the Word outside himself beckoned, apart from a total surrender effected by grace he was powerless to achieve a stable, secure orientation towards the God he momentarily glimpsed and loved. He began to open himself to a further action of God within him, a transformation of his powerless will, of his divided heart. His quest came to a crescendo as he reread the epistles of Paul.

In later texts Augustine clearly links the ensuing conversion which took place in a garden in Milan to the infusion of the *HOLY SPIRIT*, but this is not obvious to one who narrowly inspects the text at the end of Book 8 in which Augustine relates his own experience. It contains light rather than love imagery: " . . . it was as though the light of confidence flooded into my heart and all the darkness of doubt was dispelled".[25] But that light is not purely intellectual. It brought confidence and, what is more important, enabled his paralyzed will to move.

The conversion account brings out another feature of the justification experience which is somewhat underplayed in later polemical texts. The gift of inner, sanctifying grace is accompanied by outward graces as well. The story told by Ponticianus led Augustine to the garden. There the famous "tolle lege" led him to the New Testament, to the words of Paul which gave focus to the powerful movement being born within his spirit. The overall transition Augustine describes in Books 7 and 8 is from the illumination of his mind to the transformation of his will. Yet in another sense these were concomitant. The

shift was not so much from intellect to will, from knowledge to love, as it was
from an imperfect knowledge still full of illusion, accompanied by an inefficacious will, to a deeper knowledge accompanied by an efficacious and loving
will. Without love illumination is not only lifeless but also incomplete. Apart
from the response, the call is only imperfectly understood.

Where then is this transformation of the will spoken of in the *Confessions*,
since, as we have seen, this theme does not stand out in the conversion passage
of Book 8? A wider perusal of the *Confessions* brings this theme out quite
clearly, as for instance in the following sequence of texts:

> *(BEFORE)* I was astonished that although I now loved you and
> not some phantom in your place, I did not persist in enjoyment of
> my God. Your beauty drew me to you, but soon I was dragged away
> from you by my own weight and in dismay I plunged again into the
> things of this world. The weight I carried with me was the habit of
> the flesh. But your memory remained with me and I had no doubt at
> all that you were the one to whom I should cling, only I was not yet
> able to cling to you.[26]

> *(DURING)* You called me; you cried aloud to me; you broke
> my barrier of deafness. You shone upon me; your radiance enve-
> loped me; you put my blindness to flight. You shed your fragrance
> about me; I drew breath and now I gasp for your sweet odour. I tasted
> you, and now I hunger and thirst for you. You touched me, and I am
> inflamed with love of your peace.[27]

> *(AFTER)* My love of you is not some vague feeling: it is posi-
> tive and certain. Your word struck into my heart and from that mo-
> ment I loved you.[28]

The first text tells us about the inefficacious love which accompanied his philosophic conversion. The second demonstrates that his conversion is no mere
intellectual illumination: Augustine is at pains to show us, by referring to the
five senses, that conversion touches his entire person, and entails a transformation of his power to love. The third text describes the secure orientation of
love which this conversion brought about, and also shows how the word was
active in the very conversion process. To harden the distinction between cognitional and volitional elements in Augustine's conversion is to do his careful
account an injustice.

The fuller grasp of the truth that accompanied the gift of love which
changed the "weight" of Augustine's life is of great moment in an insightful

account of his theology of grace. As he was struggling towards that final movement of surrender, he was also being led by his study of Paul to an insight into the Word which went far beyond what the Platonist books offered. They enabled him to acknowledge the Word that was with God, but now he is able to acknowledge that the Word became flesh in the man Jesus of Nazareth (a scandal for the Platonists of the fifth century as it was for the *illuminati* of Paul's Corinth) and that this Jesus is the only mediator between God and sinful humankind.[29] At the same time he comes to a new personal knowledge of himself as a sinner in need of conversion:

> [having read the Platonists] I used to talk glibly as if I knew the meaning of it all, but unless I had looked for the way which leads to you in Christ our Saviour, instead of finding knowledge I would have found my end. For I had now begun to wish to be thought wise. I was full of self-esteem, which was a punishment of my own making. I ought to have deplored my state, but instead my knowledge only bred self-conceit. But how could I expect that the Platonist books would ever teach me charity?[30]

The kenotic overtones of these texts and of the conversion they recount are striking. Only when Augustine became able to acknowledge the humble, self-emptying Christ was he ready for his conversion. The kenotic Christ offered him the strength and the inspiration needed for the self-emptying process of his own conversion, helped him to let go of the vaunted intellectual self-sufficiency to which he clung in spite of its sterility proved many times over, and to recognize himself as a sinner in need of mercy. Only when he was willing to become humble in imitation of the humble Christ, was he lifted up towards God:

> The lesson is that your Word, the eternal Truth . . . raises up to himself all who subject themselves to him. From the clay of which we are made he built for himself a lowly house in this world below, so that by this means he might cause those who were to be made subject to him to abandon themselves and come over to his side. He would cure them of the pride that swelled up in their hearts and would nurture love in its place, so that they should no longer stride confident in themselves, but might realize their own weakness when at their feet they saw God himself, enfeebled by sharing this garment of our mortality. And at last, from weariness, they would cast themselves down upon his humanity, and when it rose they too would rise.[31]

There is scarce reference to the Spirit in Books 7 and 8. It is only in Books 12 and 13 that the role of the Spirit in the transformation of the human will is brought to light. For instance:

> It is in your Gift that we find our rest. It is in him that we enjoy you. The place where we find rest is the rightful one for us. To it we are raised by love. To it your Spirit lifts us up, lowly creatures as we are, 'from the gate of death'. It is in goodness of will that we find our peace.[32]

The "love of God poured into our hearts by the Holy Spirit which is given to us" (Rom 5:5) becomes a *leitmotiv* of Augustine's mature theology of grace. The cognitional aspects of his conversion come to a focus in relation to the Word, and the volitional aspects in the transforming activity of the Spirit. Just as the distinction of Word and Spirit does not take away from oneness of the Godhead, so too these aspects of Augustine's conversion, though quite distinct, mutually inhere. And let us not forget to include within his doctrine of a grace in the image of the Trinity the underlying constant in his life, his innate desire for fulfillment in the Father, powerless prior to his conversion, efficacious thereafter.

Augustine's conversion was not an end but a beginning. Having surrendered to the Lord, how was he to serve him? He began by leading a life of quietude and study: a few persons joined him in Cassiciacum and they formed a community dedicated to Christian converse and the search for wisdom. Not long afterwards he decided to return to North Africa to continue this way of life on a more secure and organized basis. The account of events in the *Confessions* comes to a close in Book 9 with the death of his mother Monica at Ostia during the return trip. The *Confessions* do not relate the events surrounding his ordination to the priesthood in 391 and his installation as Bishop of Hippo in 396. This call was a difficult one for Augustine to accept, but accept it he did. He had moved out of the hurly-burly of life as a rhetorician and aspiring politician into the genteel retreat of a Christian philosopher. He was attracted to this monastic and scholarly form of existence, but he now found himself thrust back into the hurly-burly of the North African Church and the declining Roman Empire.

The naïve enthusiasm of his Christian beginnings clearly contrasts with the realism of his mature years as a bishop. With nostalgia but also with serenity he came to recognize the continuing unredemption of the world and of his own self. In Book 10 of the *Confessions* he recounts with extraordinary acumen his inner trials and tribulations as a bishop, using images and terms which to our ears and eyes are strikingly contemporary.[33] His account of the vast caverns of memory remind us of the Freudian unconscious. When he tells us about a narrower part of himself bathed by the light of consciousness and a wider self which remains unknown to him and needs redemption, he foreshadows the ego/self distinction so characteristic of the Jungian school, reflected in the diagram we developed in Chapter 3.[34]

This latter point is worth developing. For our purposes we will roughly define the ego as that area of conscious control which is situated close to the centre of the concentric circles in the diagram, and the wider self as the area which covered by the entire set of circles, including the *pneuma*, *psyche*, and *soma*.[35] This will help us to delimit three significant stages in Augustine's journey: the pre-conversion phase, the conversion itself, and the post-conversion phase. Briefly, before his conversion Augustine experienced the relationship between his ego and wider self as problematic and painful. The conversion experience for him was a breakthrough, but that breakthrough entailed the typical dangers of inflation, of mistaking transformation in the central area of his self for the transformation of his total self. After his conversion his active life as a mature Christian provided the needed corrective. As a bishop, he gratefully acknowledged the inner conversion of his heart, but at the same time fully realized how fragile and incomplete that conversion was. His wider self was not yet permeated by the light of grace and his response to God not yet total and irreversible. Let us examine these stages in turn.

The life of Augustine prior to his conversion was marked by restlessness and dissatisfaction. The more he sought God by wandering away from himself and pouring himself out into created things, the less he found God. His alienation from God and his alienation from himself were of one piece. He tells us about his "wound":

What agony I suffered, my God! How I cried out in grief, while my heart was in labour . . . For the light was within, while I looked on the world outside. The light was not in space, but I thought only of things that are contained in space, and in them I found no place where I might rest. They offered me no haven where I could own myself satisfied and content, nor would they let me turn back where I might find contentment and satisfaction . . . when I rose in pride against you and made onslaught against my Lord, proud of my strong sinews, even those lower things became my masters and oppressed me, and nowhere could I find respite or time to draw my breath. Everywhere I looked they loomed before my eyes in swarms and clusters, and when I set myself to thinking and tried to escape from them, images of these selfsame things blocked my way, as though they were asking where I meant to go, unclean and undeserving as I was. All this had grown from my wound, for the proud lie wounded at your feet, and I was separated from you by the swelling of my pride, as though my cheeks were so puffed with conceit that they masked the sight of my eyes.[36]

That wound was also that of his divided will. The conscious and controlling part of him sought to live a life single-mindedly devoted to wisdom, but to no avail. He ceaselessly turned the various mysteries of existence over in his mind, but without fruit. God was not to be found by the efforts of his sharply honed intellect. Another part of him, dark, unsavory, unbridled, assailed him with enticing images and powerful feelings, and kept causing personal disarray, above all, it would seem, in the area of sexuality. He sincerely wanted to put all this behind him and without clutter strive for wisdom, but his will was wrenched in two. During his Manichean phase, he tried to repress or at least to blur the gap between his highly developed intellectual and rhetorical ego and his wider self, teeming with disorder and disintegration. In certain persons, who within our century would be styled neurotics, such a strategy may succeed, at least for a time. But this success is costly: the conscious ego becomes rigid and impermeable to the wider self. Augustine fortunately failed to escape from his "wound". His disintegration was ever a thorn in his side. Everything conspired to heighten his failure: repeated inability to find the object of his desire made him more acutely conscious of how unlimited in scope that desire was.[37] Moreover the reading of the Platonist books opened up a fruitful path of reflection for him. The ground was laid for a breakthrough.

As we saw, the intellectual beginnings of his conversion exacerbated the sense of division within himself. He came to squarely accept this division as something not only *in* him but also *of* him, something for which he was responsible: if he could not overcome it by himself, he could at least take to the Lord for healing and forgiveness. That healing entailed a conversion, a re-centering of his dispersed being and an encounter with the God he had so long both sought and eluded.[38] That conversion was a rebirth. The first flush of new integration is generally accompanied by the phenomenon Jung refers to as inflation. The newly healed ego, healed only because now it is willing to relinquish its place at the center and become the instrument of the self, in Jungian terms, or, in Christian terms, the *pneuma* transformed by God's love, is prone to expansion, to the illusion that the whole self is permeated by the light and integration is complete. In reality transformation has taken place only in his inmost heart:

> But it was in my inmost heart, where I had grown angry with myself, where I had been stung with remorse, where I had slain my old self and offered it in sacrifice, where I had first purposed to renew my life and had placed my hope in you, it was there that you had begun to make me love you and had made me glad at heart.[39]

Initially Augustine, as we saw, chose to protect that fragile seed. He stopped his ears to the alluring voices of his past, devoted himself single-heartedly to a sheltered life of personal discipline and philosophic search. He kept a safe distance from the turbulent world in which he lived, that of the late Roman Empire, its vivid allurements and its pressing problems. He was not yet aware of how much multiplicity there remained in the inner world of his psychic self and how far his restless heart still had to journey. Unlike the gnostics of Corinth, Augustine gives no signs of being fixated in the initial stages of the new life. What we do find in him is an attractive and understandable naïveté. The newly converted Augustine still had to learn within his heart that justification is not salvation, that the transformation of the *pneuma* is but the first step in the transformation of *psyche* and *soma* and that, shifting to Platonic terms, his escape from the cave had to be followed by re-entry into the cave.

Book 10 of the *Confessions* describes the mature perspective on the Christian life to which Augustine had come some ten years after his conversion.[40] His native acumen, his sharply honed reflective skills, the extraordinary vantage point on human affairs which his episcopal office afforded him led him to achieve a unique transposition in psychological terms of the already now/not yet tension operative in Paul's theology of grace.

Augustine brings to our attention the dynamic of the already now and the not yet within his own self—and within ours. Love already has transformed his inmost heart,[41] and he is secure in his relationship to God.[42] Already, as he tells us, "I have tasted you, and now I hunger and thirst for you. You touched me, and I am inflamed with love of your peace."[43] But he goes on to affirm the other side of the polarity:

> When at last I cling to you with all my being, for me there will be no more sorrow, no more toil. Then at last I shall be alive with true life, for my life will be wholly filled by you. You raise up and sustain all whose lives you fill, but my life is not yet filled by you and I am a burden to myself . . . Have pity on me, O Lord, in my misery. I do not hide my wounds from you . . . Is not man's life on earth a long, unbroken period of trial?[44]

He clings to God, but not with his whole being. Sometimes he is flooded with an inward feeling of delight, but then a heavy burden of distress drags him down to earth again.[45] He remains wounded, as he was before his conversion, but now "it is not as though I do not suffer wounds, but I feel rather that you heal them over and over again".[46] Part of him is already in the light, but so much remains in the dark:

> I shall therefore confess both what I know of myself and what I do not know. For even what I know about myself I only know because your light shines upon me; and what I do not know about myself I shall continue not to know until I see you face to face and my dusk is noonday.[47]

That darkness is vast indeed. Augustine's explorations of his inner terrain leave him with a sense of awe. Seeking God in his memory, he exclaims:

> The power of the memory is prodigious, my God. It is a vast, immeasurable sanctuary. Who can plumb its depths? And yet it is a faculty of my soul. Although it is part of my nature, I cannot understand all that I am. This means, then, that the mind is too narrow to contain itself entirely. But where is that part of it which it does not itself contain? Is it somewhere outside itself and not within it? How, then, can it be part of it, if it is not contained in it?[48]

This is a far cry from his Manichean days. He then dismissed the uncontrolled, ungrasped part of himself as belonging to an alien nature which inhabited his self and terrorized it. Since he did not acknowledge it as really part of him, he could disclaim responsibility for it. Augustine the Manichean hearer sought escape from the darkness within himself, but Augustine the bishop accepts it as part of himself, resolutely explores it, tries to bring it to the light, in the knowledge that:

> I was not myself the truth; for you, the Truth, are the unfailing Light from which I sought counsel upon all these things, asking whether they were, what they were, and how they were to be valued . . . in all the regions (of my memory) where I tread my way, seeking your guidance, only in you do I find a safe haven for my mind, a gathering-place for my scattered parts, where no portion of me can depart from you.[49]

We can discern two significant parallels here:

a) The first is between Augustine's life and Paul's doctrine. Paul was at odds with the enthusiasts and gnostics of Corinth, for they were under the illusion that with the experience of justification they had already arrived at the pinnacle of Christian life. He points out that justification is only a beginning, that its reality is distorted unless it points beyond itself and leads to a lengthy process of sanctification, a life of faithful service within a world not yet redeemed, and a loving acceptance of others with all their warts and ambiguities. In order finally to possess in salvation the gift he/she has received in justification, the Christian must let go of it in a life of sanctification which imitates Jesus' own *kenosis*. The steps Augustine was led to take in the years after his conversion are a vivid instance of justification seeking a path towards salvation. Augustine's inmost heart was transformed, but it took some time before he discovered how he was to embody that transformation, make it effective for the life of the Christian community and of the world.

b) The second parallel is internal to Augustine's own life. He is at pains to make a distinction in Books 7 and 8 between his reading of the Platonists and his conversion to Jesus Christ. The former gave him knowledge, but by itself, according to Paul, knowledge only puffs up.[50] During the brief period of allegiance to Plato apart from Christ he resembled the gnostics of 1 Corinthians. Like them, he boasted in his knowledge, but failed to recognize the gift which God had in store for him. The power of the Spirit overtook him only when, willing to recognize his own weakness, he was ready to take upon himself the pattern of Jesus' own weakness. The love which builds up replaced the knowledge which breeds self-conceit. This transition deeply marked his inner journey as he moved towards the moment of his conversion.

The same transition characterized his outer journey in the years following his conversion. What was true within him is mirrored forth in the momentous choices, momentous for him and us, he made during those years. As a newly converted Christian he may have set the attitude of boasting aside, but unwittingly he still clung to outward patterns of living in which the search for wisdom remains central, and the self-emptying of the Lord is peripheral. Later he more fully embraces the cross, when he takes up the burdens of being a bishop at a very difficult time in the life of his Church. From that vantage point he is able to carry out a mature reflection on the ambiguities of the city of God within the city of man, a far cry from the innocent enthusiasm of his earlier philosophical dialogues.[51] He allows cruciform grace to permeate his life.

To sum up, Augustine's *Confessions*, together with *The Spirit and the Letter*, present a doctrine of grace closely linked to his life experience, amazingly nuanced and contemporary. Grace does not exclusively consist in the gift of the Holy Spirit which transforms the human heart. It begins with an innate orientation which, until God is found, is a source of painful disquiet. It is continually punctuated by the events of a person's life which embody God's care for that person. The triple dimension of grace, as we saw, reflects the Trinity itself. Moreover grace has a dynamic all of its own, one to which Augustine was especially sensitive. A contemporary ego/self approach has helped us to appropriate that dynamic. Ego and self begin in disharmony with one another. The efforts of the ego to control the self are doomed to failure. The wound within festers. Intellectual clarity only heightens the pain of it all. But then comes the great breakthrough of conversion. The seeds of integration are sown within the very heart of the person and a new dynamic is operative in which the ego, now a channel for the inmost self, begins to transform and liberate the wider self. But soon one discovers that this transformation exists only in hope, that conversion has to be deepened day by day in the life of sanctification. The kenotic shift implicit in conversion has to be mirrored forth in one's entire life. Many of these points may have been latent in Paul's theology of grace, but it was left up to Augustine to express them, to correlate them with his own experience, and thus serve as a bridge between the first century and our own.

City of God

Generally students in quest of Augustine's theology of grace will concentrate on only one part of his corpus. They will describe the personal and experiential features of the theology which Augustine sharply hones as he relates his own conversion process in the *Confessions* and as he engages in prolonged controversies with the Pelagians and the Donatists. We cannot bypass the *City of God*, however, if we are to fill out our portrayal of the dynamic of grace as seen by Augustine.

Thus far different forms of apocalyptic expectation have come to the light. One is found in Paul's letters, and another is beginning to emerge in the twentieth century. Augustine's troubled era led him to generate his own stance towards the end-time. This stance emerges most clearly in his *City of God*, where he struggles to vindicate the Church against pagan thinkers who laid the blame for the downfall of the Roman Empire at her doorstep. In that work Augustine theologizes in response not so much to intra-ecclesial controversies as to questions arising from outside the Catholic Church; he relates grace to the collapsing world of his day. Consideration of the *City of God* will give balance and pertinence to our transposition of Augustine's theology of grace in contemporary terms. Our era is marked by not just personal/experiential but also social/cultural modes of reflection, and has much to learn from Augustine's apocalyptic.

If one wishes to adopt a distinction between an earlier eschatological stream within the Old Testament which expects God to deliver his people through events within the currents of history, and a later apocalyptic stream which expects God to dissolve the old age, whose miseries are beyond repair, and create an altogether new age, one gets a sense from the *City of God* that Augustine, like Paul, belongs to the apocalyptic stream. For him this present age, secretly permeated though it is by members of the city of God in its midst, is full of ambiguity. Its burdens weigh us down. It leads us to endless grief rather than to eternal happiness.[52] We will not transform it through our own efforts; rather we need to await the mercy of God who will deliver us from it and set us within the new creation coming down out of heaven from God.[53] Unlike a number of theologians popular in our day, Augustine does not pin any hope on the transformation of this world according to any particular programme of action, or on the eradication of the unjust structures which deeply permeate it.[54] He is more interested in how we are to find our way to eternal happiness, as pilgrims in the midst of this world, but as citizens of another. He looks for a modicum of peace in this world, but this minimal order can be provided for in various ways, as long as they "do not impede the religion whereby the one supreme and true God is taught to be worshipped".[55] What counts above all is the protection of that inner space within which the member of the City of God here below can relativize the achievements and failures of this world in the light of his or her absolute yearning for God.[56]

Nonetheless one can find in the *City of God* a model applicable to the transforming and redeeming activity directed to the age that is passing away, a model, which like that found in Paul's theology, depicts expansion from the inner core in which we personally relate to God to wider and wider realms of human activity. The clearest expression of this model is put in terms of the dynamic of sin rather than that of grace. It highlights how socio-political breakdown is the result of a breakdown in the relationship between God and his human creatures:

> That being so, when a man does not serve God, what amount of justice are we to suppose exists in his being? For if a soul does not serve God it cannot with any kind of justice command the body, nor can a man's reason control the vicious elements in the soul. And if there is no justice in such a man, there can be no doubt that there is no justice in a gathering which consists of such men. Here, then, there

is not that 'consent to the law' which makes a mob into a people . . .
I consider that what I have said about 'a common sense of right' is
enough to make it apparent that by this definition people amongst
whom there is no justice can never be said to have a commonwealth.[57]

Is the positive counterpart to this negative dynamic ever realized according to Augustine? Yes, but only in the City of God, which exists fully only in
the next world. In this one it is found only latently and imperfectly:

It follows that justice is found where God, the one supreme God,
rules an obedient City according to his grace, forbidding sacrifice to
any being save himself alone; and where in consequence the soul
rules the body in all men who belong to this City and obey God, and
the reason faithfully rules the vices in a lawful system of subordination; so that just as the individual righteous man lives on the basis
of faith, active in love, so the association, or people, of righteous
men lives on the same basis of faith, active in love, the love with
which a man loves God as God ought to be loved, and loves his
neighbour as himself.[58]

Indeed the inhabitant of the city of God is never at home in this world.
He passes through it as a pilgrim, because his real home is elsewhere.[59] Rather
than put her every effort into creating tranquillity of order within this passing
world, the Church is satisfied with the ambiguous, unreliable and uneasy patterns of peace which the earthly city provides.[60] The main concern of religion
is not to transform the present world but to carve within it a space in which it
enjoys the right of untrammeled exercise. It is satisfied to live a life of captivity, as long as it can preserve a certain harmony with the world in matters which
relate to the support of this mortal life.[61]

In this Augustine resembles Paul more than he does many of our more
optimistic contemporary authors. He is convinced that the dynamics of good
and evil are inextricably entwined in this world,[62] and refuses to prematurely
separate out the wheat of the heavenly city from the chaff of the earthly.[63] He
does not pretend to offer a clear apocalyptic perspective on the events of his
age, but he certainly has a vivid sense of the dynamics which inexorably lead
the city of man away from God and towards dissolution, a powerful longing
for deliverance which parallels that of Romans 7,[64] and a conviction that in the
end the City of God will prevail.

In Book 14 he discusses these two dynamics in more general terms. One city follows the standard of God (or of the Spirit), the other that of men (or of the flesh):

> We see then that the two cities were created by two kinds of love: the earthly city was created by self-love reaching the point of contempt for God, the Heavenly City by the love of God carried as far as contempt of self. In fact, the earthly city glories in itself, the Heavenly City glories in the Lord. The former looks for glory from men, the latter finds its highest glory in God, the witness of a good conscience. The earthly lifts up its head in its own glory, the Heavenly City says to its God: 'My glory; you lift up my head.'[65]

The sequel to that quote will help us come to grips with the different dynamics at work in the two cities:

> In the former, the lust for domination lords it over its princes as over the nations it subjugates; in the other both those put in authority and those subject to them serve one another in love, the rulers by their counsel, the subjects by obedience. The one city loves its strength shown in its powerful leaders; the other says to its God, 'I will love you, my Lord, my strength.'

Failure to put the service of God at the center of our lives irremediably distorts the service we ought to render to one another in love. Power relationships set in, a form of idolatry, a form of boasting analogous to that which was so disruptive in the Pauline communities. In the city of God, *kenosis* leads to *koinonia*; in the city of man domination creates what turns out to be a travesty of the true commonwealth. Its peace is at best the uneasy compromise of conflicting forces.[66]

   This striking contrast dovetails with the scarcity/abundance, competition/cooperation, and oppressor/oppressed binomials which we developed in Chapter Three. First as regards the city of God:

> Isaac therefore, who was born as a result of a promise, is rightly interpreted as symbolizing the children of grace, the citizens of the free city, the sharers of eternal peace, who form a community where there is no love of a will that is personal and, as we may say, private, but a love that rejoices in a good that is at once shared by all and unchanging—a love that makes 'one heart' out of many, a love that

is the whole-hearted and harmonious obedience of mutual affection.[67]

Then as regards the city of man:

> For this is how Rome was founded, when Remus, as Roman history witnesses, was slain by his brother Romulus . . . Both sought the glory of establishing the Roman state, but a joint foundation would not bring to each the glory that a single founder would enjoy. Anyone whose aim was to glory in the exercise of power would obviously enjoy less power if his sovereignty was diminished by a living partner. Therefore, in order that the sole power should be wielded by one person, the partner was eliminated; and what would have been kept smaller and better by innocence grew through crime into something bigger and worse.[68]

Augustine reflects on the key differences at work here:

> A man's possession of goodness is in no way diminished by the arrival, or the continuance, of a sharer in it; indeed, goodness is a possession enjoyed more widely by the united affection of partners in that possession in proportion to the harmony that exists among them. In fact, anyone who refuses to enjoy this possession in partnership will not enjoy it at all; and he will find that he possesses it in ampler measure in proportion to his ability to love his partner in it.[69]

The affinity to the scarcity/abundance theme developed in the last chapter is remarkable. The goods pertaining to the city of God are radically abundant. I rejoice in what my neighbour possesses, and my neighbour rejoices in what I possess. Apart from this sharing, there is no possession. The goods pertaining to the city of man are marked by scarcity. The more there is for me, the less there is for others. Rather than rejoice in my neighbour's achievement of those goods, I envy him, I enter into conflict with him. This results in a commonwealth that is no genuine commonwealth, because it is at root built on patterns of domination, oppression, of uneasy compromise threatening at any moment to break down.

Another drawback of the city of man is the isolation of parts from other parts and from the whole. In this insight Augustine adumbrates the growing perception of fragmentation within our own society. As he puts it, each department of life in the earthly city has its own god to be placated, whereas the

Heavenly City only knows and worships one God,[70] and because of that is able to serenely knit together the fragments into a variegated but organic whole:

> While this Heavenly City . . . is on pilgrimage in this world, she calls out citizens from all nations and so collects a society of aliens, speaking all languages. She takes no account of any differences in customs, laws, and institutions, by which earthly peace is achieved and preserved.[71]

Augustine sees the idolatry of the earthly city in clear religious terms. Our secular city, as we have seen, is blemished by the idolatry of fragments gone wild, worshipping their own relevance and power in isolation from each other, competing with each other in a ceaseless and fruitless war, failing to find their true selves in each other. Rather than to the smaller and better, Augustine tells us in terms evocative of Schumacher and other contemporary advocates of humanly dimensioned enterprises, the earthly city is addicted to the bigger and worse. Each part secretly aspires to be a whole, whereas its only true fulfillment is to be a part within the whole.[72]

Many have seen in Augustine a precursor of the existential, introspective concerns of the twentieth century. But he too is a trail blazer for the incisive social and cultural analysis which also marks our age. In both of these areas, he makes a strong positive contribution and is open to further development, as we will see.

CONCLUSION: AUGUSTINE'S LEGACY

The data for this section has been largely displayed in our account of the *Confessions* (397–401), *Spirit and Letter* (412), and *City of God* (413–427). In the first two of these works, Augustine formulates the inward dimension of grace with a happy blend of theological acumen and psychological experience. In the third we find in seminal form some insights needed for a theology of grace alert to the dynamics of a society marked by profound disruption. We will recapitulate points already made in the last section and offer reflections and correlations under the following headings: grace as inward; grace as prevenient; grace as freeing. Augustine's contribution under two of these headings was affirmed in the Councils of Carthage in 418 (the internal nature of grace defined vis-à-vis the Pelagians) and Orange in 529 (the prevenience of grace defined vis-à-vis the semi-Pelagians) and was received in the Western Church.

This section aims to point out the positive contributions of Augustine. Yet we cannot leave unspoken our assent to the commonly held view that he also introduces certain elements of distortion in Western theology, partly because he reflects the assumptions of his age, and partly because, like everyone else, he has his own blind spots. Providentially the Councils of Carthage and Orange crystallize for us the main elements of his positive contribution, and leave out some of the areas where his thought did not show mature development and balance. Before proceeding to the positive, let us briefly allude to this negative and ambiguous side of Augustine.

1. Augustine shared with his age an inability to conceive of salvation apart from an explicit reference to Jesus Christ and to the Church.[73] The *massa damnata* was no theoretical construct for him. For him unbaptized infants and pagan adults had no access to the fulfillment in God for which God had created them. He felt he had no choice but to affirm that the universality of grace implied its scarcity, that mercy to really be mercy had to appear against a backdrop of justice. His difficulties in accepting the saying of 1 Timothy 2:4 that God wants all human beings to be saved have often been mentioned in this respect.[74] This fretful and severe Augustine, however, sharply contrasts with the one who reflects on the dynamic of grace in *The City of God*. More relaxed, less polemical in that setting, he rejoices, as we saw,[75] in the utter abundance of a goodness which does not have to be restricted in order to be gracious.

2. Why then does God choose this person for salvation and leave that one to damnation? Augustine was right in condemning the semi-Pelagian answer to that question, an answer which makes the bestowal or non-bestowal of divine favour dependent upon the occurrence or non-occurrence of some prior human gesture, actual or anticipated, towards God. But his own position on the predestination by which God positively chooses those to whom he bestows the powerful grace needed after the fall, the *auxilium quo* which makes the unwilling will willing, brings its share of problems, as is attested by the controversy it engendered down through the centuries, much of it fruitless.[76] It is very difficult to draw the line in Augustine between a grace which is efficacious and one whose irresistibility makes a mockery of human freedom.

3. The universality of sin was a constant preoccupation of Augustine. He wanted to make sure that sin was recognized in all its malevolent and pervasive power. However right he may have been in rejecting the view according to which the transmission of original sin is purely and simply a matter of imitation, his own view that links it with biological propagation and the sexual pleasure it entails betrays an attitude towards the human psyche and the human body—his attitude towards women may be tied to this as well—which contrasted with his perceptive and subtle evaluation of the wide range of human functioning in Book 10 of the *Confessions* and in the *City of God*.

Having expressed these caveats, which are not condemnations so much as reminders of the unfinished dimensions of Augustine's thought, we are ready to return to our positive task of retrieval.

Grace as Inner Transformation: The average thumb-nail sketch of Augustine's theology of grace tells us that Augustine rightly grasped the internal nature of grace and its prevenience: while Augustine's mind generated other brilliant insights on grace, some of them unbalanced and hasty, the solidity of these two has been ratified by widespread ecclesial assent from Augustine's time onwards.

We are concerned here with the first of these two themes, grace as an inner transformation indispensable for salvation, which emerged fairly early in Augustine's theological career. The Pelagian notion of human freedom and divine grace to him was superficial. It did justice neither to the great tradition of the Church nor to his own lengthy experience of pilgrimage towards conversion. Grace is not just exhortation and good example galvanizing a will that is already able to move towards God: it is the removal of the heart of stone, replacing it with a heart of flesh, the infusion of a power and a willingness that were not there before, the transformation of an interiority that otherwise remains utterly powerless to move towards its own true fulfillment. Grace does not coerce me into acting against my will, but changes my will itself:

> He who comes is drawn in a marvellous way to want, drawn by the One who knows how to act interiorly within the hearts of men, not to make them believe against their will—this is impossible—but to bring them to want to believe, when they did not want beforehand.[77]

The issue for Augustine is spontaneity. Unless I want to take a certain course of action out of my own inward inclination and delight, any effort to get me to take that course will at best from time to time lead me to perform the outward simulacrum of an act which falls far short of genuineness. I cannot by doing good acts acquire a spontaneous, inward, personal inclination to do the good but rather I will only do good acts if the spontaneity is already given as a gift. As far back as 396 in his response to Simplicianus, Augustine offers a striking image:

> Fire does not heat something in order to be hot but because it is hot: the wheel does not turn in order to be round but because it is round; likewise no one does good in order to receive grace but because he has received it. For how can one love justly without having been justified, live as a saint without having been sanctified, or simply live without having received the gift of life?[78]

Indeed, as Brown points out, the basic lineaments of Augustine's doctrine of interior grace were already given at that time.[79] The transposition of the Pauline conception of the eschaton dwelling within the human heart into the psychological category of delight was already in place: from early on Augustine's doctrine is not just a theoretical construct but experientially based. A classic statement of that is the *amor meus pondus meum* of the *Confessions*.[80] Concupiscence draws downwards and scatters; love reverses the pull of that gravity and leads me inwards and upwards in the Spirit.

Augustine's position emerges out of a protracted and painful experience. The will stands out as a distinct entity requiring specific action of God precisely because of the conflict which so obviously takes place within it. To be free for Augustine is to be freed from his own self, from the division which plagues that self from within. Pelagius did not have such a sense of what conflict or freedom are. Inwardly he always remains free to say yes or no, to determine himself. If conflict there is, it is between him and the realm of the not-him impinging upon him, and for that conflict to be alleviated it is sufficient that some intervention occur within that exterior realm, such as a salutary exhortation or a good example.

For Augustine freedom is in its deepest root opposed to coercion. Whether my response is necessary or not, as long as it is spontaneous and in accord with my deepest innate desires, it is truly free. The highest instance of freedom is the fulfillment in God to which I cannot say no, because it is what I most desperately and constitutively want.

For Pelagius freedom is opposed to necessity. Its essential feature is my self-determination, my ability, undiminished at all times, to say yes or no without external hindrance. For Augustine the human predicament cuts deeper than in Pelagius, and though he fails to appreciate as he should the authentic values of adult responsibility rightly stressed by Pelagius, on this precise point the vast experience of contemporary psychology on the psycho-spiritual roots of the conflicts which prevent human beings from acting in accord with their deepest aspirations will generally bear out Augustine's conclusions. This we will see from an account of the views of Rollo May, Herbert Fingarette, and Gerald May.

Rollo May's *Freedom and Destiny*[81] struggles with some of the same issues as did Augustine, and can serve as a helpful contemporary reference point. His distinction between freedom of doing and freedom of being, especially when the latter is seen in its relationship with destiny, has affinities to the notions of freedom advocated by Pelagius and Augustine respectively.

Freedom of doing is freedom in the domain of every day actions, the "capacity to pause in the face of stimuli from many directions at once and, in this pause, to throw one's weight towards this response rather than that one.''[82] This freedom does not deal with the ultimate issues of human fulfillment but with such mundane things as purchasing this necktie or that, or none at all, to use an example from May's book. This freedom of doing, of saying yes or no, is akin to the freedom of self-determination Pelagius vindicates against Augustine.

When we move to the more weighty issues of human living and fulfillment, freedom becomes more elusive and paradoxical. May would title it essential freedom, or freedom of being. This freedom "refers to the *context* out of which the urge to act emerges''.[83] Pointing to the deeper level of one's attitudes, it is the fount out of which "freedom of doing" is born. Outwardly I may be bound, incapable of effective doing, but the very adversity which afflicts me can lead me to discover the inviolable inner core, the secret private place where I am myself and relate to myself.[84] Indeed freedom of being comes into its own precisely when I struggle with my destiny. Destiny is "the pattern of limits and talents that constitutes the 'givens' in life'',[85] "the design of the universe speaking through the design of each one of us''.[86] Destiny "cannot be canceled out; we cannot erase it or substitute anything else for it. But we can choose how we shall respond''.[87]

For Augustine as for Rollo May the freedom that is linked with authentic fulfillment is situated on the level of being rather than on that of doing. It is not absolute, monadic. It is freedom-in-relation-to, freedom within a flow of life which is given and to be accepted, of which the strongest undercurrent is the *cor inquietum*. In the presence of the God who fulfills my restless heart, freedom of self-determination pales into insignificance. At this final stage of my human quest, freedom is the delightful inevitability of saying yes to who I am and who God is.[88]

A facile reading of May would lead us to believe that once I have come up against the inevitable limits of freedom of doing, it is very simple for me to take retreat in the freedom of being. In the example he adduces,[89] I could be unjustly cast into prison, thereby rendered incapable of exercising a whole range of choices, but at least my self-possession would be inviolable, my freedom of being remaining under my own control. Augustine's *Confessions* appear to be diametrically opposed to May on this point. Nothing is more desirable and natural than to find my authentic self and enjoy freedom of being, but nothing is less accessible to my unaided powers. Self-determination on the level of superficial choices never was a concern for Augustine. It is his quest for freedom of being that repeatedly brought him to the painful realization of his passivity and helplessness. For Augustine freedom of being is bound up not only with destiny but also with the gift of a transforming love which enables one to accept destiny with grace.

Unlike Augustine, Rollo May does not adopt an explicitly religious viewpoint. However in the last two chapters of his book he does intimate that freedom of being is precarious. The outcome of the struggle with destiny which leads to essential freedom is not to be taken for granted. That struggle passes through despair, defined as "that emotion which forces one to come to terms with one's destiny . . . not freedom itself, but a necessary preparation for freedom".[90] The favourable outcome of this struggle May describes in terms which, while they fail to do justice to the personal context of divine grace, do evoke Augustine's own experience:

> When a person has "hit bottom"—i.e. when he has reached ultimate despair—he then can surrender to eternal forces; this is the dynamic in all authentic conversions. I would describe this process as giving up the delusion of false hopes and, thus, acknowledging fully the facts of destiny. Then and only then can this person begin to rebuild himself. It is a superb demonstration of the hypothesis that freedom begins only when we confront destiny.[91]

Augustine plumbed other paradoxical dimensions of willing and freedom which have been articulated in the recent literature. Rollo May deals with one of them in his *Love and Will*. The will so extolled within the old culture for its power to achieve is in crisis. More and more we realize how powerless it is.[92] Is there a solution to the problem? Rollo May seeks it within the human spirit in what underlies will and decision. He begins with a discussion of wish and will. The following passage brings out their contrast:

> "Will power" expressed the arrogant efforts of Victorian man to manipulate his surroundings and to rule nature with an iron hand, as well as to manipulate himself, rule his own life in the same way as one would an object. This kind of "will" was set over against "wish" and used as a faculty by which "wish" could be denied.[93]

Following different paths, Freud and other modern healers of the psyche have rehabilitated "wish". For Rollo May:

> "Will" and "wish" may be seen as operating in polarity. "Will" requires self-consciousness; "wish" does not. "Will implies some

possibility of either/or choice; "wish" does not. "Wish" gives the
warmth, the content, the imagination, the child's play, the freshness
and the richness to "will." "Will" gives the self-direction, the maturity, to "wish". "Will" protects "wish", permits it to continue
without running risks which are too great. But without "wish",
"will" loses its life-blood, its viability, and tends to expire in self-
contradiction. If you have only "will" and no "wish", you have the
dried-up, Victorian, neopuritan man. If you have only "wish" and
no "will", you have the driven, unfree, infantile person who, as an
adult-remaining-an-infant, may become the robot man.[94]

May goes on to pursue his development of this theme in terms of intentionality, love, and care. The relationship of love and will appears to be similar
to that of wish and will: love brings us back to an original oneness with the
universe, a primordial "yes" whereas will is the "no" which each one of us
must speak in order to assert ourselves as distinct from the world.[95]

Herbert Fingarette in *The Self in Transformation* brings a sharper focus
to our transposition of Augustine's categories on will and freedom into a twentieth century context. Like Rollo May, he distinguishes instantaneous "deci-
sions" between trivial alternatives from choices of significance for the person:

In trivial choices . . . we have the closest nearest approximation to
a single, momentary "act of will". Go left or go right; sell or buy;
move the lever up or down . . . Either what we choose in these matters does not matter or it is effectively governed by pre-existing
rules, goals, techniques . . . However, if we turn to our own important private deliberations, and certainly if we turn to the crucial
deliberations which take place in psychotherapy, we see that responsible choice by no means consists simply in decisively "taking
the initiative" at some crucial instant. On the contrary, significant
choice involves the "free" production of thoughts, feelings, fantasies, memories; it involves the willingness to contemplate these, to
"savor" them, to explore them, to give them scope to operate, if
only within limits and in tentative fashion . . . Finally serious
choices, the choices which make one a new person in a new world,
involve that sometimes sudden, sometimes gradual, but always involuntary, fusion of the whole into a meaningful pattern which then
"takes over." "*Now* I see how I must act." "Now I understand
what I must do." We *discover*, when deliberation is successful, that
"this is it."[96]

For Fingarette while the neurotic is plagued with an excess of willfulness,[97] the psychologically mature person in personally significant choices experiences the mystic paradox of complete freedom coexisting with utter passivity. What the mature person can and the neurotic person can't do is surrender. Here too we have a striking parallel with Augustine's experience. He experienced a rebirth of freedom in his conversion, but at the same time that freedom emerged through a number of inner events over which he had no control. Many years of striving had got him nowhere. At root his conversion was an event which took place in him but not from him. At core his freedom was passive.

Augustine goes beyond Fingarette on certain points. He suggests that the radical passivity of will is passivity vis-à-vis the infusion of the Holy Spirit, and he formulates the profound continuity between his earlier self and his converted self in terms of the restless heart which was there from the beginning and which, at that crucial moment, received God's gift, not that of final rest in God but that of steady and secure movement towards God.

The final author in this brief survey is Gerald May. The distinction between willingness and willfulness which he develops in his *Will and Spirit* will help us to pull together many strands[98] (See table on p. 178.)

In his struggle to defend and illustrate the grace that had transformed his life, Augustine shows an awareness of the issues quite compatible with that of these contemporary students of the human psyche. It is clear that Augustine, unlike Pelagius, had an appreciation of the role in human development of willingness and passivity, convinced as he was that the willful flexing of psychic muscles would achieve perfection. These contemporary authors do not claim that the willingness which is of such fundamental importance in human development is in final analysis God's gift of love poured within the human heart. Yet they are open to a mystery of profound gratuity within human life, and they help us to better understand and transpose the insights offered by Augustine. Chapter One of this book suggests that the powerlessness of our world is in large part due to a spontaneity which is shackled and paralyzed. Augustine and these contemporary authors have much to contribute to an analysis of that powerlessness, and to the transformed spontaneity that can overcome it.

Grace as Total Prevenience: As we have already seen, in the heat of the controversy with Pelagius the inward dimension of grace seems to occupy the entire stage in Augustine's reflections, but, if one considers the fuller picture which he offers us in *Spirit and Letter* and above all in the *Confessions*, one appreciates the balance of his doctrine, its easy correspondence with the trinitarian pattern which so deeply permeates his contemplative gaze.

Willingness[99]	Willfulness[100]
"Spirit has something to do with the energy of our lives, the life-force that keeps us active and dynamic." (3)	"Will has more to do with personal intention and how we decide to use our energies." (3)
"Spirit has a quality of connecting us with each other, with the world around us, and with the mysterious Source of all." (3)	"Will has qualities of independence, of personal freedom, and of decision making." (3)
(*Will flowing with spirit*): "At such times, it is indeed as if something in us had said yes. Then, at least for a moment, we are whole." (3)	(*Will pulling away from spirit*): "At such times something deep within us is saying no, something is struggling against the truth of who we really are and what we are really called to do" (3)
"willingness implies a surrendering of one's self-separateness, an entering-into, an immersion in the deepest processes of life itself." (6)	"willfulness is the setting of oneself apart from the fundamental essence of life in an attempt to master, direct, control, or otherwise manipulate existence." (6)
". . . saying yes to the mystery of being alive in each moment" (6)	". . . saying no, or perhaps more commonly, 'Yes, but. . .' " (6)

Let us remind ourselves of the three elements of his doctrine of grace. (See p. 179.)

These three elements of grace are linked together in a dynamic flow. In first place, unless we are primordially created with an orientation which only God can fulfill, the external and internal elements of grace, in which God powerfully approaches us, are a violation rather than a fulfillment of our beings. There would be no spontaneity, in Augustine's sense no freedom, in our response to the divine initiative. Because of this primordial orientation inscribed within our nature, grace liberates rather than shackles nature,[101] and the final irrevocable yes to God is the pinnacle, not the abolition, of freedom. In second place, unless the external promptings of grace culminate in the Spirit's inward

The three experiences:	The three elements:	The three Persons:
The restless heart, the irrepressible yearning for beatitude with God, the necessary ground of receptivity towards God within the human being, which, apart from the two other elements, remains a nameless undertow.	**PRIMORDIAL** Yearning or Desire	The **FATHER** who creates the formless void. *(potency)*
The constant external promptings of providence, leading, suggesting, cajoling, convicting of sin, teaching, illuminating, which, apart from internal grace, leave one powerless.	**EXTERNAL** Teaching or Illumination	The **WORD** who illuminates it. *(form)*
The inner transformation of the self through the love of God poured into the heart: on this point Augustine adds something not found in Pelagius.	**INTERNAL** Stable love or Inner Delight	The **SPIRIT** who stabilizes it. *(act)*

transformation of those whose attention they beckon, the orientation to God which arises within those prompted in this way will remain fleeting, unstable, incapable of effectively moving them towards God.[102]

This dynamic is in the image of the triune God. While it is true that for Augustine the three persons inhabit in the soul of the person who is justified,[103] the above doctrine shows the three persons also dynamically present in the very process by which a person moves from the original endowment of a restless heart through the intermediate stage of justification to final rest in God. The image of the Trinity is embedded within us not just in *stasis* but also in *dynamis*.

Thus in final analysis grace is a comprehensive reality for Augustine. There is no person, event, aspect of his human existence which did not come under the intent of God to bring him by mysterious ways to fulfillment. The conversion which he describes in Book 8 of the *Confessions* is not the beginning of grace for him, but the privileged moment from which he can begin to appreciate the presence of grace from the very beginnings of his life, leading up to that conversion, and leading him still further towards the beatitude which he had always sought so earnestly. Absolutely nothing about his life escapes the constant prayer of gratitude to the Father which weaves in and out of the *Confessions*. Wherever he finds himself, God is there first.

Another way of putting this inescapability of grace is to say that grace is absolutely prevenient. There is no human initiative, movement of heart or mind, desire, which is not preceded by the presence of God who not only sustains our hearts with a holy restlessness but also continually calls us. In the final analysis grace is always response rather than initiative.

Thus while Augustine developed precise views on the prevenience of grace under the stimulus of discussions he had with those later termed semi-Pelagians, especially when suggestions were made linking the gift of grace to a prior initiative, real or anticipated, on the part of the one seeking it, the inner ground of that doctrine of prevenience is found in the very experience of his life. Its constant undertow was an emptiness which God implanted within him and which only God could fulfill, and the providence of God, relentless and unfathomable, leading him to that fulfillment.

Striking contemporary parallels to Augustine's doctrine of internal grace can be found in the thought of sensitive authors of our own day; we have put forward some of them. The basis for a similar transposition of the other dimensions of grace, primordial and external, is perhaps not so readily at hand. This is above all true of the limitless yearning which underlies every human act towards or away from God: contemporary non-theological authors leave this area relatively undeveloped. By contrast it has emerged as a significant theme in the theology of this century. Rahner's supernatural existential is the best illustration of this fact.

The basis in contemporary study of human experience for speaking about the external dimension of grace is less tenuous. Students of human development within a social context make it abundantly clear that without a suitable outer constellation, in part facilitated by an appropriate social order, of significant events and persons, human development is thwarted. Along these lines practitioners of liberation theology attach great importance to the transformation of outer structures. Apart from the struggle for liberation from oppressive structures, both oppressors and oppressed are condemned to remain truncated as human beings. Authentic structures of society enflesh the dynamics of grace, inauthentic ones those of sin. Other disciplines will help us reflect on the difference between manipulative and liberating interpersonal relationships. Reflection on the ways by which human beings can exercise genuine influence on each other may help us grasp less inadequately the mystery of a God who as persuader is at once most effective and most respectful. Moving the question to a broader context, Rollo May, as we have seen, wishes to integrally respect the dialectic of freedom and destiny. There is no such a thing as freedom in a vacuum. Freedom always functions within a context over which it has no control. I am free to react, but I do not often choose the situation I react to. Thus a grace that touches the freedom and ignores the context is only half a grace.

Grace as Kenotic Freedom: Freedom is a leit-motiv of Augustine's theology of grace. As we saw, for him freedom increases in proportion as grace is operative. In *Spirit and Letter* he makes a sharp distinction between free-will (*liberum arbitrium*) a basic inalienable human endowment utterly ineffective without grace, and the freedom of the will (*libertas arbitrii*) which enables it to act effectively towards its only fulfillment, beatitude with God. This *libertas* is power (*posse*), love, grace as the infused gift of God.[104]

As we saw, for Augustine freedom is primordially opposed not to necessity but to a servitude which coerces me into acting contrary to my authentic nature. Its deepest realization is not an act in which I remain equally able to say yes or no, but an act in which, determined from within and not from without, I spontaneously say an irreversible yes to the only One who can fulfill me. In other terms Augustine stresses freedom of authentic fulfillment rather than freedom of choice. Though this latter plays an essential role in my human journey, it is superseded when that journey has reached its goal. Indeed when freedom of choice enters into play in moments of deep significance to me, e.g. moments of conversion, a sense of passivity prevails, as we have seen, a sense of "I can do no other." At those times especially it is akin to the freedom of fulfillment towards which it inescapably points.

Augustine's perspective on freedom dovetails with the Pauline theme of kenosis and sheds light on the painful re-birth of freedom taking place in our day. For him the passage from velleity (*velle*) to freedom (*posse*) does not take place by a clenching one's psychic fists or by asserting oneself against all odds. It requires a letting go, a flowing with the spontaneity which alone brings effective power. In this sense vulnerability (*pati*) is at the heart of freedom (*posse*). While Augustine does not develop the kenotic theme as explicitly as do Paul and certain contemporary authors, that theme does emerge at three significant points in his thought.

In first place Augustine closely links his conversion with his ability to appreciate not only "The Word was God" with the Platonists but also "The Word became flesh" with the followers of Jesus incarnate. The Platonists were quite at home with the Son's entitlement to the attributes of Godhead, but not with his kenosis, his assumption of the form of a slave.[105] Only in his kenosis can our kenosis take place, as we humbly acknowledge our own weakness and surrender to the living God:

> From the clay of which we are made he built for himself a lowly house in this world below, so that by this means he might cause those who were to be made subject to him to abandon themselves and come over to his side. He would cure them of the pride that swelled up in their hearts and would nurture love in its place, so that they should no longer stride ahead confident in themselves, but might realize their own weakness when at their feet they saw God himself, enfeebled by sharing this garment of our mortality. And at last, from weariness, they would cast themselves down upon his humanity, and when it rose they too would rise.[106]

In second place the subsequent decision to leave the well-ordered monastic life to become a bishop, plunging back into the complexity of the world, making his psyche vulnerable to innumerable pushes and pulls, is a form of kenosis even more closely patterned on kenosis in the original Pauline sense. Paul uses the example of the one in the form of God who takes the form of the servant to motivate Christians in Philippi and in Corinth not to cling to what gives them security but to let go and enter into the state of vulnerability which alone builds relationship and community. In the case of Augustine the equivalent to the *forma Dei* is the new found state of conversion which he originally planned to perpetuate by means of the sheltered monastic-cum-academic existence he was hoping to lead with his companions, and the equivalent to the *forma servi* is the unsettled life of the bishop of Hippo, which would only accentuate the complexities and the unfinished integration of his own psyche, plunging him into the ambiguities of history.[107]

Book 10 of the *Confessions* lets us view a mellower Augustine willing to accept the ambiguities within and without, to trust in the stable orientation towards God which prevails in his life and to derive from it a pervasive inner peace. The conversion of our hearts does not snatch us away from the battlefield in which our psyches search for fuller integration, but, flowing from and leading to kenosis, it makes that battle redemptive, incorporates it within the agonic struggle which will lead to the new heaven and the new earth. Book 10 of the *Confessions* is a powerful statement of how grace, having freed the heart with the love of God, moves into the psyche, permeating it with that love, gradually and imperfectly here below and perfectly in the next world.

The third instance of this freeing dimension of grace follows from the second. When Augustine as bishop entered into the realm of world events, he saw writ large in them the threads of ambiguity which ran throughout his own psyche. As he tells us in *City of God*, this world is a vale of tears, marked by a profound longing which will never be totally satisfied here below. Even those endowed with genuine virtues have to suffer:

> . . . they [the genuine virtues] do not profess to have the power to ensure that the people in whom they exist will not suffer any miseries; genuine virtues are not such liars as to advance such claims. But they do claim that though human life is compelled to be wretched by all the grievous evils of this world, it is happy in the expectation of the world to come, just as, in expectation, it is saved . . . We are beset by evils, and we have to endure them steadfastly until we reach those goods where there will be everything to supply us with delight beyond the telling, and there will be nothing any longer that we are bound to endure. Such is the salvation which in the world to come will also be itself the ultimate bliss.[108]

For Augustine, those who belong to the city of God do not settle into this world. They will make use of the patterns by which the earthly city ensures a modicum of peace and order, but expect little of them, because they are profoundly convinced of their transitoriness.[109] The present life is full of misery. Yet the one who sets his heart on the other life may rightfully "without absurdity be called happy even now, though rather by future hope than in present reality".[110] Indeed, as Augustine goes on to tell us:

> . . . the present does not bring into play the true goods of the mind; since no wisdom is true wisdom if it does not direct its attention, in all its prudent decisions, its resolute actions, its self-control and its just dealings with others, towards that ultimate state in which God will be all in all, in the assurance of eternity and the perfection of peace.[111]

Nothing is ever definitively achieved or maintained in this world by human effort. What appears good may be secretly vitiated by the seeking of what is not God. The sober virtues by which the ancient Romans prospered were naught else but splendid vices. Even the Church on earth is subject to the same vicissitudes. Only at the end can the wheat be safely separated from the chaff.[112]

Wisdom invites us to let go of the anxious concern which leads us to unduly focus on our activity here on earth as if it were self-enclosed and self-motivated, investing that activity with an efficacy and its intended goals with an ultimacy which they cannot bear. We are always invited to discern the patterns of a providence which takes up the strands of our activity and with them achieves what is beyond our scope, a fulfillment not in this world but in the next, and to entrust ourselves to the flow of that providence, no matter how paradoxical it may seem. Kenotic detachment from the immediate results of one's action is the key to inner peace in the midst of outer turbulence and ambiguity. That detachment is the gift of freeing grace.

Augustine gave that detachment a somewhat pessimistic hue. Etched into his mind was the helpless senescence of the Roman Empire falling into ruins all around him. He dwelt not so much on the inner freedom that helps us in the toil and pain of our determined striving to achieve the good possible in a humanly intractable situation, as on the inner freedom, grounded in God, that enables us to be reconciled to our helplessness in the midst of events over which we have no control: we will never be able to ever achieve anything solid and definitive here below, anything clearly and unambiguously good.

If we are to situate Augustine's thought within the kenotic framework, we would say that he concentrates on the downward movement of kenosis, the assumption of the *forma servi* which in this case is the intractability of human history. Other authors, sensitive to the disarray and helplessness of the first world, adopt an emphasis akin to that of Augustine.[113] By contrast a more optimistic contemporary theology stresses what human effort can and ought to achieve. Unjust structures are not there to be put up with but to be transformed by a human activity which is creative and co-creative. Pushed to its extreme this theology would hold that the final ultra-terrestrial fulfillment Augustine so intensely longs for is but a symbol of the terrestrial achievements within our power. In a more balanced version this theology accepts that the fulfillment of this world has a transcendent dimension, but stresses the elements of continuity that link this world and the next: our activity hastens, prepares the way for the coming of the kingdom.[114]

Using kenosis as a frame of interpretation, we can line up the positions on this key issue as follows:

a) The Augustinian position concentrates on the downward movement within kenosis, and attaches very little significance to the corresponding upward movement as it touches the world we live in.[115] We are to free ourselves from undue expectations about what we can do here below and live in hope that God will in his own time and way be our future as he comes to us. Our stance is one of waiting rather than building.

b) The position at the opposite end of the scale would deny the path of kenosis and foster the illusion of an exaltation without crises or set-backs by which, with our own resources, we create a new heaven and a new earth. It would offer us a movement from humankind to God without the need to assume the prior movement from God to humankind, an exaltation by means of human activity without the prior kenosis which brings about detachment from the re- sults of that activity.

c) A third position attempts to occupy the middle ground where kenosis and exaltation are kept in proper equilibrium. This position ranges between a more creation-centered approach in which our efforts to transform the world are seen as co-creative, and a more redemption-centered approach in which we are called upon to enter into Jesus' struggle for liberation in our own day, suffering with him as we engage in the transformation of the structures of our existence. The latter emphasis seems more appropriate to our day and more in harmony with the Gospel's unmistakable call for kenosis. It is precisely in the measure that action is detached, that it is free from the illusion of self- generated power and self-enclosed expectation that it can achieve something of real signifi- cance, of significance for the kingdom.

A Few Words of Recapitulation: While open to the Johannine emphasis on divinization, Augustine's theology of grace builds on the Pauline pattern. Though a concern akin to Paul's for the broader context of salvation history emerges in *City of God*, the contribution for which Augustine is above all re- membered is his personalization and internalization of the Pauline patterns of grace. Highly sensitive and articulate, he was able to identify the processes of justification and sanctification as they occurred within his own personal jour- ney, and put them across in terms and images that have lasted to this day.

Unlike Paul, prior to his conversion Augustine was a catechumen and had many years of sympathetic contact with Christianity, a contact which only sharpened his own awareness of a deep desire for beatitude that only God could fulfill, akin to the longing of the one who in Romans 7 exclaims "Who can deliver me from this body of death?" In his *Confessions* he discerns that longing as a thread that runs through his life both prior and subsequent to his conversion, and relates it to the outer and inner impact of God as God graces him in justification and sanctification. This makes it possible for him to leave to his theological posterity the makings of a triad which supplements the justification/sanctification/salvation triad of Paul and which has unmistakable trinitarian overtones, that of primordial, external, and internal grace.

NOTES

1. Cf. K. Stendahl's "The Apostle Paul and the Introspective Consciousness of the West", in *Paul among Jews and Gentiles* (Philadelphia: Fortress, 1976), esp. pp. 84–85 and 90.

2. A key text is found in *Letter 140*, 4,10.

3. *Confessions*, 4,9; 4,11.

4. Cf. Laporte, "Grace, the Mystery of God's Abundance," in *Word and Spirit* (Toronto: Regis College Press, 1975).

5. Indeed, unlike Paul and Augustine, only Aquinas among the authors we will consider in this book lived in an era marked by newness, development, a sense of as yet untrammeled horizons.

6. Peter Brown, *Augustine of Hippo: A Biography*, (Berkeley: Univ. of California Press, 1969), p. 177.

7. *Confessions*, 1,20.

8. *Confessions*, 2,2; also cf. 3,1: "I was struggling to reach you, but you thrust me back so I knew the taste of death. For 'you thwart the proud'." (*Confessions*, 4,15)

9. *Confessions*, 1,11; 7,5.

10. *Confessions*, 3,4.

11. *Spirit and Letter*, par. 5.

12. Cf. *Confessions*, 10,6 as compared to *Confessions*, 7,7. A most helpful discussion of the notions of free-will, freedom, and beatitude in Augustine is to be found in M. Huftier, "Libre arbitre, liberté et péché chez S. Augustin," in *Rech. Théol. Anc. Méd.*, 1966, 187–281.

13. *Spirit and Letter*, par. 60. At this point in his career Augustine was something of a congruist: he had not yet clearly linked this mystery of persuasion with the infusion of the love of God in the heart of the one predestined. In this text Augustine refers to these promptings as both external and internal. The external promptings come from

side the person, i.e. through the providential series of events which mark each one's life. The internal promptings are God's action within the mind and psyche of the person. Both internal and external promptings are external to the will itself, which says yes or no to God. Cf. discussion of this in Appendix B of Laporte, *Les structures dynamiques de la grâce*.

14. Cf. Gisbert Greshake on how Pelagius conceives the innate endowment from God more positively and inclusively than Augustine: *Geschenkte Freiheit: Einführung in die Gnadenlehre*, (Freiburg: Herder, 1977), pp. 77–80.

15. Eugene TeSelle, *Augustine the Theologian*, (New York: Herder & Herder, 1970), pp. 135 ff.

16. The Thomist triad of potency, form, and act, so influential in the thought of Lonergan, is quite pertinent here: innate desire corresponding to potency, illumination to form, the stabilization of love to act. Augustine himself in reflections on trinitarian traces within creation adumbrates this Thomist triad: "There are also three things looked for in any artist: natural ability, training, and the use to which he puts them. Those are needed for any real achievement; and his ability is judged by his talent, his training by his knowledge, his use of them by the enjoyment of the fruits of his labours." And a bit further, but in broader terms: " . . . our nature has God as its author; and so without doubt we must have him as our teacher, if we are to attain true wisdom; and for our happiness we require him as the bestower of the delight in our hearts which only he can give" (CG 11,25).

17. *Confessions*, 5,10. This account is phrased in terms which have a remarkable affinity with the language of contemporary psychological writers such as R.D. Laing. Cf. his account of the schizoid condition in *The Divided Self*. For him the schizoid person is afraid of the impingement of a hostile reality upon himself. There occurs within him a dissociation between an inner self, which is unembodied, and an embodied self which he regards as false, as not really pertaining to himself. Thus that impingement, which touches his embodiment considered to be false, no longer threatens him or touches him. Milder forms of this defense mechanism appear to be at work in the common phenomenon of repression.

18. Cf. J.J. O'Meara, *The Young Augustine* (Staten Island: Alba House, 1965), pp. 140 ff.

19. *Confessions*, 5,2.

20. *Confessions*, 7,10.

21. *Confessions*, 7,17.

22. *Confessions*, 7,3.

23. *Confessions*, 7,16.

24. *Confessions*, 8,8–10.

25. *Confessions*, 8,12.

26. *Confessions*, 7,17.

27. *Confessions*, 10,17.

28. *Confessions*, 10,6.

29. *Confessions*, 7,9; 7,18.

30. *Confessions*, 7,20.

31. *Confessions*, 7,18

32. *Confessions*, 13,9. Also cf. 13,7–8, and the famous passage in Chapter 9 which compares the downward "weight" of concupiscence to the "weight" of the Spirit which draws us upwards.

33. This account complements his reflection in the *City of God* on the trials and tribulations of the entire pilgrim people of God, in exile within the city of man.

34. Cf. pp. 115.

35. This wider self is distinct from the self as center point, or *pneuma*, or, in Augustinian terms, inmost heart. In the Jungian study of E. F. Edinger, entitled *Ego and Archetype* (Baltimore: Penguin, 1972), we find this statement germane to our own struggle with the meanings of "self": "In fact the conception of the self is a paradox. It is simultaneously the center and the circumference of the circle of totality." (p. 6) In this section we will generally use self to mean the wider self, the totality which is included within the circumference, and ego as the conscious controlling component of that self. We will presume the view expressed in Chapter 3 (pp. 123) that it is only in submission to God that the self as the centre point can effectively utilize the ego as an instrument of bringing the wider self into the fullness of light and integration.

36. *Confessions*, 7,7.

37. Cf. William Desmond, "Augustine's Confessions: on Desire, Conversion, and Reflection", in *ITQ*, 1980, p. 27.

38. Desmond, op. cit., is very helpful on this point. For instance, he says: "The *Confessions* is the memory of a homecoming. Man strays from where he should be; to recover himself he returns to where his spirit is at home . . . There is the wandering out and the Odyssey back; the first alone disintegrates in dispersed externality; the second recovers the self lost to externality and restores it to its true inwardness." (p. 31) One might add that the later movement of Augustine's life as a bishop is a return to externality, but on the basis of a recovered inwardness. In other words, the conversion from multiplicity to unity is followed by a return from unity to multiplicity: "Truly it is by continence that we are made as one and retain that unity of self which we lost by falling apart in the search for a variety of pleasures." (*Confessions*, 10,29) In Pauline terms the *kenosis* of sanctification follows upon the inward gift of justification.

39. *Confessions*, 9,4

40. Chapters 15 and 16 of Brown's *Augustine of Hippo* are most helpful on this maturation process.

41. *Confessions*, 9,4.

42. *Confessions*, 10,6.

43. *Confessions*, 10,27.

44. *Confessions*, 10,29.

45. *Confessions*, 10,40.

46. *Confessions*, 10,39.

47. *Confessions*, 10,5.

48. *Confessions*, 10,8

49. *Confessions*, 10,40.

50. *Confessions*, 7,20. The reference is to 1 Cor 8:1: "Knowledge puffs up, charity builds up." The image of inflation recurs in the thought of Carl Jung, who uses it to speak of the infantile self not yet willing to accept the limitations of life. Cf. Edinger's account, *Ego and Archetype*, pp. 3–36.

51. Patout Burns in *The Development of Augustine's Doctrine of Operative Grace* (Paris: Etudes Augustiniennes, 1980), p. 21, states: "The essentialist and conceptualist character of these dialogues stands in sharp contrast to the experiential grounding of his subsequent analysis of the human condition."

52. *City of God*, 14,25.

53. Rev 20:2, cited in *City of God*, 20,17.

54. Indeed the predominant note sounded by Augustine is rather one of forbearance and patience in the midst of ambiguity and adversity than one of resolutely taking up battle against the evils of this world. The inner transformation which alone will bring fulfillment passes through the crucible of "mutual forgiveness and the great care needed for the maintenance of peace". As a result of that "change in us" we find "a greater tranquillity, here and now"; and subsequently, when we have "attained perfect peace and achieved immortality" we "will reign without sin, in eternal peace" (*City of God*, 15,6). This point is further developed in *City of God*, 19,4: "For in this state the very virtues, which are certainly the best and most useful of man's endowments here below, bear reliable witness to man's miseries in proportion to their powerful support against man's perils, hardships and sorrows. In fact, if they are genuine virtues (and genuine virtues can exist only in those in whom true godliness is present) they do not profess to have the power to ensure that the people in whom they exist will not suffer any miseries; genuine virtues are not such liars as to advance such claims. But they do claim that though human life is compelled to be wretched by all the grievous ills of this world, it is happy in the expectation of the world to come, just as, in expectation, it is saved."

55. *City of God*, 19,17.

56. A thorough and perceptive discussion of the points raised in this paragraph is found in R. Markus, *Saeculum: History and Society in the Theology of St. Augustine* (Cambridge: Cambridge University Press, 1970), especially Chapter 3.

57. *City of God*, 19,21.

58. *City of God*, 19,23; also cf. *City of God*, 19,21.

59. *City of God*, 15,1 contrasts Cain and Abel: "Scripture tells us that Cain founded a city, whereas Abel, as a pilgrim, did not found one. For the city of the saints is up above, although it produces citizens here below, and in their persons the City is on pilgrimage until the time of its kingdom comes. At that time it will assemble all those citizens as they rise again in their bodies; and then they will be given the promised kingdom, where with their Prince, 'the king of ages', they will reign, world without end." Also cf. *City of God*, 18,51; 19,26.

60. *City of God*, 19,26.

61. *City of God*, 19,17.

62. *City of God*, 1,35

63. Cf. Brown, *Augustine of Hippo*, p. 315.

64. Cf. Markus, *Saeculum . . .* , pp. 54–63.

65. *City of God*, 14,28. Also cf. *City of God*, 14,1; 14,4.

66. Cf. for instance "So also the earthly city, whose life is not based on faith, aims at an earthly peace, and it limits the harmonious agreement of citizens concerning the giving and obeying of orders to the establishment of a kind a compromise of human wills about the things relevant to mortal life" (*City of God*, 19,17). Augustine does not belittle this earthly peace, but he sees it as but a pale image of the final integration in store for those who inwardly are leavened by the heavenly city (cf. *City of God*, 19,17, towards the end). This is the uneasy state of the human psyche as well. Compromise and repression go hand in hand: "For this reason there is no perfect peace so long as command is exercised over the vicious propensities, because the battle is fraught with peril while those vices that resist are being reduced to submission, while those which have been overcome are not yet triumphed over in peaceful security, but are repressed under a rule still troubled by anxieties." (*City of God*, 19,27)

67. *City of God*, 15,3.

68. *City of God*, 15,5. For Augustine the archetype of the Romulus/Remus conflict is the Cain/Abel conflict. The issue is situated at a yet deeper level: "the one who slew his brother was not jealous of him because his power would be more restricted if both wielded the sovereignty; for Abel did not aim at power in the city which his brother was founding. But Cain's was the diabolical envy that the wicked feel for the good simply because they are good, while they themselves are evil." (*City of God*, 15,5) Brown, *Augustine . . .* , pp. 320–321, offers a perceptive comment on this. The archetypic conflict (Cain/Abel) has to do with Abel's basic goodness exemplified in his offering of sacrifice to God; the derived conflict (Romulus/Remus) has to do with the relations of human beings to each other. In his own way Augustine reflects the primacy Paul gives within human integration to a heart turned to God above all else.

69. *City of God*, 15,5.

70. *City of God*, 19.17.

71. *City of God*, 19.17.

72. One might facetiously or seriously suggest that "City of Man" should, in deference to feminist sensitivities, be translated as "City of Man/Woman". The reasons for not doing so are far from facetious. Augustine may have been more to the point than he intended. The oppressive dynamics which define the City of Man are very similar to the dynamics of the patriarchal system which contemporary feminists bemoan. In these terms, what is wrong about the city of man is maleness gone rampant.

73. This point is briefly discussed by J. Chené, *La théologie de S. Augustin. Grâce et prédestination* (Le Puy: Mappus, 1961), pp. 46–50.

74. In *Enchiridion*, 103,27, Augustine proposes two interpretations of the statement that God wants all human beings to be saved: a) No one can be saved unless God wants him or her to be saved; b) God wants human beings taken from all categories and conditions to be saved.

75. Cf. p. 169.

76. The classic instance of this is the Jesuit-Dominican-Jansenist controversies of the sixteenth and seventeenth centuries.

77. *Cont. 2 Ep. Pel.* 1,19,37.

78. *De Div Quaest ad Simp.* 1,2,3.

79. Brown, *Augustine . . .* , pp. 153–157.

80. *Confessions*, 13,9.

81. Rollo May, *Freedom and Destiny* (New York: Norton, 1981).

82. Ibid., p. 54.

83. Later in *Freedom and Destiny*, pp. 177 ff. May relates freedom of being to the psyche-self and freedom of doing to the ego-self. His use of psyche and ego is akin to our earlier use, based on Jung, of self and ego, the self being both wider and more central than the ego.

84. Ibid., p. 56.

85. Ibid., p. 89.

86. Ibid., p. 90.

87. Ibid., p. 89.

88. In *The Self in Transformation*, Fingarette in his process of reflection on this point converges with Augustine and Rollo May: " . . . the sense that 'I can do no other' is precisely the mark of the genuinely autonomous free agent in his most profound actions" (p. 56).

89. Ibid., pp. 55-58.

90. May, *Freedom and Destiny*, p. 235.

91. Ibid., p. 236. As one can readily see, for May despair is opposed not so much to hope as to presumption. To despair is to experience the full impact of the negativity which hope implies, the negativity the classical tradition refers to as the *arduum*, the difficult. Cf. Aquinas' *Summa Theologiae*, Ia–IIae, q. 40. However should one become paralyzed at the despair stage, then his or her despair becomes akin to despair in its classical opposition to hope.

92. Rollo May, *Love and Will* (New York: Norton, 1969), Chapter 7.

93. Ibid., pp. 204–05.

94. Ibid., p. 218. The affinities of this with the contemporary re-expressions of the Pauline doctrine of justification and sanctification in Chapter Two are obvious. A perceptive and creative analysis of the parallel to this point in the doctrine of Thomas Aquinas is found in F.E. Crowe, "Complacency and Concern in the Thought of St. Thomas", *Theological Studies*, 1959, pp.·1–39, 198–230, 343–395. Further developments of this will be found in the next chapter.

95. A valuable comparison could be made between May's position and the one that John Macmurray develops in *Persons in Relation*, especially in Chapter 4, where he deals with the positive and negative phases of the child's personal development in relation to the mother.

96. Fingarette, *Self in Transformation*, pp. 55–56.

97. Ibid., p. 58.

98. Gerald May, *Will and Spirit* (New York: Harper and Row, 1982). The

numbers in brackets after the entries in the following diagram refer to pages of this book.

99. Though he does not set willingness off against willfulness, Lonergan uses the term willingness in *Insight* in a way which relates to the context of this discussion. He usually refers to universal willingness, which is a readiness, an openness to do the rationally affirmed good whatever that entails. The human predicament is that such willingness cannot be easily acquired. As Lonergan puts it: "How is one to be persuaded to genuineness and openness, when one is not yet open to persuasion?" (p. 624) For Lonergan universal willingness ultimately is the love of God poured into our hearts by the Holy Spirit, or in the terms of his special transcendent solution to the problem of evil developed in *Insight*, a conjugate form which is some species of charity (pp. 696–699).

100. One will readily recognize in willfulness unchecked by willingness yet another facet of the world-view which emerged at the time of the Renaissance and later Middle Ages, and which led to the obscuring of the authentic tradition in the theology of grace.

101. " . . . Let them (i.e. the Pelagians) understand . . . that they have free will, not to despise the Lord's help with proud heart, but to call upon him with loving heart. This free will will be as free in proportion as it is sound, and sound in proportion as it is submissive to divine mercy and grace." (*Letter 157*)

102. Augustine describes these fleeting movements towards God which end up being velleities rather than effective commitments in the *Confessions*, for instance in 7,17. The Council of Orange in Canons 4, 5, and 6 suggests a two-foldness in the Spirit's work: the Spirit not only infuses (the term Augustine uses for the stable presence of the Spirit from justification onwards) but also inspires.

103. Cf. for instance *Tractatus LXXXVI*, 4.

104. Cf. Huftier, op. cit.

105. *Confessions*, 7,9.

106. *Confessions*, 7,18.

107. A striking and most helpful application of *forma Dei* to justification and *forma servi* to the path of sanctification is found in Luther's seminal *Christian Liberty*.

108. *City of God*, 19,4.

109. Ibid., 19,17.

110. Ibid., 19,20.

111. Ibid., 19,20.

112. Ibid., 18,49.

113. Jacques Ellul instances this more augustinian stance in his *Présence au monde moderne. Problèmes de la civilisation post-chrétienne*, (Genève: Roulet, 1948, pp. 56–66). For example compare the following selection with the citation of Augustine found three paragraphs back: "Les événements actuels de notre monde ne prennent leur valeur que dans la perspective du royaume de Dieu qui vient. C'est l'imminence du retour du Christ qui donne un sérieux authentique à chaque actualité, c'est par là que l'actualité reçoit son contenu véritable. Sans cette direction, l'histoire est une explosion de folie." (p. 64)

114. Perhaps Teilhard de Chardin would fit into the more optimistic category. The two approaches to the relationship between this world and the next, the first stressing continuity and the second discontinuity, can be seen in terms of their paradigm for the future. The root of future is *"futurum"*, from the Indo-European root that gives us the Greek *"phuo"* and *"phusis"* as well as the English *"be"*. The root meaning is that of growth. Inner virtualities are developed, come to the light. Continuity remains in the forefront. A contrasting model of future is contained in the word *adventus*, related in meaning to the German *"Zukunft*: the future is that which comes to me (*ad-venire, zu-kommen*), meets me as I continue my journey. Right now it is not in me but ahead of me. How the present relates to the future differs in both paradigms: we grow towards the *futurum*; we wait for the *adventus*. The presence of the images of both waiting and growing in the New Testament invites us to avoid by-passing one or the other of these images of the future, and to discern in them yet another pattern of *coincidentia oppositorum*.

115. I say "very little significance" rather than "no significance" because if Augustine does not hold out hope that this world will be transformed, at least his view enables the person to cope, to survive.

Chapter Five

THOMAS AQUINAS:
GRACE FOR AN EMERGING WORLD

Augustine offered us a vision for the first world as it experiences impasse and dissolution. Inviting us to cultivate detachment in the midst of social breakdown, to find solace in the world of interiority where God is already present, he is a prophet of freedom. Thomas Aquinas follows in his footsteps, but the context of his theology as well as its inner bent is optimistic and constructive. He is a hospitable thinker, welcoming input from any source, respectfully molding it into an architectonic whole. He offers us a model of how to harness the creative forces at work in the midst of our disarray, how to bring them to synthesis and fruition.

Nonetheless we cannot transport Aquinas into our own century and without further ado make use of his insights. Though he vehicles a profound mutation in which the personal/anthropocentric *Denkform* comes into its own, as we saw in Chapter Two, he does this with pre-critical innocence, and the nature of his achievement has remained largely hidden. On the surface, what stands out is the importation of the meta-physical categories of Aristotle. Beneath the surface, however, we find a profound effort to enliven theology and inwardly shape it according to what is most original in Christian revelation.[1] The passing of many centuries gives us the perspective needed to grasp this point. The 14th century by and large supposed that Aquinas paid scant attention to the freedom which the Christian thought-form entails, and explored alternate paths of thought which it felt more appropriate. They still deeply mark our lives.

In this chapter we will attempt to bring out the genuine achievement, Christian and personalist, of Thomas' doctrine of grace. That achievement may lie fallow in standard accounts of his thought, which stress the Aristotelian armature of his doctrine. Many of the basic points which emerged in our chapters on Paul and Augustine will recur in our treatment of Aquinas, but the latter's perspective on them will contribute greatly to our project.

Students of Aquinas on grace often heedlessly plunge right into the treatise on grace at the end of the *Prima Secundae*, oblivious to what precedes it. The first three sections of this chapter will deal with the antecedents of Aquinas' thought on grace, in the hope that we will be able to bring to the light Aquinas' sensitivity, unexpected by some, to the human person and psyche. Aquinas inserts grace into a doctrine of humanity created in the image and likeness of God and returning to God. The human reality is profoundly embodied: graced acts entail a complex interaction of different aspects of the human psyche/spirit, which is open to influences from outside (passions) and to the patterns it has already began to shape within itself (habits). In the first section we shall examine the structures and the dynamics of human activity, especially as they relate to the passions. In the second we shall focus on how Aquinas relates human activity to various kinds of habits. In the third we shall develop more fully the modalities of the specifically human form of spiritual activity.

The next section will attempt to present, in the light of the above, the key components of Thomas' doctrine of grace. The final section will attempt a sustained transposition of these components in a contemporary idiom, and draw at the very end some conclusions for a first world theology of grace.

Aquinas' contemplative vision appears to be timeless, and not without reason. Yet to prescind from the context which nurtured his thought would be a delusion. In the rest of this introduction we will evoke pertinent themes developed much more fully in works on medieval history.[2]

The myth that the Middle Ages are the final stage of the great darkness lifted only at the time of the Renaissance and Reformation needs no more refutation. The unraveling texture of the Roman Empire, so significant to Augustine's *City of God*, did lead to a period known as the Dark Ages, but by the 12th century a new world was being born, marked by developments across many areas of human endeavour. For a long time now the term "Renaissance" has been applied to that period. It featured a rebirth of human thought, aided by the translation of key texts in philosophy and science, characterized by a creativity which was at times naïve and presumptuous, but always breathtaking and full of promise.[3] At the same time people were learning new techniques of production and distribution, the economy was beginning a boom that would last until the late Middle Ages, and little by little new political structures, especially those of the new towns coming into being throughout medieval Christendom, began to challenge those fostered by the Church in its role as guardian of human and religious values in a time of eclipse.

The mood was one of optimism, of discovery. Theologians were beginning to attempt vast syntheses, confident that the most flagrant contradictions and paradoxes of reality could easily be reconciled. They were honing the new tools of Aristotelian logic and applying them to the mysteries of the faith. But to our eyes this early stage appears childlike and unreflective. It is the experience of failure and limitation that shocks thinkers/doers into self-appropriation, making them methodologically sophisticated; until opposition looms, they are satisfied to advance fully absorbed by the goal at hand, leaving the self which does the advancing in the penumbra. The emergence of this self-consciousness in the *uomo universale* of the Renaissance was a few centuries away. Aquinas belonged to a society in which personal reality was self-effaced, finding meaning and purpose within a collectivity which was both civil and ecclesiastical.

Lonergan's remarks on genuineness in *Insight* are germane here:

> The genuineness of which we think when we speak of a simple and honest soul, is the happy fruit of a life in which illusion and pretense have had no place. But there is another genuineness which has to be won back through a self-scrutiny that expels illusion and pretense and as this enterprise is difficult and its issue doubtful, we do not think of its successful outcome when we cast about for an obvious illustration of genuineness.[4]

The genuineness of Aquinas and of his era is of the first type. Applying Jungian categories[5] to this phase of civilizational development, we would situate Aquinas in a period in which the ego is about to begin the long struggle to distinguish itself from the self. The original ego/self oneness is abundantly reflected in the unclouded and uncomplicated spontaneity which allows thinkers of this era without further ado to contemplate the supremely real and to formulate it in theoretical terms.

Lonergan's second type of genuineness emerges after a long struggle which brings to the fore the key issues of self-appropriation. In the Jungian terms we evoked earlier, as the ego emerges from the original ego/self unity, it becomes inflated and alienated, loses its life-giving relation to the self. But in the course of time there follows individuation, corresponding to Lonergan's second type of genuineness, which reconciles ego and self. Put in broader terms, after the original ego/self unity of the Middle Ages there ensues a long period corresponding to ego alienation and inflation, a period now coming to its paroxysm.[6] But in the very fragments of our inflated and alienated world we are beginning to find the seeds of integration/individuation and to nurture their fragile potential. This theme of integration brings the twentieth into a secret connivance with the twelfth and thirteenth centuries, but the differences

are crucial: now integration is a task demanding a disciplined, critical awareness of interiority.

This original genuineness makes possible an innocent contemplative gaze
which takes the objectively real as it is and tries to account for it systematically
without relating it to subjectivity as such. In Lonergan's terms, at this point of
the human journey the world of theory emerges, not the world of interiority.
Nonetheless, as Metz and others point out to us, the subject-related values inherent to Christianity are profoundly embedded in the thought of Aquinas.

As a new world of human endeavour began to unfold and take its first
steps on its own, without the support of Mother Church, tension arose between
Church and state. In the earlier Middle Ages the Church had felt the need to
vindicate its own identity and prerogatives. It claimed a right to exercise ov-
ersight over civil as well as ecclesiastical affairs, as instanced by the Gregorian
reform and the canonical powers Innocent III vindicated for himself. But increasingly, and Aquinas experienced the beginnings of this newer development, men and women chafed under this tutelage. They wanted to be
themselves and to lead their own human lives without undue interference. In
the time of Aquinas this tension was healthy and manageable. The radical relatedness of religious and secular activity was not called into question. Their
opposition was seen in the context of a mutuality by that time clearly affirmed
of the persons of the Godhead themselves. This is the context in which Aquinas
developed his own approach to nature and grace, an approach, which though
it gives the primacy to grace, respects the integrity of nature and highlights the
mutuality of grace and nature. Later, and this is the story we recounted in
Chapter Two, this opposition becomes hardened.[7] Healthy tension turns into
unhealthy isolation, into disruption and conflict.

The setting of Aquinas' thought shapes the attitudes and patterns of his
theological activity in ways highly pertinent to our own twentieth century
tasks.

In first place, like his contemporaries and immediate predecessors, he
takes with utmost seriousness anything which is handed on to him from the
past. Scripture holds an indisputable primacy, but the works of any Christian
and non-Christian author available to him—with the exception of those clearly
labeled as heretics—are quoted with reverence. Reverence: rather than a sub-
servience which would destroy from the very outset the coherence of his own
thought, rather than corrosive suspicion, we find in Aquinas a hospitality
which critically yet sympathetically seeks the element of truth in anything
which is handed on to him. But in being welcomed, that truth is transformed
and reshaped as the different voices Aquinas hears are invited to dialogue with
each other.

Skills of explicitation unknown, probably unnecessary, in Aquinas' time have emerged in our age, as we struggle against the paralyzing compartmentalization and suspicion of our day. To begin with an hospitable attitude like Aquinas', but to supplement it with a sharply focused sense of the context, genesis, and method of past thought, is to make Aquinas fruitful for our age. The collaborative dimension of the theological enterprise, so important to Bernard Lonergan, is the locus where traditional hospitality and contemporary sophistication find their symbiosis.

Aquinas' attitude of hospitality presented him with a constant challenge. Critical editions of various *opera omnia* were not available to him. Often all he had was excerpts of the work of his theological predecessors intended to highlight elements of dissonance and disharmony. He would not be able, nor inclined, to achieve reconciliation by setting the discordant bits in their fuller context. Rather he attempted to create a context of his own in which doctrinal reconciliation could take place. In the terms developed at the outset of Chapter Two, he was more at home with the synchronic than with the diachronic dimension of theological interpretation.

The conflicting strands of human thought which Aquinas allowed to emerge within the horizon of his theology called for a higher viewpoint according to which they could be reconciled and related to each other. His extraordinary architectonic powers enabled him time and time again to meet the challenge this entailed. At the same time in many areas of his thought we find an incomplete knitting together of various strands of the tradition. They are allowed to simply stand in juxtaposition. Even when some measure of integration takes place, it does so unobtrusively, and usually will become apparent only after careful structural scrutiny.[8] We find in his writings a number of integrating insights which have become the backbone of the classical tradition on grace, those which relate grace (the supernatural) and nature (the connatural), healing and elevating grace, habitual and actual grace. In some of these integrations Aquinas is attempting to reconcile the different emphases of Eastern and Western theologies of grace, emphases which we find juxtaposed in the thought of Augustine, rather than integrated in a fuller theoretical perspective. Aquinas' willingness to deal with the East as well as with the West is a sign that he was instinctively aware of the need for balance. He was a theologian of the Western Church, but the Western Church did not engulf him.

HUMAN ACTIVITY AND THE PASSIONS

As we have seen, the person-related dimensions of reality do not loom large on the thirteenth century horizon. In structuring his thought on grace

Aquinas enthusiastically exploits the recently rediscovered meta-physical, cosmocentric categories of Aristotle. Nonetheless resources for a more person-oriented and psychologically developed understanding of the human reality lie just beneath the surface of his thought. By delving in the fuller anthropological context of his treatise on grace we hope to bring some of these resources to light.

The fullest expression of Aquinas' mature theology of grace comes at the end of the *Prima Secundae*, that part of the *Summa* where he deals in general terms with the human activity by which men and women journey towards their fulfillment in God. Grace touches that activity and transforms it, but at the same time the many facets of that activity, the feelings that undergird it and the habits that shape it, structure its embodied reality. In this section we will deal with Aquinas' intricate description of human activity, and in the next we will consider how habit empowers and facilitates that activity.

Bernard Lonergan has set aside the "faculty psychology" of Aristotle and Aquinas for an approach which is more contemporary, more attuned to intentionality analysis and to genuine self-appropriation.[9] This move has its advantages. It counters a mechanistic view of faculties that function like the spatially distinct parts of an engine. It encourages one to avoid reification and to use more contemporary analytic tools, so as to continue and at times to correct the work Aquinas did in his own time. Yet there is ample evidence in Aquinas' work of a rough yet perceptive phenomenological analysis of human consciousness and behaviour, and his view of the human soul is far from mechanistic. He does refer to various powers—rather than faculties—of the soul, but as he conceives them, these powers are interior to one another, engaged in constant interaction within the field of a consciousness vitally present to the entire self. Indeed these powers do not act: it is the self (supposit) that acts through them. Consciousness can focus only on one thing at a time, but its non-thematic, vital presence to a much broader range of events means that stimuli arising from one area of that consciousness can draw focused attention to themselves, in spite of one's prior resolve to concentrate on a particular object in another area.[10]

The distinction of powers which Aquinas makes is meant not to erect barriers but to reflect various specifically distinct patterns of activity present within consciousness. Indeed consciousness has no barriers within itself except those which human waywardness erects, such as, in Thomas' terms, the errant person's refusal to consider the judgement of conscience at the moment of making a sinful free choice, or in contemporary terms, neurotic defenses erected around parts of the psyche in order to keep out stimuli that would threaten a vulnerable ego.

We will continue to use concentric circles with the self in the centre as a basic symbol of the field of consciousness,[11] confident that this model is consonant with Aquinas' thought. As objects from outside impinge upon the human self, that self, which as incarnate spirit is in and of itself only latently self-present, becomes aware of them and reacts to them, and in the process awakens to itself. From that awakened self there ensues a multi-layered and intricate conscious activity, comprising discrete momentary events as well as sequences of events constituting complete human acts. The world impinges upon the self; the self shapes the world. In the process the self discovers and shapes itself.

As symbols of each conscious event within the self we will use the model of the musical note played by an instrument. That note has a dominant frequency which situates it on a scale. But what gives it its timbre, its special resonance, is the complex set of background harmonics that fill out the dominant frequency. Differences in harmonics explain why the same note played by a violin and a trumpet sounds quite different. Any momentary event within the field of consciousness has its clearly dominant note or foreground, but there are a multitude of volitional/cognitive harmonics which, though remaining in the background, give that act its appealing or discordant characteristics. More precisely, that act might be one of choice, velleity, insight, love, enjoyment, on either sensitive or spiritual level, but other components in a recessive but unmistakable way contribute to its unique timbre.

But then a complete human act does not take place in any given instant. Comprising many discrete events within consciousness, it has a beginning, a continuation, and a dénouement, positive or negative. For instance, I begin by experiencing an attraction for something, then I intend it, then I seek means to obtain it, then I choose appropriate means and implement them, facing obstacles with a mixture of hope, fear, daring, and despair, then I overcome obstacles with anger, and finally come to enjoy the possession of the object which drew my attention in the first place. Thus we need to supplement the image of the single note with that of the melody, with its chords and counterpoints, its tensions and its resolutions, an image which better expresses the intricacy—which ultimately surpasses human understanding—of human conscious activity and of the grace that transforms it.

We shall speak later about the sequence which makes up a complete human act. We first need to identify the major bi-polarities of human conscious activity, which is at once cognitive and appetitive, spiritual and psychic, direct and reflective, affective and conative.

Conscious Acts as Cognitive/Appetitive: The first bi-polarity which emerges within Thomistic anthropology is that of the cognitive and the appetitive. The cognitive and appetitive modes of relating to being are irreducibly distinct though intimately intertwined. Cognition for Aquinas is centripetal: I know something to the extent that it is present in me, that I have received it, possess it intentionally, whereas appetition is centrifugal: when I love something, I move towards it as it is in itself, I cherish the unique being it has apart from me.[12] In other words by my intellect I am oriented to the true, by my will to the good.[13]

For Aquinas these two powers are interior to each other: I know not only my own knowing but also my own willing; I know what I am attracted to, intend, choose; I will not only my own willing but also my own knowing; I am attracted to knowledge, and I will my intellect to strive towards knowledge.[14] My will and my intellect constantly enter into relations of mutual causal interdependence within the unity of the same self which acts through both of them. Indeed I cannot act except through that intimate symbiosis.

Conscious Acts as Spiritual/Psychic: For Aquinas our human nature is at the intersection of two worlds, that of the spirit and that of the body. Like Aristotle he defines us as rational animals; in the more properly personal terms that correspond to the anthropocentric *Denkform*, he also considers us as incarnate spirits.[15] Thomas clearly differentiates between the human spirit and the animal sentience (psyche) which it conjoins to itself. The first is open to being as such, and, since it is present within its own unrestricted horizon, it is radically self-reflective, and thus able to master and originate its own activity.[16] The second, according to the design of nature, responds spontaneously but automatically to a preordained specific range of objects within the realm of being (Aquinas uses the technical term "formal object"), and is not self-reflective. Thus animal instinct is determined to respond in set ways to certain stimuli, whereas with human freedom I can originate my own response.

In the realm of spiritual beings the human spirit is the lowest. Though I emerge out of the realm of matter, my nature requires that I be incarnated within that realm: I need a material and sensing body as conjoint instrument. Without the ceaseless stimuli of sensory knowledge and affective resonances (passions) I have nothing to become present to in acts of knowing and willing. Unless I actualize my primordial self-presence by being present to what is not me, I cannot elicit reflexive acts, knowing my own knowing, willing my own willing; and I can never actualize myself as a spiritual being who originates rather than responds. The inward light that constitutes me remains latent.

The differences between animal and human sensory life are crucial.[17] The sensory apparatus of an animal brings to a point the reality of that being, and is complete in itself. It serves the purposes of the biological organism, its need to develop, protect, and reproduce itself. In the case of the human, that sensory apparatus has a further and more essential purpose: it also serves as the indispensable instrument of an unfolding self-presence, of spirit in process.[18]

Because both sensory and spiritual acts occur within one consciousness which is at root marked by the self-presence of spirit, it is difficult to sift out in that consciousness what is sensory and what is spiritual. There is no such thing as a purely animal sensation or passion in the human being. At every instant of activity there operates a self-presence which promotes the object of sense to an object of spirit. In sum, though human acts of spirit and psyche are distinct they are not separate. The boundary between them is an osmotic one.[19]

The symbiosis of the spiritual and the psychic is evidenced by the parallel lines along which spiritual and psychic appetition progress:

	Psychic Level	**Spiritual Level**
Good as such	love	simple volition
Good as absent, to be acquired	desire → hope, fear, etc.	intention → election, etc.
Good as present	joy	fruition

The intertwining of these two levels is further evidenced by the frequent use of terms originally pertaining to the psychic level, as depicted in the above diagram, in order to denote realities on the spiritual level. In Thomas' theology, love, hope, joy, for example, bespeak basic affects common to human and beast as well as the highest realm of spiritual transformation wrought by God.

Situated within one conscious field, the spiritual and the psychic cannot but elicit a reaction in each other. In one direction, the passions evoke a reaction of my spiritual self, i.e. a will act. But this redounding, as Aquinas sees it, too easily clouds the control of reason and is to be carefully monitored, even shunned (for instance, a spontaneous movement of anger in my psyche might incline me to choose a vengeful action which more likely than not will be disordered). In the other direction, I can by a deliberate act of the will arouse a movement of my sense appetite in order to accomplish a certain deed more promptly and easily (for instance, I choose to take revenge and to work up my feelings so as to be able to take action vigorously and effectively); or else a vehement act of my will (e.g. the spiritual abhorrence of some injustice) spills over into my psyche (e.g. brings about feelings of indignation with the appropriate bodily changes), making of that will act the expression of my entire person.[20] In sum, even if the spiritual always keeps the primacy, for Thomas

Aquinas there is no authentic human spiritual act without an element of passion, and no authentic human passion without its corresponding spiritual element.

Conscious Acts as Direct/Reflexive: Incarnate spirit, or spirit in process, moves towards its fully personal acts in stages. The following diagram, which introduces the distinction between direct and reflexive acts of spirit, will help us grasp these stages:

	Cognitive Function	**Appetitive Function**
Sense-Level		
	sensory data which I *experience*, ask questions about	various *passions* which entail bodily changes and repercussions in my spiritual self
Spirit-Level		
First Act spontaneous, direct, natural:	*simple apprehension:* I possess the intentional form of the other which I experience	*simple volition of the end:* in consonance with passion I reach out towards the good-in-itself of the object: VOLUNTAS UT NATURA
Second Act: reflex, more properly personal:	*judgement:* I reach out and affirm the existence of the other which I experience and grasp	*intention/election:* I deliberately strive to possess that goodness I now judge to be perfective of me: VOLUNTAS UT RATIO

As a sentient being I respond in many different ways, cognitively and affectively, to the physical environment that surrounds me. This response, though not spiritual, is the indispensable basis for my spiritual activity. In a first moment, my spirit responds with the same spontaneity and passivity as my psyche, reflecting, or redoubling, as it were, the latter's movement. In a second moment, the spirit, now awakened to itself, is able to act in a properly spiritual way. Knowing that it knows, it emits a judgement. Aware of its first spontaneous reaction, it chooses to go along with it or turn aside from it. Willing its own will acts, it freely chooses the ends it will pursue, choosing suitable means and implementing them.

In this way knowing and willing for Aquinas are twofold. In any complete act of knowing or willing there is first an underlying act, natural, direct, spontaneous, or in which my intellect or will responds to its proper object. This act, akin to that of infra-spiritual beings whose action is always a re-action, lays the basis for a second act which reflects on the first. In this second act I take a stance as a spiritual being, personally commit myself as a knower (by judging) and/or as a willer (by intending/choosing). That second act does not share the first's infallibility.[21] In it my intellect acts not as nature but as intellect, my will not as nature but as will.[22] Though the first act of my will does not express the active, self-positing reality of spirit, it is indispensable for the second act. I need to be moved towards an end (e.g., to experience an attraction towards another person) before I can move myself, intending that end (e.g., intending to build a relation with that person), and selecting the means through which I will strive to achieve it. In sum my first direct spiritual act mediates between my sensory affect and my properly personal second spiritual act.

This distinction enables Aquinas to offer a more theoretical formulation of the basic anthropological issue that divided Augustine and Pelagius, and recurs in contemporary terms under the heading of will and wish, willingness and willfulness. Pelagius is mesmerized by what Aquinas would term the subsequent act of the will, active, free, oriented towards the practical implementation of chosen objectives, but he bypasses the primordial act in which the will is passive rather than active. Augustine, by contrast, insists that my choice to live my life according to a pattern of virtuous activity leading to beatitude in God is not possible without a prior act of willingness which is received as gift, and which powerfully attracts me to God and life with God. Without this energizing gift my will remains a *velle*, a velleity unable to ground effective action. With it my will can become a *posse*, and I can be a source of effective action towards God. As a created, incarnated spirit, the only acts of choice which I can originate are grounded in a prior state of receptivity, and that receptivity is the theatre *par excellence* of God's grace.

Moving to the contemporary transposition of this issue, we can see that Aquinas in his own way offers a rationale for opposition by authors such as Rollo and Gerald May[23] to the view of the will which centers on striving rather than assenting, on concern rather than on complacency,[24] on technology rather than on value. Our era suffers from a surfeit of a willful yet ultimately ineffective striving towards goals, and needs to cultivate the primordial surrender of spiritual affectivity at the root of any constructive effort to achieve what is humanly worthwhile. This issue warrants fuller development, which it will receive later in this chapter. The contrasts which have thus far emerged can be put as follows:

Augustine	Aquinas	Contemporary
velle (inefficacious wish for beatitude in God) — — — — — — — *posse* (will energized by God's grace)	*simplex volitio* (powerless apart from grace) — — — — — — — *Infusio gratiae* (energizing the will)	wish, or willingness (value)
agere (effective action towards goals)	*intentio finis/electio*	will, or willfulness (technology)
plenum posse (beatitude)	*fruitio*	(fulfillment)

Our inclusion in the above diagram of the final moment of *fruitio*/fulfillment enables us to discern a dialectic pattern at work in direct/reflexive acts of the will. The initial attraction by which I am drawn outside of myself towards a value viewed absolutely as good, and spontaneously will it, is the thesis. This is followed by a rude awakening both to the antithetical reality and to myself, in which the distance between myself and that value becomes an obtrusive, at times painful, reality. I enter into a laborious process of intending, choosing, implementing. But then there emerges the final moment of synthesis, of fulfillment. Now I enjoy the value which originally drew me and which I have effectively sought. Presence follows upon absence. Refusal to leave the initial state of well-being and well-wishing, which is promise rather than fulfillment, in order as a responsible agent to deal with the absence of the attractive value, cuts off the only access to that fulfillment. In simple terms, the luscious apple on the top branch will remain a mere object of attraction and not be savoured unless I get the ladder and do some climbing. This is the point Paul was making against the enthusiastic Corinthians.

The notion of difficulty in striving for the good has now emerged. We are ready to move to the next section, which expressly deals with it.

Conscious Acts as Affective/Conative: Aquinas' distinction of direct and reflex acts of the spiritual self has its counterpart in the psyche. He develops the latter distinction within the treatise on the passions in the *Prima Secundae*. That relatively neglected treatise offers subtle insights for a contemporary theology of grace. Its basic lineaments are found in Plato and Aristotle, and its often fascinating details on human feelings evince considerable phenomenological acumen.

Aquinas divides the eleven passions known to him into the passions of the concupiscible (or affective) and those of the irascible (or conative) appetite.[25] Here are these passions in diagrammatic form. (The arrows in the diagram indicate their progression):

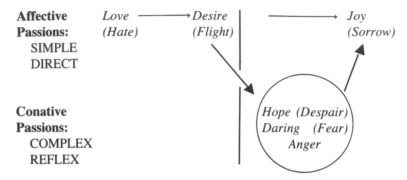

The more basic *affective* passions share the dialectical pattern of the will acts. First a particular good elicits a positive (or negative) response of love (hate), to which there corresponds in the will the act of simple volition. Secondly there emerges a desire for that good as not yet possessed, to which there corresponds intention. Finally, there is the spontaneous reaction of joy or pleasure in the good which now fulfills me, a joy which corresponds to the will-act of fruition. Aquinas refers to these passions as concupiscible, a term that focuses on desire more than on love or joy. The term "affective" more accurately hits off what is common to these passions: a simple affect of attraction or repulsion, which can be modified by presence or absence.

The *conative* passions flow out of and resolve into the more basic affective passions. Once I desire a good, they will be aroused and accompany my action until a resolution is achieved, either the joy of the good possessed or the sorrow caused by my inability to possess it. They emerge to the extent that the good that I pursue is difficult, requires a heightening of my power, an assertiveness that will enable me to overcome obstacles. They help me resolve the inner struggle between being attracted towards the difficult *good* and shrinking from the *difficult* good.

At this point it will be helpful to view the conative passions synoptically. The next diagram reflects Aquinas' presentation in *De Veritate* 26 4.

The conative passions are boldfaced. Joy and sorrow are given as the two possible resolutions of the process of contention entailed by the conative passions. The lines of demarcation between these conative passions are rather fluid. At any one time one of them will predominate, but the others will be

The Conative Passions:

centering on a good	I am now enjoying	(no difficulty ergo no conative passion, rather JOY)
	I do not yet enjoy, but which is difficult to obtain	the difficulty exceeds my power: **DESPAIR** I feel I will be able to handle it: **HOPE**
centering on an evil	I do not yet suffer but which is difficult to avoid	the difficulty exceeds my power: **FEAR** I feel I will be able to handle it: **DARING**
	I am now suffering	I feel I can overcome it: **ANGER** (it exceeds my power: no conative passion, rather SORROW)

there as recessive components. Thus with hope there will be some measure of despair in the background, with some daring and possibly some fear as well. This is not to mention the underlying affective passions of love and desire which are ever the mainspring and companion of the conative passions.

The conative passions have in common their concern with difficulty. I wish to achieve some good, but that good is difficult, and I will have to exert an effort to achieve it. For Aquinas hope is the most fundamental of the conative passions, but anger the most climactic: the angry person sees evil not as a future threat to be averted but a presence to be overcome here and now, and marshals his or her resources in full force. Because the evil is present, anger has a note of hatred and sorrow in addition to that of desire. Aquinas uses the term ''irascible'', from ''ira'', anger, to denote these passions. The term ''conative'', from ''conatus'', striving or contending, would appear to better convey their full range.

The terms ''irascible'' and ''concupiscible'' used by Aquinas came from the translations of Aristotle available to him. Like myself, other contemporary authors have sought less obscure translations of them. In the process they have highlighted different dimensions of Thomas' doctrine. We can learn much from them.

The psychiatrists Conrad Baars and Anna Terruwe use the Thomistic doctrine of the passions in describing their own therapeutic practice, translating "concupiscible appetite" by "pleasure appetite" and "irascible appetite" by "utility appetite".[26] The concupiscible appetite responds simply and directly to what is perceived to be good or bad, pleasing or displeasing. However to get that pleasurable object, the sentient being needs the assistance of the utility appetite to effectively face and overcome obstacles in the way. In the real world, once we enter into the process of choosing means, we encounter difficulty, once we implement our choice, we encounter resistance. If we pursue further the parallelism between the psychic appetites and the acts of the will, it would seem then that the affective passion of desire is seen to be related to intention, and the conative passions to the will acts of choice (*electio*) and of application (*usus*) of the means that will result in the desired goal.

In translating the questions of the *Summa* that deal with the passions, Eric d'Arcy seeks guidance from the Greek terms used by Aristotle, which hark back to Plato's tripartite division of the soul.[27] The highest part is the *logistikon*, or reason, the lowest part is the *epithumia* or desire, and the intermediary part is the *thumos*, or spirit (spirit in the sense of animal spirits, of vitality, but spirit also in the sense of reason's ally in taming the irrational desires of the *epithumia*). As a result he renders irascible by spiritual, and concupiscible by affective. This translation has the benefit of highlighting the greater affinity of the conative or irascible powers to the domain of the properly spiritual, to the reflex acts of the will acting as will, the *voluntas ut ratio*.[28]

This greater affinity of the conative passions to self-reflection emerges in a transposed fashion within some contemporary theories of human development. Let us begin with a simple example. Through the movement of my pleasure appetite I am fascinated by an attractive object, totally caught up into it, merged into it, as it were, but once the note of difficulty is sounded, I am shocked into awareness of myself as distinct from my environment, as having needs and desires which that environment does not easily support. In developmental theory this point is often expressed in terms of the primary environmental "other", the mother. The infant originally exists with its mother in a state of warm symbiosis, but little by little establishes differentiation from her, its conscious ego emerging from its undifferentiated self. This process is painful and marked by conflict, but eventually leads to the development of the self-reliant adult who enters into mature relations with others. The initial warmth of the secure self is related to the affective, and the struggles of the developing ego to the conative. Edinger offers a helpful Jungian perspective on this:

The child experiences himself quite literally as the center of the universe. The mother at first answers that demand; hence, the initial relationship tends to encourage the child's feeling that its wish is the world's command, and it is absolutely necessary that this be so . . . However, before long, the world necessarily begins to reject the infant's demands. At this, the original inflation begins to dissolve, being untenable in the face of experience . . . He is exiled from paradise, and permanent wounding and separation occur. Repeated experiences of alienation occur progressively right into adult life . . . we are exposed to the reality encounters which life provides, and which are constantly contradicting unconscious ego assumptions. This is how the ego grows and separates from its unconscious identity with the Self.[29]

In broader existential terms Rollo May reflects on the same phenomenon in his *Love and Will*:

We have a memory, a "reminiscence" in Plato's sense, of a time when there was a union of ourselves with our mothers in the early experience of nursing at mother's breast. Then we were also at union with the universe, were wedded to it, and had the experience of "union with being". This union yields a satisfaction, calm happiness, and elation. This is the "first freedom", the first "yes". But this first freedom always breaks down. And it does so because of the development of human consciousness. We experience our difference from and conflict with our environment and the fact that we are subjects in a world of objects—and even mother can then become an object. This is the separation between self and world, the split between existence and essence . . . This is why human will, in its specific form, always begins in a "no". We must stand against the environment, be able to give a negative; this inheres in consciousness.[30]

Rollo May's contrast of "yes" and "no" leads us to the insightful views of the English personalist philosopher John Macmurray as he traces the withdrawal and return, central to the full development of the person, that occurs between caring adult and helpless infant. In the positive phase the needs of the infant are met by the mother in a recurrent and reliable way. In the negative phase the child experiences the mother's refusal to satisfy his expectations as a "no" hostile to himself or herself, and the child is thrust on his own meager resources. In reality, however, that refusal intends to be life-giving, it is an invitation to the child to explore his own powers, to learn how to satisfy his own needs:

> The expectation, persistently unfulfilled, becomes a demand. His cry for what he expects passes into an angry insistence, even perhaps a paroxysm of rage. This is the genesis of will, which always implies a self-assertion against the Other, an opposition to be overcome, and therefore an awareness of self as opposed to the Other. The conflict of will individualizes the child for itself; and the mother who opposes him, for him. He recognizes himself as an agent through the opposition of another agent, who seeks to determine his future against his own will.[31]

While Eric d'Arcy's translation of "irascible" by "spiritual" has the merit of showing the hidden affinity of the Aristotelian/Thomist doctrine of the passions with contemporary ego-psychology, it is confusing because of the other sense of spiritual as opposed to sensory. J.P. Reid, who continued the Blackfriars translation of the *Summa* in the subsequent volumes, adopts "impulse emotions" and "contending emotions" for the emotions of the concupiscible and irascible appetites. The use of "contending" hits off the element of difficulty, of opposition. We have adopted the slightly variant form of "conative".

The above, with a few additional details from Aquinas, can be synoptically summarized as follows:

	Affective	*Conative*
Baars translation	*pleasure* appetite	*utility* appetite
D'Arcy translation	*affective*	*spiritual*
Reid translation	*impulse* emotions	*contending* emotions
Points of comparison	*simplicity* of attraction /repulsion	*complexity* added by note of difficulty
developed by Aquinas:	strives to acquire what is good for it: *reception*	strives to destroy/conquer what is harmful to it: *action*[32]
	desires *pleasure*	desires *victory*[33]

	Affective	*Conative*
Correspondence with:	the *direct* act in which the will is moved	the *reflex* act of the will, in which the will moves itself
	simple volition	intention/*election*/*use*
In Edinger's terms:	original *identification* of the ego with the self	*differentiation* of ego from self
In May's terms	yes: *wish*	no: *will*
In Macmurray's terms:	*positive:* original state of total dependence	*negative:* development of the distinct personal agent

The Complete Human Act: We have been engaged in dissecting the harmonic elements which at any given instant may be present in the note sounded within consciousness. Single notes, however, make up melodies, as we have seen, and we need to clarify the complete human act whose elements we have already begun to discern.

A complete increment of human activity comprises a number of distinct and interrelated acts of intellect and will underpinned by corresponding acts of the psyche. The intellectual and volitional components on each level are simultaneous, the first providing specification, the second exercise. As, moving from level to level, we wish, will, choose, do, enjoy, we are engaged in a temporal sequence. This is shown diagrammatically on p. 212.

Since my incarnate spirit cannot move itself unless moved, it must await its awakening, which is prompted by sensory input and affect. This prompting yields a first spontaneous movement within my spiritual self, one in which, present to my own sense reaction, I apprehend the goodness of the object (simple apprehension) and am moved towards it spontaneously and naturally (simple volition). I apprehend this goodness as such, not in relation to myself and to my own personal purposes. Such personal commitment emerges in intention, a subsequent act which entails a measure of reflexivity and leads to action. Simple volition is a "This I find pleasing; this attracts me; this I would like; this I wish"; intention is an "I will this; I intend to do this; I really want to achieve this."

Though crucial, the transition from simple volition to intention is relatively undeveloped in Aquinas' work. What is put forward here amplifies his

Intellect	*Will*	*Example*
Simple apprehension of the good attractive in itself	Simple Volition (Wish)	Wouldn't it be nice to go to the beach?
Judgement that the good is attainable and worth striving for me.	Intention (Will)	I intend to go to the beach.
Deliberation yielding various means to achieve the intended end.	Consent to all the means	Look at all the beaches I can go to, and how I can get there!
Final practical judgement settling on the means	Election of the means	I choose Sunnyside beach and will go by car.
Ordering of the various powers required to implement the election (command)	Use (Application)	I rouse myself to implement my choice, setting in motion different parts of myself.
(Judgement that good has been achieved)	Fruition (Enjoyment)	I enjoy my time at the beach.

thought rather than simply interprets it. Simple volition of some particular object or other offers matter for the incarnate spirit's self-reflection. Having willed something, its own willing self and its own will are able to come within its own purview. Self-coincidence is replaced by the duality which objectification entails. As a result the particular object which has triggered the spontaneous movement of the will now stands within the horizon of the will's prevailing orientation, and is an object of possible choice. This prevailing intentionality is complex: it includes the fundamental orientation of the will towards or away from God (more on this later) and it also includes orientations acquired over a period of time which can be foundational, in the absence of a fundamental orientation towards God, or which are subsumed under the more basic orientation towards God which relativizes all other orientations. For instance, what triggered off an affective response to the movie "x" which I saw advertised is my predisposition, ordered or disordered, towards spectacles or movies. Such as I am in my personal orientation, so will the end appear to me.[34] Sometimes intention and subsequent choice of means emerge within me with great ease. But at other times, in the process that takes place between simple volition and action, I am moved to interrupt the flow and go back to a more foundational level of intentionality. To pursue the same example, in considering what is involved in going to this movie, I might realize that there is a conflict between two values: getting work done that I had agreed to do and going to the movie. To sort this out I need to go deeper into my fundamental intentionality: in this case, I might ask myself in the light of my primordial orientation to my total personal fulfillment, which value shall I pursue here and now: the movie? the work that beckons me? the fulfillment of a commitment? the relationship to the friend who has asked me to do the piece of work in question? the relationship to the friend who wants to go to the movie with me? At this point the fundamental orientation towards or away from my fulfillment in God comes more explicitly into play.[35]

Thus as I move from simple volition to intention, the object that prompted my awakening to myself is bathed in a new light: it becomes a potential object of my personal commitment, a means to my personal fulfillment, something seen to be particular within a more universal horizon, and even within the most universal horizon of being which is mine as an enfleshed person. I take a stand towards this good present to me, promoting it from a good which is willed absolutely to a good willed in relation to the means by which I will attain it and in relation to my incarnate self which will be perfected or harmed by that good.

The cognitional component corresponding to intention is not totally clear in the writings of Aquinas. Traditionally it has been described as a judgement by which I affirm this good to be possible of attainment and in harmony with my disposition at the moment.[36] Inasmuch as the non-thematic empowerment of intention is my orientation to the good as such—an orientation which will only be satisfied in God—this act towards a limited good is free.[37] Necessarily moved towards the good as such, I am able to move myself freely towards particular goods. Indeed as I shift from choice of what to strive for—and such choice can mount to high levels of generality as I scrutinize goods that present themselves as possible objects-for-me—to choice of the most appropriate and technically effective means of achieving the goods I intend to pursue, I am passing from a central to a peripheral area of freedom, from purposes to goals, to use Stephan Strasser's terminology.[38]

My intending a good implies a resolve to seek out and implement the means necessary for its obtention. First, in an act that corresponds to simple volition, I seek out means to the end, deliberate about them, and, unless I recoil from any of them in particular, give them my overall *consent*, until the moment of choosing which one I will adopt. Secondly, I take a personal stand towards the means I will actively pursue, terminating the process of deliberation with a final free judgement accompanied by the act of will known as *election* or choice. Having done this, in an act termed *application* (*usus*) I implement my choice according to the ordering (*imperium*) of my intellect.

After the process of implementation is completed—it may involve not only my own abilities and skills but resources, instruments, networks of human cooperation—I reach the final stage of willing with regards to the end. I now recognize the presence of the good I intended in the first place and enjoy the fruition of my activity. A complete sequence of human willing has come to its fulfillment.

In Aquinas' description of the sequence which comprises a full human act there emerges a distinction between will acts regarding the end and will acts regarding the means. If we put the pair of acts side by side, and connect them with the affective and conative feelings, there occurs a remarkable patterning of Aquinas' intricate thought about embodied human activity:

	Will Acts Regarding the End (also affective feelings)	Will Acts Regarding the Means (also conative feelings)
Viewed absolutely, without commitment	I consider possible goods to intend: **VOLITION** (Love) **THESIS:** Direct/Affective	I consider possible means to choose: **CONSENT** (Hope)
Viewed in relation to my personal commitment	I personally commit myself towards a good: **INTENTION** (Desire) **ANTITHESIS:** Reflex/Conative	I personally commit myself towards a means: **ELECTION** (Daring)
Viewed in relation to its fulfill-ment:[39]	I am personally engaged with that good: **FRUITION** (Joy) **SYNTHESIS**	I am personally engaged in using that means: **APPLICATION** (Anger)[40]

Human Activity and the Habits

In our chapter on the plight of the first world, we drew a link between power and gracefulness and showed how grace-ful action, marked by spontaneity, is free of obtrusive consciousness, and done with skill, out of habit.[41]

Paul adumbrates this theme when he speaks of grace as unction, but Augustine is the theologian *par excellence* of grace and inner spontaneity. Aquinas deals with this topic under the heading of habits and their role in human fulfillment. After considering human free will and the passions, he moves to an analysis of habits and virtues (Ia–IIae 49–67). To bypass this analysis and move on directly to his treatise on grace—as well as to ignore the broader analysis of habit he develops in question 24 of the *De Veritate*—would be to render our transposition of Aquinas' theology of grace woefully superficial. Moreover interaction with contemporary reflection on habit and skills—that of John Macmurray and Michael Polanyi comes to mind—will help us to sharpen our understanding of how Aquinas builds on Augustine and to offer a helpful context for some contemporary themes.

The sources of Aquinas in this area are wide ranging. When dealing with the acquired habits which make human endeavour here on earth more proficient and effective, he borrows heavily from Aristotle. But then he also considers habits in a much more personal mode, seeing them as stable orientations towards various values, resulting from repeated past free choices and impinging upon the fundamental option of the person for or against God.[42] At that point he enters into the realm of infused habits, to use the Pauline image for love of God bestowed by the Spirit given to us. He attempts to relate these two realms, integrating Aristotelian themes which have a more cosmocentric ring with Christian themes consonant with the anthropocentric/personal form which deeply permeates his thought.

Habits and Passions Compared: For Aquinas, habits and passions both impinge upon me as I engage in the process of determining myself freely. On the surface, they both appear to limit that freedom, bringing an element of necessity to bear upon it.

As an incarnate person I am situated in a world over which my free choices have no control. My attention is constantly solicited by a succession of stimuli arising from that world, and my spontaneous inclinations, psychic and spiritual, are being constantly drawn in different directions. Thus even if I have freely chosen to be attentive to a particular task, I cannot determine that the phone will not ring, that some demand put upon me will not stimulate a whole new set of feelings, absorb my psychic energy to the detriment of my original intention, even leading me to reassess that intention. The intricate life of the passionate psyche in symbiosis with an ever changing world is akin to the hustle and bustle the nature-lover discovers in a swamp. Nonetheless that life serves as the indispensable grounding of human freedom, which does not unfold except out of a self-presence which has been awakened by such stimuli. Thus, paradoxically, passion both energizes my freedom and limits it. It may at times suggest to me disordered personal choices, but as long as I live in this world, it is the ever present source of new possibilities, preventing me from being confirmed in evil,[43] and it is the source of energy I need to achieve anything.

Habits are marked by a similar paradox. As a free person, I strive to establish various stable patterns and orientations within the randomness of my psyche. While I do not attempt to exercise rigid surveillance of my affective responses—I would only end up repressing the spontaneity of my psyche, erecting neurotic barriers, and hampering my fuller human development—I can aim to achieve "political" as opposed to "despotic" control over my psyche, training it to act or respond in certain ways, while allowing it to act on its own as well. To the extent that I have done this with success, I have introduced what appears to be yet another limitation to freedom, which is habit. Habits offer an easy path to my will, a default option, as it were. They impel me from within whereas the passions impinge upon me from without. They are the successful traces left in me of my own prior intentions, choices, consistent use of the energies available to me, they lead to enjoyable activity conducted with a minimum of conscious strain. To act against them requires me to swim against the current through an arduous and self-conscious process of deliberation.[44] In the long range, habits heighten, prolong, express my freedom; in the short range they restrict it.

This latter point bears further comment. The ultimate act of freedom is the one in which I commit myself irreversibly, with fully actualized uniqueness and intensity to the person in whom I find unsurpassable fulfillment, namely God. Habits are a straining towards that kind of relationship, a half-way house between the isolated act of free choice (singled out as normative by more mechanistic contemporary accounts of freedom) without continuity with the person's past and future, and the irreversible act of freedom in which I consent to my total fulfillment in God. Ultimately the fidelity and the commitment which habit entails do not diminish but prolong and amplify freedom, enabling it in some small way to transcend the limitations of the incarnate spirit caught in the here and now.[45]

In sum, while passions are the material out of which I am constantly solicited to new possibilities, new choices, habits are the traces within me of what

I have already chosen to be. As we continue our survey, we shall attempt to describe habits more fully and account for some of the different kinds of habits.

The Nature of Habits: Let us begin with a simple example in four steps:

1) I am a human being endowed with the basic ability to learn mathematics;
2) I set about learning mathematics;
3) I have become a mathematician;
4) I am actually doing mathematics.

The first step is that of an unfulfilled and unrestricted potentiality. My basic endowment as a human being allows me to enter into a wide range of academic endeavours, including but not restricted to mathematics. Many disciplines can beckon my attention and attract me. Prior to my becoming a mathematician, however, I must learn mathematics by the ordered repetition of mathematical activities, little by little shaping within myself the intricate complexity of the *habitus mathematicus*. This second step brings into focus the agent who shapes habits within himself or herself by dint of repetition, often with the assistance of persons who already possess them. The third step brings a measure of fulfillment. I have become a person who at a moment's notice can attend to a problem in mathematics with interest and ability, and others rightfully expect that I can help them within this area of competence. In the fourth step I have reached the pinnacle of my actualization as a mathematician, a state of fruition, as it were. Without undue strain, I find myself absorbed in doing mathematics, and I experience the pleasure of doing something which has very much become part of me.

In the diagram on p. 218, we will relate this example to the precise terms used by Aquinas.

This analysis can apply to any number of cases, ranging from learning to walk, to dance, to regulate my spontaneous cravings, to be well disposed towards the rights of others. It offers us a context to situate habits. Now we must more carefully determine how habits function.

In the first place habits determine me in some way. I am radically able to love any person, but my habitual inclination is specified to this and that particular person and not to someone else. I could learn geology, philosophy, computer science, or anything else, but the *habitus mathematicus* determines my intellect towards mathematics rather than towards something else.

In the second place the habit enhances the quality of my power's operation. In his *De Virtutibus in Communi* Aquinas accounts for this enhancement:

AGENT or **ACTIVE POWER:**		In a laborious process, I implement a choice to learn mathematics, and thus shape my own self: I am receptive to myself and to those who teach me.
POTENCY (passive)	or POWER (passive)	I have the basic ability to enter into the study of mathematics.
FORM or HABIT	or FIRST ACT	Having completed a programme of study, I am qualified as a mathematician.
ACT	or SECOND ACT	Here and now, I am engaged in doing mathematics.

. . . we need virtuous habits for three reasons: First, that there may be uniformity in our acts. For those things which depend solely on human actions are easily varied, unless they are firmly fixed by some habitual inclination. Secondly that a perfect operation may be readily performed. For unless the rational powers in some way are inclined by a habit to one definite object, it will always be necessary, whenever it is time to act, to begin an inquiry concerning the manner in which to act. This is evident in one who lacks the habit of science and yet wishes to consider a speculative question; and in one who wants to act virtuously, although he lacks the habit of virtue . . . Thirdly, that a perfect operation be performed with pleasure. This is effected by a habit which, inasmuch as it becomes a second nature, renders natural the acts proper to it, so that it is delightful to perform them . . . [46]

This quotation of Aquinas shows the affinity of habits, at least of habits once acquired (*in facto esse*), with the affective dimension of the psyche and with *voluntas ut natura*. To act out of habit is to act out of an acquired spontaneity, a second nature. In sum it is to act out of love, and love is the primary act of psychic affectivity, as we have seen.[47] Conation deals with the difficult, whereas habits make things easy for me, incline me to them with a whole-hearted affection that does not need reflection and deliberation to be operative. I relax and let the habit take over.[48] I enjoy the ease of familiar terrain.

Habits enable me to by-pass the process of deliberation with respect to the means by which I will achieve my goals, whether my ultimate fulfillment as a human person or any particular purpose I choose to pursue along the way. Finding myself already inclined to one value rather than another, one pattern of action rather than another, I need not go into a lengthy consideration of what value within the unlimited horizon of my spiritual openness I choose to pursue and how I am to pursue it. I need not in every case enter into a state of heightened, at times agonizing, self-presence. I throw myself into my action. I live out who I am. I enter into a kenotic stance, forgetting myself and focusing on the act in its overall *Gestalt*. In other words to be endowed with well-ordered habits is to be able to live the life of self-forgetfulness and presence to the other which is the opposite of neurosis.[49] Habits are central to the healing process to which Chapter One alluded.

We have already referred to the work of Michael Polanyi on skills. In Chapter Four of his *Personal Knowledge* he offers some most illuminating examples of skills at work. Skills allow me to forget about the instrumental components of my action, allowing my vital presence and learned patterns of activity to take over. As a result I become free to concentrate on the broader pattern, the intended outcome of my action. That I am only tacitly present to the pressure of the hammer on my hand, for instance, liberates me to be focally present to the contact of the hammer on the nail. That I need not worry about the basic movement and balance of different parts of my body liberates me to perform artistically and creatively as a dancer. The more skillful I become, the more intricate and wide-ranging will be the patterns of coordinated activity on which I can call as second nature. Interestingly enough, Aquinas shows his awareness of the same dimensions of skill in the following passage:

> Both choice and execution are necessary in a virtuous deed. Discernment is required for choice. For the execution of what has been decided upon, alacrity is required. It is not, however, highly necessary that a man actually engaged in the execution of the deed deliberate very much about the deed. This would rather stand in the way than be of help, as Avicenna points out. Take the case of a lute player, who would be greatly handicapped if he had to give thought to each touch of the strings; or that of a penman if he had to stop and

think in the formation of each letter. This is why a passion which precedes choice hinders the act of virtue by hampering the judgement of reason necessary in choosing. But after the choice has been made purely by a rational judgement, a passion that follows helps more than it hurts, because even if it should disturb rational judgement somewhat, it does make for alacrity in execution.[50]

To dwell on the pleasure that arises out of habits already acquired without adverting to the struggle, so familiar to each of us, which the acquisition of habits entails is to be unrealistic. Habits in the process of being acquired (*in fieri*) bring into play the conative as opposed to the affective dimension. In this case, rather than wrestling with recalcitrant materials as I attempt to build something outside myself, I wrestle with the multiplicity within myself, I become the material of my own self-making. I may want to determine myself in this or that particular way, but my spiritual powers are radically undetermined and my psyche is at the beck and call of every impact upon it from within or without. What I can do with my particular psyche and my particular body is limited. A heightened and sometimes painful attention and self-consciousness are required if I am going to overcome these limitations, and, especially in the initial stages, I must give careful and consistent attention to each particular component that makes up the emerging graceful pattern of a learned activity: practicing the scales, doing stretching exercises, finding out by trial and error how to deal with a particular person, how to constructively channel a particularly strong psychic drive, and I must reinforce each pattern of activity that proves effective. I am plunged in the realm of the conative, of the difficult. Not having the habit already, I am obliged to produce the regular sequence of acts which will enable me to acquire the very habit which would make that regular sequence feasible. This is at best an uphill battle, and at worst a source of frustration, especially when I am bereft of instruction, encouragement, example.

A final note: for Aquinas habits in this life do not exceed the effectiveness of nature itself, which is consistent only for the most part (*ut in pluribus*). Breakdown, outside interference, strong distraction can draw me from what I spontaneously love. The habits I acquire I can lose, though I will not lose them easily.

Types of Habits: In the course of our discussion thus far we touched upon various types of habits. The differences between them are crucial to Aquinas' account of grace. More than any other the distinction between *infused* and *acquired* virtues is crucial. Presented in a proportional equation, here are its ramifications:

$$\frac{\text{acquired virtues}}{\text{infused virtues}} = \frac{\text{imperfect beatitude in via}}{\text{perfect beatitude in patria}} = \frac{\text{connatural fulfillment}}{\text{supernatural fulfillment}} =$$

$$\frac{\text{ruling mainly the psyche}}{\text{ruling mainly the spirit}} = \frac{\text{acquired by human agency:}}{\substack{\text{repetition and learning} \\ \text{infused by divine agency}}} =$$

$$\frac{\text{specification by way of limitation}}{\text{specification by way of expansion}}$$

Human nature, according to Aquinas, is in the paradoxical position of being naturally oriented towards a fulfillment, intimacy with God, which only divine initiative can bring about. Indeed the genuineness and the perfection of any *personal* fulfillment is in proportion to our lack of control over it. Such fulfillment is relational. It either comes from the inmost freedom of the other or it is sham. It cannot but be super-natural, absolutely so in terms of God, relatively so in terms of human others. The *infused* habits attune us to the infinite reality of a God who is utterly beyond us but who chooses to be intimate with us; they specify us by expanding us to the infinite rather than by limiting us to this or that object within our world. They make it possible for us to move towards and enjoy perfect beatitude in God. As we journey towards that beatitude we shape ourselves in various ways, learn to enjoy the relative and imperfect beatitude of our earthly state, the only beatitude of which Aristotle had a clear grasp in his philosophy. This we do through *acquired* habits. What is true of infused habits is also true to a lesser extent of acquired habits. The help of others can be indispensable for us to acquire them. The personalist philosophy of Macmurray makes this point pellucidly clear: the form of the personal implies the constitutive interdependence of human beings in their becoming fully actualized persons. Hence the genuine but relative "supernatural" dimension of acquired habits: we need God not directly and immediately, as in infused habits, but through the mediation of fellow human beings acting connaturally.[51]

The acquired virtues regulate human activity, adapting it to the imperfect fulfillment available as I journey in this life. That activity, especially as it emanates from the lower psychic powers, needs to be channeled in such a way that it helps rather than hinders human development. Temperance and fortitude regulate my feelings of affection and conation in such a way that they sustain and foster my balanced authentic development rather than detract from it. With prudence, my intellect is ready and prompt to make appropriate practical judgements in matters that concern my right action. Justice lifts my will itself from the narrow perspective of my individual human organism and its needs to that of a spiritual being which sees the other as precious as myself.[52] Thus, already by nature oriented towards the preservation of my own rights, I become ready and prompt to treasure the rights of others. For Aquinas these four virtues are not an inbuilt mechanism but something acquired by dint of practice, experience, learning.

The infused virtues regulate human activity, adapting it to the perfect fulfillment which comes beyond this life, a fulfillment utterly beyond the power of human nature to achieve. Central among the infused virtues that regulate human activity is the love of God, poured into our heart by the Holy Spirit.

Another pertinent distinction, not developed with the same thoroughness by Thomas as that of infused and acquired habits, is that of prudence and art. Prudence regulates my action with a view to my integral human fulfillment (*recta ratio agibilium*); art regulates my action with a view to conformity to its objective canons and requirements (*recta ratio factibilium*). Prudence touches the fulfillment of the subject, it deals with how the subject is to be disposed towards things outside the subject,[53] so as to find in them authentic fulfillment; art touches the objective dimension of human action, it deals with how those things are to be.

Aquinas' text on the lute player and the penman[54] will help us put this latter distinction in the broader context of virtues and skills. Virtues—and prudence—intervene at the point of choice, of personal commitment, helping me to choose rightly in the midst of the conflicting stimuli arising from a complex environment. They preside over my fulfillment as a human person. Skills—and art—intervene at the point where, having decided what to do, I execute my decision. They make it possible for me to act effectively, gracefully, and economically, in harmony with the inner norms and requirement of the deed I am about to accomplish. Skills focus on the outer action, virtue on the inner fulfillment which that action is designed to achieve; skills on techniques, virtues on values.

Implicit in the above two distinctions is a gradation from the *central* to the *peripheral* dimensions of the human person. The infused virtues have to do with the transformation of the heart; the acquired virtues with the transformation, flowing from the transformed heart, which facilitates good human behaviour; and the various skills I learn are instrumental in making that behaviour effective. As I move from the peripheral to the central, I enter more deeply into the domain of values and of personal commitment, and my utter dependence on others and on God becomes more crucial. As this occurs, I enter into the realm of grace. At its deepest level, the form of the personal is bound up with the mystery of God.[55]

In this way Aquinas' doctrine of habits amplifies and sharpens Augustine's own reaffirmation of the inner spontaneity of grace, the primordial orientation which grace renders effective, and the external helps without which grace is not operative.

THE DISTINCTIVENESS OF HUMAN ACTIVITY

Having related human acts to the passions which undergird them and the habits which shape them, we are ready to explore the broader context of Aquinas' anthropology. We will begin by situating human activity in a broader context; then, in relation to the flow of time, we will attempt to define the modalities of that activity according to Aquinas.

Human Activity within the Hierarchy of Being: For Aquinas, among animals only the rational animal is capable of having habits because of its rationality, its unrestricted orientation towards being. Its spiritual powers—and by extension its psychic ones—have the plasticity necessary to be shaped by habits, which determine their completely unrestricted orientation to specific patterns of action appropriate (or not) to their complex environment. Because of this unlimited malleability, the earlier stages of human development are marked by a vulnerability, a fragility which are not found in the young of the animal kingdom. Indeed for Aquinas animals do not develop habits.[56] Not extending to the full range of being and incapable of the self-coincidence which defines spirit, their powers have a strictly limited scope. Built into them, and operative from the beginning, are specific orientations towards suitable action within their biological environment. Birds do not have to learn how to build nests nor dogs to define their territory. They behave by instinct, and their specific patterns of behaviour unfold in relatively automatic ways. Human beings by contrast learn behaviour from scratch, in constant interdependence and communication with caring adults. In this way from the beginning they develop as persons-in-relation. Their unrestricted openness to all forms of behaviour makes it necessary to learn those forms of behaviour which are appropriate—a task whose successful outcome is by no means certain.[57]

Human nature is not only defined as rational within a physical cosmos but also as incarnate within a world of spiritual, personal beings. The contrast Aquinas draws between incarnate human and pure angelic spirits is most illuminating.[58] In sum, humans experience a gap between act and habit which is overcome only in the final act of human existence, whereas pure spirits do not: their first act determines for them a total and irreversible orientation towards (or away from) God and is thus their last act.

The incarnate spirit is poured out into the spreadoutness of space and time. It needs the constant stimulation of beings within a physical cosmos to come to itself. Its fulfillment is shaped over a period of time, and comes only at the end of that period. Until that moment, all its acts of personal freedom are provisional, tentative, reversible. By contrast, once created the angel is totally present to itself, and proceeds to totally dispose of itself, saying yes or no to its fulfillment in God in one irreversible and total act.

Thus in the angel act and habit can rightly be said to coincide. The intensity and the focus of act are allied with the permanence and stability of habit. In the incarnate spirit *in via* (on the journey towards God) they do not. In my present state my individual will acts are focused, at times with fierce intensity; but they are always fragile and ephemeral. The next stimulus coming from my psyche can distract me, draw my attention to something else. My habits are stable, offer my efforts the consistency which comes from a second nature; but they cannot sustain the intensity and the focus of my individual act in any given here and now. Sooner or later, allowing them to revert to their latency, I must attend to something else. Thus their permanence is only relative. While increasingly effective in prompting the action of my will, they cannot determine it in advance. What I have learned in the course of time I can unlearn. The options closest to my heart I can neglect. This ability to turn away from what I have chosen limits the effectiveness of my act of freedom. I can decide only for the moment, and not for the entirety of my life. I can enter into long-range commitments; but strain as I will to emulate the fierce power and fixity of angelic self-determination, I cannot absolutely guarantee that I will be faithful to my own will.[59]

Human Activity within the Flow of Time: What we have just said about acts and habits profoundly relates to the complex structure of human action/ passion which we considered earlier in this chapter. Any given increment of human freedom involves a multiplicity of factors and elements and is but partial. Human persons shape themselves through a multiplicity of acts over a lifetime. By contrast, the mode of angelic freedom, as Aquinas conceives it, is quite different.

In spite of their differences, angelic and incarnate spirits have a profound kinship, that of being created. This means that in relationship to God their first cause and their final end they are in a state of radical dependence and receptivity. This communality applies most particularly to the three will acts regarding the end. Created spirits find in God both the originating impetus of their activity and the ultimate fulfillment to which that activity leads. Before they can freely turn towards God (the pivotal act of intention) and find fulfillment in God (the ultimate act of fruition), they must be moved by God (the primordial act of volition).

This is the only sequence of will acts needed for the fulfillment of the pure spirit, and these acts occur instantaneously and irreversibly at the very moment of its creation.[60] Incarnate spirits, by contrast, are set within a physical universe, depend on other incarnate spirits for their unfolding, and are caught up in the flow of time. In this they encounter both support and resistance.[61] Struggle is the necessary law of their being: they must little by little by repeated, multiple acts organize, integrate an often refractory "tohu-we-bohu" both outside and within their own psyche. This is a task of great subtlety, since integration of the disparate elements involved must fully respect their genuine spontaneity. Time stretched out before them, and the gap between the now of their intention and the then of their fruition is a constitutive part of their experience. To overcome this gap, they must, in addition to willing the end in various ways (volition, intention, fruition), enter into an often lengthy and often repetitive process of willing the means (consent, election, use), with the assistance of the conative passions. They can never avoid the difficult. Their achievement is fragile: orientations and patterns may become more and more deeply rooted within them, but there is always the possibility of reversal. In this life the human person is confirmed in the path neither of good nor of evil. Only having completed their journey, made and implemented countless choices, experienced toil and pain, expended energy, will their deepest intention flower into fruition.

Most essentially, the first act and the last act of the pure spirit freely disposing itself towards God radically coincide, whereas in the case of the incarnate spirit they are separated by a multitude of acts of freedom, none of which exhaust the virtualities of that spirit for personal commitment. At the same time the first act and the last act of the human person in his or her journey towards God play a crucial role in the thought of Aquinas. In the last act, that which occurs at the time of death, the choice of the person towards or away from God becomes irreversible.[62] In the first act, the person who has just come to the age of reason has no choice but to deliberate about his or her stance towards salvation in God, and to determine the fundamental option (*conversio ad Deum* or *aversio a Deo*) which will influence all subsequent will acts, until such time as it is changed by the gift of grace or by a fall from grace.[63] This first act of self-determination is free, but with respect to all subsequent acts it is an act of intention which need not itself be made the subject of deliberation. The last act of self-determination is free and irreversible, a fruition which leads to God seen face to face or the irremediable absence of that fruition. The acts in between are the theatre in which the destiny of each human being is played out.

This element of struggle endemic to the incarnate spirit has a two-fold origin. Most directly and immediately it arises from the opacity, multiplicity, and resistance of the matter in which that spirit is embodied. In Aquinas' view these limitations had been overcome in the state of original justice by the gifts of integrity and immortality, but they are not only released but also heightened by original sin; and incarnate spirit is left to its own innate resources as it struggles with them.[64] Spirit's integration of matter becomes aleatory and fragile. The ultimate disintegration of death becomes inevitable. In the paradoxical pattern of redemption, however, death becomes a moment of liberation, of transition to a state in which the incarnate spirit is akin to the pure spirit in its power to achieve an irreversible free surrender to God.[65] The uncertainties, ambiguities, sudden reversals of the present state explain why a special providential assistance of God is needed to shepherd the human person towards the fulfillment of his or her journey.[66] This is why, when Aquinas in the *Secunda Secundae* considers in their full panoply the virtues which regulate the conative passions, he offers a corrective to the stress on anger which emerged in his account of the passions in the *Prima Secundae*. Yes, anger is the culminating passion of the conative appetite. Yet for the incarnate spirit on the path to redemptive fulfillment, the perfection of the conative appetite resides not in the anger that attacks and removes obstacles but in the sustaining power which faces difficulty with equanimity from deep inner resources.[67] Human fulfillment cannot be forced. Waiting in patience is the only way: just as the origin of one's volition so too its fulfillment is received from another.

AQUINAS ON THE DYNAMICS OF GRACE

Thus far we have surveyed key elements which have emerged in Aquinas' thought as he moved towards the treatise on grace of the *Prima Secundae*. These elements provide the basis for his more systematic transposition of the foundational insights on grace received from his predecessors. It is fitting that we should begin with Aquinas' reformulation of the foundational triad bequeathed by Paul. In subsequent sections we we shall explore how Aquinas builds his own theology of grace on both Paul and Augustine.

Justification/Sanctification/Salvation: The elaborate structure of the human act which Aquinas unfolds has keen affinities with Paul's presentation of grace as essentially time-bound and fraught with struggle. This above all emerges in Paul's doctrine of the between-time: I am in a state of struggle, caught between the already now of justification and the not yet of salvation. The time of my sanctification stretches out before me. In a fuller presentation:

Primordial Act by which God moves me: **JUSTIFICATION**	**SIMPLE VOLITION**	The Age to Come breaks into This Present Age
	— **INTENTION**[68] —	
Journey by which I set on the path towards God: **SANCTIFICATION**	**CONSENT/ELECTION/ APPLICATION**	The Age to Come germinates in This Present Age
Final fulfilling act in which I am drawn into God: **SALVATION**	**FRUITION**	The Age to Come vanquishes This Present Age

In the act of *justification*, my will is moved by God to an act of simple volition which is fundamental to all else: I spontaneously love God above all else; my heart of stone is plucked out and replaced by a heart of flesh; my unwillingness is translated into willingness.[69]

Once justified, I begin a journey towards God by concrete spatio-temporal acts. In other words, I enter into the Christian struggle, the process of *sanctification*. At the root of my journey is a hope which allows me to move towards the good even though there are obstacles in the way. As the obstacles take on their full dimension when I move towards commitment to a particular path of action, I might be invited to daring. And in the midst of the struggle, there sometimes is room for anger, for a disciplined, aggressive, and effective use of energy against evil. More than anything else, however, patience, a less intense but ultimately more effective and significant mode of conation, is needed.

When I come to the third stage, that of *salvation*, I will enjoy that which from the very first I have desired and for which I have struggled through my life of sanctification. The whole process began with a simple yet powerful affective impulse given to me by God, and comes to its fulfillment in the affective presence of God which totally and irrevocably envelops me.

Thus in the life of grace the conative and the affective play distinct roles: **a)** The *Affective*: The primordial "already now" transformation wrought by grace is situated on this level, and it underlies everything else. Unless my basic affectivity is in some sense changed, conation is sterile and ineffective. In other words, I cannot intend something unless I am first spontaneously attracted to it, and this without any control or premeditation on my part. In conversion the change godward of my basic affectivity takes place through the infused gift of love, a gift rightly described as a second nature since I receive it rather than acquire it through my efforts; and since it operates within me tacitly, undergirding the functions which I carry on with my deliberate will. This initial gift of love, faced with the ''not yet'' dimensions of my existence, blossoms into desire and hope, which are the mainsprings of my conation.

b) The *Conative*: To remain in the affective is to be arrested at an infantile stage of development. The child must become an adult. I must as person emerge from the spontaneities of my nature. In Jungian terms the self must allow the ego to emerge, and this move towards the embodied, the explicit, the personally appropriated always entails an effort. Indeed it is only by wrestling with myself, learning how to marshal my limited resources, when to be aggressive and when to be patient, that my self-scrutiny is sharpened to a fine point and I achieve the authenticity of my being.

The affective/conative bipolarity has recurred in different guises throughout the chapters of this book. This analysis of Aquinas' thought brings it to the light. It can most usefully prolong the bipolarities with which we ended our chapter on Paul. The elements of this bipolarity can be expressed in the following equation:

$$\frac{\text{Child}}{\text{Adult}} = \frac{\text{Justification}}{\text{Sanctification}} = \frac{\text{Affective}}{\text{Conative}} = \frac{\text{Natural}}{\text{Personal}} = \frac{\text{Self}}{\text{Ego}} =$$

$$\frac{\text{Tacit}}{\text{Explicit}} = \frac{\text{Passive}}{\text{Active}}$$

To by-pass affectivity, natural or infused, to pretend that at the deepest level of ourselves we are not passive, is to render all conation essentially fruitless. That is the illusion so commonly cultivated in our first world, whose vaunted technology leaves us powerless in matters of ultimate moment. But on the other hand to refuse to go beyond the comforts of the first stage of affectivity is equally to condemn ourselves to a fruitless existence. We would never become self-appropriated, and our emergence within the cosmos as persons, as spiritual beings who take in hand their own destiny, would be aborted. While Aquinas' theology offers us the elements of a right balance between affectivity and conation, the emphasis suggested by his own century was one of nature unfolding with ease rather than one of effort and of sharp self-scrutiny.

We first identified this basic bi-polarity as we tried to account for Paul's attempts to deal with the struggles between judaizers and enthusiasts within his communities. The *judaizer* type of Christian is caught up in the conative side of things. What counts above all is to be an adult, proud of hard-earned accomplishments—in this case the faithful performance of the prescriptions of the law. Disciplined effort comes to the fore, not spontaneity. Spirituality becomes a subtle form of technology. The stress is on a well-developed ego function which effectively controls everything. The *enthusiastic* type of Christian is arrested at the stage of the earlier affective, undifferentiated self. Rather than enter into the struggle towards achievement, the enthusiast would rather pretend that the warmth of initial contact with God is fruition rather than promise. Everything is spontaneity and possibility, nothing is discipline and actuality. Spirituality centers around maintaining the primordial state of comfort. Paul offers us a path towards and a rationale for integration. Aquinas contributes to a more sophisticated restatement of the issue grounded in his perception of the dynamics of human activity.

The Context of Grace: Our discussion of infused and acquired virtues has already pointed us towards the foundational distinction of the natural and the supernatural. Elements of that distinction had emerged before Aquinas, but he drew them together in a contextual whole.

The relationship of the connatural and the supernatural is paradoxical. Deriving from the distinction of God and creatures, this distinction at first glance appears to be an abyss. Yet nature and the supernatural could not be more intimately related. If we look at created spirit as created, God, and the supernatural which is bound up with God, is utterly beyond it; if we look upon created spirit as spirit, as constitutively open to all reality, God is its only total fulfillment. This theme has been thoroughly studied in the modern era by authors such as Henri de Lubac and Karl Rahner, and needs no further discussion at this point.[70] If one persists in conceiving persons on the analogy of the infrapersonal realities most familiar to our experience, the paradox becomes a contradiction. But if one adverts to what makes the human reality stand out within our earthly environment, the paradox becomes a mystery. In other words the personal thought-form plays a most significant role in this doctrine of nature and grace. Aquinas did not bring this thought-form into sharp focus, and the coherence of his doctrine with what is most central to Christian revelation was massively misunderstood in later centuries, as is documented in de Lubac's work. John Macmurray offers a statement of the human dimension of that paradox in *Persons in Relation*:

> We need one another to be ourselves. This complete and unlimited
> dependence of each of us upon the others is the central and crucial

fact of personal existence. Individual independence is an illusion; and the independent individual, the isolated self, is a nonentity. In ourselves we are nothing; and when we turn our eyes in search of ourselves we find a vacuum. Being nothing in ourselves, we have no value in ourselves, and are of no importance whatsoever, wholly without meaning or significance. It is only in relation to others that we exist as persons; we are invested with significance by others who have need of us; and borrow our reality from those who care for us. We live and move and have our being not in ourselves but in one another; and what rights or powers or freedom we possess are ours by the grace and favour of our fellows. Here is the basic fact of our human condition; which all of us can know if we stop pretending, and do know in moments when the veil of self-deception is stripped from us and we are forced to look upon our own nakedness. (p. 211)

For Macmurray persons are intrinsically relational. In the last chapter of his *Persons in Relation* he shows how God is the key-stone of this relational network. For persons to define themselves in a self-enclosed rather than a relational way is a delusion. This is above all true of the relation to God, which empowers the relation of human persons to each other. That relation, which entails God's freedom as well as human freedom, is of primordial significance for human fulfillment.[71]

The Functions of Grace: Ia–IIae 109 2, a key article in the treatise on grace, offers a broad presentation of the dynamic aspect of grace for Aquinas. It alludes to a differentiation of the modalities of grace, corresponding to but richer than the scholastic distinction of actual and habitual grace, but we will postpone its consideration until the next section.

What concerns us in this section is the distinction between the two functions of habitual grace. Grace both heals and elevates us. Yet in *healing* and *elevating* grace we do not encounter a parcelling out of grace into hard and fast categories of thought, but the one grace of God which functions in different ways. In brief, healing and elevating are participles, i.e. adjectival verb forms. Their verbal, dynamic role is quite clear from the direct objects they often take in Aquinas' text.[72] These functions bring alive the paradox of nature and the supernatural. Grace elevates us to a fulfillment utterly beyond our natural endowments; it heals the wounds of our nature; it does both inseparably.

If persons are at core relational, then it is not surprising that it is precisely by a welcoming of the not-me that I find myself, by a limitless broadening of my horizons that I deepen my appropriation of who I am. Elevating and healing are terms that highlight the particular broadening and deepening that take place in my relationship with God.

What occurs in this relationship is not marked by the particularities and limitations that inhere in any human relationship. Rather it is a radical break-through—termed elevation—into the limitless mystery of Persons-in-Love. Grace in its deepest meaning is precisely the breakthrough into the mystery of God which occurs only at God's free initiative. By radically heightening my powers through the infused virtues, God makes it possible for me to effectively move towards the fruition of that mystery. I become a person-in-love-with God, and the power of that love penetrates and gives meaning to all my actions.

Elevating grace as received by me heals me. It is not an entity foreign to my nature but corresponds to its deepest aspiration. Thus in giving me himself in grace God gives me to myself. The deepening effect goes far beyond the measure of self-knowledge and self-acceptance which I achieve when I am in love with another human person. Grace deals with me as I am in my total personal history, my sin, my weakness, the obstacles that beset me, and releases within me the authentic power of who I am as a human being. I am affirmed, confirmed, healed, empowered to become my genuine self.[73] In setting me on the path of perfect happiness, grace liberates me to acquire the virtues whose presence make up the relative, imperfect happiness which I can achieve in this earthly life.

As we saw before, this connatural human development is problematic: I must overcome the severe handicap of having to act with regularity and consistency in order to acquire the good habits which I need in order to act with regularity and consistency.[74] In the area of skills and proficiency, I may be able to achieve satisfactory results on my own or with the help of other qualified persons, especially in areas where I have a special interest and pre-disposition. But in the area that ultimately counts, my integral human development, I am stymied. The consistent and discerning choices to be made in an environment whose impact on me is at best ambiguous are beyond my power if I am not already in a state of integrated development. The development of the human person is far more fragile than the training of a technician. This limitation inherent to embodied spirit, together with the dynamic of sin at work in the world, leads to what the classical doctrine refers to as moral impotence. I can avoid any particular act of sin, but apart from sin I cannot in the long run avoid sin. Wounded by sin, warped in my fundamental intentionality, it is impossible for me to achieve the full and balanced development of myself apart from the healing effect of grace. This point Aquinas makes in Ia–IIae 109 2: I am like the sick person who has a certain limited power of movement but is quite hampered, unless proper medical care supervenes.

How does the grace which elevates me also heal me? The elevating function of grace entails the infusion of virtues which endow me with an effective willingness to love God above all else, and to love all other beings with the genuineness and discretion which alone arises from my loving them in God. Healing ensues: my choices, animated by an infused love which is stronger than the vivid solicitations of any moment, can little by little shape the orientations of my psyche, adapting it to my authentic self.[75] The many created values which draw me are relativized by this love and there is created within me the inner space required for the emergence of an ordered and integrated intention in their regard,[76] one in which no created value is invested with a commitment which only the limitless mystery of God should evoke in me. Ordered action becomes more natural to me, an object of delight. I begin to acquire the virtues which preside over my development here below. The vicious circle of moral impotence is broken.

At the same time I come to possess myself only in patience and the struggle remains till my dying day. The initial impact of the grace which elevates me is in principle complete, but the grace which heals me operates over a period of time. I must learn to go with the flow of grace and not against it. Of central moment in the healing process is my gracious assent to the requirement that as an incarnate spirit I must live in time and develop in time. While anger and forcefulness are sometimes called for in the struggle to become myself, in the final analysis the sustaining force of patience is more essential, especially since in the matter of my own development I have no ultimate control. The terms of that development are set by a Providence which alone can devise the strategies that overcome the power of sin still at work in the between-time.[77]

A final reflection: By contrast with the gracious approach of human persons to each other, God's offer of intimacy is without bounds or limits. For it, Aquinas often uses the traditional image of the sun whose rays no one escapes except by the deliberate interposition of an obstacle,[78] an image which powerfully evokes the cosmic universality of grace which contemporary theology has begun to take with great seriousness. What is more, the power of God's offer is such that it can effectively meet each person at a level of ultimate penetration and remove whatever impediments he or she has interposed to prevent the light from flooding him or her. That power is such that it is all the more effective the more vulnerable it makes itself, the more respectful of the unique history and freedom of each one of us.[79] These topics will be developed in a later section on the efficacy of grace.

A summary of this section in a proportional equation:

$$\frac{\text{elevating}}{\text{healing}} = \frac{\text{infused virtues}}{\text{acquired virtues}} = \frac{\text{perfect beatitude}}{\text{imperfect beatitude}} = \frac{\text{broadening}}{\text{deepening}} =$$

$$\frac{\text{supernatural}}{\text{connatural}} = \frac{\text{cosmic, universal}}{\text{particular, personal}} = \frac{\text{instantaneous}}{\text{gradual}} = \frac{\text{opening me to God}}{\text{restoring me to myself}}$$

The Modalities of Grace: Always present in the background of Aquinas' theology of grace is the distinction between *grace as a habit* infused by God which empowers me to act in a radically new way and *grace as a motion* in my will by which God actualizes my powers both innate and infused. God moves me to act by applying my powers and habits to their objects. He providentially sets in my path suitable objects for those powers, providing the setting of my world: the situations, challenges, opportunities, persons which will best stimulate me through the mediation of my psychic affectivity.[80]

This motion from God takes place according to the two phases, direct and reflex, which, as we saw, characterize the activity of incarnate spirits. In a first phase, the world has an impact upon me through the primary response of my psyche/will as nature; it awakens me to myself, to what I am, a radically unlimited emptiness which only God can fill. The impact of that world is chaotic, random, radically plural. If I am not at heart in love with God, I am defenseless before that plurality. It assails me. I cannot avoid at best the scattering of my energies, at worst their absorption into something less than God. But if the self that is awakened has already been transformed by love, that awakening—the *first* phase—releases within me a powerful sense of direction. It makes me able in a second phase to craft genuine and constructive responses to that which has had an impact upon me, painstakingly to shape my psyche and the world in such a way that they reflect what God has already achieved in my heart. In this *second* phase, that of responsible intention of ends and selection of means, of diligent application, of heroic effort at times but always of patience, I deliberately assume who I am and live out my journey.

Put in the terms which Aquinas inherited from his tradition, the primal rectitude of the spirit or self in its relationship to God, received in the first phase, in the second phase expands beyond itself in widening circles: through its responsible activity the rectified spirit tends to rectify the psyche in its life of affectivity and conativity, the soul (which includes both spirit and psyche) tends to rectify the body, and the total human being (including both soul and body) the external world.[81] The eschatological state of salvation is the one where every human self and the world have been totally and irreversibly permeated by this inner transformation, such that "not only the heart but also the flesh will exult in God".[82] From first-fruits and down-payment, the Spirit becomes permeator and uplifter of all reality in glory.

The first rectification, which corresponds to Pauline justification, takes place instantaneously in the affective core of the self: the love of God is poured into our *hearts* (Rom 5:5). The others, which correspond to sanctification, take place gradually and in this world never achieve their full effect. They involve self-knowledge, self-acceptance, responsibility, wise choice, diligent effort. Above all they involve patience, since the process of integrating our own selves and the world in which we live is never complete. The temptation is to polarize the native orientation of our restless spirit around some particular value which, vividly present to us, gives us the illusion of security in the midst of ambiguity, and crowds out the obscurity in which alone we know God here below. We must struggle to allow the emptiness, the non-fulfillment to exist, rather than attempt to overcome it prematurely. The radical passivity which marks the beginning of our activity, accompanies it throughout its course, and culminates in the surrender of our death.

As this gradual process of rectification takes place, my psychic affectivity and conativity are shaped by my repeated acts in such a way that what they propose to me is more and more in tune with my authentic self. For example, the one who has been justified begins with the virtue of continence which enables right sexual choices in the face of constant solicitations mediated by psychic affectivity. As a result of repeating these choices, that person acquires the virtue of chastity which endows psychic affectivity with a spontaneous bent towards right sexual response. The feelings more and more reflect the firm orientation of the spirit towards God in this area of behaviour.[83] Spontaneity begins to predominate over struggle. My body and the world in which I live also begin to acquire a similar transparency, but the process entails constant setbacks and comes to its fulfillment in another experience of radical passivity, which is death.

The Efficacity of Grace: We need to take one final step in our account of the dynamic of grace according to Aquinas. According to him, the divine assistance that moves us to do what is good (actual grace) is differentiated into *operating* and *cooperating* grace, as is habitual grace itself.[84] This distinction between an operating grace in which God acts and we are passive and a cooperating grace in which God's action elicits our free response should not surprise us at this point. We have already come across the distinction between simple volition, in which I spontaneously find myself resonating in spirit with what my psyche proposes, and intention, in which I take the deliberate personal step of making that good-attractive-in-itself a good-for-me, one which I will pursue by all deliberate means. We are also aware of the distinction between the first phase in which I am passive, simply responding to my environment, and the second, in which I self-possessedly reach out to shape both myself and my environment.

Taking this further distinction into account, we can summarize the doctrine of Aquinas as follows:

1. *HABITUAL GRACE*: As infused by God into my heart it is an operating grace regarding which I am totally passive. As giving rise to acts of free response on my part (cf. 3 below), acts which, empowered by grace, lead to God, it is seen as a cooperating grace.

2. *ACTUAL GRACE: Initial OPERATING Stage*: Through his providential care over events both within and outside me, God orchestrates the succession of stimuli to which I naturally respond in spontaneous acts of simple volition which in and of themselves are inefficacious. These motions in my will, caused by God, are operating graces which activate my will, and through them I become present to my will and its prevailing orientation.

3. *ACTUAL GRACE: Subsequent COOPERATING Stage*: If an actual grace meets me as a self already transformed by habitual grace, then the me that emerges in the self-presence activated by that grace is a self in-love-with-God-unrestrictedly, and a positive response on my part to that grace would further embody my relationship with God in acts meritorious of salvation. If that grace is concomitant with the infusion of habitual grace, then a positive response on my part is the act of conversion by which I perfectly prepare myself, under grace, for what Aquinas terms the *consecutio gratiae*. If I am not yet transformed by habitual grace, the self that becomes present, though constitutively oriented to God as its only possible fulfillment, is not yet graced with habitual love, and a positive response would be one of preparing myself imperfectly for that transformation.[85] In both cases, I move myself in the power of the one who has moved me. In response I responsibly intend, resolve to discover, choose, and implement the means by which I can fulfill God's call. I pass from mere velleity to firm will. Grace not only operates in me but cooperates with my own personal appropriation of my life history.

If to actual and habitual grace we add the natural desire to see God, we come to an understanding of how Aquinas builds upon and clarifies the trinitarian pattern which emerges in Augustine. The radical openness by which we secretly yearn for God's approach—our natural desire to see God, as Aquinas puts it—can be linked to the *Father* as absolute mystery from which we derive and towards which we are pointed; the habitual grace infused inwardly and welcomed within this emptiness is linked with the gift of the *Spirit*; the actual graces which come to us through our world, which awaken within us a personal presence to our own yearning and desire to act out of the power we have received are linked with the sending of the *Word*.

This three-fold gift results in our responses, totally empowered by God and totally free, which in their sequence constitute a long process of shaping ourselves and the world we live in. *Shaping ourselves*: we adopt prevailing patterns of intention for our own activity and make of our psyches much more eager and willing instruments of those intentions; we achieve integration, order, spontaneity within. *Shaping the world*: together with others we shape the structures in which human beings are nurtured and, having achieved their maturity, help nurture others, in this way becoming instruments of an intention that transcends our own, that of God towards his reign to be established on earth. Just as God acts through others in shaping us, God acts through us in shaping others. This process is a lengthy and fragile one. The materials with which we work—aspects of ourselves that call for further integration or aspects of the world in which we live—cannot be brought to integration except in loving patience. Never in this life will we achieve the totality of what we intend, of what God intends. No matter how effective or felicitous, our efforts will never overcome the gap between intention and fruition. We cannot ourselves achieve the transition between this world and the world to come.

This ties in with the Pauline triad of justification/sanctification/salvation. Justification is God's act in me; sanctification my response; salvation the fruition beyond all my efforts of those responses. Just as initially there is a discrepancy between my innate aspiration and my power, which God closes through the gift of justifying grace, so too finally I am an unprofitable servant: the fulfillment of everything I do depends upon a culminating intervention of God by which this world is transformed into the next.

CONCLUSION: AQUINAS IN A NEW KEY

Our reading of Aquinas' theology of grace in this chapter was based mainly on a structural reading of his texts,[86] but it owes much to the perspectives of two contemporary followers of Aquinas, Bernard Lonergan and Karl Rahner. In their own way they would agree with Metz' assessment of Aquinas' epochal significance and discern in the form of the personal, such as expressed, for instance, by John Macmurray, not a betrayal of his thought but an expression of what animates it from within. They are men of this century, and out of their struggle with the thought of Aquinas has come a widely appreciated contribution to contemporary theology, Rahner's from a more existential and pastoral perspective, Lonergan's from a more epistemological and methodical one.

Anthropocentric/Cosmocentric Thought-forms: That the anthropocentric or personal thought-form has woven in and out of this chapter should not surprise us by now. Just as it clearly presides over the work of numerous contemporary followers of Aquinas, so too it runs as a thread through Aquinas' own work. Tacitly, unobtrusively, it knits together his thought, fosters some of its most fertile insights, underpins its attractive sense of equilibrium. Thus far in this chapter we have attempted to bring that personal thought-form to the fore. To consider the workings of grace described by Aquinas in the light of the characteristic transactions which make up the warp and woof of human relationships is not only to pave the way for pertinent contemporary insights, but also to be profoundly faithful to his intention.

As we saw in Chapter Two, the cosmocentric aspects of Aquinas' thought arise from his use of Aristotle's categories. Derived from a reflection bearing on physical reality, these categories were termed meta-physical (after or beyond physics). Physical reality is created by God, reflects him in some distant way, can lead to some glimmers of understanding in the realm of God's mystery. But it clouds as much as it reveals. It can hinder us in the pursuit of liberating insights into God's mystery. The breakdown of the medieval synthesis is a good indication of its limitations.[87]

Anthropocentric/personal categories are derived from a reflection on personal reality, on the inner life which distinguishes that reality from purely physical reality. Rather than meta-physical, these categories are *meta-human* (meta-psychological, meta-sociological). They are less inadequate for the purposes of theology than our traditional *meta-physical* categories, since the mystery of God is less inadequately reflected in our human mystery than in that of physical creation.[88] How we relate with each other as persons will tell us more about how God relates with us than our reflections, no matter how profound, on acorns becoming oak trees and fire broiling steaks. This is not to imply that the metaphysical categories of Aristotle lose all usefulness. To the extent that they reflect structures and dynamics proper to all created beings, they were of great assistance to Aquinas and will assist us. There is, however, a point beyond which they need supplementation.

Grace as Quality/Grace as Relation: Essential to Aquinas' understanding of created grace was the Aristotelian category of quality. Grace is not a quality in the same sense as greenness is the quality of a leaf or heat of the sun, to use proper Aristotelian examples, but quality is the least inadequate category Aquinas, within his context and with his background, could come up with for grace. He used it to point to the spontaneity and inner harmony of graced activity.

His multiple references to Scripture and to the Fathers, however, as well as the care of his formulations, invite us as he did to release the category of quality from its material analogate and to avoid the pitfalls of reification. With the shallow mind that mistakes imagination for insight nuances are set aside, quality is taken too literally and eventually becomes hardened into quantity. Only too easily there emerges the caricature of grace familiar to many generations of Catholics: habitual grace as a magic fluid poured into the soul, actual grace as the pellets of a celestial BB gun designed to rouse us from our complacency. Such reification was far from Aquinas' intent. Against it, as we saw in Chapter Two, Martin Luther rightfully reacted.

When we move from the cosmocentric to the anthropocentric thought-form, relation displaces quality as the basic category.[89] Aristotle did have a category for the relations existing in the physical cosmos. Aquinas did not use it explicitly for grace—this would have evidenced the full emergence in his work of the personal thought-form—though in fact his thought was relational through and through, and the universe for him at core personal.[90] Aquinas transformed the category of quality and made it a meaningful vehicle for his thought, but at a deeper level it would appear that persons-in-relation were his operative principle of discernment and organization.

The last section has offered us the lineaments of Thomas' doctrine of grace. We will now sketch out, in consonance with the contemporary personal thought-form, a transposition of that doctrine. As we have already begun to see, in the inter-human relationship we can easily find elements which correspond to the nature/grace, habitual/actual, healing/elevating, and operating/cooperating components of grace on which Aquinas focused in his own work. We will continue to explore these correspondences.

Nature/Grace: This bipolarity needs to be approached from both human and divine perspectives:

a) *From the human perspective*: Human beings experience a basic need for interpersonal relationships without which they cannot be fulfilled. Yet paradoxically I cannot lay claim to the friendship or love of any other person. The only fulfilling relationship is the one which comes as the free gift of the other, as the uncontrived expression of the other's core-freedom. To the extent that I bypass the freedom of the other in an attempt to establish, without fear of refusal, some relationship with the other, I manipulate the other, and any relationship I might succeed in establishing thereby will be neither personal nor fulfilling. Genuine relationship is a grace-event, a mystery; it can only be received as a gift, as something unexpected and undeserved.

What most deeply constitutes me is desire for a relationship with God. Only in friendship with God will I find my total fulfillment. As is true of all personal relationships, I await the fulfillment of this relationship as a free gift which I neither claim nor control; if it were to come to me out of anything except the utterly gratuitous mystery of God's love, it would not satisfy my deepest yearnings. Thus the form of the personal is at the root of the nature/ grace relationship, and apart from it the paradox inherent to that relationship becomes a contradiction. Cosmocentric thought as such has no point of reference beyond the organic necessities of nature, and later medieval thought misunderstood Aquinas because it was not able to situate both divine and human freedom in the unique context of personal relationship. It saw no alternatives but an organic necessitarianism and a mechanical juridicism, and opted for the latter.

b) *From the divine perspective*: human beings find fulfillment not only in receiving friendship but also in giving it. Indeed there is always in me a coincidence of need and gift. In giving myself, I fulfill myself. In God there is only gift.

God's decision to share his inner life, to be a be-friender, has been revealed to us in abundant ways. What comes first in God's plan? It is the sharing beyond himself of the personal mystery God is. However God cannot do this unless there is someone with whom to share that mystery. The gift calls for and presupposes the recipient of the gift. Since the gift is of himself as person, the recipient must be such as to be able to receive it freely, as a person. To experience the gift as gift, the recipient must experience it as fulfilling an aspiration, an openness within himself/herself. Human persons are such recipients. Their nature is intrinsically ordered to the gift of grace which God wishes to bestow upon it.[91]

In both human and divine self-gift, mystery and the familiar come in vital contact with each other. My intention to share my inner life with a friend embodies itself in day-to-day events shared with him or her. The "grace-mystery" of this human love takes flesh in a realm which by comparison is natural, familiar, ordinary. Likewise God's grace takes flesh in a nature, which, mysterious enough, does not share the intensity of God's own mystery. The extraordinary in the form of the ordinary, the divine in the form of the human: what we have here is the *kenosis* which is part and parcel of the movement by which any person reaches out to another person, and which comes to its culmination when the one who is in the form of God takes on the form of the servant.

To sum up: from our viewpoint nature comes before grace, from God's grace comes before nature. Our nature is made for grace, desires grace as its only real fulfillment; grace fulfills that desire by embodying itself in nature, to the point of emptying itself out.[92]

Actual/Habitual: Personal relationships between humans have two modes of intensity. First the habitual mode: any such relationships are relatively permanent. They prolong in fidelity an act of freedom that intends to commit itself beyond the here and now. "She is my friend" and "he is my husband" retain their truth even at times when the relationship is not being attended to or actualized. Indeed if our personal relationships were to be attended to at all times we would be dealing with a form of unhealthy obsession. For the most part, they ought to remain in a state of latency. This latency can be complete (e.g. deep sleep), but it often consists in a greater or lesser conscious presence which perdures, which remains on the periphery of one's awareness. Thus we often enjoy a feeling of being-in-love, of being loved, of inner peace and harmony as we attend to the many other aspects, sometimes fraught with concern and tension, of our daily existence.

Nonetheless from time to time every inter-human relationship must be actualized, brought to a higher mode of intensity at the call of one or other partner. One partner will think of the other, desire to be with the other. The partners will converse, collaborate in common tasks, support each other, express their love in word and/or deed. If they do not do this at certain times, their relationship as a habitual reality is in danger of being whittled away and vanishing altogether. Given the vagaries of the human psyche and the uncertainties of the world, our relationships are fraught with a great deal of precariousness. They require assiduous cultivation.

The same two modes of intensity apply to the relationship between God and human beings. If I love God, I am in a state of being-in-love, experience within myself a fundamental orientation towards God loved above and in all things. This relationship can be completely latent, but it is mostly experienced as a dynamic state-of-being-in-love which suffuses, gives colour and significance to the rest of my human activities which focus on what is other than God. This relationship is termed habitual or sanctifying grace.

At times that relationship is actualized. I need to express, to concretely embody my state-of-being-in-love with God. Indeed that state is a mind-set which keeps me on the lookout for signs, tokens of God, enfleshed in the spontaneous movements of my will, speaking to me and inviting me to actualize my relationship to God. These invitations are termed actual graces. Since grace embodies itself in nature, most of these invitations will not lead me to perform professedly religious acts but will set before me opportunities for graceful human living in the circumstances of my life.

It is appropriate to subsume under this heading the conative/affective bipolarity we developed earlier in this chapter. Personal relations find their beginning and their fulfillment in spontaneity. They begin when I am swept away beyond my intentions and deliberations in a first movement of spontaneity; and they find their fulfillment in a state of second spontaneity, as I become able to let go, rest, enjoy what I have cultivated and has become a precious part of myself. In between the two there is a period characterized by conativity rather than by affectivity. It calls for vigilance, heightened attention, a sustained effort to find the appropriate moments to actualize the relationship. I must discern when to be patient and when to take an active, even an aggressive stance. In moments of crisis I will become excruciatingly present to the mystery of myself as I come up against the mystery of the other. In sum, as I enter into the alternation of habitual and actual modes of intensity, I am called upon to trust that just as the source of my spontaneity is not in me so too its fulfillment relies on a provident God.

Healing/Elevating: Inter-personal relations better me in two ways. They broaden my horizons, enable me to enter into the world of the other, to share the other's feelings, desires, perspectives. Contact with what is uniquely and irreducibly other is most enriching. But in addition to that the relationship deepens, strengthens, supports me, liberating me to lead my own life and challenging me to carry on my own personal development. In this way contact with what is irreducibly other brings me to a deeper contact with myself. Broadening and deepening are inextricably entwined, because my relationality is intrinsic to myself. As I lose myself in the other I find myself.

When God initiates a relationship with me broadening and deepening also take place. In this case Aquinas has termed the broadening effect *elevating* and the deepening effect *healing*.

When God be-friends me, I enter into the world of God's thoughts and affection. The broadening here is on much more than a human level: I am taken up, elevated into a realm which is totally above what I can lay claim to as a human creature. I am super-naturalized, divinized, brought into intimacy with God.

When God be-friends me, I enter into contact with myself, with my own basic resources and goodness. But this takes place on a much deeper level than in human friendship. God's friendship meets me where I really am. It can pry loose the barriers I have erected against others and even against my own true self. In all cases it releases more deeply within me the forces of authentic human development. If I am alienated, powerless to be the person I want to be, God's friendship can liberate me, heal me, forgive me such that I am not just declared to be forgiven but my burden is really lifted. In sum, it not only enables me to become like God, but it also enables me in the process to become myself as a human being in the fullest and the most authentic sense. Transformed by the love of God, I can begin to pursue my authentic good, which is inextricably bound with the good of others, rather than my illusory, isolated, private good.[93]

"Grace heals and elevates" can appropriately be re-expressed today as "grace humanizes and divinizes." I cannot fully and authentically be a human person living a human life unless God pours his love into my heart, setting me on the way to divinizing union with himself. Apart from the gift of grace, my humanity is broken, deficient, scattered. Conversely, there is no process of divinization which does not entail my humanization. God cannot draw me to himself without my being more integrated within myself. Though distinct, these two functions are inseparable.[94] As Augustine puts it, God is both *superior summo meo* and *intimior intimo meo* (higher than the loftiest part of myself, elevating me; and more intimate to me than I am to myself, healing me). In giving himself to me, he restores me to myself: the two gifts are distinct but indivisible.

Operating/Cooperating: Thus far we have been bringing to the light continuities between human relations and the divine/human relation. As we try to express the doctrine of operating and cooperating grace in a language coherent with the form of the personal, the radical discontinuity between them will emerge. The relationship between the personal God and the persons God has created is asymmetrical.

The initiative can come from either side in human relationships. As human persons the two partners are basically equal and their mutuality is symmetrical. Though in any given relationship initiative may come more easily from one side rather than from the other, this reflects specific factors which attach to that relationship.

In the relationship between God and myself, God is always the first initiator. Not that God's prior initiative cancels out my own initiative and blots it out. Rather that initiative comes before my initiative and allows it to take place. Before God my primordial stance is one of passivity. The free response by which I cooperate with God always depends upon a prior operating grace. In affirming this, Aquinas was faithful to scriptural passages such as "You did not choose me, no I chose you" (Jn 15:16) and "We love because he loved me first" (1 Jn 4:19), and to the Council of Orange, which in 529 took pains to vindicate the prevenient nature of grace.

A human person can call another human person to friendship, but does so only with the antecedent conviction that the other is already empowered to respond to his invitation. The other's power to respond is a given which the human initiator does not control or grant. God not only calls me to friendship but also gives to me the very power, the very willingness by which I respond to that call. The response is just as much gift as is the call, the acceptance just as much gift as the offer. "No one can come to me unless the Father draw him" (Jn 6:44).

My call to another human being is not a continuous one. It is marked by intermittence. I wait for the propitious occasion. I approach another in this set of circumstances and not in that, now and not then. Other tasks, other concerns, press upon me and claim my attention. By contrast God continually calls, in every situation, encounter, person, challenge. There is a rhythm of consolation and desolation in how God deals with me, variations in intensity and explicitness, but no intermittence.

Our invitation to another to enter into friendship supposes a prior, usually tacit, response to the lovability of that other. God's offer of friendship to me does not presuppose that I am lovable but creatively constitutes me as lovable.[95] God loves me from non-being into being, from being an enemy into being a friend. The point is made by Paul in Romans 5:6–11 and also by Augustine as quoted by the Council of Orange: "God loves us such as we are to be through his gift, not such as we already are through our own merits" (Canon 12).

I can invite and persuade the freedom of another human person, but I cannot work within it as God can because I only have available to me a small cross-section of the totality of that other person's life. My power to invite and to persuade with effectiveness is radically limited. If I strive to infallibly get another person to respond in a certain way, I will have to manipulate that other, find a way of bypassing his or her freedom, because over that freedom I have absolutely no control. If on the other hand I sincerely wish to respect the freedom of the other, I will never be certain of the outcome of my initiative, because that person's freedom is incompatible with my attempt to control it.

God's power to invite and to persuade effectively is not limited in this way. God has the whole range of a person's life to work in: God can bide his time, allowing for the secret maturations of human purpose to take place. God knows when and how to invite and persuade from without, and through his Providence God orchestrates the set of circumstances that are congruent for each unique human "yes" to grace. In addition God can also work within my freedom, giving that freedom a new power, a new willingness. Thus, while remaining utterly respectful of my human freedom, God can attain what he wills to attain with efficacious certitude, not by forcing me against my free will, but by being infinitely patient, by working with the flow rather than against the flow of my being. Putting this in terms of aggression and patience, it is not that God is infinitely more forceful than we are but that God is infinitely more patient, more adept in dealing with the complexity of who we are with a total respect which is totally effective.

This infinite respect for human freedom puts God in a position of total vulnerability. God does not force my no into a yes. But at the same time the ultimate efficacy of God's will puts God in a position of infinite strength. How can God be both infinitely strong and infinitely weak? This mystery we can contemplate only as it is embodied in the Paschal mystery: Christ crucified embodies the weakness of God, God's infinite respect for my wayward freedom; Christ risen embodies the power of God, the efficacy which changes bad will into good will, brings me freedom and life.

A mechanical model of force and counter-force is utterly incapable of leading us into the mystery of grace. Divine activity and passivity, divine efficacy and divine vulnerability would be at loggerheads rather than reinforce each other. A model which derives from human relationships at their best, which are effective because they are respectful, discerning, and patient, does give us a glimmer of understanding, and would have been most helpful to the Jesuit and Dominican debaters of the 16th and 17th century who locked up considerable energies in their fruitless battle on God's energies at work in our lives.

In sum, the personal model gives new coherence and power to the synthesis achieved by Aquinas. It helps us express what was at the heart of his thought, and to do so in terms that are cogent for today. Some of the themes I have developed in the course of this analysis are of great moment for a theology of grace for our world. The themes of spontaneity, fidelity, and patience stand out among them.[96] They must animate any effort to deal with the broader socio-political issues of our world.

Concluding Remarks: Thomas Aquinas has a signal contribution to make to the conspiracy that would transform our age. However his contribution will be all the more effective the more pertinently it is transposed into a contemporary language. This contribution can be only heightened if we nurture the symbiosis of his thought with that of Augustine and Paul, and if we treasure the integration of Eastern and Western perspectives which occurs in his thought.

In contrast with Paul, Aquinas is relatively less attuned to the properly social dimension of human life. The organic fabric of the high Middle Ages was remarkably solid. Thus Aquinas could assume that a supportive social body was in place, and did not, like Paul, make reconciliation between opposing forces into a urgent theme of his thought. Aquinas was not constantly bedevilled with the intractable opposition of Jew and Gentile, of Judaizer and Enthusiast. There was less call for him to sharply etch out in dialectical terms the paradoxical dimensions of his thought. Yet Aquinas was profoundly indebted to Paul and some of the dialectical patterns of the latter were deeply embedded in his own thought. This we have seen in his presentation of the will acts and the passions, shot through as they are with a thesis/antithesis/synthesis structure not unrelated to that found in the basic Pauline triad of justification/ sanctification/salvation.

The thought of Aquinas in and of itself is remarkably balanced, but Aquinas still needs to be complemented by Paul. Aquinas lends himself more readily to a meta-psychological transposition, and he points out the constructive and developmental role of grace within our psyches and in our world. Paul lends himself more readily to transposition in meta-sociological or meta-political categories, and those categories are especially useful to us as we try to address the deep set oppositions that mark our own world.

By contrast with Augustine, Aquinas expresses his theology in more theoretical terms, and manifests a basic optimism with regard to human nature and its possibilities which Augustine does not share. This does not imply that Aquinas lays before us a programme of inexorable development onwards and forwards: the healing grace of God is needed for human nature to be in touch with the forces of authentic development within itself; and at every step of the way the orchestration of Divine Providence is required. Moreover, even with such powerful assistance human efforts do not yield automatic and assured results. Aquinas develops the conative side of human action; but he also reminds us that in the things that ultimately matter the final word is patience, not aggressivity, a patience modeled after the divine patience that achieves its purposes infallibly while totally respecting our resistances.

Again in this case, to set Aquinas in complementarity with Augustine will assist us greatly. Like that of Augustine, our age is dying, falling apart; like that of Aquinas, our age bears within itself the seeds of a new era. The discernment needed for action today is especially delicate. The danger is that we will try to achieve quick results by unduly narrowing the base on which solutions to human problems are devised, and by relying too heavily on our vaunted technological prowess and too little on honest assessment of the values and implications of our actions. Aquinas offers us a theology that supports patient, long-range human action. Augustine offers us the motivation for the inner freedom, the detachment from this present age, which will enable us to be both free and effective in that action.

The above considerations pertain to the domain of healing and liberation. Let us never forget that Aquinas is the first theologian of the West to carefully distinguish the healing from the elevating function of grace, nature from the supernatural, only to bring them into a sweeping integration which runs through all the categories of his theology. Humanization and divinization for him are utterly inseparable. The former is inescapably oriented to the latter, the latter totally poured out in the former. The habitual grace that utterly transforms our horizon towards God is the same grace that gives us the power to act with ease, spontaneity, promptitude in the things that lead us to our own fulfillment as human beings. In other words, Aquinas develops a theology of grace as habit which encompasses dimensions of both quality and relation. He laid a firm basis for a theology dedicated to unfolding the many virtualities, intra-personal and inter-personal, social, political and economic, of the personal thought-form.

NOTES

1. As we saw in Chapter Two, this is the main burden of Metz' *Christliche Anthropozentrik*.

2. Cf. the introductory chapter of Laporte, *Les structures dynamiques de la grâce*, esp. pp. 26–34. Also cf. Jean Gimpel, *The Medieval Machine: the Industrial Revolution of the Middle Ages* (Harmondsworth: Penguin, 1977).

3. One can evoke here Anselm of Canterbury and Richard of St. Victor, who seemingly treated revealed doctrines as the conclusions of reasoning processes. Aquinas continues to use the resources of reason to deal with the mysteries of faith, but he clearly limits himself to an attempt to show that these mysteries are not unreasonable, i.e. that they have a certain fittingness and coherence, and cannot be disproved.

4. *Insight*, p. 477.

5. The analyses of Edinger in *Ego and Archetype* are most helpful at this point, as well as those of Erich Neumann, *The Origins and History of Consciousness* (Princeton: Princeton University Press, 1970).

6. For Neumann, this paroxysm entails a regression to an earlier collectivism, which he discusses under the heading of "Mass Man and the Phenomenon of Recollectivization", ibid., pp. 436 ff.

7. A good source for this is Georges de Lagarde, *La naissance de l'esprit laïque au déclin du Moyen Age*, 2 Volumes (Paris: Béatrice-Nauwelaerts, 1956).

8. I have developed this point in *Les structures dynamiques de la grâce*, pp. 7–22, and 25–26, and in "The Dynamics of Grace in Aquinas: a Structural Approach", in *Theological Studies*, 1973, pp. 203–226.

9. Cf. for instance "The Subject", in *A Second Collection* (Philadelphia: Westminster, 1974), p. 79, and *Method in Theology* (London: Darton Longman and Todd, 1972), p. 343. The earlier Lonergan of *Insight* does speak in terms of the faculties of intellect and will, but the doctrine of conjugate potency/form/act he develops there does offer a helpful lead towards a better approach to the analysis of consciousness. To speak, as Aquinas does, of "the power of intellect", "the power of imagination", "the

power of irascible appetite'' evidences not an explanation of human behaviour but what Lonergan calls a heuristic structure, a recognized area of emptiness to be filled by later investigation. To pretend otherwise would be equivalent to claiming that one understands how a sleeping pill works by affirming that it has sleep inducing power (the Latin ''virtus dormitiva''). The term ''power'' for Aristotle and Aquinas was not a magic spell warding off the need to do further research. To the contrary.

Paul Ricoeur in his *Philosophie de la volonté*, (Paris: Aubier, 1950), pp. 180–186, engages in a phenomenological analysis of the will in the course of which he takes a negative position towards Aquinas' analysis which in some ways appears akin to that of Lonergan. For him Aquinas is too much caught up in cosmological categories, and does not sufficiently respect the properly irreducible nature of subjectivity and freedom. Central to Ricoeur's thought here appears to be a Cartesian vision of subjectivity, marked by the tendency to see the self as primordially a-relational. By contrast, Stephan Strasser in his *Phenomenology of Feeling. An Essay on the Phenomena of the Human Heart* (Pittsburgh: Duquesne University Press, 1977), considers it worthwhile to retrieve Aquinas' doctrine of the powers of the soul within his phenomenological analyses. Cf. p. 169.

10. This analysis is carried out when Aquinas tries to explain how the human self, lowest in the order of spiritual beings, can deal with things only piece-meal, and is easily distracted from its pursuit of the good by a more vivid and intense stimulus or by ingrained habit. The self's force of attention, apart from grace, is insufficient to enable it to avoid giving consent over a period of time to promptings towards what is objectively sinful. Cf. De Ver 24 12.

11. Cf. page 115 in Chapter Three.

12. De Ver 22 10 c.

13. De Ver 1 1 c, 21 1 c.

14. De Ver 22 12.

15. To my knowledge Aquinas does not use this precise definition of human nature. However he does situate human nature within a wider spiritual realm which encompasses the divine, the angelic, and the human. This approach implies that the spiritual side is viewed as genus, and the incarnate ''animal'' side as specific difference (cf. Ia 51 1 c; De Spir Creat 1 c & ad 11, 5 c; Ia 79 2 c, Ia 89 1 c. De Ver 24 3). For the more cosmocentric Aristotle, the physical cosmos is the backdrop (genus) and the rational dimension the specifying mark.

16. Transposing this into the contemporary terms made popular by Lonergan, the spiritual being is able to generate methods and principles, whereas the sentient being automatically follows predetermined paths. On this view, the transition from classical to historical consciousness is a breakthrough in the emergence of the properly spiritual dimension of a being who can only too easily be immersed in the routines of mere sentience. One readily finds not the evidence of but the roots for 20th century methodological sophistication in Aquinas' anthropology.

17. The terms ''psychic'' and ''psyche'' are not used by Aquinas. He prefers to use ''sense'', ''sensitive'', and their cognates to denote the lower level of conscious-

ness available to both animal and human levels of being. In modern parlance, however, psyche often denotes the particularly human form of sense-level consciousness. We will generally use the more evocative contemporary term.

18. Lonergan makes this point very clearly in *Insight*, ch. 15. He thus reflects Aquinas' own position, for whom, for instance, the higher function of sensitivity plays an instrumental role in providing the materials for intellection. In the animal, the highest sensory function is the *vis aestimativa*, which enables the animal to make correct instinctive evaluations of the environment in which it is to survive. In the human being this becomes a *vis cogitativa* which collates similar instances of concrete events and paves the way for simple apprehension.

19. In cognitional terms, there is never any experience which is not accompanied by simple apprehension of the intellect. The simple apprehension that occurs at this initial stage might be quite rudimentary, but it serves as a basis for further insights. Unless I understand the object to be an object liable to further understanding, I cannot raise a question about it, and trigger off a process which leads to more precise knowledge. In volitional terms concupiscence as it specifically occurs in the human being offers a striking example of the same principle. Suffused by the self-presence of spirit, it is in the human being potentially infinite rather than moderated by the control of instinct as it is in the animal. Cf. Ia–IIae 30.

20. As a person grows in virtue, this overflowing of the spiritual upon the psychic leaves its traces upon the psychic. Repeated good choices render the psyche so attuned to the spirit that its spontaneous reactions, even those which occur prior to the action of the will, can be trusted because they are already authentically spiritualized. This attunement is known as virtue, or operative good habit.

21. A simple example. A pleasant gastronomical odor wafts my way. In an act which is both sensory and spiritual, there arises in me a positive resonance to the object which it evokes. That positive resonance is necessary and infallible. I cannot but experience it, and on this level, which implies a simple complacency in what is good in itself, my reaction cannot but be good and wholesome. However the next step is neither necessary nor infallible. Once I raise the reflexive question "Do I want to eat in this restaurant now, or is there something else more important for me to do at this moment?" I have created the space within which I am free to say yes or no to the original impulse, and to choose either rightly or wrongly.

22. This language is more explicitly developed by Thomas in terms of the will. The first act of the will is that of *voluntas ut natura*, the second is that of *voluntas ut ratio*, or of the will as will. The volitional sequence implied here, that of feeling, simply willing, and intending, corresponds to Lonergan's cognitional sequence of experience, understanding, judgement.

23. Chapter Four, pp. 173–78.

24. The complacency/concern terminology is that of F. Crowe. He develops the main point I am dealing with here in three seminal articles, "Complacency and Concern in the Thought of St. Thomas", *Theological Studies*, 1959, pp. 1–39, 198–230, 343–395.

25. His analysis has roots in Greek philosophy, as we shall see. It is not without pertinence to contemporary work in this area. One has only to refer to Stephan Strasser, op. cit., esp. pp. 203–243, where he transposes the "concupiscible" to the the pre-intentional level of impulse, and the "irascible" to the intentional level. Ricoeur's analysis centers much more on the will itself; but in speaking about what motivates the will, he distinguishes between a number of affective movements which in some way or other have to do with "well-being" from a series of others in which the will is attracted to difficulty, to struggle, to domination over obstacles. Cf. ibid., pp. 111 ff.

26. Cf. Anna A. Terruwe, M.D., and Conrad W. Baars, M.D., *Psychic Wholeness and Healing. Using ALL the Powers of the Human Psyche* (New York: Alba, 1981), esp. Chapter 1. As they put it: "sensory beings also seek things which of themselves do not give pleasure, but are nevertheless sought because through them we can obtain something that does give pleasure". Having offered the example of the dog who exerts effort to get a piece of meat out of his reach or a student hard at work, they go on to say "It is not the pleasure appetite that causes the animal and the student to exert the effort because that which is difficult cannot constitute an object of the pleasure appetite, which is activated only by a pleasurable good. Consequently we are forced to postulate the existence of another emotive power which moves one to seek things that are not desired in themselves but only as useful for obtaining some other pleasurable object. This we call the *utility appetite*." (p. 11)

27. Cf. Vol. 19 and 20 of the translation published by Blackfriars, London, 1967. He addresses this issue in the introduction to Volume 19, p. xxv. The references in Plato are *Phaedrus*, 246–247 and *Republic*, Book 4, 436–441.

28. A text of Aquinas clearly confirms this point: "The fact that an animal seeks what is pleasurable to its senses (the business of the concupiscible power) is in accordance with the sensitive soul's own nature; but that it should leave what is pleasurable and seek something for the sake of a victory which it wins with pain (the business of the irascible) belongs to it according as it in some measure reaches up to the higher appetite. The irascible power, therefore, is closer to reason and the will than the concupiscible." (De Ver 25 2 c) Strasser makes a similar point. He terms the concupiscible feelings pre-intentional and highlights their affinity with the biological level: they are simple responses to felt good and evil (cf. op. cit., pp. 212–213). The irascible feelings are intentional; they pertain to a conscious being which needs to act purposively within an environment in which good and evil are related, often as dimensions of the same being (pp. 221 ff).

29. Edinger, *Ego and Archetype*, p. 12. Edinger further develops his position on pp. 38–40, and there refers to the work of Erich Neumann.

30. Rollo May, *Love and Will* (New York: Norton, 1969), pp. 283–284. May goes on to speak about the fuller integration of "yes" and "no". We need to be shaken out of our original state of "bliss", to enter into conflict and ego-development, in order to find at a later stage in life a mature integration of "love" and "will". Here again we find the dialectic that leads us from initial pleasure through strife to final fulfillment.

31. John Macmurray, *Persons in Relation*, pp. 95–96.

32. De Veritate 25 2 c.

33. De Virt Comm 4 ad 10.

34. This Aristotelian phrase is often quoted by Aquinas. Cf. for instance Ia–IIae 9 21 c.

35. This particular dynamic is evoked by Aquinas in his account of moral impotence in De Veritate 24 12. In the case of the person who is fundamentally oriented away from God and towards a particular created value which plays the role of ultimate fulfillment, the natural bent will be to fall in with a particular good suggested to the will in accord with that flawed orientation. But there is always the possibility of a *deliberatio attentior et major* which will call into question the advisability of acting in accord with that prevailing intentionality. However, in the long run, without the gift of grace healing that disordered orientation, the human spirit will be unable to stifle the free expression of what it has chosen to become in its most fundamental project of self-fulfillment.

36. The judgement of convenience is one of personal convenience rather than moral convenience, because I can judge that in spite of the moral disorder entailed in pursuing a certain good, it is still what I want to pursue. The judgement of possibility is one of negative possibility. In other words, at this stage the good does not appear as impossible of attainment. But I might subsequently discover that there are no appropriate means available for me to attain it.

37. The non-thematic consciousness of the self oriented towards the good as such which is at the core of its spontaneous orientation to this particular good (simple volition) is expressed in the first principle of the moral order: good is to be done, evil avoided. In Aquinas' terms, the judgement which determines the content of my intention is a conclusion from this general principle. The discrepancy between the good as such (Good is to be done) and this particular good (This is a good) ensures the contingence of the conclusion (This is to be done). Only the final presence of God satiates this orientation of the will to good as such and necessitates the will. In this life God is present only through created effects, and I remain free to intend to strive towards some value which excludes God.

38. Strasser, op. cit., pp. 246–253.

39. Paul Ricoeur's analysis of the will and its acts also adopts a tripartite sequence. First the will *chooses*: this is akin to the moment which Aquinas refers to under the heading of election and intention. Then the will executes, or *acts*. Finally, in the carrying out of action the agent meets a number of inevitabilities to which the will must *consent*. Apart from this consent action is inefficacious. Ricoeur puts consent at the end of the process, whereas Aquinas puts it earlier in the sequence: on the latter's view, in the strict sense consent is the first act of the series of will acts regarding means; but more significantly still, simple volition entails a broader consent to being as being as in its many forms it constantly impinges on the human psyche/spirit. For Ricoeur the will appears more to be over against nature, needing reconciliation with it in a subsequent moment of consent, rather than as from the very outset symbiotically plunged in

the world of nature and natural causes. Given the differences between the context of our own century and that of Aquinas, it is understandable that Ricoeur, unlike Aquinas, would bestow such significance upon this final moment in which I come up against and consent to that which in one sense limits the scope of my will but in another sense undergirds it: my own character, my subconscious, and the terms of my history which are not of my own making.

40. The parallelism of love (hate), desire (flight), joy (sorrow) with the acts of the will regarding the end is fairly clear. The parallelism of hope (despair), daring (fear), anger with the acts of the will regarding means is not explicitly found in Thomas. It nonetheless rounds out the systematic coherence of Aquinas' account of human willing. In greater detail: the act which triggers off the consent/election/application sequence is intention, and intention always deals with the possible. Once we enter into the realm of what is possible and impossible, difficulty becomes a pertinent issue. Thus conative feelings will accompany will acts pertaining to means. Hope belongs to an earlier phase which focuses more on the good to be obtained and its feasibility than on the obstacles in the way. It shares the open-endedness of consent. As I move towards concrete engagement, the obstacles loom larger on the horizon. Thus hope ripens into daring: in contemporary terms, choice implies a risk. As I engage with the means, face the difficulties, a greater or lesser degree of assertive force is released within me. If I am struggling against a notable evil in my effort to implement my choice, the feeling is one of anger. Lesser versions of anger might be titled animus, aggressiveness. In the absence of strong assertive feelings, however, there will always be that self-control and consistency in the midst of present difficulty which is motivated by the long-range good. Under the name of patience or perseverance it is given a highly significant role by Aquinas, especially when he deals with the virtuous operation of the irascible (conative) power: cf. IIa–IIae 123, esp. 6 10 ad 3.

41. Cf. Chapter One, pp. 12–13.

42. Aquinas speaks of *aversio a Deo* and *conversio ad Deum*. Contemporary Roman Catholic thought will speak in this context of fundamental option towards God or away from God. Severino Dianich has sought out the bases for this contemporary approach in *L'opzione fondamentale nel pensiero di S. Tomasso* (Brescia: Morcelliana, 1968).

43. De Ver 24 11.

44. De Ver 24 12 c.

45. Ricoeur in his *Philosophie de la volonté* puts what he terms emotion and habit under the heading of the involuntary dimension which is in constant creative tension with the voluntary dimension of freedom. Emotion erupts, it catches me by surprise; habit is a familiar pattern which I learn and make my own, a second nature, as it were. (pp. 266 ff.)

46. *De Virt. in Comm* 1 c. Translation of J.P. Reid, *On the Virtues* (Providence: The Providence College Press, 1951).

47. This is confirmed by the fact that Aquinas tells us in a passage which parallels

the one we have quoted: " . . . those things which are done out of love are done with firmness, promptitude, and delight. The love of the good towards which the virtue operates is required for the virtue." (De Car 2 c: my translation)

48. We do not deny the role of conation in the *acquisition* of habits. The ease of which we speak relates not so much to simple volition as to fruition, which follows upon a period of struggle against difficulty. Thus the positive affectivity which is at the heart of habit is marked not only by love but also by joy. Hence the graceful quality of habit.

49. This theme of self-forgetfulness emerges in a striking way in the work of Herbert Fingarette, *Self in Transformation*, esp. ch 7. The well-integrated self is not forced to obtrude on itself because of conflict or anxiety. It simply decides, does, is.

50. De Ver 26 7 ad 3.

51. This dimension, which Macmurray develops in *Persons in Relation*, pp. 58–59, remains relatively undeveloped in the thought of Aquinas.

52. Justice in a sense mars the symmetry of Aquinas' system, in which the infused virtues are the ordering of the highest part of the self by God and the acquired virtues the ordering of the lower part by this highest part. The acquired virtue of justice puts order in the will itself, which pertains to this highest part. Nonetheless justice operates differently than the love which is the infused habit pertaining to the will. In acquiring justice the will, endowed with the gift of love of God above all things (infused virtue), develops the power and the willingness to transcend the essential selfishness of the biologically extraverted sentience in which it is incarnate. In Lonergan's terms this entails the passage in the practical order from counter-position to position, from biological extraversion to the objectivity which alone befits the pure desire to know (cf. *Insight*, p. 473, and Chapters 7 and 18). It entails the overcoming of individual and group bias (ibid., pp. 218–223). In the terms of Paulo Freire we might refer to the transcendence of the spiritual as victory over the us/them dichotomy, the division between oppressor and oppressed to which the radical insecurity of our incarnate situation gives rise.

53. Cf Ia–IIae 57, esp 1,3,4, and De Virt in Comm 8. There is no sub-category of art in Aquinas which would include skills such as those related by Polanyi and Macmurray. The external *opus* is not as clear when we consider something like learning to walk, for instance, but at the same time the body is in some sense external to the inner self, and there are objective norms to be followed in acquiring such a skill. One could also further develop Aquinas' thought in the sense that just as prudence orchestrates the acquisition of good operative habits in the psyche, so too art orchestrates the acquisition of graceful and effective patterns of activity embedded in the body itself.

54. Cf. pp. 219–20; *De Ver* 26 7 ad 3.

55. There are other distinctions operative in this area which we will not touch on here, between habits of the appetitive powers and those of the apprehensive powers, between virtuous habits and vicious ones.

56. Their sensory powers act according to the instinct of nature. They are not at

the service of a self-reflective being able to choose patterns of activity and implement them. Nonetheless—Aquinas notes this—domestic animals can be trained by their human owners. Thus they acquire habits in an extended sense. Cf. Ia–IIae 50 3, esp. ad 2.

57. The above paragraph draws from Macmurray, who does not as Aquinas use the language of unrestricted openness, of the human spirit as able to become and to do all things (*potens omnia fieri et facere*). However his stress on the personal dimension of human learning and habit moves along parallel lines. Cf. *Persons in Relation*, pp. 54 ff.

58. As we contrast the pure and incarnate modalities of spiritual being/action our purpose is not so much to endorse or reject Aquinas' doctrine of pure spirits as it is to make use of it to achieve greater clarity on what it is to be a human spirit and to act as one.

59. A development parallel to this one is found in Rahner's article on "Theological Notion of Concupiscentia", in *Theological Investigations*, Vol I.

60. One could argue that in the case of the angelic spirit, volition as the prior (not temporally but causally) act of receptivity to God's grace is distinct from the subsequent act of free response which is at once an intention and a fruition, a first and a last act, whereas in the case of the human spirit, intention and fruition are clearly distinct not only from volition but also from each other.

61. The two are not unconnected. What enables me to walk is that the floor not only supports my weight but offers a certain resistance to me. Making use of that resistance, I am able to suitably balance and propel myself. Transposing this in personal categories, the difficulties we experience are as positive as they are negative in our unfolding. Cf. Macmurray, *Persons in Relation*, pp. 17 and 79. This point is developed with regard to Aquinas' theology of concupiscence in *Les structures dynamiques de la grâce*, pp. 182 ff.

62. Cf. for instance, SCG 4 95; Comp Theol c. 174, De Ver 24 13. Aquinas' sober approach to the mystery of death offers clues which are developed in contemporary approaches to the theology of death. For them death is a final summing up of the person's life, "moment of truth", opportunity for conversion.

63. This recondite topic is studied by Severino Dianich, op. cit. He presents key texts on pp. 15–27: II S 28 1 3 ad 5; II S 42 1 5 ad 7; De Ver 24 12 ad 2; De Ver 28 3 ad 4; De Malo 5 2 ad 8; De Malo 7 10 ad 8 and ad 9; Ia–IIae 89 6 c and ad 3. Thomas' presumption appears to be that this act occurs fairly early in life, as reflected by the classical doctrine which perdures to this day that one has a sufficiently developed rationality to be able to sin and confess sin at the age of six or seven. Contemporary psychology offers a much more nuanced account of human development than was available to Aquinas, and it likely will impel us to radically rework what he left us on these questions.

64. Aquinas' phrase for this is "natura sibi relicta".

65. Ia–IIae 109 9 c.

66. This dimension is reflected—though this specific position is not endorsed—in

254 PATIENCE AND POWER

the last chapter of Ricoeur's *Philosophie de la volonté*. If there is to be any lasting achievement of human freedom, it will pass through consent to limitation, above all the limitation of death. Ricoeur alludes to resurrection but does not make of it a theme of his philosophical analysis. He sees it rather as belonging to a poetics than to a philosophy of the will.

67. Aquinas tells us that the most essential aspect of fortitude is the power to sustain rather than the power to attack. In and of themselves obstacles exercise a moderating force over daring and aggression. Thus fortitude is less essential in this respect. To stick to one's resolve in the face of difficulty, of suffering, of fear, is much more dependent on fortitude. We shall use the general term of patience to refer to this particular dimension of fortitude, though Aquinas distinguishes between patience, perseverance, constancy, and longanimity (IIa–IIae 137–138).

68. In this diagram intention purposefully straddles the fence between justification and sanctification. The personal act of turning towards God for Aquinas is both the culminating act of the justification of the adult and the first of the series of meritorious acts which make up the process of sanctification (Ia–IIae 112 2 ad 1). As flowing from the transformation of the inmost heart of the person by God, it is a free act, a *motus liberi arbitrii* as Aquinas puts it in Ia–IIae 115. As the foundation for further will acts regarding means to beatitude, it is an already set act of intention. In the case of the child as yet incapable of a free act, justification consists in the first step, which is that of the heart's transformation by the gift of habitual grace. The second step, which is the free act by which the person makes his or her own that transformation in an act of conversion, comes later.

69. In adults, however, justification is not complete except in a free response by which they personally cleave to God and renounce their sinful past, an act akin to the intention which flows from simple volition. Indeed, for Thomas the first free act of the human person sets the person in a fundamental orientation towards or away from God. This complex problem is studied by Dianich, op. cit.

70. Cf. for instance his *Le mystère du surnaturel* (Paris: Aubier, 1965).

71. Macmurray's approach has the advantage of showing the secret connivance between Aquinas' doctrine of the Trinity and that of the relationship of nature and grace. In both case the key issue is one of authentic genuine personal relationships, which do not take place without kenosis.

72. Cf. *Les structures dynamiques de la grâce*, pp. 137–150.

73. This point is developed in terms of the states of integral and of corrupt human nature in *Les structures . . .* , pp. 179–180.

74. An excellent statement of this handicap of the incarnate spirit is found in Lonergan, *De Deo Trino: Pars Systematica* (Rome: PUG, 1964), pp. 196–204. He puts it in terms of the gap between the temporal and the eternal subject.

75. Cf. M.D. Chenu, "Les passions vertueuses. L'anthropologie de S. Thomas", *Rev Phil Louvain*, 1974, pp. 13–18.

76. Rahner develops this point in a broader context in his article "Theological Reflections on the Problem of Secularization", *Theological Investigations*, Vol. 10

(New York: Herder and Herder, 1973), pp. 318–348, esp. pp. 341 ff. The psyche-in-relation-to-the-world continually solicits the spirit with an incredible plurality of objects. The temptation is to focus in on this or that one, and make of it the integrating principle of all the others. The grace which elevates me makes it possible for me to love God above all else, to choose God as the integrating principle, even in the face of God's absence: in other words love is accompanied by faith and hope. By the same token that grace empowers me to resist the temptation to focus on this or that object, person, value as the absolute integrating factor, and thereby to be fixated and arrested in my development. Loving God above all things, my adherence to whatever presents itself to me from within my world is marked by a healthy relativism. I am willing to live at peace with the absence of God's fulfilling presence, and feel no need to conjure up the illusion that the absence has been removed.

77. Ia–IIae 109 9 c.

78. Cf. *Les structures . . .* , pp. 159 ff.

79. That statement brings out what I am convinced is at the root of Aquinas' approach to the mystery of grace and free will. He states without any sense of embarrassment that God's dominion extends not only to what creatures do, but how they do it, freely or necessarily. How can God infallibly move a creature to act freely? The key to this is not so much meta-physical as it is meta-personal. In the final analysis vulnerability and respect of the other do not diminish but enhance the impact of personal relations. God's dominion does not consist in his escaping vulnerability but in espousing it, does not consist in forcing the issue of a person's consent but in being infinitely patient. The paradox of the personal is fully respected. For the Christian its ultimate expression is in the mystery of the cross.

80. This second role is absolutely universal in scope: all powers, whether endowed with infused habits or not, are moved to their acts by God, who, in Aquinas' perspective, directs each event because he directs them all. For a clear and helpful account of this matter one might refer to Bernard Lonergan's *Grace and Freedom* (New York: Herder and Herder, 1971).

81. Cf. In Rom 5,3. This text is explained more fully in *Les structures dynamiques de la grâce*, pp. 171 ff.

82. De Malo 7,2, ad 17.

83. A lengthy text develops this point in terms of infused and acquired virtues: cf De Virt in Comm 10 ad 14: "The passions which incline us towards evil are not completely suppressed by either acquired or infused virtue . . . However, these passions are subdued by both acquired and infused temperance, to the extent that a man is not violently disturbed by them. Acquired and infused virtues accomplish different effects in this subduing of the passions. Acquired virtue effects that the attacks of concupiscence be felt less. This effect results from the causality of acquired virtue; by the frequent acts whereby a man grows accustomed to virtue, he gradually grows unaccustomed to obey his passions and begins to resist them. From this there ensues that he senses their attacks the less. Infused virtue is of value in that, even though the passions be felt, still they in no way gain control. For infused virtue effects that

a man in no way obey the concupiscences of sin; and while this virtue remains, it does this infallibly.'' Cf. *Les structures* . . . , pp. 199–201.

84. Cf Ia–IIae 111 2. A helpful analysis of this text is provided by Lonergan, in *Grace and Freedom*, pp. 128–137. I attach more importance to the distinction between intention and simple volition than Lonergan does in this context.

85. Aquinas' doctrine on this finds its most mature development in Ia–IIae 115. Cf. also Appendix A of Laporte, *Les structures* . . .

86. Cf. my article, ''The Dynamics of Grace in Aquinas: A Structural Approach'', *Theol Stud*, 1973, pp. 203–226.

87. Cf. pp. 63–64.

88. Cf. Lonergan's *Method in Theology*, pp. 288–89, 343.

89. This shift was keenly highlighted by Luther, as we saw in Chapter Two. But there is a world of difference between a relationship of internalized trust and one fraught with anxiety and requiring constant reinforcement from outside.

90. In addition to relation as an Aristotelian category—a category Aquinas did not use for grace—in him one also finds transcendental relation, relation as it transcends the categories, permeates all being, and even, in Christian revelation, finds its root in the Godhead which is triune. The relations which emerge in Aquinas' theology of grace are transcendental relations. Lonergan's development of this point in his *De Deo Trino: Pars Systematica*, pp. 291–315, is most helpful.

91. This perspective emerges quite cogently in Rahner's article on grace in the *Sacramentum Mundi*. In the thought of another great medieval thinker, Duns Scotus, it takes on a most attractive Christological hue.

92. This latter point ought to enable us to develop a theology of anonymous grace as opposed to grace in an explicitly ecclesiological context. Grace need not draw attention to itself to be grace.

93. Ia–IIae 109 3 c.

94. The basic paradigm of this relationship is Christological. The divine and the human in Christ are as inseparable as they are distinct. As the definitive embodiment of grace, he shows forth in himself both the divinizing and humanizing functions of grace realized to their utmost.

95. Ia–IIae 110 1.

96. At this point we could continue with an analysis of Aquinas' doctrine of created and uncreated grace in terms of this personal model. This would open up for us yet another area where the dissimilarity between God and humans is crucial.

Very briefly put, in friendship I give everything to my friend except the very inner core of me that does the giving: I share my thoughts, communicate my feelings and affections, give my possessions, even my body to be burned (1 Cor 13), but the ''I'' that gives remains the giver and not the gift given.

God's gift of self is more radical than that. God is infinitely more able to give of himself than I am able to give of myself. In giving me his thoughts, God is giving me himself, because God's Word is God in person. In giving me his love, God is giving me himself, because God's Spirit of Love is God in person. Remaining

Father, Son, and Spirit God divests himself of himself in order to dwell in me. My thoughts and affections may dwell in my friends, but I do not dwell there in person. God's thought and love is God in person. For the Divine Persons to hold me in their thoughts and affections is for them to dwell in me. Thus God is both giver of a gift and gift given.

Chapter Six

RECAPITULATION:
GRACE AS PATIENCE AND POWER

Some threads of convergence running through this work are already dyed in vivid colors, others will stand out only with careful scrutiny. The time has come to pull them together. We will begin by recalling broader concerns and themes that have recurred in our work.

THREADS OF CONVERGENCE

1. The *apocalyptic* theme introduced in Chapter One has resurfaced in each chapter of this work. In its Pauline origins the doctrine of grace intends to correct various attempts to elude the end-time tension of the already now/not yet in which the first Christian communities were called to live their lives. Augustine saw the collapse of society around him with apocalyptic eyes, and sought a refuge in the world of interiority in order to find inner detachment amidst uncertainty and turmoil. Aquinas appears to have been less sensitive to this tension. The Dark Ages having dissipated by his day, he looked out on a world marked by the hope of brand new endeavours rather than by the sadness that everything is inexorably moving to its end.[1] Yet his thought offers an apt foundation for one who wishes to explore the constructive side of apocalyptic, the newness which we hope will emerge out of the old irreversibly wasting away.

Cast adrift from these apocalyptic moorings, the doctrine of grace loses its vital nerve. The momentous forces for both good and evil unleashed in our own era cannot but rekindle our awareness of the apocalyptic matrix of grace. As we saw in Chapter One, a sense of impending doom pervades our world, but in the detritus of the old the seeds of a new order have already been planted. Many are seeking to cultivate these seeds, looking back to the past and across to other religious traditions for the ingredients that will make them grow. Our task has been to seek and identify those ingredients as they are to be found in the Christian tradition which nurtured our world, and to show how the epic struggles of our day are a form of the eschatological *thlipsis* so central to Paul's thought, as well as an invitation to patient and trusting surrender to God.

2. The horizon analysis carried out in Chapter Two offers us a valuable perspective, that of the *personal* thought-form. As we saw in Chapter One, some contemporary thinkers, sensitive to the inter-webbing of all reality, would have us move from the form of the mechanical which permeates our world to the form of the organic. At best an exercise in superficial nostalgia, such a move fails to recapture what is most vivifying in the earlier tradition of the West. Praiseworthy though it may be, by itself the rejection of extrinsic relations and brute survival fails to protect the irreducible uniqueness of each human person. Something more is needed.

It is the form of the personal, rooted in the Christian tradition, gradually unfolding century by century, brought to our attention by Metz and Macmurray, which recapitulates and brings into vivifying interchange the contrasting but authentic bipolar values of relationality and uniqueness. The form of the organic affirms relationality, but apart from uniqueness the distinct terms which are required for a genuine relation are absorbed into each other. The person fails to emerge. The form of the mechanical affirms individuality, but apart from the unique set of relations which constitute an authentic self that individuality becomes sterile and isolated, fails to accede to the level of a uniqueness which for each person is utterly unrepeatable. The person is stifled. The authentic heritage of the West, bound up with the form of the personal, allows both relationality (*ad aliud*) and uniqueness (*in se*) to reinforce and enliven each other.

Person-in-relation, for the Christian grounded in the mystery of the Trinity, is a theme central to the many concerns of this study. There is no person without community. The link between the development of human persons and the appropriate community context which by turns fosters and embodies that development is integral to our purpose and has been reflected when appropriate in the chapters of this book. More broadly still, the notion of person-in-relation undergirds and authenticates the attractive features of twentieth century ecological and holistic sensitivity. Extending beyond the confines of human society, the relations which constitute human persons solidly implant them within the cosmos and give the cosmos the only context in which it can with realistic hope await the liberation promised by Paul in Romans 8.

3. In addition to the apocalyptic and the personal, a *structural* theme has constantly recurred throughout this work. Paul, Augustine, and Aquinas each

left behind a basic structure for understanding the dynamic of grace. In a cumulative process which goes on into our own day, their legacy has been treasured, and its patterns transposed and handed on.

Paul's doctrine of justification/sanctification/salvation, formulated mostly in response to the various deviations which occurred in his communities, caught as they were in the crucifying tensions of the between-time, has served down through the centuries as a unifying structure for the dynamic of grace.[2] Even today, the parameters set by that doctrine and the equilibrium it suggests can be set aside only at great peril. *Augustine* transposes Paul's doctrine, but at the same time develops a triadic pattern of his own, one with clear trinitarian affinities, comprising the restless heart which is foundational to all grace, the grace that beckons us from without, and the grace that transforms us from within. *Aquinas* builds on both Paul and Augustine, but offers a set of distinctions between grace and nature, healing and elevating grace, grace as movement within the person (actual grace) and grace as habit (sanctifying grace) which offer a theoretical clarity which has yet to be surpassed, though unfortunately at times it has been subject to undue simplifications and distortions. In the very last section of this chapter, we will return to some of these structural themes.

4. The final theme that we wish to mention at this point is that of grace as *dynamic*. We began Chapter One with a contrast between first and third worlds that set this dynamic in proper perspective. Experiencing oppression in blatant and explicit forms, the third world finds in the term ''liberation'' a powerful focus for its need of grace. Oppression, however, entails oppressors as well as oppressed, and our first world as a whole experiences oppression predominantly from the side of the oppressor rather than from that of the oppressed. Oppressors are just as dehumanized and in need of liberation as the oppressed.

The oppressors' need for grace may not be immediately apparent. The first world controls massive resources. Nonetheless its power is being more and more clearly recognized for what it is: unreal and ineffectual, a form of domination rather than of integration, power over and against rather than power with. For our first world the absence of grace occurs under the subtle guise of real powerlessness in the midst of apparent domination. Technology has offered us a panoply of sophisticated means, but what ends shall we achieve with them? Agreement on constructive objectives and the harnessing of the available means to achieve them is beyond our grasp. The longing of our first world is for a grace that, in the most genuine sense of the word, *empowers*. Since, as Paul of Tarsus and Paulo Freire agree, liberation comes to the oppressor through the oppressed, that empowerment will only come if the first world is willing to learn from and enter into the patient and courageous struggles of the rest of humankind for liberation.

The theme of power has run through the many chapters of our essay. In the opening chapter we contrasted the grace-ful power of the ballet dancer with the cluttered distractedness of our world. This concern with gracefulness re-emerged in the chapter on Paul under the heading of *kenosis*, that self-forget-fulness after the pattern of Christ of which the ballet dancer's art is a secular counterpart, acquired in her case by much practice rather than received as gratuitous gift.[3] Augustine developed this theme under the heading of the God-given spontaneity to which we are to abandon ourselves if we wish to journey towards beatitude. Aquinas offered us a more technical analysis, systematically transposing the classical doctrine of acquired habits (such as the skill which makes the ballet dancer so graceful) to the realm of infused grace. In the gracefulness of grace, its kenotic abandonment, its unobtrusive harmony, there is found an antidote to the repetitive mechanisms and fruitless endeavours of our technological world.

What is the secret of the grace that bestows genuine power on its recipients? Genuine power is opposed to violence: it knows how to respectfully wait for the right moment, and because of this it is able to gather together all the dispersed strands of a broken reality. Without patience grace has no power. The only grace that integrates is the grace that waits. Put in Christological terms, there is no resurrection without passion and death.

The waiting is not only ours but also God's. We wait for grace, but grace also waits for us. There is a rhythm to this waiting. Grace is mostly tacit, unobtrusive, yet, when the time is at hand, it is more powerful than any power conjured up by our mechanically proficient world. The secret of this rhythm is its respect for the unique worth and destiny of each person, a respect that calls for infinite patience. In the end this patience will prevail.

The dynamic of sin which grace overcomes is ultimately self-destructive. Because of the fragmentation it fosters, that dynamic is at cross-purposes with itself. Integrating grace takes the narrow and slow path that leads to reconciliation in depth, achieving partial increments of integration in this world, and in the next the full recapitulation of all reality of which the graced achievements of this world are but the first fruits, the down payment.

The next sections of this chapter will develop more fully these aspects of the dynamic of grace. Having first attended to the patterns and rhythms of grace, we will offer a recapitulation of our work under the headings of the patience of grace and the power of grace.

THE PATTERNS OF GRACE

The bi-polarity of the waiting/integrating, patience/power dynamic is absolutely crucial to grace. Just as personal uniqueness and personal relationship, for example, grow in direct rather than in inverse proportion to each other,[4] so do patience and integration. The more grace knows how to wait, the deeper will it knit reality together. The more sensitive grace is to the ecological and the relational dimensions of God's creation, the more will it be willing to wait for its *kairoi*.

The bipolarity of waiting and integrating grace can be related to the many others which have emerged in this work: childlike passivity and adult activity; affection and conation; nature and grace; the healing and elevating functions of grace; the habitual and actual modalities of grace; personal relationship (*ad aliud*) and uniqueness (*in se*). It would be very helpful if we could collapse all of these pairs into a unique pair, an all-pervasive yin and yang of grace. To do this, however, may well be to fall prey to an illusion. It is better to accept the ambiguity and tension that flows from unresolved plurality than to get stuck in a premature synthesis. We cannot, however, fail to note elements of affinity between a number of these pairs:

a) Obviously waiting and integrating grace relate to personal uniqueness and personal relationships respectively. More than all else, it is the personal uniqueness of the other which prompts us to wait, to be respectfully patient, and our own personal uniqueness, to the extent that we have appropriated it, which gives us the inner peace and security which makes it possible for us to wait. Being ourselves in a nurturing and accepting way, we are willing to let others be themselves. By contrast, to build up, celebrate, and maintain the network of relationships which corresponds to the fulness of Christ's body is the object of the integrative function.

b) Habitual grace is tacit, unobtrusive, always waiting for the right moment. In a sense actual grace is that moment: in our creative response, empowered by divine assistance, to what is novel, different, other, we reach out and seek fuller integration with that other. This affinity between habitual and waiting grace, between actual and integrating grace must not however be pushed to the extent of forgetting that habitual grace constitutes us in an intimate relationship with God or that actual grace is configured to the uniqueness of each one of us by the same God.

c) One can readily link actual and habitual grace to the distinction between the two modalities of God's self-communication. The Word is spoken in space-time, there to be acknowledged or rejected; the Word is actual grace *par excellence*, confronting us from without, challenging us to collaborate in the task of transforming the world. The mission of the Spirit touches and transforms our hearts from within in a habitual, non-explicit way beyond our fathoming, making it possible for us to respond to the Word, under whatever guise the Word comes to us.[5]

Again we must not explore this affinity in a single-minded way. This contrast between two facets of God's approach must never be allowed to degenerate into a dichotomy. While the Word's coming into the world is public, we are also told that the light shone in the darkness and the darkness did not comprehend it, and that the Word became flesh in the form of hiddenness and anonymity. Indeed, unobtrusive presence ultimately is more revealing than the showy trappings of willful self-affirmation. Moving to the other side of the contrast, while the gift of the Spirit as we have studied it in the tradition of the West is a hidden one, our lives are punctuated by precious moments in which the nameless mystery within us, at the prompting of certain circumstances of our lives, does come to some measure of explicit focus.

In sum, actual grace, God's operation from without, is explicit and, without being intermittent, approaches us in distinct momentary events;[6] habitual grace, God's operation from within, is the implicit and relatively permanent undertow of our lives. Habitual grace is the love of God poured into our hearts by the Holy Spirit who is given to us; all actual graces find their center and their meaning in the primordial action of God in history, the event of the Word-made-flesh, to which human hearts are invited to respond as they collaborate in building up the fulness of the body of Christ.

d) The affinity between the theme of patience and power and that of healing and elevating grace is also worth noting. Habitual grace as received by me deepens, transforms, gradually creates within me a space of interiority and spontaneity which leads me to grace-ful action in accord with the truth of my being. If habitual grace encounters me in a state of sin, it heals me, brings me to myself, in a way that is gradual, painstaking, unique for me as it is for each individual.[7] At the same time habitual grace, like every habit, has an object. It puts me in relation with what is not me, in this case with the living God, a relation of intimacy which, utterly beyond my scope, shatters the parameters of my created being. Thus elevating grace is the ultimate integrating grace: it brings about an unprecedented union between God and the human self, which fully respects the nature of both and makes possible every other integration within the human sphere.

e) Other affinities ought to be brought to light. The waiting dimension of grace links up with the passive, the child-like, the affective side; it puts me in touch with my primordial receptivity to God's gift of an authenticity and security unique to my own self. The integrating dimension of grace links up with the active, the adult, the conative side: having received as gift the inner resource of a self rooted in God, I reach out towards others, hoping both to give and to receive, to express and to deepen the mystery of who I am.

THE RHYTHMS OF GRACE

As we have seen in our discussion of patterns and bi-polarities, the patience and the power of grace are bi-polar, ultimately not to be separated or extricated from each other. Yet there is a distinction between them. The natural way of experiencing that distinction is by a to and fro passage from one to the other. In this section we will reflect on that rhythmic movement. What we say applies specifically to patience and power, but it applies as well to the other bipolarities we have mentioned.

Rhythm and grace go together. This is true not only for the dancer but also for the lover of God. Grace is mostly silent, tacit, hidden, but it is punctuated by moments which manifest the power of God. It constantly moves back and forth from the habitual to the actual, from the implicit to the explicit. It waits, it achieves, and then it waits again.

We will begin by adverting to this rhythm as it marks any harmonious human consciousness. To go around in a stupor, even a "mystical" one, impervious to what is going on around us, is one form of excess; to be constantly focusing upon certain elements within our conscious field, fostering within ourselves a state of obsessive hyper-alertness, is equally excessive. What is called for is a rhythmic ebb and flow between two states, one in which we carefully focus our awareness on our basic commitments, relationships, and patterns, try to understand them, affirm them, deliberate about them with a view to shaping ourselves and our world; and another in which they are left to influence us as a tacit perspective, a light, a standpoint from which we can gracefully attend to the myriad details of our lives.[8] Putting this in terms that emerged in our chapter on Aquinas, what we need is the proper balance of the affective and the conative, of relaxed surrender to the fundamental movements of our spirit and deliberate, intentional focus on this or that particular concern.

Examples will help to clarify this rhythm. Let us begin with going for a walk on a particularly beautiful day. My purpose as well as yours is to enjoy the scenery, and I am able to do so precisely because I can forget about the walking and concentrate on the scenery. If I am transfixed by the sidewalk in front of me, anxious about possible obstacles, constantly checking whether my shoes are properly tied and whether the sidewalk is clear, I enjoy nothing. If, conversely, I am totally oblivious to these factors, I eventually will stumble or bump into something, and my walk comes to a premature end. There is a right balance in which I never lose my alertness concerning the peripherals, while thoroughly enjoying the central purpose, which is the scenery. In this state, I implicitly trust that at the right moment I will awaken to any hindrance before me and attend to it in the appropriate manner. I allow myself to enter into a rhythm by which I alternate between explicit attention as required to any element within my total field of consciousness and implicit presence to all of them. I let go and allow the "automatic pilot" to take over.

The same applies to relationships, as we have seen in Chapter Five.[9] Insecure about a relationship, I constantly dwell on it, bring it up with the other person, and end up making myself and the other person miserable. The relationship becomes its own narcissistic object and is in danger of destroying itself. But I can go to the opposite extreme. Oblivious of a relationship, I never take the opportunity to celebrate it, to actualize it; the relationship cools and eventually dies. With the proper rhythm of attentiveness and letting go, the relationship flourishes. As a relaxed awareness, the relationship colours and heightens my dealing with all else, but without obtrusion or awkwardness, much as the ballerina's graceful and tacit presence to her finely attuned body allows concentration on the *Gestalt* of her dance as an artistic whole.

Moving from personal to intra-psychic relationships will help us bring to light a dimension, to which we have not yet clearly adverted, of this obsessive actualization. Over-actualization of certain elements within consciousness has as its counterpart the repression of other unwanted elements from consciousness. My obsessive focus on a particular object or relationship or pattern of behaviour leads me to keep in the dark other elements which, introduced to my consciousness, would threaten me and heighten my anxiety. I refuse to accept the waiting, the suffering entailed by the process of integrating those alien elements, and in that way deprive myself of the enrichment only they can bring to me. Instead of an osmotic membrane, an easy flow, between the explicitly conscious and the implicitly conscious parts of my psyche, there is a rigid barrier between them, in more technical terms a neurosis. The actual becomes obsessive, the habitual becomes repressed. The dance becomes a stand off.

This approach to grace within the more intimate inter- and intra-personal spheres extends to the world as a whole. The particular disorder of consciousness which marks the oppressed of the third world, if one is to believe the account of Paulo Freire, is a numbness, a narcotization which blocks out from their awareness the fact that they are being oppressed. Liberation from that disorder begins with the process of conscientization, as we have seen in Chapter Three.[10] Going to the other end of the scale, we found in Chapter One that the opposite disorder is prevalent in the first world: consciousness is galvanized to the point of obsession.

Neurotics invest their threatened security in particular self-definitions, particular patterns of behaviour. They exhibit the appearance of self-control and effectiveness, but on closer examination show signs of awkwardness, rigidity, even paralysis. They stifle their own authentic growth and creativity. They erect barriers to protect themselves against contents of consciousness that are threatening and confusing.[11] They fear the shadow side of their own selves.

Our first world culture as a whole is neurotic, it is encumbered by the repetitive and self-conscious nature of its own processes, and blocks out whole areas of the global reality. Advertising helps us to forget the shadow elements within our world; political manipulation blurs our awareness of an oppressed third world without which we would not be able to maintain the trappings of our own comfortable existence. The correlation of anxiety and repression in the individual is found writ large on our planet: the first world tends to be anxious and over-conscious, the third, apart from those who have joined together in the struggle for liberation, repressed and lethargic.

This contrast between harmonious and disharmonious consciousness also applies to our relationship to God. Anxiety about that relationship leads to an undue focusing and narrowing of consciousness. One's relationship with God, as in the case of Paul's Galatian opponents, for example, is defined in terms of clearly formulated patterns of behaviour designed to wrest God's approval. The ambiguous and threatening areas of consciousness are not allowed to impinge upon this area of pretended clarity. Feelings of anger, resentment, or lust, are repressed, and self-righteousness prevails. Not only are they repressed but, as we find in the case of Augustine the Manichee, they also are disowned, not acknowledged as really belonging to the person whose they really are.[12] A lesser form of this deviation is found in the fundamentalist who hastens to impose his or her orthodoxy upon anyone, already in this life seeking to separate the sheep from the goats. By contrast genuinely religious persons refuse to prematurely judge what is good and evil, according to the example offered in the parable of the wheat and the tares.[13] Exuding a quiet, self-effacing power grounded in their security before God, they respect the mystery of God's own ways, the rhythms of grace.

Whatever the bi-polarity we deal with, grace as tacit/explicit, inner/outer, healing/elevating, patient/powerful, actual/habitual, we are called to surrender to a rhythm not of our own making, by which the complementary facets of grace ceaselessly point towards and lead to each other in every area of our human endeavour. Because of this rhythm the distinction between the next two sections, on the patience and on the power of grace, though useful for the purpose of orderly exposition, bears a certain artificiality.

THE PATIENCE OF GRACE

It is easy to discern in the archetypical kenotic text, found in Philippians 2, how power and patience are inseparable. The power of the resurrection emerges only under the contrary appearance of death on the cross, of a life lived in radical patience. Christ Jesus unreservedly enters into the human condition, refusing to impose an *a priori* definition of himself upon others, to cling to his prerogatives as the one who is in the form of God. That would be to go through the motions of incarnation without its commitment, to remain fixated at the initial stage of the human journey where all is possible and nothing is actual, to refuse struggle and self-sacrifice, the only anvil on which the self can be forged. Christ Jesus does not give up the form of God. Rather, absolutely secure in the mystery of who he is, he lets go of that mystery, surrenders it into the realm of the tacit, the hidden, the habitual,[14] enters into the human condition, takes the form of a servant. The self-definition and the acknowledgement by name to which he is entitled come only at the end of this process of self-abandonment, not from his own hand but from that of the One who graces him with the name that is above every name. Like all humans, he must wait in patience for his *kairos*.

To allow our relations with God and with other persons to become a rigid preoccupation is precisely to refuse kenosis. To let go, to surrender, to allow a power which is from beyond us to flow through us, is to embrace kenosis. The habitual patterns acquired by the ballerina enable her to let go and give herself entirely to her dance. The gracelessness of the adolescent arises from an understandable anxiety about how he is seen by others to walk, a heightening of self-consciousness, because he has not yet had the time to acquire the skills of graceful gait.

This kenotic understanding applies to Augustine's doctrine of willfulness and willingness. To try to do good without the prior transformation of a grace that makes one good is to engage in a futile exercise in willfulness. It is to be like the wheel that thinks that it will become round by turning, rather than recognize that it is because it has been shaped to be round that it can turn.[15] Unless willingness to love God above all else is given and received, there is no willing of the good, except superficial and precarious. Without surrender the will is not healed.

Aquinas' doctrine of moral impotence can be similarly understood. For him the person without habitual grace is unable for long to avoid serious sin because, given a prior orientation of the will away from rather than towards God, the effort of concentration needed to act each time as befits one in communion with God is beyond his or her human capacities. Such an effort would be a willful attempt to make of oneself what one is not rather than a kenotic surrender to the only power that can act creatively in our depths. In other words conation without underlying affection, activity without underlying receptivity, eventually turns into frustration.

The hymn to Christ Jesus in Philippians evokes one kenosis but, as Augustine implies, we really need to surrender twice.[16] The first surrender is that of justification: we consent to the divine power as it permeates the very roots of our being and transforms us. Then we are called to the surrender of sanctification, of obedience to the God who unceasingly operates from without, orchestrating the events, situations, and persons which we encounter during our lives, and who finally calls us to the ultimate kenosis of death.

As we move from achievement in this or that precisely delimited sphere of human activity, such as ballet dancing or walking, to the achievement of our total human maturation, interpersonal, intrapersonal, religious, this second surrender becomes much more significant. The intricacy of who I am to be surpasses my understanding. To become who I am to be means to embrace in faith the unique challenges, limitations, opportunities that come my way, to accept them and live them out. To exclude them according to a narrow and pre-determined programme of self-development is to wither and die.

In the course of that journey, I will time and time again face the unexpected, and my vision of what lies at the end of my struggle will evolve. I must be discerning yet open-minded. Not every new path opening up before me leads to my fulfillment in God. At the same time, when hard pressed by disappointing turns in my life, I am to avoid becoming locked into visions of what could have been which masquerade as visions of the future, visions of envy rather than visions of hope. To look behind rather than ahead is, to use the scriptural image, to be turned like Lot's wife into a pillar of salt.[17] The illusion in such a case would be that of movement into the future, but the reality that of a frozen structure.[18]

When we move from the realm of individual destiny to that of the human family as a whole, the need for a discernment open to mystery must be underlined even more. A new and attractive vision of what needs to be done in our world is now emerging. A convergence of opportunities and perspectives for the first world has been described in Marilyn Ferguson's *The Aquarian Conspiracy*. Injustice and oppression in so many sectors of human activity and parts of our planet cry out for our labour of love. We are beginning to clearly discern the holistic dimensions of this labour: our rebuilding of the first world must go hand in hand with our collaboration with brothers and sisters of the third world in overcoming global structures of oppression.

Yet, and this is the point which Augustine effectively makes in *City of God*, apart from surrender to the mysterious designs of Providence, without detachment from the goals we intend for our action, that action is ultimately futile.[19] It is too easy for us to isolate a set of factors that we think we can control, pretending that our action on these factors will move us towards a better and more compassionate world. This would be to allow the dynamics of individual neurosis to poison our collective action, and to condemn ourselves to the same paralysis and ineffectiveness which vitiate our own individual efforts when we give way to the illusion that we control the mystery of our own person and destiny. Rather we must respect the intrinsic limitations of human activity, allowing the twists and turns of Providence inexorably to bring them to our attention. Put in Christian terms, the law of the cross applies to our collective as well as to our individual endeavours. We do not inexorably evolve from one success through another and so on all the way to the triumph of the new world, but rather we work out our collective purposes in fear and trembling, celebrating moments of partial triumph, yet awaiting the final and decisive moment of God's intervention in history. Though this final moment is in continuity with the best desires and efforts of humankind throughout history, it alone brings them to a close, definitively judging their positive or negative place within the pattern of that history,[20] fulfilling them in a way which utterly transcends them. At that point the futility of any choice to withdraw from the lordship of God will become inescapably and universally manifest.

The relativity of human action, the fact that this action finds its fulfillment and meaning within a whole which only God orchestrates, is an invitation to patience. This ought not surprise us. As we know, the kenotic love Paul brought to the attention of his beloved Corinthians is patient and kind, bears with all things; the fruits of the spirit he lists in the letter to the Galatians include patience and gentleness. Moreover, as we saw, Aquinas when dealing with the healing of our conative appetite by the infused virtue of fortitude stresses not the burst of anger sometimes needed for immediate results but the patience that collaborates with the long-range action of God.

This patience is God's as well as ours. We are to be patient and peaceable in the midst of the most strenuous efforts, the most ardent strivings, the most heart-breaking disappointments. In this we reflect the mystery of a God who is patient and long-suffering, who waits for the right moment before acting. Human patience reflects divine patience.

The theme of divine patience sheds considerable light on the classical sixteenth and seventeenth century debates on grace and free-will. Yes, divine dominion efficaciously achieves its purposes while leaving us free, but how? To recognize that God exercises that dominion in patience and peace, in long-suffering and compassion, the only mode of dominion that befits the form of the personal, rather than in the despotic and a-personal mode that befits the form of the mechanical, will help us overcome sterile approaches to this mystery.

On the mechanistic view success comes to those who isolate precise objectives and situations and pursue them with a full panoply of quick-acting technological means. The form of the personal, which gives first place to the mystery of person-in-relation, suggests that such a mode of action is short-sighted and stupid. We need to move slowly, in full cognizance of the organic interrelatedness of all persons and events, aware of long-range effects, especially of patterns according to which the very massiveness of our intervention will bring back the very evil we were trying so vigorously to eradicate.[21] We must work with and not against the grain of our intricately interrelated world.

Is the God we believe in the God of the quick fix or the God of painstaking love? The answer, fully embodied in the career and destiny of Jesus, is clear. God is the latter. The mechanistic strategy, which Jesus clearly rejects when he encounters Satan in the desert, is a recipe for disaster. Even its most notable triumphs are doomed in the long run to oblivion. The personalist strategy may not achieve results right away, but, recognizing the embodied nature of human activity, does not fear struggle with a complexity which is usually recalcitrant but which ultimately can be harnessed. The first strategy is relentless and often massive in its deployment. It pretends that it will be able to hasten the *kairos* but ends up acting prematurely. The second, allowing itself to be carried by a current which ebbs and flows, waits for the right moment, the moment of *kairos*, to intervene in a decisive but surgically precise way.

The sixteenth and seventeenth century debates on grace and free will brought to the fore the question of how we are to understand the reconciliation of efficacious divine grace and genuine human freedom, but achieved no resolution of that question. These debates were conducted when the form of the mechanical was in the ascendant. The approach that form suggests is futile: it focuses the mind on how God influences individual human acts, and is unduly influenced by an underlying quantitative image of physical force and counterforce.

Lonergan's *Grace and Freedom* offers us a most valuable retrieval of the classical tradition of Aquinas on this point. Aquinas' doctrine is remarkably holistic. For him, in the final analysis, God directs each event because he directs all events, God masters the interrelation by which they diverge, converge, coalesce, and come to term. The mechanical thought-form would have us isolate individual actions and events, and raises for us the ultimately spurious question of how God is able to control each one of them in such a way that human freedom remains intact. In Lonergan's view, the efficacy of God's grace has nothing to do with mysterious pushes or pulls which can force our will without taking away its freedom, but everything to do with the fact that God has the entirety of our span of life and all the circumstances of our lives to work with. God, not each one of us, determines the setting in which we are created and are to work out our destinies. God does not need to precipitate, to force issues, but can wait for the right time and the right situation. Ultimately God's action in our hearts and in our lives is infinitely efficacious not in spite but because of the fact that God is infinitely respectful of our freedom. Our graced action shares in the effectiveness of God's action to the extent that it is similarly patient and aware of the intricate web of relationship in which it is inserted. The kenosis exemplified by Jesus is not an arbitrary choice but derives from the inmost characteristics of God and God's action in our world.

THE POWER OF GRACE

Our reflection on patience and power needs to be continued from the perspective of the fulfillment which ensues from kenosis. As we saw, our world's headlong rush into activity is futile; trampling on the delicate holistic texture of creation, disregarding the mystery of personal existence, this activity, though technologically sophisticated, only succeeds in amplifying and hardening the patterns of fragmentation it aims to overcome. By contrast, graced activity, because it bears the secret of how and when to wait, has the power to gather together, to reconcile, to undo fragmentation. We have dwelt on the waiting; let us now dwell on the integration that ensues, first briefly recalling its roots, then attempting to characterize the dynamic at work within it, and finally surveying its range and its architectonics.

The Roots of Integrating Grace: Grace-ful action cannot but lead to integration since, empowered by habit, it is already within itself a paradigm of integration. That gracefulness enables me to let go of the individual components of my action and dwell upon the action as a whole, which has a purpose and a meaning of its own. To evoke a familiar example, if I had to be present to each finger striking the keys of my computer terminal, I would soon be exhausted and paralyzed. I would have no energy to concentrate on the overall *Gestalt* of the text as it takes shape in my mind and on the screen. Following the lead of Polanyi, we have already briefly developed the significance of this contrast in Chapter One,[22] using the image of the graceful ballet dancer and the awkward adolescent, and in Chapter Five we have in similar terms considered the role of habits and skills in Aquinas' thought.[23]

The distinction which emerged in the chapter on Aquinas between the conative and the affective is highly pertinent to this analysis. The conative is characterized by effort, concentration on technique, concern with obstacles, and heightened consciousness. The affective bespeaks a sense of ease and well-being as we are drawn by values attractive on their own terms and derive from them a sense of unity. Our conative involvement with means is effective only if it is preceded and empowered by an affective involvement with ends. The conative—on the wider scale this means technology—has crowded out affectivity and value in the shaping of our world. We are highly proficient in devising means to achieve goals, but we find it very difficult to assess which goals are genuine and deserving of priority. Under the painful guise of special interests and lobby groups, the compartmentalization of our world becomes noisy and obnoxious. We lack the ready ability to discern—here I am stressing communal as opposed to personal discernment—the movements of our affectivity with a view to committing ourselves together to encompassing goals and values. Unbridled, technology exacerbates rather than allays the fragmentation of wholes into isolated parts, and the awkwardness of action at cross-purposes with itself.

The Dynamics of Integrating Grace: The patient dynamic of grace leads not to the suppression of differences but to their affirmation, since the secret of becoming one's true self is letting go of self and reaching out to the other. Failure to rise to the level of kenosis leaves us with a choice between an organicist blurring of distinct personal entities[24] and a mechanistic fragmentation into isolated parts. Using Laing's terminology in *The Divided Self*,[25] the self is either engulfed—in the case of our world as a whole by the anonymous and impersonal organizations on whose efficiency so much is made to depend—or it is isolated and left to wither. Only by assenting to the paradox of self affirmed and surrendered in the same act do we have access to the form of the personal.

The difficult requirements of integration in our world have already emerged in the chapter on Paul. To strike up new relationships might seem to be a nice romantic thing to do, but in a world deeply scarred by sin, the *terminus a quo* of such relationships is often not simple non-acquaintance but hostility and misunderstanding. Breaking down the ensuing barriers is painful and fraught with risk. It calls for a long-suffering patience which only grace bestows. It leads to an integration which sees the uniqueness of the other as a treasure rather than as a threat, and builds the rich synthesis of the one and the many expressed in the image of a living body with its members. Paulo Freire transposes this Pauline dynamic in more secular terms. He does not advocate forcing oppressors to switch places with their erstwhile victims but radically overcoming the structures of oppression, turning differences which were a source of conflict and diminishment into a source of dialogue and new life.

Thus grace shapes humankind into a body which recapitulates, orchestrates, and brings to authentic fulfillment every value, every person, every activity, in every time and in every place. On the broadest scale, the distinctiveness of East, West, North, and South is to remain, but each of them will discover and deepen its unique identity only in affirming the others. This points us in the direction of Paul's vision of the final *pleroma*, of the cosmic Christ who is all in all, of the kingdom Christ presents in the end to the Father.

The Architectonics of Integrating Grace: Grace links together many different realms of activity and relationship within human persons and communities. It not only establishes a line of communication between elements hardened into us/them opposition in any given realm, but also brings together in fruitful interaction the realms themselves.

These different realms were presented in Chapter Two by means of a diagram made up of concentric circles. The inmost circle is that of the self in its relationship to God; next there comes that of the psyche and its different components, conscious and unconscious; next there comes that of the I/thou of inter-personal relations; next that of we/they social and political relations; finally in the broadest circle the ecological realm of relations between humankind and the physical world.[26]

The communication grace fosters between these "circles" takes place both inwards and outwards. Reconciliation on the broader levels of human life, social, political, and economic, facilitates the proper inner development of the person in his or her relation to self and God; the healing of the inner self contributes to the healing of the oppressive structures which define the relationships of peoples to each other on our planet. There is no realm of graced activity which does not have its impact on all the other realms. Thus while one may seek to discern and implement a preferred strategy, and wish to highlight this or that form of action as more immediately pertinent to a situation, the ultimate fact is that wherever one is called to act in the continuum from the centre to the periphery, or from the periphery to the centre, all realms of the continuum will receive the impact of that action.[27] The effect of grace is not only to achieve a measure of reconciliation within any one of these realms, but also to bring to light and affirm the integration between each realm and all the others.

More and more we are coming to see that the integration within and between the realms is foundational. Together they make up a universe at one with itself and with all its parts. Concern for the holistic and the ecological are not a monopoly of the twentieth century. The tradition on grace may not have used those precise words, but under the image of the total Christ in which the whole universe is recapitulated it has affirmed the reality they point to. This brings us back to the patience of grace. The intricacy of this recapitulation is such that its ultimate pattern will not emerge in full clarity until the human journey is over. At times one is called to decisive witness and energetic action. Yet one must be ready to move slowly, carefully, by adjustment, creatively responding to the surprises and challenges on the way, patient and hopeful in the midst of adversity.

Above all it is this architectonic dimension of grace which holds together the many concerns of this essay, allowing me in the chapter on Paul to bring out the religious ramifications of the Freirian analysis of the third world socio-cultural context and show the affinities of his analysis with the work of some contemporary psychology, and in the chapter on Augustine and Aquinas to give pride of place to more personalist categories, in the confidence that what I formulated there does indeed apply to the broader social realm.

Indeed the point of this book is that a single-minded concern with the religious, the psychological, or the politico-economic is futile. Differences of emphasis and of starting-point are legitimate, but ultimately the garment of grace will be not only without patches but also without seams. The architectonic dimensions of Paul have emerged clearly in Chapter Two. With his trilogy of *Confessions*, *City of God*, and *On the Trinity*, Augustine "is a model of theological illumination concerning the intersection of divine, personal and social transcendence".[28] The bent of my chapter on Aquinas has been more personalist, but at the same time the basic structures uncovered there apply to the wide panoply of human effort. I would single out the analysis of Aquinas on feelings, which may seem somewhat irrelevant but, if we are to believe Robert Doran on psychic conversion, illuminates an area of vital concern if good will is to be effectively harnessed in the struggle for social transformation.[29]

Other first world theologians addressed themselves more explicitly than I to the application to the first world reality of principles shaped in the crucible of the third world.[30] Their insights are both cogent and balanced. What I have tried to do is to draw into a process of mutual enrichment:

a) basic principles and themes from the liberationist perspective,
b) a body of literature emanating from first world sociologists and

psychologists who have been alert to the dynamics of our society
from their own distinctive humanist standpoint,
  c) foundational structures animating the classical tradition on grace.

I hope I have been able to show that these partners not only can carry on a very interesting and constructive interchange, but are indispensable to each other.

This three way conversation has neither intended nor yielded quick results. Like those theologians who have dealt more specifically than I with the political dimensions of grace, I have come up not with sharply delineated practical strategies for action to be applied to our complex predicament, but with a method and a context. Indeed I have offered a rationale for maintaining a critical distance from strategies such as the enthusiastic endorsement of the technological marvels of the first world, supposed to painlessly usher in utopia without calling for far-reaching changes in the structures of our world, as well as from the rigid observance of specific lines of socio-politico action intended to right an unjust order. That we ought to use technology to our advantage, or that we ought to resolutely address the injustices of our world, even to the point of putting ourselves in jeopardy, is not in question. What I would insist on, however, is the relativization which protects us from naïve enthusiasm and doctrinaire rigidity.[31] The stakes are too high and the intricacies of our historical situation too intractable for anything else in the end to guide our action but the divine patience enfleshed in a human patience which respects the holistic context of all human action. The ambiguities and uncertainties which surround our every step, if assumed in faith, can occasion a purification and a surrender which will prove essential for the long-term effectiveness of our action.[32]

A FINAL SUMMATION

Not surprisingly, this summation will be ternary in structure: first we shall remind ourselves of three categories for grace which have played a role throughout this work; second we shall bring out more closely some of the trinitarian affinities of the dynamic of grace; finally we shall return to the theme of the three worlds with which we began in Chapter One.

The Three Categories: Three Aristotelian categories have been applied to grace over the centuries, quality, relation, and quantity. As has emerged in our work, relationship and quality are appropriate categories for grace, but quantity is not.

We have linked gracefulness, inner security, habit, and patience to the category of quality. Endowed with a secure self-presence which does not fear to abandon itself to the mostly tacit rhythms of life and the mysterious patterns of a Provident God at work in the world, the graced person radiates an intrinsic harmony, an integration which readily attracts and persuades.

That secure self-presence is as closely linked to the category of relation as it is to that of quality. Isolation breeds anxiety, leads to obtrusive and painful self-consciousness. The presence of significant others, above all of the Other who is source of all significance, gives us the security we need to be graceful as we exist within ourselves and reach out to others. The contemporary emphasis on grace as a relationship between ourselves and God and the medieval affirmation of grace as quality converge rather than diverge.

Aristotle is not the only source of insight into quality and relation. The constitutive bipolarity of grace which these two categories of his help us formulate emerges in other ways as well. To begin with, the God of grace is no isolated monad but a Trinity of subsistent relations. The three persons exist both in themselves and towards each other. To this theme we shall return.

The etymological antecedents of the word "grace" suggest a similar convergence of quality and relation. The Greek and Latin words for grace (*kharis*, *gratia*) both mean inner gracefulness, charm, elan, spontaneity, but are also used to mean the undeserved favour someone bestows on me as well as the thanks I freely give in return, in that way bespeaking the realm of personal relationship.[33] Both the favour bestowed and the thanks returned are marked by personal, free, gratuitous spontaneity. Grace is the favour and the thanks (relation), as well as the spontaneity (quality) common to favour and thanks.

Personal relationships are to be sharply contrasted with business relationships. In the latter the category of quantity becomes primordial. Yes, there can be a measure of relationship in business transactions, but the personal dimension of that relationship is muted. What comes to the fore in business is not qualitative states of being but quantitative descriptions of the objects stipulated in explicit or tacit contracts: for example, so many pounds of sugar, made with such and such chemically verifiable specifications, to be delivered by such and such a day for such and such a sum of money, with such and such conditions attached to non-payment or delayed payment. As we saw in Chapter Two,[34] the urge to specify and to calculate is abetted by the anxious concern that accompanies real or supposed scarcity. The less there is of a commodity, the more stringent are the conditions that define its exchange. In the business transaction the relationship is extrinsic, grounded not in the inner propensity of persons to freely give and receive of their spiritual selves, but in the urge to assure material survival and growth, protected by carefully drawn up contractual documents. Quality and personal relationship go together, as do quantity and contractual relationship. As we delve in the mystery of grace, we are invited to divest ourselves more and more of the latter and enter into the former. A more personalist theology of grace has already in our century gained the favour of many theologians. Our own task has been to develop more fully the rationale and ramifications of such a theology.

The Three Persons: The favour/thanksgiving relationship which exists between God and human beings underlies the foundational justification/sanctification/salvation triad which Paul introduces into the Christian tradition, and which John, Augustine, and Aquinas transpose in their own terms. The following diagram presents that triad, showing how grace as quality and grace as relationship might relate to it, and opening up striking trinitarian affinities:

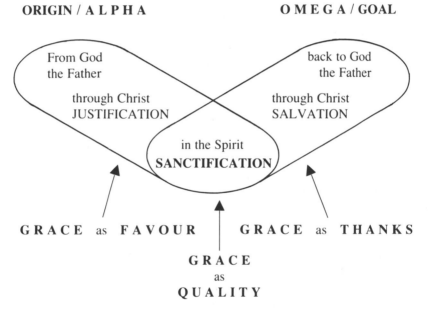

ORIGIN / A L P H A   **O M E G A / GOAL**

From God the Father

through Christ
JUSTIFICATION

back to God the Father

through Christ
SALVATION

in the Spirit
SANCTIFICATION

G R A C E as F A V O U R   G R A C E as T H A N K S

G R A C E
as
Q U A L I T Y

The quality of grace, its spontaneity, its inner harmony, links up most closely with the gift of the Spirit which graces our lives and our action. The two movements which constitute grace as relation, God's favour to us and our thanksgiving to God, unfold in a trinitarian pattern. The favour originates in God: it unfolds as the Father reconciles us to himself through the Son and in the Spirit, justifying us, and making us able to live the life of sanctification. In the Spirit we respond, doing deeds of service which build up the body of Christ and give thanks to the Father. In this way we live out the classical doxological pattern of praise to God the Father through Christ and in the Spirit. The culmination of this process of ongoing sanctification is our return to the Father, our salvation, in which the body of Christ is brought to its completion and handed over to the Father (1 Cor 15:20–28). Augustine, as we have seen, is the one who most clearly expresses the trinitarian dimension of this dynamic of grace:

a) Grace finds its origin and goal in the First Person, the Father, and this is reflected within us in what Augustine calls the restless heart, which God has created (origin) in such a way that no one less than God can fulfill it (goal); in what Aquinas terms the natural desire to see God; in what contemporary theologians such as Rahner term the supernatural existential.

b) In the economy of grace, the Second Person, the Word, is intimately linked with the exteriority, the embodiment of grace. Every event, every facet of human history is a reflection of that Word, definitively spoken to us in Jesus Christ. Every event that challenges us finds its power in the event of events, which is the Paschal Mystery into which we are baptized. Thus the gift of grace is mediated to us through various embodiments, related to the central embodiment of God's purpose, the body of which Christ is the head. In our response, we enter into the movement of reaching out to others, building, shaping, articulating the fulness of that body of Christ, and we become to others what others have been to us in the dynamic of grace, embodiments and sources of mediation. The body of Christ in its absolute universality is the ultimate context and significance of the integrating function of grace which has come to the fore in this concluding chapter.

c) The Spirit poured within our hearts is pivotal in the movement of grace. It is at once the termination of the movement that begins from God and ends in the gift of a transformed heart, and the beginning of the movement of our heart which terminates in gratitude and service rendered to the same God. The Spirit is the very interiority of grace, without which our response to God fails to engage the depths of our persons, remains ineffective and superficial. The Spirit is the secret of grace's gracefulness, of its compliance to the rhythms of providence and its ultimately all-conquering patience.

The Three Worlds: The grace that is triune in pattern is both efficacious and vulnerable, powerful and patient. The vaunted techniques and instruments of our first world offer the empty shell, not the reality of power. There is no genuine power without patience, and no lasting patience without the gift of grace. At the same time, the efficacy of grace goes beyond the first world and its plight, with which we began this essay. The only healing possible for the first world is one that entails integration with the second and the third world. Close relations between the three worlds need to be fostered, as well as the mutual enrichment of the contrasting religious and human values they embody. The integrating activity of grace will not cease until, transformed and authenticated, absolutely all values, ideas, events, persons, achievements devised by humankind find their proper place in the body of Christ. In our terms this "all" must include first, second, and third worlds in their totality.

We have clearly developed this point with respect to the third world and its emerging Church. Our analysis of the oppressor/oppressed relationship in Paul of Tarsus and Paulo Freire bids us recognize that apart from collaboration with the third world, we will never discover patterns of oppression within and between ourselves, and will continue to live in the neurotic and futile sterility of the oppressor, clinging to a power of domination which ultimately destroys itself. Liberation comes to the oppressor only through the oppressed. If we allow ourselves to be challenged in depth by the third world and its call for justice, our theology of grace will much more easily move from the realm of the intra- and the inter-personal into the wider realm of the social, political, and economic, acquiring in this way a maturity and a realism which would otherwise elude it.

The point of cultivating our relationship to the second world and its ancient Church is more difficult to pin down, but is just as crucial. Whether dwelling in the inter- and intra-personal spaces which our own world has opened up, or claiming the wider social, political, economic spaces opened up by our involvement with the third, we focus on the healing side of grace. We become caught up in a project of embodying the patterns of authentic human living as much as possible on this earth. The danger, however, is to forget the transcendent space which is at the inner core of any humanizing endeavour. We have been created in such a way that our only total fulfillment is in God; grace, Aquinas tells us, puts us in touch with the human only to the extent that it elevates us to the realm of the divine. The Church as it has been able to survive within the second world, has given and gives an especially vivid witness to the yearning for the utterly transcendent and mysterious space where God dwells, and by its patience in the midst of persecution it forcibly reminds us of our need to relativize anything we do in this world, to cultivate, like Augustine, detachment in the midst of our involvement.[35]

Grace opens us to the mystery of otherness, and that otherness, for those of us who belong to the first world, is made present in our brothers and sisters of the second and third worlds. As we become present to them, we are invited to include within our compassionate concern all the domains in which we need to be reconciled, not only with them but also among and within ourselves. Any attempt to move towards a renewed first world will fail unless we take the time and trouble to listen to voices within other worlds and collaborate with them in a project of liberation that, in spite of its slowness and reverses, shares the breadth of God's apocalyptic promise of a total Christ in which there is no Jew or Greek, slave or free, male or female, East or West, North or South, oppressor or oppressed.

NOTES

1. This sense of newness was very much in the air in the 13th century, but by the 14th there began to emerge an exalted sense of the millennium just around the corner, fostered for example by Joachim of Fiore, which later became associated with a sense that the times were out of joint.

2. Cf. pp. 95ff.

3. One could also claim that it emerges under the heading of unction, an unction which bespeaks the suppleness and well-being which Augustine put under the heading of spontaneity and Aquinas under that of habit.

4. A striking expression of this is found in R.D. Laing's *The Divided Self*: Referring to the state of the ontologically insecure person prone to psychosis, he tells us "Instead of the polarities of separateness and relatedness based on individual autonomy, there is the antithesis between complete loss of being by absorption into the other person (engulfment), and complete aloneness (isolation). There is no safe third possibility of a dialectical relationship between two persons, both sure of their own ground, and, on this very basis, able to 'lose themselves' in each other." (p. 44)

5. The basic pattern of this is to be found in 1 Thessalonians. Not only did the word come to the Thessalonians but it came in power, in spirit, in full conviction, such that they were able to receive it and such that it could bear fruit in them. A more technical expression of this occurs in Rahner's theology of the Trinity, when he contrasts the two missions (of the Son and of the Spirit) in terms of offer and acceptance, of history and transcendence, and in Lonergan's *De Deo Trino. II: Pars Systematica*, pp. 240 ff.

6. Momentary does not mean intermittent. Some events within our world speak to us more vividly of God, but God is present in all of them. Cf. my article, "Grace: The Mystery of God's Abundance" in *Word and Spirit*, esp. pp. 378–379.

7. Cf. *Les structures* . . . , pp. 165–170.

8. Gerald May offers a parallel analysis of the states of consciousness in *Will and Spirit*, pp. 210–243. His categories are most germane to our considerations.

9. Cf. pp. 240–41.

10. Cf. pp. 110–111.

11. Cf. my article "Kenosis: Old and New" in *The Ecumenist*, 1974, pp. 17–21, which offers references in the work of Herbert Fingarette and R.D. Laing on this point.

12. Cf. Chapter Four, pp. 155, 161, 163.

13. Mt. 13:24–30.

14. The kenotic dimension of habitual grace is aptly expressed in the image used by Paul in Philippians to describe the dynamic of grace. The first moment in which I receive the infusion of habitual grace is described as a being grasped (in justification by faith). This leads to the subsequent moment in which, transformed by grace, I am able to take an active stance which will eventually enable me at the end of my journey to grasp as the "prize" the one who has already grasped me. This passive dimension of habit is highlighted by the fact that *habitus* is a passive verb form, denoting not a possessing but a being possessed.

15. Cf. Augustine, *De Div. Quaest. ad Simp.*, 1,2,3.

16. As we saw, Augustine was converted in 387, and in later years accepted the invitation to further reorient his life in kenotic obedience by becoming a bishop. Cf. Chapter Four, pp. 159ff., 182ff.

17. This reflection may offer a helpful perspective on the problem of evil. The fulfillment in God of someone whose life is exactly like my own except that the injustices, the scars, the sinful patterns are magically taken out, and no longer need to be dealt with creatively, is not *my* fulfillment but that of another person. I am not a monad disassociated from the circumstances of my life. My relation to each one of those circumstances is intrinsic, it is part and parcel of who I am and who I can be. The issue of why God allows so much evil in my life is a non-issue: if that evil were not there to face it would no longer be my life but that of some other person that I would be living.

18. Cf. Eugene T. Gendlin, "A Theory of Personality Change", pp. 126 ff., for this term of "frozen whole" which plays an analogous role to the image of the pillar of salt.

19. Cf. Chapter Four, pp. 183ff.

20. It should not be difficult to discern here the reality of parousia, of final judgement, and of definitive salvation.

21. The vicious circles we have cited from Philip Slater's work in Chapter One offer good instances of this short-sighted action.

22. Cf. pp. 12–13.

23. Cf. pp. 219–220.

24. In their own way Morris Berman's musings about the advantages and pitfalls of what he calls "holism" in the last chapter of his *The Reenchantment of the World*. He envisages that possibly in the holistic society the ego will not be reformed, or complemented, but simply abolished (p. 302). Yet this is fraught with danger. Fascism, guruism, the abdication of personal responsibility, the realization of an Orwellian night-

mare are real dangers. I would suggest that the missing ingredient in Berman's analysis is the presence of a personalist perspective which transcends and encompasses the tensions of the organic and the mechanical with which he struggles, but without achieving clear resolution. Macmurray's analysis of mechanistic and organicist models of society in Chapter Six of his *Persons-in-Relation* is far more satisfying. It suggests that if society gets stuck in either the organic or the mechanical, it can too easily collapse into the opposite extreme. This explains the totalitarianism lurking behind the optimistic holistic vision of today.

25. Cf. note 4 above.

26. Cf. Chapter Two, p. 115.

27. These are the centripetal and centrifugal movements alluded to in Chapter Two, pp. 116–123.

28. D.J. Fasching, "Theology and Public Policy. Method in the Work of Juan Luis Segundo, Jacques Ellul, and Robert Doran", in *Method. Journal of Lonergan Studies*, 1987, p. 72.

29. Cf. Doran, *Psychic Conversion* . . . Also cf. Fasching, op. cit., p. 72.

30. One might refer here to the political theology of the later Metz, which antedates much liberation theology, to the work of Matthew Lamb and of John Coleman. It would have been very instructive for me to do my work in constant conversation with these authors, but that would add a note of complexity warranting another book or article. It is also important to acknowledge that some theologians have explored alternative models more directly connected with the experience of the first world. Having in my own reflection come to an appreciation of the central role which patience plays in empowerment, I happily recognized the convergence—a convergence entailing some tacit indebtedness—of my own approach to the theology of grace with the themes of inclusion, hospitality, and patience so creatively and cogently developed in Frans Jozef van Beeck's *Christ Proclaimed: Christology as Rhetoric* (New York: Paulist, 1979).

31. A reader who would make a connection between this reflection and Paul's advocacy of a middle way between Gnostic enthusiasm and Pharisaic observance (Chapter Three, pp. 102–103, 129ff.) would not be missing the mark.

32. I have no intention of denying that the position I have adopted here is motivated by not only my theological convictions but also my standpoint as a Canadian. The Canadian ethos is not one of asserting a manifest destiny, nor is it one of undergoing massive oppression. Rather it is one of surviving, in a constant attempt to keep together with reasonable harmony diverse cultural and economic elements. Canada's geographic location contributes to this ethos. Its experience of the forces of nature, especially of winter, has marked its psyche with a sense of patience and resiliency. Its spread-outness, its strong regional profiles make it almost ungovernable. This has taught its citizens to appreciate small but repeated increments on the road to progress, to seek the careful balancing of deeply set tensions. This does not exclude a passionate commitment among them to profound social transformation, both national and international. This commitment, however, has characteristics of its own. Many Canadians have learned to discipline and temper it in the interests of long-range collaboration, as

evidenced by Canada's major Christian denominations when together they deal with a wide range of social issues.

33. It is to that order of relationship that contemporary thinkers such as John Macmurray would have us lift our sights. It is to that order of relationship that Aquinas would have us accede when he affirms that grace is at once gratuitous, beyond the claim of our nature or its power of accomplishment, and indispensable for the authentic fulfillment of that nature. Only on the level of personal relationships can such a paradox be sustained.

34. Cf. pp. 60–61.

35. At the same time, we must not fall in the trap of erecting barriers between second and third worlds by the ways we speak about them. Differences between them clearly emerge, but at the same time the poignant openness to the mystery of God which alone adversity shapes is also a reality of the third world, and the burning thirst for a just world a reality of the second. First, second, and third world are not different compartments but different syntheses of our common humanness and its values.

BIBLIOGRAPHY

ARTICLES:

Chenu, M.D., "Les passions vertueuses. L'anthropologie de S. Thomas", *Rev Phil Louvain*, (72)1974, 13–18

Crowe, Frederick E., "Complacency and Concern in the Thought of St. Thomas", *Theological Studies*, (20)1959, 1–39, 198–230, 343–395

Deason, G.B., "The Protestant Reformation and the Rise of Modern Science", *Scot. Journ. of Theol.*, (38)1985, 221–240

Desmond, William, "Augustine's Confessions: on Desire, Conversion, and Reflection", *Irish Theol. Quart.*, (47)1980, 24–33

Fasching, Darrell J., "Method in the Work of Juan Luis Segundo, Jacques Ellul and Robert Doran," *Method. Jounal of Lonergan Studies*, (5)1987, 41–91

Gendlin, Eugene T., "A Theory of Personality Change", *Personality Change* (P. Worchel and D. Byrne, editors), New York, John Wiley & Sons, 1964, 100–148

Hacker, Paul, "Martin Luther's Notion of Faith", *Catholic Scholars Dialogue with Luther* (J. Wicks, editor), Chicago, Loyola Univ. Press, 1970, 85–105

Huftier, M., "Libre arbitre, liberté et péché chez S. Augustin", *Rech. Théol. Anc. Méd.*, 33(1966), 187–281

Käsemann, Ernst, "Justification and Salvation History in the Epistle to the Romans", *Perspectives on Paul*, Philadelphia, Fortress, 1971, 60–78

Laporte, Jean-Marc, "Grace: The Mystery of God's Abundance", *Word and Spirit*, Toronto, Regis College Press, 371–409

———"Kenosis Old and New", *The Ecumenist*, (12)1974, 17–21.

———"The Dynamics of Grace in Aquinas: A Structural Approach," *Theological Studies*, (34)1973, 203–226

Lonergan, Bernard, "The Natural Desire to See God", *Collection*, London, Darton, Longman, & Todd, 1967, 84–95

Metz, Johannes Baptist, "Freedom as a Threshold Problem between Philosophy and Theology" (Eng. Trans.), *Philosophy Today*, (10)1966, 264–279

———"Future of Faith in a Hominized World" (Eng. Trans.), *Philosophy Today*, (10)1966, 289–299

Rahner, Karl, "Dogmatic Questions on Easter", *Theological Investigations*, Vol. IV, Darton, Longman, & Todd, 1966, 121–133

———"Grace", *Sacramentum Mundi* (6 Vols.), New York, Herder and Herder, 1968–1970

———"Nature and Grace", *Theological Investigations*, Vol. IV, London, Darton, Longman, & Todd, 1966, 165–188

———"The Theological Concept of Concupiscentia", *Theological Investigations*, Vol. I, London, Darton, Longman, & Todd, 1961, 347–382

_____"Theological Reflections on the Problem of Secularization", *Theological Investigations*, Vol. X, New York, Herder and Herder, 1973, 318–348

Ratzinger, Joseph, "Zum Personenverständnis in der Theologie" in *Dogma und Verkündigung*, München, Wewel, 1977

Rotstein, Abraham, "The Apocalyptic Tradition: Luther and Marx", *Political Theology in the Canadian Context* (ed. B. Smillie), Waterloo, Wilfrid Laurier University Press, 1982, 147–208

Schlegel, Jean-Louis, "La gnose ou le réenchantement du monde", *Etudes*, (366)1987, 389–404

Sesboüé, Bernard, "Esquisse critique d'une théologie de la rédemption", *NRT*, (106)1984, 801–816, and (107)1985, 68–86

Stendahl, Krister, "The Apostle Paul and the Introspective Consciousness of the West", in *Harvard Theological Review*, 56(1963), 199–215

BOOKS:

Augustine of Hippo, *Opera Omnia*, Paris, Migne, 1841–1877

Barth, Karl, *Church Dogmatics* (4 Vol.), Edinburgh, T. & T. Clark, 1936–

Beker, J. Christiaan, *Paul's Apocalyptic Gospel: The Coming Triumph of God*, Philadelphia, Fortress, 1982

_____ *Paul the Apostle: The Triumph of God in Life and Thought*, Philadelphia, Fortress, 1980

Bellah, Robert N., et al., *Habits of the Heart: Individualism and Commitment in American Life*, New York, Harper and Row, 1985

Berman, Morris, *The Reenchantment of the World*, Ithaca, Cornell University Press, 1981 (references are to the Bantam Edition, 1984)

Boff, Leonardo, *Liberating Grace* (Eng. trans.), Maryknoll, Orbis, 1979

Bouillard, Henri, *Conversion et grâce chez S. Thomas d'Aquin*, Paris, Aubier, 1944

Brown, Peter, *Augustine of Hippo: A Biography*, Berkeley, Univ. of California Press, 1969

Brown, Raymond, *The Community of the Beloved Disciple*, New York, Paulist Press, 1979

Bühlmann, Walbert, *The Coming of the Third Church: An Analysis of the Present and Future of the Church* (Eng. trans), Maryknoll, Orbis, 1977

Burns, Patout, *The Development of Augustine's Doctrine of Operative Grace*, Paris, Etudes Augustiniennes, 1980

Campbell, Jeremy, *Grammatical Man: Information, Entropy, Language, and Life*, New York, Simon & Schuster, 1986

Capra, Fritjof, *The Tao of Physics: An exploration of the parallels between modern physics and Eastern mysticism*, London, Fontana Paperbacks, 1983

286   PATIENCE AND POWER

————*The Turning Point: Science, Society, and the Rising Culture*, New York, Simon and Schuster, 1982 (references are to the Bantam Edition, 1983)

Chené, J., *La théologie de S. Augustin. Grâce et prédestination*, Le Puy, Mappus, 1961

Copleston, Frederick, *History of Philosophy* (Revised Edition), London, Burns, Oates, & Washbourne, 1951–

Cox, Harvey, *The Feast of Fools*, Cambridge, Harvard University Press, 1969

Dianich, Severiano, *L'opzione fondamentale nel pensiero di S. Tomasso*, Brescia, Morcelliana, 1968

Doran, Robert M., *Psychic Conversion and Theological Foundations: Towards a Reorientation of the Human Sciences*, Chico, Scholars Press, 1981

Edinger, Edward F., *Ego and Archetype*, Baltimore, Penguin, 1973

Ellul, Jacques, *Présence au monde moderne. Problèmes de la civilisation post-chrétienne*, Genève, Roulet, 1948

Ferguson, Marilyn, *The Aquarian Conspiracy: Personal and Social Transformation in the 1980's*, Los Angeles, Tarcher, 1980

Fingarette, Herbert, *The Self in Transformation*, New York, Harper Torchbooks, 1965

Freire, Paulo, *Pedagogy of the Oppressed*, New York, Herder and Herder, 1971

Fuller, Reginald, G., *The Foundations of New Testament Christology*, London, Collins, 1965

Gendlin, Eugene T., *Focusing*, New York, Bantam, 1981

Gimpel, Jean, *The Medieval Machine: The Industrial Revolution of the Middle Ages*, Harmondsworth, Penguin, 1977

Greshake, Gisbert, *Geschenkte Freiheit: Einführung in die Gnadenlehre*, Freiburg, Herder, 1977

Hampden-Turner, Charles, *Radical Man*, Doubleday, New York, 1971

Hansen, Paul D., *The Dawn of Apocalyptic*, Fortress, Philadelphia, 1975

Holland, Joseph, and Henriot, Peter, S.J., *Social Analysis: Linking Faith and Justice*, Washington, Center of Concern, 1980

Johnson, Paul, *Modern Times: The World from the Twenties to the Eighties*, New York, Harper and Row, 1983

Käsemann, Ernst, *New Testament Questions of Today*, Philadelphia, Fortress, 1969

Kegan, Robert, *The Evolving Self: Problem and Process in Human Development*, Cambridge, Harvard University Press, 1982

Kertelge, Karl, *Rechtfertigung bei Paulus*, Münster, Aschendorff, 1967

Kossel, C.G., *Relation in the Philosophy of Saint Thomas Aquinas*, University of Toronto (doctoral manuscript), 1952

Krempel, A., *La doctrine de la relation chez S. Thomas: exposé historique et systématique*, Paris, Vrin, 1952

Kuhn, Thomas S., *The Structure of Scientific Revolutions*, Chicago, University of Chicago Press, 1962

Kuss, Otto, *Der Römerbrief*, Pustet, Regensburg, 1963

Lagarde, Georges de, *La naissance de l'esprit laïque au déclin du Moyen Age* (2 Vols.), Paris, Béatrice-Nauwelaerts, 1956

Laing, Ronald D., *Knots*, Harmondsworth, Penguin, 1970

———*Politics of Experience*, Harmondsworth, Penguin, 1967

———*The Divided Self. An Existential Study in Sanity and Madness*, Harmondsworth, Penguin, 1965

Laing, Ronald D., and Esterson, A., *Sanity, Madness, and the Family*, Harmondsworth, Penguin, 1970

Laporte, Jean-Marc, *Les structures dynamiques de la grâce: grâce médicinale et grâce élevante d'après Thomas d'Aquin*, Montréal, Editions Bellarmin, 1974.

Lonergan, Bernard, *Collection*, London, Darton, Longman, & Todd, 1967

———*De Deo Trino, Pars Synthetica*, Rome, Pont. Univ. Gregoriana, 1964

———*Insight: A Study of Human Understanding*, New York, Philosophical Library, 1956

———*Verbum—Word and Idea in Aquinas*, London, Darton, Longman, & Todd, 1968

———*A Second Collection*, Philadelphia, Westminster, 1974

———*Method in Theology*, London, Darton, Longman, & Todd, 1972

———*Grace and Freedom*, New York, Herder and Herder, 1971

Lubac, Henri de, *Augustinisme et théologie moderne*, Paris, Aubier, 1965

———*Le mystère du surnaturel*, Paris, Aubier, 1965

Luther, Martin, *Christian Liberty* (trans. by Lambert), Philadelphia, Fortress, 1957

———*Luther's Works* (55 vols.), St. Louis, Concordia Publishing House, 1958–1967

MacIntyre, Alasdair, *After Virtue: A Study in Moral Theory*, Notre Dame, University of Notre Dame Press, 1981

Macmurray, John, *The Self as Agent* and *Persons in Relation*, London, Faber, 1957 and 1961

Markus, Robert, *Saeculum: History and Society in the Theology of St. Augustine*, Cambridge, Cambridge University Press, 1970

May, Gerald, *Will and Spirit: A Contemplative Psychology*, San Francisco, Harper & Row, 1982

May, Rollo, *Freedom and Destiny*, Norton, New York, 1981

———*Love and Will*, New York, Norton, 1969 (references are to the Delta Book edition)

———*Power and Innocence*, New York, Norton, 1972

———*The Meaning of Anxiety* (revised edition), New York, Norton, 1977 (references are to the Washington Square Press Edition, 1979)

Meeks, Wayne, *The First Urban Christians: The Social World of the Apostle Paul*, New Haven, Yale University Press, 1983

Metz, Johann Baptist, *Christliche Anthropozentrik*, München, Kösel Verlag, 1962

Moody, E.A., *Studies in Medieval Philosophy, Science, and Logic*, Berkeley, U. of Cal. Press. 1975

Moore, Sebastian, *Let This Mind be in You: A Quest for Identity Through Oedipus to Christ*, New York, Winston-Seabury, 1985

Munck, Johannes, *Paul and the Salvation of Mankind*, London, SCM Press, 1959
Neumann, Erich, *The Origins and History of Consciousness*, Princeton, Princeton University Press, 1970
O'Meara, J.J., *The Young Augustine*, Alba House, Staten Island, 1965
Ogilvy, James, *Multi-dimensional Man: Decentralizing Self, Society, and the Sacred*, New York, Oxford University Press, 1977
Pesch, Hans Otto, *Theologie der Rechtfertigung bei Martin Luther und Thomas von Aquin*, Mainz, Grünewald, 1967
Plato, *The Dialogues of Plato* (trans. B. Jowett), Oxford, Clarendon Press, 1953
Polanyi, Michael, *Personal Knowledge, Towards a Post-Critical Philosophy*, Chicago, U. of Chicago Press, 1958
Rahner, Karl, *Geist in Welt: zur Metaphysik der endlichen Erkenntnis bei Thomas von Aquin*, München, Kösel, 1964
Reich, Charles A., *The Greening of America*, New York, Random House, 1970 (references are to the Bantam edition 1971)
Ricoeur, Paul, *Philosophie de la volonté*, Paris, Aubier, 1950
Rifkin, Jeremy (with Ted Howard), *The Emerging Order: God in the Age of Scarcity*, New York, Random House, 1983
Roszak, Theodore, *The Cult of Information: The Folklore of Computers and the True Art of Thinking*, New York, Random House, 1986
_____*Person/Planet: The Creative Disintegration of Industrial Society*, New York, Anchor Press/Doubleday, 1979
_____*Unfinished Animal: The Aquarian Frontier and the Evolution of Consciousness*, New York, Harper Colophon Books, 1977
Roszak, Theodore, *Where the Wasteland Ends: Politics and Transcendence in Postindustrial Society*, New York, Anchor Books/Doubleday, 1973
Rowland, C., *The Open Heaven. A Study of Apocalyptic in Judaism and Early Christianity*, London, SPCK, 1982
Saussure, Ferdinand de, *Cours de linguistique générale*, Paris, Payot, 1971
Schillebeeckx, E., *Christ, the Experience of Jesus as Lord*, New York, Seabury, 1980
Schmithals, Walter, *Die Apokalyptik: Einführung und Deutung*, Göttingen, Vandenhoeck und Ruprecht, 1973
Schumacher, E.F., *Small is Beautiful: A Study of Economics as if People Mattered*, London, Abacus, 1974
Segundo, Juan Luis, *Grace and the Human Condition* (Eng. trans.), Maryknoll, Orbis, 1973
Siegwalt, Gérard, *La loi, chemin du Salut*, Neuchâtel, Delachaux et Niestlé, 1971
Slater, Philip, *Earth-walk*, New York, Doubleday, 1974 (references are to the Bantam Edition, 1975)
_____*The Pursuit of Loneliness: American Culture at the Breaking Point* (revised edition), Boston, Beacon Press, 1976
Stendahl, Krister, *Paul among Jews and Gentiles*, Philadelphia, Fortress, 1976

Strasser, Stephan, *Phenomenology of Feeling. An Essay on the Phenomena of the Human Heart*, Pittsburgh, Duquesne University Press, 1977

Terruwe, Anna, and Baars, Conrad, *Psychic Wholeness and Healing. Using ALL the Powers of the Human Psyche*, New York, Alba, 1981

teSelle, Eugene, *Augustine the Theologian*, New York, Herder and Herder, 1970.

Theissen, Gerd, *The Social Setting of Pauline Christianity*, Philadelphia, Fortress, 1982

Thomas Aquinas, *Opera Omnia*, Roma, Typographia Polyglotta, 1882–1906

———*Summa Theologiae* (Latin text and English translation in 61 vols.), London, Blackfriars, 1953–

———*Truth* (*QQ. De Veritate* translated in 3 vols.), Chicago, Regnery, 1952–1953

Toffler, Alvin, *Future Shock*, New York, Random House, 1970 (references to the Bantam Book Edition 1980)

——— *The Third Wave*, New York, Bantam Books, 1981

van Beeck, Frans-Jozef, *Christ Proclaimed: Christology as Rhetoric,* New York, Paulist Press, 1979

Voegelin, Eric, *The New Science of Politics*, Chicago, University of Chicago Press, 1952

Weber, Max, *The Protestant Ethic and the Spirit of Capitalism* (trans. T. Parsons), New York, Scribner's, 1958

Yankelovitch, Daniel, *New Rules: Searching for Self-Fulfillment in a World Turned Upside Down*, New York, Random, 1981 (references to the Bantam Edition, 1982)

GENERAL INDEX

(N.B. Italicized numbers in brackets after the page number refer to endnote numbers on that page.)

Vicious circle 10, 19–21, 60, 86, 231–32, 247(10), 250(35), 267–68

Voegelin, Eric 82(76), 83(87)

We/they: see I/thou

Weak: see Strong/weak

Weber, Max 26, 76(25)

Western church: see Church

Willingness/wilfullness 177–78, 192(99,100), 204–05, 267

Wish/will 175–76, 204–05, 211

Word/Spirit 91–92, 262–63, 278, 280(5)

World, First/Second/Third 1–6, 30(3), 265–69, 273–75, 278–80, 283(35)

Yankelovitch, Daniel 19